Copyright ©2023 by John Humbert

Photos provided by John Humbert.
All rights reserved.

ChalicePress.com

978-1-60350-090-6 Hardcover
978-1-60350-091-3 Paperback
978-1-60350-092-0 Ebook

CBP

Printed in the United States of America.

CLAIMING A LEGACY

A Memoir by John O. Humbert

CBP

Foreword

Rev. Teresa "Terri" Hord Owens

I first met John Humbert on the morning of the day I would be elected as General Minister and President (GMP). My husband and I were in the hotel garage headed to worship that Sunday morning at my home church, and who should approach but John Humbert. With his warm smile and kind eyes, he extended his best wishes and said that he was excited about my nomination, and that he would be praying for me. I felt the historical weight of that moment, and it began a friendship and conversations that have blessed and informed my own ministry as GMP.

John has always served and led with a pastor's heart and he brought that to his calling as GMP. He emphasized that a Christology that understands Christ as "Prince of Peace, justice and compassion," as well as "personal savior," is the foundation of all Disciples mission. He focused on finding ways to bring Disciples from various theological and social justice perspectives together. John emphasized that we are a global church, called to make a difference in the world as a contributing force for peace and justice in crucial issues of the day. As a pastor in the D.C. metropolitan area, he was a staunch supporter of the Civil Rights movement, preaching on it, supporting it even when many of his local leaders initially resisted. A witness to history, he was present for Martin Luther King, Jr.'s iconic "I Have a Dream Speech" during the March on Washigton for Jobs and Peace on August 28, 1963. Later, shortly after Dr. King's assassination, he took Dale and Betty Fiers and John Compton to the Poor People's March in Washington, on June 19, 1968. He supported DOM in their decision to offer a grant to the African National Congress in SouthAfrica for their anti-apartheid resistance. He also worked with DOM to build relationships with Central American and

Cuban partner churches, leading delegations to Cuba and Nicaragua. He publicly opposed U.S. support for the Contras, and was even arrested with a handful of other heads of communion in the Capitol Rotunda to protest that support.

John's ministry has always reflected his firm belief that we Disciples must be the church we say we are, and that all voices are not only welcome and needed to engage in decision-making across the church. John worked to advance the role of women in top leadership across the church, especially in the general ministries. He appointed the first woman deputy general minister, Claudia Grant.

As Deputy GMP, he staffed the committee on structural reform that revised the resolution process for General Assembly, creating among other things the "sense of the assembly" resolutions. He opened churchwide planning to all Disciples, conducting "listening conferences" through the US and Canada, making our first significant use of the internet to invite remote participation in church decision making. As I write this in the spring of 2022, I'm grateful for this example, as the church will once again be holding listening conferences as we prepare to consider new ways to make decisions together, working to ensure that voices across the church are engaged, can speak, and are heard. John worked to advance computerization throughout the church, and was the first to use utilize the internet for churchwide strategic planning and decision-making.

John worked across the staffs of our general ministries to foster a growing sense of unified mission and ministry. He also focused on unifying general and regional staff across the life of the church. Those staff were more numerous at that time, and his efforts represented an important understanding of the covenantal relationships across every expression of the church.

As GMP, John's emphasis on pastoral care from the Office of General Minister and President reflected his great love for the whole church. He worked to model and strengthen openness and access between local churches and general church leadership to bridge the perceived gap between congregations and the general church. I daresay that every GMP since has sought to continue that work, recognizing the importance of being pastor to the whole church.

I always enjoy conversations with John, listening to his many stories of what he has witnessed and experienced in his ministry, being encouraged by his joyful spirit, and being strengthened by his loving support of me as one of his successors. Long before we had language that identified us as a movement for wholeness, becoming an anti-racist church, or bearing witness to God's limitless love, John has always understood that we Disciples must be the church we say we are. Thank you, John, for all you have done to shape and nurture our church. I pray that we may always remember and learn from you, holding your example close in memory and in heart now and always.

Preface

John O. Humbert served as Deputy General Minister and President of the Christian Church (Disciples of Christ) from 1977 to 1985. In August 1985 at the Disciples' Des Moines General Assembly the Reverend Dr. Humbert was elected General Minister and President, the chief executive of the 1.2 million member denomination. Before serving as Deputy for eight years, Dr. Humbert was pastor of congregations for twenty-eight years in Ohio and Maryland.

He is the fourteenth ordained Disciples minister in his family's line of ministers dating back six generations to his great-great-great-grandfather, James Foster, a colleague of the Disciples founders, Thomas and Alexander Campbell. Foster was the first in the family line of ordained ministers leading to Humbert. Mrs. James Foster, Martha, along with her parents Thomas and Lucy Hodgens, and family, were members of Thomas Campbell's Presbyterian congregation in Ahorey, Ireland, before the three families' immigrated to Washington Township in western Pennsylvania.

Introduction

Rick Lowery, President,
Disciples of Christ Historical Society

John Humbert, the third General Minister and President of the Christian Church (Disciples of Christ) in the United States and Canada, served the church in a variety of offices during an enormously consequential period in the history of our church and the world. He was witness to and an active participant in some of the most significant national and international events of our time. He has been a friend and colleague of some of the most important Disciples and ecumenical church leaders of the day. As the spiritual leader of Disciples in the US and Canada at the time the Cold War was about to wind down, he challenged the political leaders of our two nations on a number of important policy issues to work for justice and peace. He called the church to love and to express that love by listening to one another with respect and patience, even as we work fervently to heal and repair injustice. He was and is a great leader who continues to inspire us by his wisdom and example.

As a biblical scholar, I am compelled to say a bit about "genre" and reading strategy as you approach this narrative. This book is not a critical biography, a work of historiography. It is John's memoir. It represents his own memory and self-assessment. It has a point of view – John's point of view. John is appropriately self-critical at points, but he is not a disinterested, "objective" observer – which can be said of any author, of course, but is especially true of those who write memoirs. That fact brings its own strength to the still unfinished story John tells of his own life in his own words. But it also means that, for historians and others interested in understanding the unique significance of this important leader and his life in the long history of our church, this memoir will necessarily be read alongside other sources, other contemporaneous documents and subsequent critical points of view to get a richer sense of this history and John's place in it.

That being said, this memoir is a treasure trove for historians, full of first-hand contemporaneous observations and reflections on some of the most historic events of the last six decades from someone who was there in the thick of it. Drawing extensively from the personal journal he has kept throughout his ministry, John offers a real-time record and reflection on his life's experience now tempered by hindsight and the wisdom of many years of life in the church.

The title *Claiming a Legacy* is aptly chosen. John's story is closely interwoven with the story of our church during his lifetime. In an important sense, however, it is shaped by the church's story long before John was born. His personal identity and experience is profoundly shaped by his deep faith and his lifelong membership in the Christian Church (Disciples of Christ). A multigenerational Disciple, from a long line of Disciples ministers that stretches back to the beginning of the great American reformation that gave birth to our church, John rightly begins his story with the stories of his ancestors. His great-great-great grandfather, James Foster, was a founding member of the Brush Run Church in Bethany, (West) Virginia, and in 1809 signed *The Declaration and Address*, written by Thomas Campbell, one of the two documents that historians consider foundational for Disciples and the broader Stone-Campbell tradition. Foster was trained for ministry by Thomas and Alexander Campbell and ordained by them at Brush Run.

John's memoir continues, telling the stories of a long ancestral line of deeply committed men and women who devoted their lives Christian witness and ministry, to spreading the gospel of unity and healing embodied in the "primitive gospel" championed by the Campbells, Barton W. Stone, and other early 19th Century Christian reformers.

John tells the stories of his grandfather and grandmother Orth and Ella Humbert, both of whom were ordained as Disciples preachers, called as co-ministers to the church in Corvalis, Oregon, and later to Eugene Bible College in Eugene where, in addition to serving as ministers, Grandpa Orth served as college vice president and Grandmother Ella taught world missions. For many years, Disciples missionaries to what was then the Belgian Congo studied with her. Ella was such an outstanding and well-known preacher that she was asked to preach at the historic Disciples Centennial International Convention in Pittsburgh in 1909 that celebrated the 100th anniversary of the signing of *the Declaration and Address*. Pregnant with John's uncle, she was unable travel, but she sent a written copy of her address which was read publicly at the Centennial Convention. Ella and Orth were both heavily involved in soliciting funds for a Disciples medical steamship, the famous S.S. Oregon, which sailed up and down the Congo River delivering essential health care along the way. The Disciples printing press that sailed across the ocean from the U.S. and then up the river from Kinshasa to the Disciples mission station in Mbandaka on the S.S. Oregon sits today just inside the entry of the Disciples of Christ Historical Society on the Campbell farmstead in Bethany, West Virginia.

John tells of his own experience as a Disciples "preacher's kid" and his experiences at church camp and in athletics, including his time playing at Butler University under the legendary coach Paul D. "Tony" Hinkle whose name now adorns the basketball center where the movie "Hoosiers" was filmed. He tells the story of his various early romances and, most importantly, his lifelong love JoAnne. He chronicles his sense of calling to ministry and his theological training, ordination, and early pastorates.

As a local pastor in the greater Washington, D.C. area and as Deputy General Minister in the 1960s and early 1970s, John helped Disciples refine and then live into the vision of the church embodied in *The Design of the Christian Church (Disciples of Christ)*, the foundational document of the newly restructured denomination. He offered courageous and bold leadership, sometimes at significant personal risk, as the church grappled with the issues raised by the Civil Rights and anti-war movements. He was an outspoken ally for women's leadership as feminist consciousness grew in the church.

With a pastor's heart and a deeply Disciples commitment to diversity of thought, John encouraged and listened respectfully to those who had opposing views on the important issues of the day. His loving pastoral demeanor, however, did not restrain him from bold prophetic leadership. During his tenure as GMP, the church, with John's encouragement, began to sort through moral, theological, and ecclesiological issues related to human sexuality and the full participation of LGBTQ persons in the life and ministry of the church. As the leader of the denomination Ronald Reagan grew up in, John became a key leader during Reagan's presidency in the ecumenical and interfaith movements to limit and reduce nuclear weapons, traveling with other world religious leaders to Geneva to pray for peace at John Calvin's Cathedral while Reagan and Mikhail Gorbachev met in 1985 to discuss ending the Cold War and restarting nuclear arms talks. He was one of two US religious leaders selected to appear at a press conference announcing a petition with a million signatures that would be delivered to the two world leaders urging bold steps to ban nuclear weapons, something they almost did the next year at a follow-up summit in Reykjavík, Iceland. John continued to advocate for nuclear disarmament throughout his tenure as GMP. He took a lead role in opposing US support for the Contras in Nicaragua, speaking and presenting a letter from religious leaders to the Speaker of the US House of Representatives on the steps of the US Capitol before joining a handful of religious leaders in an act of civil disobedience, kneeling in prayer and being arrested and taken away in handcuffs from the Rotunda of the Capitol. John was a courageous and key public religious voice for compassion and justice at the height of the AIDS epidemic, which tragically took the life of his own beloved son, his namesake. John's description of his final words with his son at the end of his life is profoundly moving, heartbreaking and inspiring.

John was a strong advocate for women's leadership in every aspect of the church's life, appointing the first woman, Claudia Grant, to the office of Deputy General Minister.

In his own earlier role as Deputy General Minister, John helped change the resolutions process for General Assembly, creating "Sense of the Assembly" resolutions as a way for the church to speak boldly and urgently on sometimes contentious moral and political issues, while respecting the freedom of congregations and individuals to hold divergent views. As GMP, he focused on bridging the divide between more "social activist" and more "evangelically" inclined Disciples. He instituted and participated in a large number of churchwide "listening conferences" as an essential component of strategic planning for the general church. As part of that churchwide planning effort, he inaugurated DiscipleNet as a means to empower church members throughout the US and Canada to participate, contribute and vote remotely via the still relatively young Internet. He launched a concerted, extensive effort to computerize the general church that transformed the way all of our ministries conduct their work. Recognizing the need for a new church headquarters, he led the church to launch a churchwide capital campaign to raise money for mission and for a new facility. That campaign ultimately was unsuccessful, but it laid the groundwork for the church's move to the headquarters we have today. He worked diligently to create a greater sense of community among general ministry presidents and staff, initiating the first General Cabinet retreat for prayer, recreation, and cooperative planning and reports among the ministry presidents. He worked to build a common commitment to work and witness grounded in a Christological understanding that the Risen Christ is the "prince of peace and justice" whose living

Spirit is working in and beyond the church to heal and transform the world.

In short, John's ministry as local pastor, Deputy General Minister, General Minister and President, professor, mentor, and revered elder of the church has been a testament to bold witness for justice, compassion, patience, and genuine openness to the glorious diversity of the Disciples church. His life is an ongoing lesson in justice grounded in Christian love. It is a life well lived, deeply rooted in family, in faith, and in deep appreciation for the countless ways grace and mercy appear in the great and the everyday moments of our lives. This memoir tells the story of this remarkable church leader in his own words.

Acknowledgements

I want to give a heartfelt thanks to my daughter, Deborah Humbert, for her immeasurable help with my computer when it played hijinks with me as I prepared the manuscript for my memoirs. She was the line-by-line editor for the final copy. Thank you, Debbie.

Brad Lyons, President and Publisher of the Christian Board of Publication was of major help in moving my manuscript to book form.

I am grateful to Disciples of Christ Historical Society and its President, Dr. Richard Lowery. Rick and his wife Dr. Sharon Watkins, also a former General Minister and President, have long been dear friends. He took the possibility of the Society publishing my memoirs to his Board, with a positive response, and the "project" moved forward.

Remarkably, Dr. Duane Cummins—historian, author, former President of Bethany College and President of the Disciples Division of Higher Education—and Rick Lowery were volunteers in the final editing of the manuscript. What a major contribution of time and energy. My deepest gratitude to these two lifelong friends.

Rachel Bell, of Clyde Custom Publishing, was a gift to us in the actual printing of the book, published by the Christian Board's Lucas Park Books.

A generous gift to the Historical Society by my niece, the Reverend Diana Spangler Crawford, in support of the publication was then most significant.

I will always be deeply indebted to Rick Lowery and the Historical Society for bringing my story to "the light of day." Thank you, my dear friend, Rick.

CHAPTER 1

"Brother Humbert's Baby"

"The preacher's baby needs to be born in a hospital where Mrs. Humbert and the baby will receive the finest medical care!" So spoke Mr. Dunn, a lifetime member of the First Christian Church of Richmond, Missouri, where Rev. M. Dale Humbert was the pastor. Mr. Dunn had grown up in Richmond, about forty-five miles from Kansas City. He was a wealthy industrialist who now lived in Kansas City while keeping his strong ties with his hometown church. He had achieved notable wealth and was known for his generosity. Not only did he strongly recommend Lakeside Hospital in Kansas City, but he insisted that Brother Humbert and Mrs. Humbert should come and stay in his mansion in the city in the week of the expected birth.

The invitation was accepted, and on October 26, 1927, Frances Elizabeth Humbert gave birth to a baby boy, John Orth Humbert. He was named for his maternal grandfather, John Longston, and his paternal grandfather, Godlove S. Orth Humbert.

During the hospital stay and the recovery of mother and son at the Dunn mansion, there was discussion of transportation home to Richmond. The Humbert family car was a 1924 Chevrolet Coupe. Mr. Dunn insisted the new mother and son should have a more comfortable ride home than in a '24 Chevy Coupe. He would provide his limousine and butler driver for the trip. My very first automobile ride was in style, with the caravan of the limousine leading the way, trailed by the Chevy Coupe and my father. We arrived on the Richmond Street of our parsonage home just as school was out. The children were running down the street clamoring loudly, "Here comes Brother Humbert's baby!" (In the 1920s, in the days of Disciples starting on the road to maturing, some laypeople referred to their minister as "Brother" rather than "Reverend.") My mother was aghast that they were not recognizing she had something to do with this baby!

I don't remember much about my first week in the parsonage. But I do know that within days I received my first letter in the mail. It was postmarked Manson, Washington, and was from my grandfather, John Longston. He was the minister of the Christian Church in Manson, on Lake Chelan, Washington. He welcomed me to the family and the world with some instructions. I was to be a good show baby. I would be receiving much attention at church, especially from the ladies, and should be generous in allowing their affection, since some of the older women might rarely have an opportunity to give kisses. (He actually said "old maids," but I cleaned it up for him.) Furthermore, I was to carefully supervise my mother, to see that for the next six weeks she did not try to carry me upstairs to the nursery. He noted that my father was quite strong and capable enough to tote me upstairs and should regularly do so. He wished for me "a long, wholesome and healthy life, knowing that with my parents' loving and Christian upbringing, I would make outstanding contributions to the world."

CHAPTER 2

John A. Longston

John Longston was an Englishman reared in Great Britain. There is a story related to his coming to America as a late teenager. His brother, Luke, was out hunting and shot a rabbit. It turned out that he had shot the rabbit on the lands of a lord, or some such. At any rate, the word was that he was going to have to go to jail for poaching. He decided that instead he would emigrate from England. John decided he would go with him. Then their parents also made that choice. The question was, shall it be Australia or America? They literally flipped a coin to decide. It was tails, America! I thank God, or I would not now have come to be born in Lakeside Hospital in Kansas City or anywhere for that matter. (There are some other factors, of course!) My knowledge of those years is limited to a photograph of a handsome young man in a band uniform with his instrument, a trumpet.

As a young man John was a member of the Christian Church (Disciples of Christ) and received a "call" to the ministry. I know nothing about that period. But he attended the College of the Bible, a Disciples of Christ seminary, in Lexington, Kentucky, and graduated in the class of 1898. I have a photograph of that graduating class.

The Reverend John A. Longston, then became the minister of the First Christian Church of Independence, Kansas, a congregation which was to have significance on the other side of my family in years to come. But in 1898, Lexington to Independence was a major distance geographically and in the life of the Christian

Church. I can only conceive that there must have been some relationship between the Seminary and a leader in Kansas who steered my grandfather to the Independence Church.

At this point John Longston was single. However, he was soon to meet a young lady from Atchison, Kansas, named Elizabeth Luckman Ramsey.

CHAPTER 3

John and Elizabeth

John and Elizabeth. I have never known how they found each other, though I surmise it must have been through something connected with the meetings of the Disciples churches in that area, or somehow through their mutual British Isles background. Elizabeth Ramsey had emigrated with her family from Cuper in the County of Fife in Scotland, the town just seven miles from the famed all-male University of St. Andrews. Lizzie Ramsey was in a program designated the LLA Examination for Women. Our family has in its possession Elizabeth Ramsay's University of St. Andrews certificates declaring, "We hereby certify that Elizabeth Luckman Ramsey has passed the University written examination in English, History, Geography, French and German," dated 1886. Lizzie was obviously a very bright and industrious young lady in the university's study program for women.

The Ramsey family lived in Dunfirmlin, Scotland, when Elizabeth was born, but moved to Cuper in the County of Fife, where they established a flourishing dry goods store called Ramsey's. Robert Ramsey, her father, was respected and popular in the community of Cuper as a businessman, which led to his election as mayor. In 1985, when JoAnne and I visited Cuper, a gracious gentleman showed us into the historic Town Hall where my great-grandfather presided over the town council. Displayed on the walls were photos of past mayors, dating back to the mayor who succeeded my great-grandfather. The gentleman hosting us said my relative's photo had been installed in an Edinburgh museum.

The timing of this knowledge was unfortunate, for we had just traveled that day from Edinburgh. After visiting the commercial block where our family store had been, we then drove on to St. Andrews where, our son John was finishing his junior year abroad at the university. Small world!

The Ramsey family immigrated to the United States to Atchison, Kansas. One wonders how they settled on Atchison, Kansas, from Cuper, Scotland. But Atchison was a thriving city around the close of the nineteenth century. Located on the Missouri River, it was also the hub of the famous railroad, the Atchison Topeka and the Santa Fe. It was there that the Ramseys chose to begin their operations for their dry goods store, which later would have stores across Kansas and Missouri. John Longston and Elizabeth Ramsey were married, and he had a strong ministry at the First Christian Church in Independence through 1908. On January 16th, 1903, my mother, Frances Elizabeth Longston was born. In 1908, John Longston was called to serve the Christian Church in Fairfield, Iowa. The family, now including a son Robert, and another daughter, Jessica, moved on. Subsequently John served as minister of Disciples churches in Wenatchi and Manson, Washington. In Manson he served not only as the minister, but they were able to buy acreage on which he established a fruit orchard ranch which would supplement the minister's salary and would then become young Robert Longston's next generation livelihood.

CHAPTER 4

Godlove S. Orth Humbert

Somewhere around the winter of 1920, the Manson Christian Church welcomed a guest minister to its pulpit, G. S. O. Humbert, the vice president of Spokane University in Washington. He traveled widely among Disciples churches in the northwest, raising money for the university and recruiting students. He successfully recruited Frances Elizabeth Longston, then seventeen, to attend Spokane University where Morton Dale Humbert was also a student.

Godlove S. Orth Humbert was born in Americus, Indiana, on March 2, 1867. He was named for a state legislator his father greatly admired by the name of Godlove S. Orth. The family never learned what the S stood for. As a young man he followed the call, "Go West young man!" He was very successful as a traveling salesman. Then he apprenticed to become a lawyer.

At some point, probably through the Disciples church, he met Mary Eleanor Fuller, the daughter of a Disciples minister. Mary Eleanor was born in Oregon on December 28, 1868. Mary Eleanor and Godlove S. Orth were married June 22, 1892. As a young adult, Ella, as she was called, was an outstanding church leader and eventually was ordained. G.S.O. also felt called to the ministry and was in the first graduating class of the Eugene Bible College in 1900, later to become Northwest Christian College.

It is through my grandmother, Ella Humbert, that I have a truly remarkable Disciples family linage, dating back to Thomas Campbell and the founding of the Disciples of Christ Church, with fifteen Disciples ordained ministers in my family's seven generations.

Ella Humbert's great-grandfather was James Foster, an Ahorey friend and colleague of Thomas and Alexander Campbell and a trusted participant in founding the Disciples of Christ movement.

CHAPTER 5

James Foster

Thomas and Lucy Hodgens lived in Rich Hill, Ireland, and were members of the Presbyterian Church in Ahorey, near Rich Hill, about thirty-five miles southwest of Belfast. Thomas Campbell was their pastor as the minister of the Ahorey church, and the founder of the Ahorey Academy where the Hodgens' children sat at his knee. The Hodgens' daughter Martha, married James Foster, a strong member of the Haldane Independent church. The two families became good friends of the Campbell family, especially with their son Alexander. Years later there was some question about Alexander Campbell's date of birth. Robert Richardson, in his definitive two volume, *Memoirs of Alexander Campbell*, published in 1868, quotes James Foster as one with knowledge regarding Alexander Campbell's age and birthdate.

> James Foster, who is yet living in the full exercise of his faculties, and has always been remarkable for his power of memory, states that the first time he saw Alexander was at Rich Hill, and that then he was a mere lad of 15 or 16 years of age, and engaged in boyish sport, having in his hand a long pole with a net attached with what he was catching small birds along the eaves of the thatched houses of the outskirts of town. James Foster, himself was, he says, then a young man, and he could not have been more than 3 and a half or 4 years older than Alexander. James Foster was

born March 1, 1785, and adding to this 3 and a half years, we are brought to September 1788.[1]

For Thomas Campbell, the two burdens of teaching and preaching took their toll. Many of his Ahorey friends had migrated to America, or were about to, because of the economy and the religious violence between Protestants and Catholics. He determined to go to America and, with good fortune, to bring his family later. On April 8, 1807, Thomas embarked on the ship *Brutus* from Londonderry, arriving in Philadelphia on May 13, 1807. By coincidence, the Anti-Burgher Association Synod of North America was in session in Philadelphia when he arrived, and it cordially welcomed him. At his request, the Synod assigned him to the Chartiers Presbytery of Southwest Pennsylvania. Many of his Ahorey friends had settled there, near Washington, Pennsylvania. Less than three months after leaving Ahorey, Thomas Campbell was preaching to a circuit of communities on the frontier adjacent to Washington, Pennsylvania, among people who appreciated his ministry.

Meanwhile, Thomas Hodgens, in the midst of hopeless prospects in Ireland for large families, sold his land for three hundred guineas, resolved to emigrate and purchase land in America. One of his daughters was married to James Foster, and he urged his son-in-law to accompany him.

> James Foster was destined to take no unimportant part in Thomas Campbell's future religious movement. He was one of those men who, from a retiring disposition, or other circumstances, do not put themselves prominently forward but who exerts nevertheless, an important influence within a limited sphere, and often make that influence felt through other minds. He was

---

[1] Robert Richardson, *Memoirs of Alexander Campbell* (Philadelphia: Lippincott and Company 1868), 28. A number of excellent histories have been written of these early years, but Richardson included numerous references to my ancestors with whom he was personally acquainted. Hence, I have chosen to reference and quote Richardson's work in this part of my narrative.

a young man of more than ordinary piety and religious attainments. Possessed of a remarkable retentive memory and devoted to the study of the Bible, his mind became a complete Treasury of the word of God, so that he could, with utmost accuracy repeat from memory its sacred teachings at his pleasure. Having become convinced that there was no authority in scripture for the baptism of infants, he would never consent to its administration in the case of his own children.[2]

James Foster...urged to go to America...was induced to consent, and the whole party, the Hodgens and the Fosters having made their arrangements, set out about two weeks after the departure of Thomas Campbell.[3]

A few weeks after Thomas Campbell arrived, James Foster and Thomas Hodgens and their families arrived in Pennsylvania and settled upon a farm near Mount Pleasant, sometimes called Hickory. It was a small village about 10 miles North of Washington Pennsylvania. Thomas Campbell thus found himself situated in the midst of old friends and neighbors, who were impressing their own high estimates of Mr. Campbell's qualifications and character upon their neighbors and acquaintances of different religious parties. With this, Mr. Campbell soon became popular as his many excellencies and his liberal religious spirit became known.[4]

Suspicions began to arise in the minds of his ministerial colleagues because Thomas Campbell was disposed to relax too much of the rigidness of their ecclesiastical rules.[5]

As Thomas was preaching and visiting scattered communities in Washington and Allegheny counties, towards Pittsburgh, he was accompanied by a young minister, a Mr. Wilson. Thomas offered communion to these folks, who probably had not had the opportunity for some time for sacramental celebration, and to

---

[2] Richardson, Memoirs, 81–82.

[3] Ibid., 83.

[4] Ibid., 223.

[5] Ibid., 227.

all who were gathered, though they might have been members of other branches of Presbyterian churches, or even Methodist. A theologically narrow and irascible John Anderson, at the next meeting of the Presbytery, proceeded to lay before them a case of "libel." The Presbytery presented formal questions. Thomas's pleadings on behalf of Christian liberty and fraternity, and his appeal to the Bible as the only true standard of faith and practice, were disregarded and he was found deserving of censure for not adhering to the "Secession Testimony." His case was submitted to the Synod in Philadelphia. There he made his declaration.

> "To refuse anyone his just privilege, communion, is it not to oppress and injure? You can labor under no difficulty about my teaching and practice whatever as expressly taught and enjoined in the divine standard, the Holy Bible.[6] I plead the cause of the scriptural and Apostolic worship of the church, in opposition to the various errors and schisms which have so awfully corrupted and divided it...acquiescing in what is written, as quite sufficient for every purpose of faith and duty, to promote and secure the unity and purity of the church." The final ruling of the Synod was declared. "He has expressed sentiments very different from the sentiments held and professed by this church and are sufficient grounds to infer censure."[7]

The hostility of his opponents was intensified by the issue of the trial. He came to the conclusion that he would present the Synod his withdrawal from ministerial connection. But his action did not interrupt his ministerial labors. He had great personal influence in the counties of Washington and Allegheny. The novelty and force of his plea for Christian liberality and union on the basis of the Bible caused large numbers to attend his preaching and services, often in the deep shade of Maple Groves. These were worthy and religious people who collected

---

[6] Ibid., 228.

[7] Ibid., 227.

from various "parties," seeking better things than could be accomplished in the existing forms of Christianity. They were not all settled in their convictions and there were some among them, such as James Foster, who had been an Independent in Ireland.

Mr. Campbell proposed a special meeting in order to elicit a clear and distinct statement of the principles they advocated. The meeting was held, "reviewing the ground they occupied in the Reformation they now felt it their duty to urge on religious society."[8] Campbell went on to announce in simple and emphatic terms the great principle, or rule, on which they were acting. He declared, "Where the *Scriptures* speak, we speak, and where the Scriptures are silent, we are silent. Henceforth, the plain and simple teaching of the word of God itself was to be their guide. It was from this moment when the significant words were spoken and accepted were dated the formal and actual commencement of the Reformation of the Disciples of Christ."[9]

In the discussion that followed the question of infant baptism arose and the adoption of the principle meant an end to infant baptism. Thomas Atchison of Washington spoke with great emotion, "I hope I may never see the day when my heart will renounce the blessed saying of scripture, 'Suffer the little children to come unto me...'" At which point James Foster, not willing that this misappropriation of scripture pass unchallenged, cried out, "Mr. Atchison, I would remark that in the portion of scripture you have quoted there is no reference, whatsoever, to infant baptism."[10] This exchange foreshadowed some of the trials of the future. Some who were loosely connected with the movement began dropping away.

While in Ireland, James Foster became convinced that there was no scriptural foundation for infant baptism and spoke forcefully about his views. Thomas Campbell, however, was not yet

---

[8] Ibid., 236.
[9] Ibid., 236.
[10] Ibid., 238.

prepared to admit that the principle they had adopted would necessarily involve direct opposition to infant baptism. For the sake of peace, it could be considered nonessential and left to private judgment.

About this time, Thomas Campbell was riding one day with James Foster, urging their views with considerable warmth. At length, James Foster turned toward him and asked with great emphasis, "Father Campbell, how could you, in the absence of any authority in the Word of God, baptize a child, 'In the Name of the Father, and of the Son, and of the Holy Spirit?'" Mr. Campbell was quite confounded at this question. His face colored, he became irritated for a moment, and said in an offended tone, "Sir, you are the most intractable person I have ever met!"[11] (That was my great-great-great-grandfather. A family trait?

At any rate, though having differing sentiments on particular points, the people felt united in promoting Christian union and peace in the religious world. At a meeting on August 17, 1809, it was resolved that they would seek to carry out this purpose more effectively by forming a regular association under the name of the Christian Association of Washington. Twenty-one of their number were appointed to meet and confer together with Thomas Campbell to determine the proper means to carry on promoting Christian union and peace. Five members of my family from two generations were members of the Christian Association of Washington. Thomas and Lucy Hodgens, their son James Hodgens, and their daughter Mary Foster as well as her husband, the noted James Foster.

At this point, Thomas Campbell, spent most of the week between Sunday meetings in study and in writing. The result of which was a document entitled "The Declaration and Address",[12] to set forth to the public at large, in a clear and definite manner,

---

[11] Ibid., 240.
[12] Ibid., 241.

the objective of the movement in which he and those associated with him were engaged. Among the declarations, "This society by no means considers itself 'church,' but merely as volunteer advocates for church reformation in the promotion of Christian union."[13] And the basis for union was to be the restoration of the New Testament church in its pristine purity and perfection, a pure evangelical reformation by the simple preaching of the gospel and the administration of the ordinances in exact conformity to the divine standard.[14]

Thomas Campbell then developed thirteen propositions as "The Declaration and Address." First, "The Church of Christ on earth is essentially, intentionally and constitutionally one." The watchword of the Society became "in essentials, unity, in nonessentials, liberty, and in all things charity."

It was noted that "James Foster, already intimately acquainted with the Bible, and remarkable for the fullness and accuracy with which he could quote and apply its language, soon began to take a public part in the meetings that were held; his pious instructions, exhortations and prayers being always most acceptable and edifying."[15]

About this time the rest of the Campbell family arrived from Ireland, notably son Alexander, who had studied for the ministry in Ireland. Upon discourse and studying The Declaration and Address, he came to be a powerful advocate of the position of the restoration movement and the Association, taking his place alongside his father.

He often held talks in the homes of Christian Association members, but on Sunday, July 15, 1810, he was to preach his first sermon at a farm called Templeton's Grove, eight miles north of Washington, Pennsylvania. It had been advertised in *The Washington Reporter* newspaper. A crowd of supporters, some out

---

[13] Ibid., 244–245.
[14] Ibid., 245.
[15] Ibid., 277–278.

of curiosity, and others who opposed the Christian Association had gathered. Father Thomas had insisted that James Foster preside at the meeting so he could hear his son as one of the congregation. After an opening prayer, James Foster led a responsive reading of Psalm 100, and then he said, "Alexander Campbell, candidate for the ministry from the Christian Association of Washington County," and left the platform.[16]

As powerful as the restoration position was, the Declaration and Address did not cause much of a ripple in the churches of the frontier. The Christian Association accomplished none of the things it set out to do in reforming the parties in churches. Its own existence under the name in its original form, continued less than two years.[17]

At the semi-annual meeting of the Association on May 4, 1811, the Christian Association constituted itself as Brush Run Church. With this action they were no longer a group of reformers from the inside of the Presbyterian Church, but they had become reformers from the outside. They became a separate denomination, consisting of one small country church with thirty members. Without a bishop, presbytery, or presiding elder they committed themselves to the autonomy of the local congregation. As the members of the Association came forward one by one to qualify as members of the church, Thomas Campbell propounded the test question: "What is the meritorious cause of the sinner's acceptance with God?" Only two failed to give satisfactory answers and their admission was postponed. However, a prominent leader of the Association, James Foster, was out of town that Sunday. During the next week there was a discussion of their position, "No Creed but Christ," which led to the church receiving James Foster the next Sunday, simply upon his confession of faith in Jesus Christ as Lord and Savior, with no other test. From his historic admission to membership in this manner

---

[16] Ibid., 277–278.

[17] Louis Cochran, *The Fool of God* (New York: Duell, Sloan and Pearce, 1958), 132–133.

May 11, 1811, Disciples of Christ have never used any other test for membership.

In the Brush Run Church, Thomas Campbell was elected elder. Four deacons were elected, with James Foster as one, and Alexander Campbell was "licensed" to preach.

On January 1, 1812, Alexander Campbell was ordained with the "laying on of hands" by Elder Campbell and the four deacons

At some point, James Foster and Abraham Altars of the Association, anxious to promote the Reformation, began a course of study with a view to the ministry of the Word under the direction of Thomas Campbell. With Thomas Campbell's busy schedule however, they were remanded to study with Alexander Campbell. Subsequently James Foster was ordained in the Brush Run Church with the imposition of hands by Thomas Campbell, Alexander Campbell, and two others.

In 1826, the Fosters sold their farm at Hickory and moved to Beales Station, where James founded a Disciples church where he preached for forty years.

James and Martha Foster had a daughter who married a Stewart, also a Disciples minister. The Stewarts had a daughter, Mary Jane, who was born near Beale Station in December 1845.

Mary Jane Stewart married Benjamin Franklin Fuller, who was born in 1840 near Washington, Pennsylvania. My great-grandparents Mary Jane and Benjamin were married in May 1866. Subsequently, they moved to Cottage Grove, Oregon, where my grandmother, Mary Eleanor Fuller was born.

CHAPTER 6

Godlove S. and Mary Eleanor Humbert

Married in 1892, Godlove S. Orth Humbert and Mary Eleanor Humbert—also known as Orth and Ella—had two children, Harold Franklin, born October 26, 1893, and Madge Pearl, born February 6, 1896. Then on June 7, 1900, just days after G.S.O. had graduated from Eugene Bible College, my father, Morton Dale Humbert, was born in Eugene, Oregon.

In August, Orth and Ella were called to be the co-ministers of the First Christian Church of Corvallis, the town where Oregon State University (then named Oregon Agricultural College) was located. The Humberts alternated the Sundays they preached. On the Sundays Ella preached, Orth would serve one of the smaller area Disciples churches as a visiting minister. Ella was an outstanding speaker and preacher. In 1909 she was invited to speak at the Disciples Centennial International Convention in Pittsburgh, but was pregnant with her son, Royal. Since she could not travel, she sent her address, "The Investment of Life," which was read at the convention in her absence.

G.S.O. and Eleanor served the Corvallis church for three years. They received an invitation to return to Eugene Bible College where Orth would serve as vice president, raising money for the school, and Eleanor would teach world missions. For a number of years, Disciples missionaries in the Belgian Congo studied with my grandmother. My father Morton Dale was named after Stanley Morton, an early Disciples missionary in Latin

America. My uncle Royal was named after Royal Dye, an iconic missionary in the Belgian Congo.

During this period, my grandparents were deeply involved in raising money to build a steamship to be used in the Belgian Congo. Our mission stations in that country were strung out along the Congo River, and transportation was by canoe. Money was raised, the steamship *Oregon* was built, and it was birthed at a river dock in Pittsburgh for the 1899 International Convention. One session of the convention was orchestrated so that the delegates could go on board the steamship and make a contribution to funds for transporting the steamship to the Belgian Congo. The ship was disassembled, packed up, and the parts were transported by commercial ship to the Congo.

When my grandfather Longston was the minister in Wenatchee, Washington, there was a young man, a member of the church, who wanted to be a missionary and widely shared his dream. His personality was rather rough and coarse so most thought he could never qualify. However, he ultimately became the captain of the steamship *Oregon*, transporting missionaries and Congo leaders between mission stations on the river.

My father's boyhood years were spent in Eugene. Transportation in his early years was by horse and buggy, and he would tell us stories about Dan, his favorite horse. In his high school years, the family moved to Washington where my grandfather became the vice president of Spokane University, another Disciples of Christ established institution of higher education. The university also had an academy where Dale finished his high school education. He was committed to the pastoral ministry as he began his freshman year in college. He preached his first sermon at eighteen years old and served student churches during his college years. Another Spokane University student was Theodore Dunton, an extraordinary athlete, who starred on the baseball team. Ted, as he was nicknamed, was such a great player that opposing coaches and observers believed he could have been a major league baseball player. He felt called to the ministry and came to Spokane for his education. He was tall and handsome with an outgoing, attractive personality. He would later marry my father's sister, Madge, who graduated from Spokane University on June 12, 1919.

Harold Humbert, my dad's brother, had also completed his studies, and went east for graduate studies at Boston University, a Methodist Seminary. Ted and Madge followed Harold there, and all three received their master's degrees from Boston University. Harold married Laverne Harrison in 1924, and they moved to Hiram, Ohio, where he came to serve as the minister of Hiram Christian Church. Ted and Madge also moved to Ohio, where Ted was called to serve as the Associate Minister at Akron High Street Christian Church.

CHAPTER 7

Dale Humbert and Frances Elizabeth Longston

When G.S.O. Humbert visited the Washington Christian Church in Manson where John Longston was minister. With his rounds of raising money for Spokane University and recruiting students, he was successful in recruiting the Longston's daughter, Frances Elizabeth Longston, to matriculate at Spokane. She had grown up in a parsonage as a PK, preacher's kid. Her brother Robert worked with her father in the orchard he had started. She had a younger sister Jessica, an outstanding athlete at anything she tried but especially basketball. She had aspirations to be a journalist and would graduate from the University of Southern California.

As a freshman at the university, Frances Elizabeth became known as "Betty" Longston. During the fall semester she dated someone else before Dale Humbert. He was a junior by the spring semester when they began spending time together. Dale had been studying voice and became well known for his baritone singing. Jesse Kellems was a well-known traveling evangelist who led congregations in weeklong revivals. The Kellems family and the Humbert family were friends. One of the key elements of a revival was the music with a vocal soloist who would also lead congregational singing. Jesse Kellems had arranged a schedule of congregational revivals which extended over months in churches in the Northwest and back to the Midwest as far as Illinois and Indiana. He invited Dale to be the soloist and travel the circuit. Dale accepted and the Kellems and Humbert team tour began, with Dale taking a full year off from his college studies. They would arrive at a community hosted by a congregation, staying in the home of a member. The revival services and worship would begin on Sunday evening, continuing through every evening climaxing the following Sunday. Each evening they would have dinner with a member family in their home. One of the stories Dad would later tell was about one of those dinners. He did not like lemon pie. At the first dinner in a congregation, the family served homemade lemon pie for dessert. Not wanting to offend the hostess, he ate it. He felt the need to respond to the pie and said, "This was good lemon pie," without going beyond to prevaricate that he enjoyed it. The word got around that Dad "loved" lemon pie, and it was consequently served by hosting families every evening the whole week.

The evangelistic tour was successful with many members added to the rolls of the churches. But as Dale returned to Spokane, he became deathly ill. Somehow he had contracted smallpox, so he was quarantined in his room in the Humbert family home. In 1921, smallpox took many lives. For him, it was touch and go as to whether he would survive. It was a difficult time emotionally for the Humbert family, Betty Longston, and the entire student body. But slowly through that summer, he recovered and returned to classes for his senior year. Betty was in her junior year by that time. They were dating and they fell in love.

Education was a signal element of the family culture. Orth Humbert spent a lifetime serving in Disciples colleges and universities. He would subsequently serve Culver Stockton College and Phillips University as vice president, raising money and recruiting students. He had an outgoing, affable personality, and "never knew a stranger." When he was working with college students, with his initials being GSOH, the students referred to him as "GOSH" Humbert. He also had acidity digestive sensitivity after meals, and always carried chewing gum, chewing a stick after each meal. He would give me half a stick of gum. He became tagged with our name for him "The chewing gum Grandpa."

My father was committed to further seminary education, preparing for the ministry. On his Kellems tour, he had visited Des Moines, Iowa, the location of Drake University, one of our Disciples colleges and its graduate seminary. One of the outstanding professors was George Medberry, who was one of the leading preachers in the Disciples denomination, and the senior minister of University Christian Church in Des Moines. Dale and Betty, looking forward to their lifetime plans, determined Betty would finish her senior year at Spokane while Dale went on to seminary for his first year at Drake. Dad would speak of the great privilege of attending University Christian Church and hearing George Medberry preach. But soon he became the student minister at the Christian Church in Exira, Iowa. During the year Dale and Betty made plans to be married in Chelan, Washington, where the Longstons were living on their fruit ranch and where Dad was still the minister in nearby Manson. They were married on July 14, 1925. Just before they were married John Longston said to my father, "Young man, if you are going to be a Disciples minister and support a wife and children, you need to go back to serve in the Midwest where we have stronger churches to support a minister's family." It was wise council.

The newlyweds then lived in Des Moines, where dad continued his seminary education while serving the Exira church on the weekends. Mother took some classes at Drake, but most notably continued her vocal training. She had studied voice at Spokane and was an outstanding contralto soloist.

Completing seminary, dad was called to serve the First Christian Church in Richmond, Missouri. I was born October 26, 1927, in Lakeside Hospital in Kansas City. After receiving the letter from Grandfather Longston in my first two weeks, I'm not sure whether I achieved the appellation of being a good "show baby." Years later, when I was General Minister and President (GMP), Fran Cradock, head of the Department of Church Women, in the Division of Homeland Ministries—who with her husband, James, had earlier served the Richmond church—called me. She said,

"We have a visitor from Richmond, Missouri, a gentleman who would like to speak to you." The visitor gave me his name, and said, "When you were a baby, whenever your mother got up to sing a solo in the church service, I was designated to hold you if you got a little fussy." Guess I wasn't a good show baby all the time.

CHAPTER 8

Called to Ravenna

In 1928, Dad was called to be the minister of the First Christian Church in Ravenna, Ohio. He began his ministry in Ravenna on October 28, 1928. Dad's brother, Royal, age twenty-one, came to help us move and traveled with us to Ohio. The story is told that my diapers were washed as best was possible, and then Royal would hold the diaper out the window to flap and dry in the breeze. This was Uncle Royal, who later graduated from Union Seminary in New York City, studying voice at Juilliard School of Music, and then earned a Ph.D. from the University of Chicago. Royal was a professor at Eureka College, one of our church colleges, for some twenty-eight years.

On our way to Ravenna, we stopped in Indiana near Muncie to visit the Burket family. Flossie Burket was G.S.O. Humbert's sister. There were six siblings in G.S.O.'s generation of Humberts, most all of whom stayed in Indiana. When I was GMP, I was engaged to preach for a District Assembly in a town north of Muncie. A gentleman named Million approached me during the business session and asked me to accompany him to a side room. There he had picture albums of the Humbert family when G.S.O. and his siblings were all adults. It was a revelation to see that generation of my family all together. Mr. Million was married to a granddaughter of my grandfather's sister.

Flossie Burket had a large family that was struggling financially. Her daughter Iola Burket, my dad's first cousin, was sixteen years old. Together they decided that Iola would come live with us in Ravenna. She would help take care of me, help mother in the kitchen and around the house, and continue her education at Ravenna High School. She became a really important member of our family at 308 North Prospect Street in Ravenna, the parsonage, our home.

The entrance to our home was a room comparable to the living room in size. Our first radio was a cabinet type, with the speaker underneath. It had enough room for me to put a pillow under it and lie under it to better hear the Indian's games since we were out in the country. (More about that later.) We would gather our chairs around the radio on Sunday evenings to hear Bob Hope, Jack Benny, and *One Man's Family*. Weekdays after school it was *Jack Armstrong, the All-American Boy, Little Orphan Annie* and her decoder rings, *The Lone Ranger* ("Hi ho Silver, Away!"), and *Tom Mix*.

On July 15, 1931, Iola took me over to the home of a family in our church for the morning and afternoon. I remember coming back and standing with her across the street, waiting to come into our house. When she finally brought me inside and upstairs to my parents' room, there, to my surprise, as I remember it, was a baby in bed with my mother. "This," my mother said, "is your baby sister Margaret Jean Humbert." Knowing my mother, I can't imagine her not sharing that she was pregnant, with all the embellishments, and that I should be expecting a baby sibling. But I only remember the astonishment when I came into the room to see a baby sister. I was three years and eight months old. I was delighted to see "Peggy."

Iola was a loving presence in our home. She was a caregiver to us as children, helped mother, and was a companion for my mother when dad was busy so often with evening meetings. My mother was twenty-five when we moved to Ravenna and Iola was sixteen. She was a high school student, graduating in 1930. She continued to help mother in the house and care for the three of us.

Dad was a strong minister with a growing congregation at the First Christian Church. He worked with the young people and had a thriving youth group. After the Sunday evening meetings, they gathered at the parsonage for games and refreshments. Iola was in the middle of all the socializing. John Riethman became a very special friend of Iola's. I was on the sidelines watching, sharing in the popcorn, and feeling their friendly affirmations as a child. Several of the young people in that group later married and became fine leaders in the congregation.

CHAPTER 9

The Cottage on Limeridge

The year 1933 was an eventful year. Dad purchased a couple acres of land five miles from Ravenna on Limeridge Road, off Freedom Road, Ohio State Route 88. Herb Kidd, was an elder in our Ravenna church, the owner of a roofing company, and a friend of Dad's. He owned a 40-acre farm at the corner of Freedom and Limeridge. He offered Dad the property at a generous price and promised himself and his stepson, Bill Hutchinson, as carpenters to help Dad build a cottage. The plan was for our family to live in the country during the summertime and cultivate a large vegetable garden.

I watched with fascination the work as the cottage went up. I was somewhat of a gopher as a six-year-old. Dad had done some carpentry around his parents' homes as a young man. Herb Kidd was a great foreman and leader of the project. The cottage was built, with Dad using his month of vacation time for labor. The whole side of the first floor of the house, front to back was the living room. On the inner side of the room, a stairway led to an open dorm-like room upstairs, to be my sisters' bedroom. The other side of the first floor contained a front bedroom and behind it a dining area, and an extension for a kitchen. Equaling the kitchen length was a generous back screened in porch. There was no basement, no water to the house, no bathroom, only an outhouse. We had a well with a hand pump on a sink in the kitchen. Cooking was with a kerosene stove. There was no electricity. Lighting in the evening and night was with kerosene lamps. We did have a party line telephone. It was a family adventure. Baths a couple of times a week for us were in wash tubs, filled with warmed pump water. We went to the parsonage for our Saturday baths, sleeping there to be ready for Dad to preach on Sunday. During the week Dad would go into town to work in his study at the church, make calls in the afternoon, and be home for dinner in the evening.

The next spring, we had a neighbor from a nearby farm come plow the family gardens on the north and south side of the house. We moved to the country in May, but of course Dad was going back into town every day for his pastoral work. I remember him taking Mondays as his day off and working in the gardens. We learned about planting vegetables and watched in amazement as they grew. We also watched the weeds growing, and I had an elementary introduction to the garden hoe.

Dad built a garage/barn for the car and a stable for our Guernsey cow and later a Shetland pony named Lena. Behind the barn in the pasture of Herb Kidd's farm, he built a pig pen. Every May he bought two young piglets to raise all summer to be butchered in the fall for pork for the Humberts and Kidds. About a hundred yards behind the pigpen was a stream that had been damned for a swimming hole. Many an afternoon from 1933 to 1938 was spent there. That's where I learned to swim.

The side yard of our country cottage became alternately our baseball field and croquet grounds. When Grandfather Longston came to visit, he brought great skill and strategy to the game of croquet and became our tutor. Many hot games were played.

When we returned to the parsonage for the school year, the Mayhew family graciously allowed Dad to stable Betsy, our Guernsey cow, in one of the buildings of the Mayhew Grain Elevator Company. One season, Betsy made Dad a celebrity she gave birth to twin calves when at the Mayhew barn. His photo with the cow and the twin calves along with an article was on the front page of the Ravenna Evening Record.

In September 1933, my uncle Ted Dutton died suddenly in Independence, Kansas, where he had moved to from Akron to be the minister. Independence, you may remember, was where my grandfather John Longston had been the minister back in the first ten years of the century. This was the same congregation Grandfather served and where my mother was born. Dad and Mother traveled to Kansas to be with his sister Madge, Ted's widow, and young Ted and Mary Ellen. Mary, Peggy, and I were left in the care of Iola. This occurred just as I was entering first grade. I had not attended kindergarten and I simply presented myself at the first grade classroom with little preparation of what to expect. Miss Beardsley was my teacher. I do not remember the content of the first day of school, but I do remember vividly that I had to go to the bathroom badly, with no idea of the procedure or location of the "boys room" at Highland Avenue School. School was out, and I gingerly walked home, which was literally right around the corner from school. I rushed to the front door to find it locked. Iola was away and I proceeded to wet my pants. I was mortified and very uncomfortable until Iola returned home. That was trauma enough, but the second day I returned to the classroom, sat down in a seat, and Nancy Lee said, "Hey that's my seat," and slapped me. I didn't realize I was to sit in the same seat as the first day. Fortunately, I learned the procedure of being excused for "going to the basement," my seat assignment, reading, writing, and numbers enough to graduate to the second grade.

CHAPTER 10

Summer in Topenish, Washington

The summer of 1935, the World Convention of the Disciples of Christ was held in Leicester, England. The church gave my father three months paid leave of absence, not only to attend the convention but to travel in Europe, Africa, Syria, and the Holy Land. While he was traveling with two other ministers for three months our mother took the three of us to Toppenish, Washington, where Grandfather now served as the minister of a combined Disciples and Congregational Church. The trip was quite an adventure—three nights and three days on the train, with Pullman sleeping service accommodations which were really cool. While we were there, our grandparents took us over the mountains to see Aunt Jessica at St. Helens, Oregon, and to the fruit orchard on Lake Chelan, where Uncle Robert and Aunt Dorothea Longston lived. One of the weekly events was attending the polo games at the Toppenish Polo Club. I fell in love with the grace, power, and speed of the polo ponies and became enamored with the local star players. Polo became one of my new sports loves. (After returning home to Ravenna, my friend Hank Piehl's father took us to a polo match at the Gates Mills Polo Grounds in suburban Cleveland.)

Since we were to remain with my grandparents until mid-October until dad returned, I entered the third grade in my grandparents' neighborhood grade school. It was a multicultural school with Native American children and a number of Japanese Americans. My seat was in the front next to a Japanese American boy who had a great sense of humor, and he became my best friend for the six weeks we remained in Toppenish. I really liked our teacher, a beautiful young woman fresh out of college. I had some trouble fitting in because I came to school during the early September warm days wearing shorts. The other boys wore long pants or jeans and made fun of me. Mother shifted me to knickers and that was worse. That really hurt until mother OK'd jeans, and the other boys ceased their hazing. After that, I enjoyed the six weeks adventure in a far-flung, unique grade school.

Our return to Ravenna was, again, a three-day and three-night train trip. At night, the Pullman car with its swaying train and the clicking of the wheels on the track was a rhythmic lulling to sleep. For years afterwards, when I heard a train whistle, I would lie very still in my bed and reimagine my Pullman sleeping compartment on the train.

We were so delighted to be home with Dad after such a long time without him. I remember worrying about his two transatlantic ship crossings praying he would be safe.

CHAPTER 11

At Home in Ravenna

We settled back into our school year back in Ravenna. I joined my classmates in the third grade at Highland School and Mary was beginning first grade. The teacher was teaching from different textbooks than the ones I began out West. I struggled to catch up. The teacher seemed strict and harsh in her approach, and though I tried to do my work well and correctly, it didn't seem to please her. She was my least favorite grade school teacher.

The summer after third grade, however, was a highlight. Dad took me to a bicycle shop, a marvelous wonderland. Together we picked out my bicycle. I had wheels! I had ridden other kids' bikes, so I knew how to ride, but I had a quick test. We were living out in the cottage, and Dad told me I could ride the five miles out while he drove in the car. I made it up and down the hills, but having never ridden that distance, I was tired yet happy.

That summer I also had another major dream come true. I can't remember when in my young life, I wasn't a rabid Cleveland Indians baseball fan. I devoured the Cleveland *The Plain Dealer* sports page for news of the Indians. I listened to the games' radio broadcasts. We could barely get the sound of the Indians radio station WHK. So, I would put a pillow underneath the speaker to listen to Jack Graney call the games. Then at 5:30 a.m., WHK had the resume of the game, telling about each out. The next morning, I would read all the write-ups and review the resume with the sports page spread out on the floor.

When Dad said we were going to League Park to see the Indians play, I was in seventh heaven! We drove to Cleveland, the big city, and as dad was in the general area of the ballpark, he stopped at a gas station to get directions. There was another customer there who said he knew exactly how to get to the park. His name was Alva Bradley, and of all things he was the owner of the Cleveland Indians. What a coincidence! We arrived, parked, bought tickets, entered, walked up a ramp toward our seats, and suddenly I was transfigured. There was all the beautiful bright green grass of the outfield, the manicured infield, and the dugouts. There was no television then, of course, so this was my first glimpse of the playing field. There were the players I knew from the pages of *The Plain Dealer* and Jack Graney's description. I stood stark still, catching my breath! It was the thrill of a lifetime! (A portrait of League Park now hangs in my home.) But then, to top it all off, the visiting team was the New York Yankees. Lou Gehrig was playing first base, a rookie by the name of Joe DiMaggio was in center field. Babe Ruth had just retired the year before. Red Ruffing started for the Yankees, with Hall of Fame catcher Bill Dickey behind the plate. For the Indians, Hal Trosky was at first (he would drive in 156 runs in one year), Hall of Fame Earl Averill was in center field, Roy "Stormy" Weatherly was in right, with Jeff Heath in left. Johnny Allen pitched. (Johnny Allen would start one season winning fifteen straight games before losing.) I was thrilled beyond imagination!

On August 23, 1936, Bob Feller made his first start pitching for the Indians. He was a seventeen-year-old farm boy from Iowa. He hadn't thrown a pitch in the minor leagues. His father, Bill Feller, had taught him to pitch. Bob had a blazing fastball. That day he struck out fifteen St. Louis Browns players, one short of the record (which he broke one month later with seventeen strikeouts). He pitched a complete game and won. He became my hero. I wanted to be a Major League pitcher just like Bob Feller, a dream I carried with me to success as a pitcher when I was sixteen. More about that later. Dad was especially interested in Bob

Feller, because his seminary student church was in Exira, Iowa, not far from Van Meter, Bob Feller's hometown. Feller completed the season with a five-win and two-loss record, and then went home to Van Meter and finished his senior year of high school! He played eighteen Major League seasons with the Cleveland Indians, finishing with 266 victories, three no hitters, a World Series title, and an induction into the baseball Hall of Fame. I would see him pitch many games.

Dad bought me a baseball glove and we often played catch. Naturally, I would pretend to be Bob Feller. And, of course, he bought me a Louisville slugger baseball bat.

I think it was on my first birthday that my prize present was a football. At a very early age, I began to practice placekicking and punting the football. Bob Heisler, a Ravenna high school football and basketball star, lived in the home around the corner. His backyard bordered our backyard. Back there, their family played softball, touch football, and had a basketball hoop. Their backyard extended all the way to a fence around my Highland Avenue grade school. It was that close to our home. Bob would cross our yard on his way over to see his girlfriend, Betty Collier, across the street. He was my local hero since, with Dad, I had watched him play for the Ravenna High School Ravens. He would stop and let me pass the football to him and be very encouraging. When I could accomplish kicking the football clear across the front yard, I thought it was quite a feat, all of about fifteen yards!

The Berlin Summer Olympics were held in 1936. All of Ravenna was excited for Bob Heisler because he had won a trip to see the Olympics in Germany. Ohioans were also energized because Jesse Owens, the track star from Cleveland's East Tech High School and Ohio State University, would be running in four dash events. This was the Olympics over which Adolf Hitler loomed with his proclamation that the Aryan race was the master race. Much to his consternation, before his very eyes, Jesse Owens, an African American, won four gold medals and was the star of the Olympics. Ravenna's *The Evening Record* carried my friend Bob Heisler's writing of witnessing the events. And of course, Cleveland's *The Plain Dealer* was filled with photographs of their native son's prodigious accomplishments.

Betty Collier's brother, Bill, was three years older than I, and I frequently played in his yard with him and several others his age, including Harry Dale Webb. When I was six, my parents were about to leave for the Ohio Disciples Ministers Institute in Lakeside. The boys and I were roughhousing in the Collier yard when Harry Dale wrestled me down, and with all of his nine-year-old weight put his knees on my shoulders and broke my collarbone. I had looked forward to going to Lake Erie and swimming. Instead I went to Lakeside with my arm in a sling, so swimming was out.

Growing up on North Prospect Street as well as in our country cottage was wonderful. My early friends, the twins Hank and Barbara Phiel, lived just behind the Colliers. We enjoyed scooters and roller skating together. They lived in what I considered a mansion, fronting on Chestnut Street, with a large yard. Highland Avenue, around the corner from our house to the west had some very large and attractive homes with beautiful lawns. However, the second house from the corner was Effie Van Meter's home. She did not countenance anyone even stepping on her lawn. If a ball of any sort ever went into her yard, it was confiscated never to be seen again. Moreover, her brother was John Goodenough, Chief of Police!

Another of my early school friends was Jack Ferguson. We both enjoyed art and drawing. He lived several blocks away and we spent many after school hours drawing, pencils in hand creating masterpieces. Later, when we both had bicycles, we enjoyed riding out to the Ferguson's celery farm to watch the harvesting, cutting, washing, and preparation of the celery to be loaded on their farm's large truck and shipped to Pittsburgh. I don't think I have ever enjoyed celery so much as then. Fresh, washed, and chilled!

The Dutter farm was just across Limeridge Road from our gardens. Vern Dutter was two years older and his brother, Gene, was three years older. We became good friends. We played baseball together at the farm and in our yard. I hung out at their farm many days, riding out to the fields on the hay wagon, watching the harvest. They had a dog who would round up the milk cattle to bring them in for the evening milking. They had two mules, Jack and Jenny, for plowing, cultivating, pulling the wagons, and raising the big barn hayfork. They also had a strawberry field and cherry trees, from which they generously allowed the Humbert family to pick.

The iconic day of the summer, however, was "threshing day." It was a day of harvest for wheat, oats, and rye. The huge mechanical threshing machine would be towed into place in the farmyard early in the morning. The wheat, oats, and rye would be cut, bound into sheaves, and then stacked in the shocks out in the grain fields. All the neighboring farmers would come clattering to the Dutter farm with their teams of horses and hay wagons. When the threshing machine whistle would blow, the horses and wagons stepped out into the fields with the slapping of reins and shouts of "giddyup," "gee," and "haw"! The grain sheaves would be loaded from the shocks, and the horses and loaded wagons would drive up to the clanking belt that ran the threshing machine. The sheaves were fed and ground, and the grain would spill out into a special wagon while straw spewed out into a haystack. Around noon a shrill whistle would sound, almost like a train whistle, followed by the procession of the teams of horses retreating to the barnyard. The Dutters, with help from other farm wives, had set the tables laden with "threshing dinner" to host their working neighbors. And the hardworking farmers dug in! As a wide-eyed young lad, I had the privilege of witnessing this humongous event at the Dutter's, with Vern Dutter as my guide. The next day, the threshing machine moved on to the next farm for a repeat performance of threshing day with the same cast of farmers, plus Mr. Dutter, Jack, and Jenny.

The Dutters had one of the nicest farms around the Freedom area, but one of the signal events for them was the Works Progress Administration (WPA) coming to their farm to build an up-to-date, modern "outhouse."

On May 6, 1935, President Franklin Roosevelt, working to overcome the Great Depression with his New Deal, established the WPA to employ unskilled laborers to carry out public works construction. I remember watching the WPA building concrete streets in our neighborhood on Elm Street, the Reithman's home street. As I recall, the pay for WPA workers was $12.50 a week.

One of the most popular programs of the New Deal was the creation of the CCC, the Civilian Conservation Corps. The work was to conserve the country's natural resources while providing jobs for young men under twenty-five. They were housed in military-like camps. They worked on preventing erosion by planting millions of trees across the country. They fought forest fires and cut out dead timbers to prevent fires. I remember passing a CCC camp just off State Route 14, the road from Ravenna to Alliance, Ohio, and seeing them working along the highway more than once.

The fall of 1936, I entered the fourth grade as an eight-year-old, soon to be nine on October 26. Miss MacArthur was my teacher, my favorite of all my grade school teachers. Another thing took place that would affect my feelings for years to come. Barbara Jean Sorenson joined our fourth grade class and would remain my classmate until ninth grade when we moved from Ravenna. She was bright, with a warm and kind personality, and I thought she was beautiful. My seat was just behind hers, and when she turned to smile and speak to me, I was thrilled. I was shy and worshipped her from afar in the fourth grade. However, in that spring she got a new bicycle. She knew we lived right around the corner from our school. She asked if she could ride to our house in the morning before school and park it there all day where it would be safer. That worked for me! I would try to await her arrival and casually time my coming out the door. I was too shy to simply ask her to walk to school with me. I just had to make it accidental. I told my mother I was in love.

Two of my very favorite movie stars were Nelson Eddy and Jeanette MacDonald, who had marvelous singing voices. They starred in two movies which were almost operettas. Nelson Eddy was a Canadian Mounted Officer in love with Jeanette MacDonald's character, Rose Marie. One of the lines in his song was "Oh Rose Marie, I love you, I'm always thinking of you," often reprised. In private, I would sing, "Oh Barbara Jean I love you, I'm always thinking of you."

With my admiration of Jeanette McDonald and Nelson Eddy and their movies and radios careers, there was an amazing coincidence in later years. When I was a student minister for two years at the Disciples church in Hanoverton, Ohio, there was a family prominent in the church by the name of Rush. Their son Malcolm Rush had gone to Bethany College and had roomed with Dwight Stephenson, who would become my homiletics professor in seminary. But more to the point, Malcolm Rush had gone West to work in Hollywood. He became the Executive Manager of Nelson Eddy, Jeanette MacDonald, Roy Rogers, Dale Evans, and Trigger, Roy's horse. I met Malcolm Rush when I performed his brother's funeral. He invited me outside for a moment of conversation, and in the process handed me a $50 bill.

Back to school. One of the important pastimes on the playground during recess or before school was playing marbles, with several variation of games. A particular favorite was a ring game, shooting our aggies with our thumb and forefinger. I became fairly proficient and held my own, including playing keepsies where you kept the marbles of the opponent you knocked out of the ring! I collected a fairly large sack of marbles. I practiced at home. The living room rug had a design that I could use as the circle ring, where I would practice by the hour down on my haunches. By sixth grade a national marble tournament was established, and a Highland school tournament was held. I won several rounds and made it to the finals. It was a tense battle, but I knocked the winning marble from the ring. I was the school champion! I jumped up to retrieve the marble. But in my excitement, I ran through the ring and was disqualified for entering the circle. I lost the championship! What a disappointment. But it was of my own doing, of course.

For some time I had wanted to play the trumpet. Mother and Dad were all for it, but stipulated I needed to take piano lessons for a year first. They felt learning the piano would help me with music theory, reading the treble and bass cleft, etc. So, I began taking music lessons early in the fourth grade. Ironically, my piano teacher and her violin teaching husband had moved into the "mansion" where Hank and Barbara Phiel had lived, so my lessons were at the piano in the front room where I used to play with the twins. Throughout the fourth grade, I took piano lessons and practiced, not always happily. After all, it was with the purpose of getting to play the trumpet, which I did in the fifth grade. I had a private teacher, Ervin Hoeffler, a member of our church. He was a great musician, playing in some big-time dance bands that came to Akron and Cleveland. He was also the band director at Ravenna Township High School. I enjoyed playing, and soon was playing the trumpet in the church's Sunday school opening session orchestra.

The church was central in our family life. As a youngster I could hardly wait to join the church, be baptized and be a real member. Dad would kindly say, "Johnny, you need to be old enough to understand what it means to make your confession of faith and be baptized." When I was nine, Dad said if I completed reading the gospel of Luke, then I could make my confession of faith and be baptized. I read passages of Luke almost every day and finished before Easter. During Holy Week, 1937, we had worship services every evening, with guest preachers. On Wednesday evening March 24, the preacher was J.H. Welshimer, who for thirty-seven years was the minister of the First Christian Church in Canton, Ohio—our largest Disciples congregation with over five thousand members. That was the evening I had decided I would come forward. All through the service, I was excited and moved. The moment the first bars of the invitation hymn "Just as I am" played, I practically bolted from my pew to come to the front. My father took my confession of faith as he clasped my hand, and I affirmed my faith in Jesus Christ, my Lord and Savior. I was thrilled. On Easter at the sunrise service, my dad baptized me. It was a beautiful, sunny day, and in the afternoon Dad and I went for a walk together. I told him how happy I was and talked about how joyous I felt when he baptized me. It was a glorious Easter Sunday.

That summer, Dad told me he thought it was time for my dream of acquiring a Shetland pony to come true. He had loved his horse as a teenager, telling us lots of stories about his family's "Dan." We answered an ad in the paper to see a pony that was for sale. We arrived at the farm. The black and white pony was in a fenced in field. She was beautiful! Dad said, "Johnny get on and ride her. You can ride her bareback." He hoisted me up. The pony took off with me holding on to its mane for dear life. There were no reins. And it ran and ran! Finally, it came back to the owner and stopped. I got off, but the pony was wheezing like crazy. "We'll think about it," said Dad. When we got in the car, he said, "That pony is not in good shape. That's why I wanted you to ride it, so we could see for certain."

We answered another ad. The even more beautiful black and white pony was named Lena. They put on a saddle and bit with reins and I rode her. She was nice and gentle. She not only had a nice Western saddle, but a cart with a car seat on the buggy and an appropriate harness. Wow! A dream come true. I enjoyed riding it around our country cottage. One particular summer evening, I remember racing around the Dutters' hay field that was partially cut. Lena against a neighbor's pony. I remember, too, harnessing Lena to the cart and driving up Limeridge Road with my sisters on the buggy's seat. I learned to feed and water Lena. There was enough room for Lena and our cow, Betsy, in the cottage barn dad built.

Nineteen thirty-seven marked a major change in our family life. Mother was pregnant! I had high hopes for a brother! I had been asking for a brother for years. The whole family pitched in sewing new diapers, sitting together in a family project.

That summer, Dad and I were hoeing in the vegetable garden when he asked me, "Johnny, what do you want to be when you grow up?" I leaned on my hoe and forcibly replied, "Well, I know one thing for sure. I don't want to be a farmer!"

Dad and I also went on a camping vacation trip to Gettysburg and Washington D.C. I was awed by the sights of the Capitol and the memorials to Washington, Lincoln, and Jefferson. The whole trip became a benchmark in my growing up.

Nineteen thirty-seven was also our last summer in the Limeridge cottage. We sold our summer home in 1938, and bought a large house at 529 Lafayette Avenue in Ravenna. The property was about two acres, with a shed where we could stable Betsy and Lena. There was also land for large vegetable gardens. After buying the house, termites were discovered in one section of the basement and under the front porch. Dad labored long and hard replacing the floor joists in both. I had my first adventure in serious sawing and painting extensively with creosote. The work was successful, and we enjoyed the larger home. The church had voted to rent the parsonage, with dad receiving the $25 a month rent as a parsonage allowance, a wonderful support in financing the purchase of the property. Ironically, the Youngs, my piano teacher and her husband, moved into the parsonage as renters.

Boy Scouts became an important part of my life, first Cub Scouts, and then our church troop led by Scoutmaster John Riethman. We met regularly at the church, and in the summer we went to Camp Manatauk for a week. I achieved the level of a Star Scout and was nearly through my merit badges for the rank of Life. My good friends were also in the troop. We spent many great times camping, hiking, and attending jamborees in Akron. I'm sure I would have gone on to Eagle Scout if we had stayed in Ravenna. But when we moved to Bellefontaine, the church troop just wasn't the same, and I concluded my scouting.

With my fifth grade teacher, I began two years of tutelage with the Holt sisters, who lived in Twinsburg. I remember her reading stories to us just after lunch. One novel was about Alaskan Huskies pulling sleds, including an exciting story of a long Alaskan race with details of the long miles and overnight encampments. This was also the year we had looked forward to because some would be chosen to be "safeties" in the Safety Patrol. We always looked up to the "safeties" as very special people and looked forward to the opportunity to be chosen. I was one of the chosen and received a badge and harness.

In sixth grade, our music teacher, Miss Williams, an attractive young woman just out of college, chose to lead the Ravenna grade schools in a presentation of the operetta *Tom Sawyer*. I was chosen for the lead, Tom Sawyer, with a number of solos and numerous lines. Barbara Jean Sorenson was chosen to play Becky Thatcher, Tom's girlfriend. I was really delighted. The operetta was presented in the high school auditorium in two showings, with acclaim. I was invited by Miss Williams to rehearse extensively with her during class time. She was wonderful with students, and I was quite infatuated. Years later when I was serving the Euclid Avenue Christian Church in Cleveland Heights, I learned that the retired Miss Williams was living in Cleveland Heights. I phoned her and was invited to stop by for a visit.

The Ravenna school system had a basketball program for sixth graders. Our Highland school team competed round-robins with the other grade schools. In our yard I put a backboard on a tree with a metal waste can with the bottom cut out for a basket. I played with a rubber ball about the size of a soccer ball and practiced shooting after I finished my chores. I made the team. It was my first experience on a team. I loved playing basketball with the other guys. We did pretty well. I had liked watching our church's adult team play league basketball in our Highland school gym and was learning about team play. Playing and observing as an eleven-year-old spawned a lifetime love for basketball.

I had broad and intense interest in sports. In addition to my outside basket, I made a small basket out of wires and string I could fit over the door to the basement in the dining room of our house, to play with a small ball. And I loved to kick the football. We played a punting game in the street where two sides would try to kick the ball beyond the opposition's goal line. I also loved to place-kick and drop-kick. I built a football goal post and installed it on our "back forty" and practiced kicking extra points and field goals in our yard. I installed five golf holes in the yard, and we had fun with my dad's golf clubs.

I had joined the neighborhood softball games at an early age. I was a left-handed batter, even though I threw right-handed. In gym class I was one of the better softball players. My good friend and I developed a game of "rubber ball" pitching and batting a baseball sized rubber ball. I had good control. Dad showed me how to hold the ball to throw a curve.

Dad played third-base on the Kiwanis softball team, and I was there for his games against other towns' Kiwanis teams. I even rode with the men to Alliance, Ohio, where they played at Mount Union College. On a few occasions when I was in junior high, I was drafted as an outfielder.

One early spring day during sixth grade, we had a snow storm. By the time school was out, the sun was shining, and it was a beautiful day. On the way home from school there must have been twenty kids who started a snowball "rumble" with snow that packed perfectly for snowballs. We fired snowballs back and forth across Highland Avenue, having fun. We were, however, violating the Highland School rules—no snowballing on the way home from school. You had to have arrived at your home before throwing snowballs.

The next morning Mr. Griffith, the principal, strode into our homeroom. He said, "I want to know who of you was engaged in the snowball fight yesterday." I was sitting in the front row, and I held up my hand. I looked around knowing that probably at least eight others were involved, but there was only one other hand up. "Come with me you two." Chuck and I went sheepishly to Mr. Griffith's office. We sat down in the outer office for a moment. Then he took Chuck into the inner sanctum. After a few minutes, I heard three smacks. Then Chuck came out. I was invited in. The principal said, "You know you violated school rules?"

"Yes, sir," I said.

"All right bend over this table," he said. I did, and he administered three hard smacks with a wooden paddle, which looked like a college fraternity paddle. "You two may now return to your homeroom. Don't do this again." Returning to our room, I couldn't help but look around at my guilty classmates who were not truthful and escaped punishment.

Well, I wondered what would happen when my father came home for dinner that evening. He had always said if I misbehaved in school enough to get paddled, I would get another lickin' when I got home. I told him about what happened. "Well," he said, "since you told the truth as the only two who faced the punishment, you won't get paddled again on your sore behind." Ah, the ides of March 30.

The Easter 1939 sunrise service was beautiful with the sanctuary elaborately decorated with lilies. Dad conducted the baptismal service and preached the 11 o'clock service, with beautiful choral music, with mother's contralto solo. She had a marvelous trained voice. We had a wonderful afternoon and evening. That evening, I had just gone to bed, when mother rushed into my room. "John, call Dr. Sivon. I think Dad is having a heart attack." With fear in my bones, I called the doctor and waited with Mother in trepidation until he arrived. They rushed Dad to Robinson Memorial Hospital for treatment for a heart attack. He was thirty-nine years old. I don't remember how long he was hospitalized, but he was homebound to the master bedroom on the second floor.

There was a balcony porch off the bedroom, where he could be moved to sit overlooking our gardens and the barn. With his commitment to serving the congregation, a family to be supported, a cow to milk, and gardens to plant, confinement to his bedroom for weeks was an overwhelming prospect. It was too much for him emotionally, and he had a nervous breakdown.

Suddenly, eleven-year-old me became the man of the house, milking the cow before school, taking care of the animals, gardens, and the heavy work around the house. Fortunately later that summer, Mr. Reed, a member of the church who was out of a job, came to do the milking and heavy garden work.

A retired Disciples minister who had come to live in Ravenna, George B. Townsend, stepped in to be the substitute minister while mother did pastoral work. Graciously, the church continued dad's salary while he recovered. He spent time at the Overlook Sanitarium in New Wilmington, Pennsylvania, with rest, physical therapy, massages, and counseling on his way to recovery. He was out of the pulpit for a full year.

Mother depended on me for moral support. After a year, dad recovered and was able to resume his work just after Easter 1940. Meanwhile we sold our cow and my pony with tearful farewells. Their demands for nurture and care were too much for a twelve-year-old school boy.

When I moved to the seventh grade, we met in the high school building. We had a homeroom and moved from room to room for classes. One exciting thing to me was having gym class. I loved playing basketball on the high school gym floor and softball and touch football on the high school practice fields. After school, the varsity football team would practice on those same fields.

The Band Director for the grade school band was also the Director for the junior high and the senior high band. The junior high band was a concert band. I was first chair in the trumpet section. Then, I was invited to join the trumpet section of the senior high school band, a concert and marching band. With uniforms! And football games! There were only two seventh graders in the senior band. The other was a clarinetist, Barbara Jean Sorenson! Our lockers were close together and we had the opportunity to walk to band practice every day for eighth period. However, I was too shy to ask if we could walk together. Instead, I tried to time my locker moment accidentally to come to band practice with her.

I decided I wanted to ask Barbara Jean to go to the movies with me, a date! The custom in our house was one movie a month, after checking with the appropriateness of a movie for kids through *Parents Magazine*. Snow White, the huge Disney movie, was playing on a weekend. On the Monday before, I was planning to ask her to go with me. We were in the same homeroom and moved from class to class between periods together. Every break I was going to ask her, but I chickened out all day. Even walking alone together to band practice, I was unable to work up the nerve. I was at home after school outside shooting baskets when I heard the phone ring. I ran in, answered the phone, and a female voice said, "I can go." "You can go?" "Yes, I can go with you to the movies on Saturday afternoon. But you will have to meet me at 12:30 at Mr. Watkin's house, after I take my clarinet lesson, and we can walk to the theater."

"That's nice," I said. She said goodbye and the conversation ended. I was stunned. It seemed my mother had phoned her mother to see if it was permissible for me to ask Barbara Jean to go to the movies with me on Saturday. That evolved into Barbera accepting. We enjoyed the movie! I was so thrilled to be sitting beside my first love on an actual date! After that it gave me the courage to pointedly wait to walk with her to band practice.

I really enjoyed the marching band. We played in parades on Armistice Day and Memorial Day, along with the U.S. Cavalry based at the armory on Freedom Road, their beautiful horses, and the Army Reserve soldiers. In June, just after the school year ended, the band was invited to play concerts at Craig's Beach Park at nearby Lake Milton—one early in the afternoon and one at seven. They were going to feed us in return. I embarked from home with one dollar. After the first concert I decided to ride the roller coaster, for the price of ten cents. It was my first ride on a roller coaster. It was scary and thrilling! I got right back on! I spent my entire dollar on ten rollercoaster rides that day.

War clouds were looming on the horizon in 1939 and 1940. Hitler and the Nazis were taking over Europe. High school debate teams were focusing on whether our country should be involved. The Federal government was buying up thousands of acres around Portage County, some not far from our Limeridge Road place. Francis P. Bolton was our congresswoman, and she owned a large farm in the area of what become the Ravenna Arsenal. One of the men in our church was the manager of her farm and her cattle, including beef and milk cattle. Our family was once invited to dinner at the manager's home on the beautiful white-fenced rolling fields. We toured the beautiful barns, amazed at them being paneled in knotty pine, like a beautiful family recreation room. Some of our church members' farms were also purchased by the government.

The summer I was twelve, Uncle Royal came to visit. He encouraged mother to allow him to teach me to drive. He took me out to Lovers Lane Road in our 1935 Plymouth, with a stick shift, to give me lessons. I was a good student, and I loved driving. I applied and received my temporary driver's permit. That summer I drove my family places a number of times, including a trip to Chautauqua, New York. The gatekeeper at Chautauqua seemed startled to note the family driver. Unfortunately, in my view, that fall the Ohio legislature passed a law requiring licensed drivers to be sixteen years of age. I knew how to drive, and was doing it competently, but had to give up driving for four years!

By the fall of 1940, my eighth grade year, we were encouraged to buy war bonds and war savings stamps. All my grade school years were during the Great Depression. The bonds were to support the government's gearing up for defense of our country. During halftime at one of our home football games that fall, I was the vocal soloist over the public address system, accompanied by the band, singing, "Any bonds today, bonds of freedom that's what we're selling, any bonds today…" At another halftime, I sang a song by Irving Berlin with the band, introduced by singer Kate Smith, "God bless America, land that I love. Stand beside her, and guide her, through the night with a light from above…" It would become a standard as you know.

One of the traumatic events of my junior high years was the callup of the Army Reserve Cavalry unit stationed at the Ravenna Armory. Many people gathered on Freedom Road to see the young men and their beautiful horses depart for active duty in the Army. My friends Jack McClain, Doug Brown, and I watched tearful families and girlfriends say goodbye.

In the summer of 1941, Dad had a visit from a pulpit committee from the Disciples church in Bellefontaine, Ohio. It was a large congregation of seven hundred members, which had been going through some difficult times—the issue being direct missions or cooperative missionary work through the United Christian Missionary Society. Gaines Cook was the State Secretary of the Ohio Christian Missionary Society, and a term later was to become the Regional Minister. He had been working with some of the elements in the congregation and believed Dad's pastoral spirit and skills could bring the congregation together for life and mission. The congregation voted to call him to serve as their minister, and he accepted. On October 27, 1941, he presented his resignation to the First Christian Church of Ravenna, thirteen years to the day from when he had begun his ministry in Ravenna.

CHAPTER 12

Bellefontaine High

I found it very difficult to move away from my school friends, my special friends Jack and Doug, my Boy Scout friends, and the church life I had always known. We left Ravenna on Armistice Day, November 11, 1941. The congregation received us warmly with the church welcome dinner and dinners in their homes. Mary, Peggy, and I entered the Bellefontaine schools: Mary in seventh grade, Peggy in fifth grade, and me in ninth grade. Our younger brother, Bobby was just four years old.

We were just getting settled in at the parsonage at 305 E Brown Street, the church, and in school when the Japanese attacked Pearl Harbor on December 7, 1941. I'm sure everyone remembers where they were when first learning of the attack. I had just come up from the basement in the parsonage, when Mr. Shauver, a church member, arrived in our living room bearing the news. We immediately turned on our radio to hear the details. The horror of the sinking of the ships and loss of lives, including one from the Derthick family in Ravenna was traumatic. We soon lived under the restrictions of rationing, with stamps for food and gasoline. The auto industry ceased manufacturing cars and became a part of the war effort to manufacture needed vehicles for combat. The draft of men into the Armed Services had begun. My hero, Bob Feller, enlisted in the Navy the next day after December 7. The athletes of Ravenna's teams I admired were going to war. We went through practice blackouts so that warplanes would not see our town to bomb it. My whole high school years would be spent during World War II.

I took my first Latin class for just over two months while still in Ravenna. The Latin textbook was different, and I struggled to integrate my Latin studies in Bellefontaine. Ravenna High School had an outstanding speech program with emphasis on debate teams. There we were encouraged to begin speech training in the ninth grade. In Bellefontaine, the speech class I was placed in was filled with juniors and seniors. They were accepting and friendly with this little freshman, but when it was my turn for a speech, they delighted in trying to rattle me.

With my trumpet, I joined the band and was welcomed as the new kid in town. It was noted I was a PK. One of my new friends from church was Dick Costin, who held the first chair in the trumpet section. He was a junior.

I joined the adult church choir as a tenor and met Dick Dodson, who was also a tenor. Dick Dodson and Dick Coston were leaders in the high school youth fellowship where I made other new friends as well. The Titus sisters were part of the Christian Youth Fellowship (CYF), one a senior whom Dick Dodson liked, and Freda, my age, whom I admired and liked. When I turned sixteen, I passed the driving examination and could drive again. We had occasional dates.

With great anticipation I went to the gym to meet the basketball coach H.A. Dodd. The gym was a beautiful big auditorium with eight hundred seats all on one side, so much larger than the Ravenna High School basketball court. Bellefontaine had outstanding football and basketball teams. Two years prior, the basketball team had gone all the way to the state finals, losing to Martins Ferry, whose star was Lou Groza, later to become the all-pro tackle and kicker for the Cleveland Browns. The 1941 football team had just concluded an outstanding 9–1 record in the Western Buckeye League. I told the coach I wanted to try out for the basketball reserve team. Traditionally the reserve team was younger players who played the preliminary game before the varsity games. At a gym exhibition night in Ravenna, I had been chosen to start for the junior high basketball team.

We aspiring players trained at a separate school gym. Just before Christmas, the freshman team, on which I started, was invited to the high school gym for a contest with the sophomore team. If we won, we would stay at the high school gym and dress for the reserve games during Christmas break. We won! We got uniforms! The second night, the reserve team was leading by a big score, so Coach Dodd put us in the game. I was so thrilled. I was fouled and had one free throw. The referee handed me the ball, and said, "Do you think you can get it up there, son." He didn't know that at the other gym I had been nicknamed "Hot Shot Humbert." Alas, I got it up there, but it rolled off. But that was the official start of my basketball career with the Bellefontaine Chieftains.

Bill Shirk was a year behind me in school. We discovered our mutual love of baseball. He was a big fan of the Cincinnati Reds. The Reds had a great team that went to the National League Championship Series. They had a great young pitcher named Johnny Vander Meer, who had just pitched back to back no hitters. I told him of my hero Bob Feller. We began playing catch and going to Mary Rutan Park to hit fly balls to each other. I started pitching to him with my fastball and curve, simulating strikes and balls and innings. He also had a great music record collection we listened to at his home. Every year, a friend of Bill's dad took me and him to Ohio State football games, where the friend had special parking by the Horseshoe Stadium because his brother was vice president of Ohio State University.

The summer after my freshman year, 1942, I had my first job. I worked on the George Ansley farm, located seven miles from the parsonage where we lived. The Ansley family were members of the church. Monday through Friday, I rode my bicycle up and down the hills to be there by 8:00. Of course, by that time, the milking and other chores had been done. I worked all morning till dinner at about 1:00, the big meal of their day. Then I worked till 5:30, and rode back to town. I drove their tractor cultivating the large acreage of field corn. I rode the hay rake to put the hay in rows that were forked by hand into shocks and then forked onto the hay wagon. When the wheat was cut with a binder, we took the sheaves and made wheat shocks, to be picked up on threshing day. I drove the tractor with a big hayfork attached to raise shocks from the wagon over to the hay mow. On rainy days, I hoed thistles in the pasture. I enjoyed the Ansley family. Jean was my age, and we worked some together on outside windows, and scrubbing down the porch walls. My pay was $5 a week, and all I could eat at noon time dinner!

That summer I also attended my first Wilmington CYF Conference at Wilmington College. The faculty was composed of outstanding ministers, including Gaines Cook as vesper speaker; Dale Fiers, later to become the Senior Minister of Euclid Avenue Church, Secretary of the United Christian Missionary Society, then General Minister and President of the Disciples; Myron Hopper, head of Christian education at the College of the Bible Seminary in Lexington, Kentucky; Myron Cole, a great pitcher for the faculty softball team, later to be senior minister at Hollywood Beverly Christian Church and Moderator of the General Assembly; John Updegraf, later to become the Regional Minister of Florida; my dad and mother; and Gertrude Dimke. In the evening before bedtime, we would meet in small groups for devotions. Dale Fiers was the counselor for our group. I was fifteen years old, and those evenings began a deep, life-long appreciation and friendship with Dr. Fiers.

The Wilmington CYF Conference, the young people I met, the worship and devotional times, the leadership of young ministers, learning of the church beyond our congregation and about the Ohio Christian Missionary Society sponsorship. All of that made an indelible impression on me. I found a new understanding and expanded appreciation of the church, even as a fifteen-year-old. And I had such a good time! Dale Fiers hit a home run in the student/faculty softball game. I learned that he was an all-state running back in high school in Florida, and a star tackle at Bethany College before attending Yale Divinity School.

Dick Coston was also at Conference, and we spent time together. Dick Dodson was also planning to be there, but his mother died just before the end of August. His father died when he was very young, and he and his siblings had lived in the county's children's home for several tough years. When his siblings graduated from high school and went out on their own, his mother was able to have Dick back in their home. Dick would become close to our family during his senior year in high school, and we become good friends. He had visited with Dad about committing to the ministry and hoped to go to Transylvania University in Lexington, Kentucky. His mother had supported herself and Dick by taking in family washings for a meager living. Dick went to live with his sister and her husband in Dayton, Ohio, and secured a job at Wright Patterson Air Force Base to save money to enter Transylvania. He entered Transy in the fall of 1943, and came to our home for school holidays. Then he lived with us the summer of 1944 while working on the New York Central Railroad.

Amazingly, Bellefontaine, a town of ten thousand, was the division point for the New York Central between Buffalo, NY, and Saint Louis, Mo. Every train changed steam engines in Bellefontaine. There was a round house where engines were repaired. Bellefontaine was a railroad town. Even during the Depression until World War II, there were railroad jobs to be had there, and Bellefontaine was better off than many Ohio towns. Bellefontaine was noted as having the first concrete streets and the shortest street on record. There are a number of famous people who graduated from Bellefontaine High School (BHS)—The Mills Brothers, a well-known, nationally acclaimed singing group; Norman Vincent Peale, whose father had been the pastor of the Bellefontaine Methodist Church; and Austin Kiplinger of Kiplinger's Washington Financial Letter. Sid Otten,

6 feet 11 inches tall, was the center on the 1939 basketball team which went to the state finals. He then became a star at Bowling Green State University and eventually the Tri City Blackhawks in the NBA. His brother, Mac Otten, was the forward on the BHS outstanding team in my freshman year, and then played for Bowling Green State.

My sophomore year, I became more and more involved in our church youth fellowship as one of the officers, working with Mary Artz, a banker who was our counselor Mary Artz. At the District 5 youth meeting in Lima, Ohio, I was elected President of the district, and Georgia (later) Meece, from Lima Central Church was elected secretary. Georgia and I became lifelong friends with our paths crisscrossing throughout the years.

In the school band, the single baritone player was drafted into the Army and left school. The band director, Mr. Stang, asked me to shift to the baritone horn. It had the same fingering as the trumpet. I said if he could get me treble clef music, I would be glad to shift. The part had beautiful countermelody parts and was really a delightful horn to play. The winter band concert for the school community was just a few weeks away when I began practicing and playing. Before the concert number, Mr. Stang announced that I had just begun playing the horn, and I would have the solo in the number. Of course, it felt like all eyes and ears were on me as I played. But I finished well, with no mistakes, to the loudest applause of the evening.

When football practice began in August 1942 as I began my sophomore year, I applied and was accepted to be one of the managers of the football team. Jim "Doc" Robinson and Jim Loehr were the other managers. I was too small to play, maybe 130 pounds. We managers worked closely with Coach Dodd, and had a good time performing the tasks. On Fridays we were excused from classes to put down the white lines on the football field. However, this meant I would not be playing with the marching band during football games. I still practiced with the band, getting ready for our winter concert.

That fall we took ten days off from school (my managing) and took a family trip to Kansas City and Independence, Kansas. By that time, Uncle Harold Humbert had left the Disciples church in Independence and was the Senior Minister of Central Christian Church in Kansas City. We visited for several days, and Uncle Harold gave Dad and me a tour of the Independence Boulevard Christian Church's new building. It was cave-like, with walls finished with sprayed on cement. It was like one of the seven wonders of the world for me. Little did I know then that I would be there more than once, years later in connection with our Kansas City General Assemblies.

We went on to Independence, where Aunt Madge and my cousins Ted and Mary Ellen lived. Our Humbert grandparents were also living with them. It was the only time we Humbert children were ever able to visit in our Humbert grandparents' home. Ted, a senior in high school, was itching to get out from under what he thought was too strict supervision by Grandfather. That coming June when he graduated, he immediately enlisted in the Navy. He was later involved in the invasion of Italy at the Anzio Beachhead in a landing craft. In his position on the landing craft, he was sitting between two other sailors, both killed by enemy gunfire as they sat. But he was spared. It was so traumatic that it really changed his bubbly personality for many years.

Mary Ellen was a delightful cousin, the same age as my sister Mary. We kept in touch through the years until her death in 2001.

I enjoyed seeing Independence, where my Grandfather Longston was minister, where my mother was born, where Uncle Ted Dunton was the minister, where Harold Humbert also served, and Uncle Royal was ordained. Years later when I was GMP, I was invited to return and was honored with the celebration of my family's roots and ministries there. They held a dinner and invited church people from surrounding Disciple churches. On that occasion they presented me with a leather-bound book of photos and news clippings about the Longstons and Humberts in Independence. Among the copies of the clippings was the announcement of my Longston grandparents' wedding in Atchison, Kansas, and a picture of the house in which my mother was born. Royal and Lois Humbert and cousin Mary Ellen Garrett surprised me by coming from Illinois and Texas for the occasion.

We came back to Bellefontaine in early November to the church youth group, school, and the finishing of the football schedule. I enjoyed working as one of the managers. With the end of the football season, basketball practice began. I was now permanently practicing at the high school gym. Coach Dodd's program was to have the "second five" play the reserve games. We sophomores were subs who only got in the games when the reserves were way ahead. But we practiced with the "big guys" and worked on fundamentals. I was put into a game on several occasions.

With me now playing the baritone horn, I would dress after the reserve game (I had hardly worked up a sweat, so I didn't shower) and join the elite pep band on the platform high above and behind the crowd, playing during the varsity game breaks and halftime. The crowd loved the pep band, especially the drummer with Gene Krupa type solos that set them wild.

The summer after my sophomore year, I worked for the county highway on the weed gang. I swung a scythe all day long, cutting weeds. A tractor mower would make the first cut on the roadsides. Then our guys came along with our scythes, cutting back to the fences or property lines. My muscles were built up, but I developed a severe poison ivy rash on my ankles and legs.

One of the events of the summer was a trip to Cleveland to see the Indians play four baseball games in three days against the Philadelphia Athletics. Dad, Bill Shirk, and I went by train to Cleveland to meet Jack McLain and Doug Brown. We stayed at the Cleveland YMCA. We attended a doubleheader and two single games at old League Park. We ate out. They could swim in the Y pool. I was a spectator for the swimming because the bad poison ivy rash on my lower legs that being in the water was prohibited. As we were leaving one of the afternoon games and crossing the street, there came the famous Connie Mack, manager of the Athletics, dressed exactly as he did on the field, in a black suit and tie and a straw hat. I asked and received his autograph.

Bill Shirk and I continued hitting fly balls to each other, and I worked on my pitching, developing my curveball.

Summer conference at Wilmington College was another very special time. The same great leaders inspired and taught us. Dick Coston and I became friends with two girls from Walnut Hills Christian Church in Cincinnati—Bobby Jean Smith and Pat Storch. That made it even more interesting and memorable. Wilmington Conference was always the last week in August.

So, it was back home to school, friends, CYF Sunday evening meetings, (where I was elected President), band practice, and working as one of the football managers. That season, Coach asked me to chart every play as it was run in games, and chart the opposition, and results of both. I studied the playbook to learn and recognize the plays as we ran them. During the games I kept a record of which play we ran, the yards marker, and the resulting yards gained or lost.

One Friday when we had an open date, Doc Robinson, Gene Eggleston, Mo Kress, and I, all of us football managers, went to Saint Mary's to scout their game. We kept a record of St. Mary's plays. Then on Saturday, we went to the Ohio State University vs Illinois football game. We sat high up in the Horseshoe. The gun sounded and the game was over. OSU had lost by two points. It took us some time to work our way down the stadium toward the exit. As we were almost to field level, the public address announcer blared, "The game is not over. There was a pass interference call on Illinois on the last play. The game cannot end on a defensive foul. It will be Ohio State's ball on the 17-yard line for one more play." The teams came back on the field, some half-dressed. Ohio State kicked a field goal and won by one point!

What a weekend!

After my sixteenth birthday, I rushed to acquire my learner's temporary driver's license. With a quick study of the laws and rules of driving, already knowing how to drive, I rushed to the State Highway garage for the test. I passed! Of course! I had my full driver's license! I could drive again!

As basketball practice began and moved along, I was promoted to the "second five." I was on the varsity! Of course, it was Coach Dodd's practice to have the second five play the reserve game. He felt that would help us develop our game more than occasionally playing in the varsity game. I started every reserve game and usually played most of the game. But after playing most of the reserve games, Coach would send me into the varsity game after the starters had played for a few minutes to play the rest of the game. I loved it! I remember one weekend we played on both Friday and Saturday nights. I played in every quarter for two nights. Eight quarters in the reserve games, eight quarters in the varsity games…sixteen quarters in two nights. I was in shape, and I loved it! In the reserve games during the regular season, we were undefeated. In one game I had eighteen points and was the high scorer for the season. The varsity was ten and four.

We looked forward to the District Tournament in the Coliseum at the Dayton Fairgrounds. I had attended tournament games there for two years when our team went deep into the playoff brackets. I was thrilled to be playing. At the three-minute mark, Coach put me in, and almost immediately I hit a shot from the corner, got an offensive rebound putback and a hook shot from the side. Six points. But we lost to the Dayton Stivers. That was the end of basketball season.

During the spring of 1943, the church decided the parsonage on Brown Street was not adequate for our family. There was absolutely no lawn for us to play. For $6,000, they purchased a large home with a wonderful expansive lot at 359 Sandusky Street, just two blocks from the church. We really enjoyed the large rooms, four bedrooms, the study for Dad, and the large backyard.

Track season. The half-mile, or the 880 as it was also called, and the high jump were my events. I won most of the dual meet high-jump events and finished first or second in the 880.

The summer of 1943, I had a great job. Coach Dodd had taken over supervising the summer park programs. He knew my love for baseball. I accepted the job of supervision for Harmon Field, the baseball field for Bellefontaine. I played with the guys who showed up every day. Coach also organized an adult baseball league for Central Western Ohio. Vacario's Shoe Repair store entered a team, and I was invited to tryout as their pitcher. They were fortunate to have a fine catcher. Before the first game, the other prospective pitcher and I threw to the catcher and showed him our repertoire. He chose me to start the first game! I pitched a complete seven-inning game, and we won! I became the starting pitcher for the season and won nine games and lost only one. We won the league championship. I was also the starting pitcher for the all-star game. Wow! A dream come true!

That spring, Gene Eggleston, Mo Kress, and I decided we needed to go the senior prom. Mary Brinkley was a new girl in town, and along with her family, was a member of our church. She accepted my invitation to go to the prom with me. Gene and Mo also had dates and we hung out together. Mary and I continued to go out that summer, until it was time for the Wilmington Conference. I wanted to be free to be with my conference girlfriend, so we kind of broke up.

Football season! Dad thought I was too small to go out for the football team. Coach Dodd asked Rudy Rudisill, one of the high school caretakers and a member of our church, to "work" on Dad to persuade him to relent. I had grown. I was six feet and 142 pounds. I was given permission by Dad to try out. I wound up as the starting left end. I knew the plays, having memorized them the year before when charting every play. We tied our opening game 7–7 with Urbana. The second game, against Marysville, we were lost 7–0. I was having trouble focusing on the plays. I had been in a pileup and got hit hard. I kept on trying to play, but I dropped a wide-open touchdown pass. I had a concussion and was "out on my feet." Our team doctor, Dr. Coston, took me to the locker room to lie down on the training table. All I could remember was the vivid picture of that yellow football in the air, that I couldn't control when it hit my hands. I can still see that ball in the air to this day. I rested for the weekend. One nice thing was that my girlfriend, Doris Richardson, came to see me. She was a member of our church and a sophomore in my sister Mary's class. She was active in CYF then. We started dating as school began in the fall. I liked her a lot.

The next week I was back on the field. The year before, we had an outstanding team with a 9–1 record, the usual good record for BHS. But we lost every game till the final one. In the second to last game, at Bluffton, in the second half, I was going deep for a pass with my arms straight high above my head, when a defender hit me low before the ball arrived. I fell face forward on the 40-yard line, and another defender landed on my head. I lay there out cold, not moving. My teammate, Bill Lewis, ran up and turned me over. He said I had line chalk and blood all over my face. He thought I was dead. They carried me off and sat me in a school bus. I began coming to, with my dad and sisters around me. I rode home in our family car. Dr. Coston examined me and determined it was definitely another concussion. He ruled me out for the last game. We beat Kenton in the final game, with me on the sidelines running the down's marker.

Basketball practice began in early November. With our undefeated season as the reserve team, and my experience with the varsity as a junior, we expected to have a good season. Coach Dodd appointed me captain to meet with the referee and the opposing captain prior to the start of games. I was the point guard and defender on the opposition's star player. We went 9–4 in the season and looked forward to the State Tournament. The night before our first game against Wilmington High School, I developed a flu-like temperature. I called Coach early in the morning, and he sent me to see Dr. Coston, who gave me some medicine to take every three hours. I traveled with the team hoping the fever would break. Coach Dodd declared I could not play with a fever. A thermometer did not leave my hands as game time approached. I sat on the bench in street clothes, with the thermometer, taking my temperature every few minutes as the game started. Our fans had no idea why their captain was not playing. The Wilmington player who I would have been guarding was key to their offense. He penetrated and passed off to the center who laid the ball in many times. I would have been able to stop that. We lost, and I was sick in more ways than one. I had missed the game I was looking forward to for my entire high school basketball career!

That fall, our band director, Mr. Stang, and his son, Dick Stang, developed a "big band" from select members of the regular concert band. They were to play a concert for an all-school assembly. Dick invited me to sing a number as the male vocalist. My singing career from Ravenna had not translated to Bellefontaine. Bellefontaine High did not have choral music groups. I was singing in our church choir, but none of my classmates knew me as a singer. I practiced the song made famous by Frank Sinatra, "I dream of you more than you dream I do, you just can't seem to see the way I feel. I want you so, more than you ever know..." When I was introduced at the Assembly, and came onstage to sing, there were some gasps and a few guffaws from my cronies. I sang it well, and when I finished I was stunned! The students were on their feet, yelling, cheering, and applauding like crazy! I left the stage and the cheering continued. I was called back for a bow, left, and the noise continued. Finally, Dick came backstage. He said, "They won't stop until you sing an encore." I performed it again. I had a new persona at BHS, "Frankie!"

Each year, in our Disciples congregation, Youth Sunday was observed, where members of our high school Christian Youth

Fellowship led the service. I was drafted to preach the sermon. I'd taken the speech class as a freshman, but as I climbed the stairs to the chancel my knees were so weak. I didn't know whether I would make it! I do not remember anything about the text for my very first sermon, but I got through it.

During my senior year, World War II was still endlessly and violently raging. My thinking for any future war years was that I would enlist in the Navy. My thoughts about my career beyond the war were leaning toward basketball coaching or ministry. I knew my parents were strongly hoping that I would choose ministry, especially Mother. At one point in my senior year, I began dating Jean Reed. My mother didn't approve, causing some negative feelings between us. She was worried because Jean's mother had told her that Jean could hardly wait to get married. Ah, the fear of the entrapment of her naive son. One morning I came down to breakfast and declared with some feeling," I'm not going to be a minister!" She just said, "Oh?" and went on with what she was doing, no remonstrance or other comments. I broke up with Jean shortly after that to go back to Doris Richardson.

In March, the war ended in Europe with great rejoicing all around. But with the Pacific War still raging, I thought I might choose the Navy. As for colleges, I thought about Hiram and Butler University, both Disciples higher education institutions. I wanted the challenge of Butler basketball over that of smaller Hiram athletics. In 1928, Butler had been the mythical National Champions in basketball.

After basketball season was over, it was traditional for the graduating seniors to play the juniors or upcoming sophomores. In that game Dick Dearwester threw a body block at me as I went up for a rebound. I fell backwards to the floor, landing on my elbows. Unfortunately, I had elbow damage resulting in bone chips which would affect my pitching that summer and in the future.

Concurrent to track season were the tryouts and rehearsals for the traditional senior class play. I tried out and was selected for the male lead part. I was Ham Ellers, a teenager with all the nuances of family life and dating. For one scene I was required to learn the basic steps of the jitterbug to perform on stage. Rehearsing, I missed some track practices, but it helped that Mrs. Dodd, the coach's wife, was the director of the play. I had a great time as "Ham."

In track season I did well in the high jump and won a number of 880s. The most memorable day was late in the season at the Lima Relays. Teams came from towns all over Northwest Ohio. There must have been fifteen high jumpers competing. Six of us made it over the 5 feet 8 inch bar with three tries to win at 5 feet 9 inches. Everyone including me missed on the first two attempts. On my third and final try, I succeeded. I watched with bated breath as the others attempted and failed. I won the high jump and seven points for Bellefontaine! The competition was so tough. Those were the only points our team won that day. I finished just out of the points in the half-mile. Since this was the first year for the Lima Relays, my high-jump height stood as the record for a few years!

The district track meet to qualify for the State Championship was held in May, the morning after our senior prom. I had a date with Jean Reed. We stayed out until 2:00 in the morning. With only four hours of sleep, our team headed to Springfield. In the high jump I finished third, missing by one place going on to State. The half-mile featured a crushing start with two rows of runners, some falling, tangled up. I was on the outside of the front row. I led the pack for the first quarter mile, but began to lose steam while runners flew by me, some with bloody knees from having fallen at the start. I finished, but definitely ingloriously.

Memorial Day in May was a major community event, with the BHS marching band leading the parade from downtown to the cemetery. At the cemetery, a program was presented from a temporary stage. I was selected to give Lincoln's Gettysburg Address. In my band uniform for the last time, I echoed the iconic prose, almost poetry, of Abraham Lincoln. I remembered how Dad had taken me to visit Gettysburg.

Graduation and its ceremony seemed surreal. Could this really be happening to us, to me? Our high school song, "Bellefontaine High, pals you and I, pride of our school days devotion..." The graduation dance at the country club was wonderful. Out into the world we were sent. But what world? Some of the guys in my class were already eighteen and would be drafted or volunteering for one of the services.

The summer world for me became working at Eicholtz Funeral Home. Les Eicholtz, the owner, was a fine amateur golfer. There was only one other embalmer and senior member on the staff, Joe Jones. I was hired to go with Joe on ambulance runs and death calls. While Les was playing golf several times a week, I helped with embalming, kept the fleet of funeral cars clean and shiny, and drove the flower car ahead of the funeral procession to the grave side. It was good experience for my future around a funeral home.

The war finally ended in early August 1945. I determined I wanted to visit Butler University, so my dad, mother, and I visited Indianapolis in mid-August. I had the grades to get in and was still considering either coaching or ministry. I brought home the forms, thinking as a seventeen-year-old, I would go ahead and begin my college career before having to register for the draft on my eighteenth birthday in October.

In the last week of August, I returned for my fourth year at Wilmington CYF Conference. The previous year, Dick Coston and Bobby Jean Smith from Cincinnati Walnut Hills Church had become a couple. Dick was now in the Navy. I was also a close friend to Bobby Jean, and we spent a great deal of time together during conference week in 1945. With the war over and college approaching in a few weeks, I was more seriously considering the future direction of my life. I loved the church. I had found such delight on occasions when extended members of my family were together, all of them involved in some form of ministry, and their deep commitment and joy in ministry. Dad's ministry was filled with positive fulfillment, and my appreciation for the church was certainly enhanced by the financial, prayerful, and moral support of the Ravenna Church during that full year when my dad was unable to work. I felt a strong call to ministry during the devotional and worship times at the conference. In the closing friendship circle Friendship Circle on Sunday afternoon, an opportunity was presented to make a commitment for ministry. I stepped forward and declared ministry would be my life's work. My friend Bobby Jean was very supportive, and we promised to keep in touch. In fact, I had fallen in love with her.

CHAPTER 13

Off to Butler University

The second Monday in September 1945, I headed to Butler University. With a trunk and one suitcase full of clothes, I boarded the New York Central Railroad early morning train in Bellefontaine. I arrived in Indianapolis at 7:00 a.m. As I struggled with my luggage, I caught a taxi to the Butler campus. I was due to report to the large Jordan Hall lecture hall at 9:00 a.m. for an English literature and composition placement test. The test was in the form of writing an essay and answering questions regarding my reading of literature.

At noon we were excused for lunch in the cafeteria on the lower level of the building. As I waited in line, other students were approaching, asking, "Are you organized?" "No, I'm certainly not organized! I don't even have a place to sleep tonight!" It turned out, of course, the context of the question was fraternity life. But I had arrived on the train that morning with no place to live for my Butler student life. My baggage was behind the door next to the lecture hall on the main floor. In 1945 Butler had no dormitories. Students lived in fraternity houses, roomed in private homes, or commuted from their own Indianapolis homes. Many times, since that first day, I have been amazed that my Mother and Dad had seen me off to college on the railroad, arriving at Indianapolis and Butler with no place live! "Well," the young man said, "after you register this afternoon, come on over to the Lambda Chi Alpha house across the street, meet my brothers and you can stay at the house tonight." I gratefully accepted the invitation.

I spent the afternoon registering for my classes and moving around Jordan Hall for the details. I trudged to the Lamda Chi Alpha house dragging my trunk and suitcase. The Brothers were friendly and welcoming. They helped me with my luggage up to the third-floor dormitory, one large room with double decker bunk beds.

Back to the first floor and the lower-level, dinner was ready and a jovial time was had by all. After dinner, the disappearing act began. By 7:00 p.m., I was the only one left at the fraternity house. I went up two flights made my bed, went back down two flights, sat down and read magazines for a couple of hours. It was back to my solitary dormitory. A window was broken near my bunk, and I was cold and miserable all night. Welcome to Butler University!

The next morning, I visited the student housing office. They gave me the names and addresses of two homes willing to receive students as roomers. The streetcar rail line, as well as a city bus route, had its terminus at the Butler campus. I took public transportation to the two homes to survey the possibilities. Neither appealed to me aesthetically, and both were too far removed from the campus to feel the university nuance. I was discouraged and homesick.

Dad had given me the name of his seminary classmate, Dr. Reisinger, a professor in the Butler School of Religion. When I returned to school, I informed the lady in the housing office I was declining both places. She called the seminary for me and made an appointment with Dr. Reisinger. When I visited with him, he invited me to his home for dinner. I accepted! The Reisingers lived just a few blocks from campus and had two sons, Don, a senior in high school, and Rick, in junior high. Both would become national leaders in the Disciples. Dinner was wonderful, and their hospitality was healing. After telling them my dilemma, they said they knew of a home nearby where a widower gentleman was open to students rooming in his home. After some phone calls, they received the information about a Mr. Forkner on Byram Avenue. The next morning, I called Mr. Forkner, visited, and had a place to live. There were two bedrooms on the second floor. One would be mine. The student in the other room was Donn Matson, a religion major from Michigan whose father was the state secretary for the Michigan Disciples Churches. Donn was a sophomore transfer from Drake University. Mr. Forkner's home was seven blocks from the campus, but two blocks from the 42nd Street trolley line with its convenient terminus at Butler's Jordan Hall.

Classes began on Wednesday. I was on the liberal arts track taking Introduction to the New Testament, Advanced English Literature, Composition, Spanish, History, and a one-hour Physical Education course.

I was struggling with life away from home. In fact, I was homesick! I met Jack, who lived in Speedway, and he invited me to spend the weekend with him and attend Speedway Christian Church where he and his family were members.

We played some basketball, and I shared my hopes about going out for Butler basketball. There were many Disciples churches scattered over the Indianapolis complex, with large memberships of over a thousand.

Late in September, Mother received word that her sister, my Aunt Jessica, would be driving through Indianapolis on her way to Bellefontaine. Jessica stopped to see me on Friday, and I drove her car on to Bellefontaine for the weekend. Jessica Longston, after graduating from Manson Washington High School, attended the University of Southern California, majoring in journalism and business. She returned to Saint Helens, Washington, where she was on the staff of the newspaper. She was outstanding at promoting, sales, advertising, and circulation, and subsequently bought the paper. During World War II she enlisted in the Women's Army Auxiliary Corps (WAAC), rising to the rank of captain, and editor of the financial page for *Stars and Stripes*, the U.S. Army's official publication. In the

Army she met Vicki Zaser, and upon discharge, they became companions. Jessica saw the future of radio in 1945, and subsequently purchased five radio stations across Idaho, Montana, and Washington. When our grandparents died, she persuaded, rather insisted, that she had the skill to turn their inheritance into a fortune and took it to use in her investments. Mother insisted that she at least needed income from the investments for my college expenses. Jessica then did send Mother $25 a month for my freshman year.

I enjoyed my visit at home, and then rode the train back on Sunday evening. Several weekends I hitchhiked home on Friday afternoon, then took the train to return.

Every year at Wilmington Conference, Gaines Cook was vesper preacher. Gertrude Dimke was the state office secretary and was dean of girls at Wilmington. Dr. Cook moved to Indianapolis that September when he became the General Secretary of the International Convention. They invited me to come to church with them, and then to the Cook's home for Sunday dinner with Gertrude. She had come to Missions Building to continue to be Dr. Cook's secretary. That was special.

After a few weeks Dad came over to visit and take me to Missions Building, our Disciples International Headquarters, at 222 S. Downey Avenue in Irvington. The building had been both part of the Butler University campus and the home of United Christian Missionary Society. We met Spencer Austin, head of evangelism, and Harry McCormick, the President of the United Christian Missionary Society, who came to that position from being Senior Minister at Lakewood Christian Church in Cleveland, Ohio. We also had lunch with my religion professor, Dr. Robert Andre.

Bobby Jean Smith and I corresponded regularly, and I was really attracted to her. She invited me to come see her for a weekend in Cincinnati, and I arranged to stay with my friend Bernie Meece, who lived in Norwood, a Cincinnati suburb. We attended the CYF Conference for four summers together and became friends. In fact, we were both nominated to be president of Conference our senior years. Bernie was elected.

I traveled by bus, and Bobby Jean and I had a great weekend with a number of Conference friends. I came back to Indianapolis quite smitten, and we continued to write almost every day. I didn't date anyone else at Butler that whole freshman year.

I needed to deal with my expenses. I applied and was hired to work the early morning shift in the school cafeteria. I also worked serving special meal functions for groups in separate meeting rooms. As a part of my pay, I could eat anything I wanted in any quantity I wished, for free as long as I recorded it in the journal in the office. What an advantage that was!

I was making friends among the religion majors, attending chapel at the seminary, and joining Ichthus, a club for undergraduate religion majors and graduate seminary students. We played some touch football in the large mall area in front of Jordan Hall. And I listened to the World Series between the Tigers and the Cubs on my portable radio. My roommate Donn Matson and I became friends.

CHAPTER 14

Butler University Basketball

Basketball! My physical education professor was one of the Butler basketball coaches. I told him I wanted to try out for the team. He gave me a form to complete with instructions to report at Butler Fieldhouse on October 15. Early in October, Butler held an open reception on the school mall in front of Jordan Hall for the return of the famous coach Paul D. "Tony" Hinkle. He entered the Navy in 1942 after coaching football, basketball, and baseball teams for sixteen years. In that time under Hinkle, Butler basketball teams had won two national titles, four Indiana Conference Championships, and two Missouri Valley Championships. In 1928, he oversaw the building of the Hinkle Fieldhouse, seating 16,000 for basketball, the first large university field house in the United States. He had just completed coaching the Great Lakes Naval Academy football team that played the likes of Ohio State and Notre Dame during the war. He had starred in football and basketball for the University of Chicago in the twenties when it was a powerhouse in the Western Conference, now called the Big Ten. He would be returning as the basketball, football, and baseball coach as well as the Butler Athletic Director.

I reported for practice on October 15 as an unknown in the midst of 115 other prospects, mostly Indiana kids and GIs. I looked around wondering what chance Johnny Humbert had. We were put through some fundamental drills. In a week, the first cut was made. Some dropped out. We were down to about fifty, and I was still on the squad. At one practice we were doing a line layup drill. Coach Hinkle was watching. As I received the pass going in for the layup, I did a certain kind of skipping move with my feet and made the basket. About my move, Coach Hinkle said to his assistant, also watching, "Who does that remind you of?" The assistant named the pre-war player. Hinkle said, "It does me too." The assistant coach said to me, "That's quite a compliment. The player he named was an outstanding all-American back before the war."

That little bit of footwork got me noticed. In another practice I was wearing my high school basketball shoes, purchased when you couldn't get true rubber soles. I was sliding around some, and Hinkle said, "We've got a skater here." And to the manager he said, "Get this skater some good shoes!" It was important in Coach's offensive patterns and plays, to be able to stop, pivot, and change directions quickly. After practice, the manager took my size and brought me a new pair of Butler shoes!

Coach Hinkle had me playing forward in drills for his wonderfully structured offense where there was always an alternative if a move was defensed. I had always played guard in high school.

The final "cuts" were made. I was among the eighteen on the 1945–46 Butler University Varsity Basketball team! I was number 32. What a thrill!

In the first game against Manchester College, Coach tried different lineups, and I was in for a few minutes handling the ball for the first time in a college game. In the second game against Wabash, I was in longer. At one point I pulled down the defensive rebound, turned, dribbled once, and on the move called out to my teammate as I passed the ball. As I did, I was tripped from behind by a Wabash player, fell literally on my face, and a foul was called. As I rose, my team bench was pointing at the floor where I had fallen. I looked down to see two partial teeth on the floor. I made the free throw for my first college points.

When I turned eighteen on October 26, 1945, I had to register for the draft. Having been on record with the Ohio Region of

Disciples churches as being committed to study for the ministry, I could apply for the status of 4-D for a military deferment. But when I received a notice from the Bellefontaine draft board to report for a physical exam, the deferment had not yet been granted. I reported with a number of my Bellefontaine classmates, and we were bused to Columbus for our physicals. Chuck Hoffman, my good buddy and neighbor, was one. He was a football tackle, and I played next to him at end "both ways." We were also at forward and guard on the same side of the basketball offense. He was not going on to college, and he did get drafted into the Army. My deferment came through, and since the war was over, I took it in order to stay in school.

On December 12, we hosted Ball State University. It was an exciting close game. The hero was Art Cook, who sank a long shot for a come-from-behind tie just as the buzzer sounded. In the opening minute of overtime, Art fouled out. Coach Hinkle called, "Humbert, go in for Cook." Nerves were on edge, the crowd of four thousand was really into it, and #32 Johnny Humbert was going in. On the first offensive play, I was driving for the basket, was fouled, and given two shots. With the score tied, I made both to put us ahead in overtime. I didn't score again, but we went on to win a thriller. To stand at 3–1.

Our next game was at Miami University in Oxford, Ohio. As we were warming up, I noticed that one of the Miami players had been the center on the Wilmington High School team that eliminated us from the tournament the spring before while I sat on the BHS bench with a thermometer in my mouth. Then as I turned to shoot a shot from the corner, who should be standing there just beyond the out of bounds but my friend from Bellefontaine, Dick Coston. He was out of the Navy and a student at Miami. He was with a new girlfriend. I stopped and said hi for a minute. The game itself was another tight one to the finish. Coach put me in for the last few minutes, which gave my confidence a boost, since again he seemed to trust me in a tight game situation. We won and now we were now 4–1.

We beat DePaul University in our next game, and then the University of Louisville came to the Fieldhouse. They were big and quick. I got tied up on a fast break and did not distinguish myself. We lost. Then Miami came to town, and we had a short break for Christmas. New Year's Day we played Indiana University, and I made my first basket against a Big Ten team, on a fake and go. Coach even commented, "Nice play."

On January 10, we went to play Earlham in Richmond, Indiana. Two things happened that were special and unique that evening. First, Coach singled me out to tell me he was awarding me a scholarship for the second semester. Half of my tuition was awarded because my father was a Disciples minister, and Butler was a Disciples school. The other half would be from the Athletic Department. However, it was to be work related, and my job was to clean Coach's office. I thought that was cool! Second, I had left something on the bus when we arrived. Before we dressed, I went out to get it. When I tried to get back into the gym, I told the person manning the door I was on the Butler team.

"No," he said, "You're just trying to sneak in."

"Really," I said. "I play forward on the Butler Team!"

"No, I've seen you around here, and you look too young to be on the team."

"Do you have a program?" I asked. "Yes," he answered.

"Look," I said. "There's John Humbert, #32. Here's my driver's license." He finally let me in. We won the game and I had six points. By this game, Coach would have me sit next to him on the bench as the game began. Then after about four minutes, he would put me in, and I would play the rest of the game.

On January 12, Illinois Wesleyan came to the Fieldhouse. We had lost to them the third game of the season in an away game. I was having muscle spasms in my back and couldn't make that trip. But I got into this game early and had an unbelievable night. I took six shots and made them all, most from the area that would become the three-point line. I shot three foul shots and made all of them. Donn Mattson was there with his cousin's family in the second row. We made eye contact as I went back on defense, and I could hardly believe how I was hitting. That night the rim seemed almost as big as a peach basket. About the game, the Butler school paper *The Collegian* wrote, "Here we go another time, after another weekend with the swell basketball game, which was really great, and we think one guy who deserves a mention is John Humbert, who couldn't miss, and all the other fellas were great too. This was the game that saw Humbert make nine baskets out of nine tries, for a hundred per cent average, and 15 points."

The next weekend we were facing Valparaiso. There was a picture of five of us in the *Indianapolis News* with the story.

> "There are a lot of little fellows in short pants in the Butler Fieldhouse this week looking for some of those shoes with the built-up heels. On Saturday night there the Bulldog basketball club faces a team reported so tall its players must surely have a permanent nosebleed. The team is Valparaiso, billed as 'The tallest team in America.' In preparation for all this 'looking up' to the Crusaders 6 foot 5 inch average, Coach Paul Hinkle asks his boys to 'reach for it.' Then a photograph showed five of us reaching for the basket, with our heights listed: 5'9", 5'6", 6'1", Humbert, 5'11", and 6'. (They fudged on mine. I was 6 foot.)"

I looked forward to the game because Dad; my high school coach, Coach Dodd; and Dr. Coston, our family doctor and the BHS Athletic Doctor, were coming for the game. They arrived early before the game, and we had an early meal. As we were warming up before the game started, it felt really great to be out there in my Butler uniform, #32, for my coach to witness this and for my dad to see me play as a Butler collegian for the first time.

And for them to attend the game in a huge Butler Fieldhouse, with Johnny Humbert playing, was so special.

Coach Hinkle put me in almost immediately after the game started. And I was sent in, to guard Valparaiso's top scorer, who was averaging seventeen points a game. He was about 6 feet 4 inches. He was dribbling in the backcourt when I stole the ball from him and scored. Later, I anticipated a cross court pass and speared it on the move and dribbled to our basket and scored. Sometime later, Dad told me Coach Dodd leaped to his feet when I did that, and yelled, "Go, Johnny!"

We stayed close to Valpo and their big guys. My guy took me into the pivot several times, but I stayed on his hips to keep the ball from coming to him. He was so upset that when a foul was called on me, he snipped to the referee, "It's about time!" But the foul was actually on my teammate. That was the only foul called on me, and I held the guy to just three points. But overall, we could not quite cope with their height, and we lost 55 to 50. I had one foul shot, made it, and had five points. But I was more satisfied with my defensive play. That had been my forte in high school, too, defense.

After the game, Dad, Coach Dodd, and Dr. Coston came down to the dressing room, and I was proud to introduce them to Coach Hinkle. It was a Friday night game with no practice on Saturday, but a game on Monday. I rode back home with them, enjoying conversation about the game with my coach, my dad, and my doc. I went to the BHS game on Saturday night and enjoyed being in church on Sunday. I caught the train back on Monday morning, in time to get to the team bus for Monday's game at Franklin College. As we were getting dressed for the game, Coach Hinkle quietly told me I would start the game at forward. Wow! I did, and for the rest of the season I was a starting forward for Butler University!

The first of February I was pleasantly surprised when I received a note from my good friend from Ravenna, Jack McLain, that he was being transferred in the Army to Fort Benjamin Harrison on the edge of Indianapolis. He came to see the next game on February 4. We went out to eat together and he stayed over with me at Mr. Fortner's. Our next game was at Ball State in Muncie, Indiana. Muncie is toward the Ohio state line closer to Bellefontaine. Dad, Mother, and my sisters Mary and Peggy came to the game. I opened the scoring with a long shot but didn't do much scoring the rest of the game. Unfortunately, we lost.

The next week, the Assistant Coach told me that Hinkle said he wanted me to shoot more. In the last three games against Louisville, at Valparaiso and Franklin, I scored twelve, ten, and twelve points. At Valparaiso, to my surprise, sitting at the end in the bleachers almost under the basket, was Joe Jones from Bellefontaine, the embalmer at Eicholtz Funeral Home. We had worked together all summer and had become friends. At one point, late in the summer when I knew I was going to Butler, I told him I wanted to go out for the Butler basketball team. He said, "I don't think you're good enough to make Butler's team."

There he was at the game. Of course, I got to speak with him as we were warming up. I started and scored the first points of the game on free throws, right there facing him under the bucket. Then, I dribbled right at him and laid one in. I scored our first six points, eight in the first half, ten overall. But we lost. However, I had a visit with Joe after the game.

With basketball season ending, I was awarded a "letter," a Butler B. Now I was a member of the "B Club," athletes who had lettered for a Butler Intercollegiate Team.

I tried out for the baseball team as an infielder, rather than as a pitcher. But I didn't make it. Coach Hinkle threw to me. But my swing was all out of kilter from my last Bellefontaine sandlot game where I had a home run and a single. I have always wished I had tried out as a pitcher to have seen what I could have accomplished. I didn't because of the bone chips in my elbow.

I continued to clean Coach Hinkle's office, and in the process got to know his student secretary. We enjoyed conversation and had a couple of dates.

CHAPTER 15

The Indianapolis 500

I learned that being in Indianapolis meant absorbing the culture of the Indianapolis 500 race, "The Greatest Spectacle in Racing." It had not been run during World War II, but the lore and stories of the races before the war were rife. I remembered as a fifth grader going across Lafayette Street in Ravenna to the Tubaughs', and their having the radio on with the race. Bob Tubaugh was my friend, though three years older. So being in Indianapolis with the race being renewed was an enervating time. A couple of times, I went with friends to watch the time trials to determine car placement for the race. The top qualifying time that year was around 115 mph. There would be thirty-three cars, in eleven rows of three cars, flanking each other.

Bob Funk, Dub Shanks, and one other friend decided we would have the adventure of ushering for the race. We applied and were accepted. We had to report at the track at 5:00 a.m. sharp. I got up at 2:00 a.m. and joined my friends going to Speedway. Yes, there is an incorporated town surrounding the two-and-a-half-mile track named Speedway. There is a Disciples church there named Speedway Christian Church. We were going to take a city bus to the track. But as the city bus approached Speedway, the street was too packed with parked cars. The bus driver announced, "This is as far as we go today." We got out and began walking. All the streets approaching the track were lined with cars and fans for one and a half miles from the entrance! When we arrived at the appointed place, we gathered with other ushers to receive our assignments. Mine was great. Lower boxes next to the track, right at the start/finish line, across from the pagoda. I took my spot, and at 6:00 a.m. they opened the gates to cars roaring into parking places inside the two-and-a-half-mile track.

The fans began to fill my section of boxes as the morning went on. The race would begin at 11:00. Around 10:15 or so, they began wheeling the race cars onto the track in the positions they had qualified for. The pre-race rituals began with the singing of "Back Home Again in Indiana," and of course, the Indiana University band played the national anthem, accompanying a soloist. And then the famous words leading up to the start of the race, "Gentlemen, start your engines!" And all that was almost literally within my reach. I was standing down, right next to the track in my section, with just the wire fence between me, the track, and the head of the pack of cars. The thirty-three engines were earsplitting. The pace car, a Lincoln Continental Convertible driven by Henry Ford II, led all thirty-three cars on the two-and-a-half-mile pace lap, then pulled into the pits as all thirty-three cars roared by, almost within arm's length. Wow! What a thrill! Then it settled down to the routine of cars blowing by and packs maneuvering for five hundred miles. There were some crashes, with the pace car leading the slowed race on the yellow flag. The winner was George Robson.

The second semester ended successfully. But I only had a few days before summer school began. To keep my 4-D draft status, I needed to be in school to make progress toward ministry. I went home by way of Cincinnati to see Bobby Jean Smith. Our correspondence had thinned down by this time, but we were still friends. Her father secured tickets for us to go to a Cincinnati Reds baseball game. In fact, we sat right next to the Reds' dugout. It was a nice visit; however, it turned out to be a farewell.

Summer school was a nice pace. On my return to Indianapolis, I brought my bicycle. Jim Cline and I were in classes together. He was a long-distance runner and had been one of the stars of the track team. Another "B" man! We were later colleagues in ministry in Ohio. I worked in the cafeteria in the evening shift. I also got a job with the head of Buildings and Grounds for the university moving all the invoices into payment vouchers. I worked in a small, closet-like office on the main hall of Jordan Hall with lots of people passing by, but I got my work done. The previous person had let the invoices pile up, and I began by catching up, then keeping pace.

Back in May, I discovered that the Ringling Bros. and Barnum & Bailey Circus was coming to Indianapolis in June. I talked with Mom and Dad and invited my brother Bobby, who was eight years old, to go to the circus. He came by himself on the train from Bellefontaine to Indianapolis and stayed with me for several days. We were both excited about it. We had a great time at the circus and with my friends. His trip was a great success.

In the late winter and spring, I had become involved in University Park Christian Church Sunday morning worship and the youth fellowship for high school and college kids. Bob Funk was the assistant minister to Louis MacAdow. Bob worked with the youth program. He had also been a bench player on the basketball team, and we had become friends.

Early in June, Betty Harper arrived in Indianapolis. Louis MacAdow had been the minister in her home church in Mexico, Missouri, before he came to University Park. Betty's brother, Bill, was studying for the ministry, and she felt called to ministry as well. The MacAdows wanted to help make that possible. Betty was coming to live with them in the church parsonage. She would help with the household chores and with the two small MacAdow children in return for free board and room. Mac, as we called him, had picked out an older ministerial student for Betty, W.H. Shanks. He had served in the Army during the war, was in Butler on the GI bill, and owned a new Oldsmobile. Dub and I were friends. Betty was very attractive, and I observed them together at church events and other get togethers at the MacAdows'. Betty let me know she was not really interested in Dub, and she hoped maybe we could have some time together. We began doing that, and we were grateful that Dub was not distressed over it.

I finished summer school. I had invited four friends, including Dub Shanks and Bob Funk, to come stay at our family cottage at Indian Lake near Bellefontaine for a week. We had a great time doing our own cooking, fishing in our two boats, swimming, and relaxing.

In August, the Ohio Disciples held the first Advance Conference at a camp near Columbus. It was a great follow-up for Wilmington Conference for me, with old and new friends and the leadership of Harold Monroe, who had succeeded Gaines Cook as State Secretary. John Updegraff was also a leader. Don Ramsdell from Columbus had been elected president. We had become friends at Wilmington. George Phearson, another Wilmington conferee, was there, and we became better friends. Later he dated my sister Mary.

In September, I returned to Indy for my sophomore year. I kept my room at Mr. Forkner's house, but Don Matson had decided to transfer back to Drake University. Bob Funk and Dub Shanks were now occupying the other upstairs room across the hall. I expanded my workload in the school cafeteria for the summer. I still had my basketball work/scholarship cleaning Coach Hinkle's office for half of my tuition. By this time Betty Harper and I were going steady, as she lived with the MacAdow's and was enrolled as a freshman at Butler. We were also both very involved in University Park Christian Church.

As I think of my first semester in classes, Greek stands out for the attention I had to give it. I even went to special tutoring outside of class, where the tutor was Bob Funk. He was brilliant, and now a junior.

Basketball practice began again in late October. There was an influx of GIs who had played on service teams during the war for three or four years and who brought sterling records with them from high school. As a starter and letterman from last year, I knew Hinkle's system well and was practicing with the highest ranked guys. When real scrimmaging began, unfortunately I pulled a groin muscle and had to sit out for two weeks. That happened over Thanksgiving vacation. On the Monday after the holiday, Coach Hinkle announced the names of those in the top fifteen and my name was not called. The next fifteen were called and I was there. I hung in there, continuing to practice with mostly freshmen, including Marvin Wood, later to be the coach of the iconic small-town team that won the Indiana State Championship. It was the foundation story for the iconic movie *Hoosiers*. We sat on the bench for the first couple of games, and then began playing the preliminary game before the varsity game. I only played as a substitute for those games, as they seemed to be developing the freshmen. The guys who came to play that fall of 1946 became a great team who, in their junior year were ranked 7th in the country.

In 1946–47 we had a good year, beating Ohio State among other Big Ten teams. We had an invitation to play in the National Invitational Tournament, the NIT, which then was more prestigious than the fledgling NCAA's Final Four tournament. But we came to Cleveland for our final game against Western Reserve, whose coach was Moe Scarry, the Cleveland Browns center and linebacker. They were also loaded with former GIs, and we lost. With the loss Coach Hinkle decided to turn down the invitation to the NIT.

As the second semester begin, Betty had a good friend, Marcy, who was also a Butler student. Marcy lived at home in the same general neighborhood as Mr. Forkner. The situation at the MacAdows' had become somewhat demanding and burdensome with Betty's work responsibilities. She left the MacAdows to move in and share Marcy's bedroom and home with her. Fortunately, she did so with the blessing of the MacAdows. Betty and I were freer to come and go at Marcy's. Ironically, Marcy and Dub Shanks were now dating.

CHAPTER 16

Niles and Joanne Trimbur

On March 16, 1947, I came home to Bellefontaine to go with my family to Niles, Ohio, where Dad was to preach a trial sermon as a prospective minister for the First Christian Church there. We arrived early and were seated in a church pew as we awaited the service. Shortly, a family came in to be seated across the aisle from us. There was a young lady with such composed gracefulness who took her place in the second row church pew with her family. She was tall and so beautiful. It may not have been love at first sight, but it certainly was admiration at first sight. As the service began, I had confidence that my father would do quite well without my help. I would leave the preaching to him, and I would handle the admiring of the young lady across the aisle. Occasionally her beautiful eyes met mine.

Our family was introduced, each being presented, I as a nineteen-year-old college junior. After the service, our family was excused so that the congregation could consider the candidate. In the next room my dad said, "Well, John, what do you think?" I replied with great enthusiasm, "Dad, this is the place for you!"

At the reception following the call and acceptance, I noted where the young lady was and worked my way over toward her side, whereupon her mother's antenna rose, undoubtedly noting the look in my eye. She introduced us by declaring, "This is our little sixteen-year-old JoAnne." That night my sisters, Mary and Peggy stayed at JoAnne's home. I came to pick them up hoping JoAnne might not have left for school yet. No such luck!

Back at Butler, Betty and I enjoyed each other's company. After Easter, my folks had moved to Niles. I came by train for two Sundays to fill the pulpit at the Bellefontaine church. One weekend Betty came with me, and we stayed at Gene Eggleston's home. Gene and I had become good friends. The summer before he had gone with me to Cincinnati when I had a date with Bobby Jean, and she had fixed him up with a blind date. Gene's mother was a good friend of ours. Betty and I continued together through the end of the school year, attending the prom and going to the Indy 500 as spectators. She went home to Mexico, Missouri, for the summer and I to Niles. When I finished my second year at Butler University, I had just three semesters to fulfill my requirements for graduation.

When I arrived in Niles, my sisters had arranged for me to take them and JoAnne somewhere every evening for about a week. I did not object! When I saw the nightly events were running out, I asked JoAnne for our first date, for June 20, 1947. We want to see the movie that was running in the Niles theater, *Duel in the Sun*. (We have a tape of that movie which we recently watched on the 60th anniversary of our first date!) I was greatly taken with JoAnne.

I talked to Betty and told her I was very sorry, I didn't want to hurt her, but I had found someone else I wanted to be with. She was really upset, and I felt extremely bad about it. However, by Christmas she was married to Bob Bond, a seminary student at Butler.

As I thought of returning to Butler in the fall, leaving JoAnne was not a course I wanted to take. I also knew that my varsity basketball days at Butler were well over. I transferred to what was then Youngstown College, now Youngstown State. I also had the opportunity to become the student pastor of Disciples churches in Hanoverton and Augusta, Ohio, serving every other Sunday. These churches had previously been served by a student from Hiram College, George Phearson, a friend who had then moved on to seminary at the College of the Bible, in Lexington,

Kentucky. The Hanoverton church had been founded in 1832. There was a morning and evening service at Hanoverton, but only a morning service at Augusta. It was 42 miles from Niles to Hanoverton and 5 miles further to Augusta.

My salary was $30 a week at Hanoverton and $25 a week at Augusta. I was able to buy my parent's car, an agate red 1937 Oldsmobile, and Dad bought a new one. I needed a car to travel to the churches, and it was nice to have my own car for transportation and dating. Incidentally, gas was $0.18 a gallon then.

At Hanoverton, I would have Sunday noon dinner with different families each week, and then make pastoral calls in the afternoon. The church was on a beautiful tree-lined street of iconic brick homes. One brick building had been a famous inn, The Spread Eagle Tavern, in Hanoverton's heyday in the 1840s. In 1947, it was broken up into apartments.

Hanoverton was established in 1813. The Sandy and Beaver Canal was built to connect the Ohio and Erie Canal with the Ohio River. The first boat traveled the canal in 1848. With Hanoverton situated half-way on the seventy-three-and-a-half mile canal, it was a perfect spot for commerce.

JoAnne and I dated all summer. It was great fun with all the activities—church softball games, Idora Park, movies, Cleveland Indian ballgame trips, and hanging out together. I really liked her family. I was told at church events I should watch out for her mischievous brothers, Bill and Dick. They had a reputation it seemed. I was advised to "get in good" with them. I liked their spirit, and I played with them after the hours I could see JoAnne in the afternoons. We became good friends.

William Trimbur, JoAnne's Dad, the Trumbull County Auditor, helped me get a job on the county highway that first summer, painting and repairing guardrails and bridges. Over the July 4th weekend, the Trimburs invited Peggy, Mary, and me to come up to their rented cottage for the holiday. JoAnne had been very welcoming to Peggy once she moved to Niles. They were both sophomores and became good friends. The day before we traveled to Conneaut that evening, our county crew was painting a bridge in Lordstown. I was on a scaffolding under a bridge scraping rust off the steel supports when the rope holding the scaffolding broke. I fell fifteen feet into the river, landing seated on a log. I was not hurt. The crew restrung the ropes for the hanging scaffold, and we were now painting with aluminum paint. A young lady came out of the farmhouse next to the bridge, and I said to Paul, my painting partner, "Take a look over here, Paul!" He began to walk over. The rope broke again. I went face first into the river. The aluminum paint fell and quickly spread over the surface. I came out of the water covered in aluminum paint from head to toe. I looked like the Tin Man from the Wizard of Oz. I walked out of the river with my paintbrush in hand and threw it as far as I could across the pasture. I had to use turpentine to clean off all the covering paint. I even had it between my toes.

When I got home to the parsonage, I soaked some more. Then Peggy, Mary and I left for Conneaut. It was a delightful weekend with JoAnne and her family.

The church had a softball team in the Niles church league. I was delighted to play third base and enjoy the camaraderie. One time after a game, JoAnne had been at the game and her mother came to pick us up. Bill and Dick were in the car, and, wanting to extoll my friendship with the boys I said to Billy, "Hi, Bucky!" Having heard Dick call him that. Whereupon JoAnne's mother said pointedly, "We don't call Billy, Bucky." (It seemed when Dick called him that it was a term of derision, short for buckteeth.) Oops!

I started my work at Hanoverton and Augusta in late July. I had my first big wedding at Hanoverton and my first funeral.

In the fall JoAnne was a junior, and I had enrolled at Youngstown College. I could transfer my credits to Youngstown, live at home in the Niles parsonage, and finish my last three semesters. If I transferred, I wouldn't be eligible to play basketball at Youngstown. I went to meet the Youngstown coach and visited with him anyway.

I did play basketball for First Christian in the Niles church league. We were undefeated coming to the last game of the season against Mt. Carmel. If we won, we would be champions. If they won, we would have a playoff because they had only lost one game to us in the first round. With seven seconds to go, they scored a bucket to lead by three points. We took the ball out, and one of their players fouled one of ours with three seconds to go. Then the guy pushed the referee. A technical foul was called. Our player, Hake, made his free throw. Two points behind. I made the technical. One point behind. We had the ball out of bounds at the center line. Our coach asked me to take the wild shot from the middle of the floor. The ball was inbounded to me as I came toward the pass, turned, and dribbled once, and let the shot go from the middle of the floor. The buzzer sounded as the ball was in midair, and swish! Nothing but net! I was manhandled in a celebration pileup! We were the champions! And JoAnne was there with Bill and Dick!

I scheduled my classes in the mornings. I could then use the library early in the afternoon and get back to Niles in time to take JoAnne home from school. I was allowed to be with her till 5:00. Then on occasion, Bill, Dick, and I would throw the football or baseball around at the school behind their house. Later I would instigate putting up a backboard with a basket in the driveway behind the house where we spent many hours shooting and competing.

By Christmas time, I was head over heels in love with JoAnne, and knew she was the one for me. She was an honor student and had been elected one of the homecoming princesses. A disadvantage for us was that I could not take her to the high school dances because I was a college student. I could, however, take her to the Youngstown College dances, though this did trouble her mother. JoAnne was active in Dad's Niles Church in Sunday school as a helper with her sister, Marilyn Thorp. We were with Marilyn and Bill a lot, and babysat for Lynn, after she was born on December 7, 1947.

During the winter, I worked at the Niles YMCA on Saturday, taking boys to the Warren YMCA on the bus. I also could have JoAnne along to chaperone junior high dances at the Niles Y building. My senior year at YoCo I coached the HiY Niles basketball team in the Youngstown Y High School Basketball League.

The summer of 1948, Dutch Elm disease was sweeping the country. Trumbull County needed a Dutch Elm disease doctor. They chose me to be trained by the Warren city forester. I was given instruction, and I could tell from a distance which trees were diseased. They sent me on a survey of the county roads. If someone called the county offices to see if someone could come look at their elm tree, I was the person making the call. I was able to diagnose the case, but the trees could not be saved.

That summer our family took a month-long trip out west. Mom and Dad, Mary, Peggy, Bob, and I headed west in Dad's new Kaiser automobile. Dad was extolling the virtues of camping. We have chuckled about our camping trip ever since. Dad slept in the car and the rest of us in the tent. We visited Uncle Royal who was the pastor of a church west of Chicago and doing graduate work toward his Ph.D. at the University of Chicago. Then we headed west with our goal being Saint Helens, Oregon, where Grandmother and Grandfather Longston lived with Aunt Jessica. It was a wonderful trip with stops at national parks along the way, including seeing "Old Faithful." We also spent time with Uncle Robert Longston and family in their beautiful home on the Fruit Ranch by Lake Chelan.

In late August I attended an ecumenical conference at Lake Geneva, Wisconsin, for two weeks. It had an impressive leadership team, and l met a wide array of conferees, including Andrew Young, who would become a right-hand person to many such as Martin Luther King Jr., a UCC minister, the mayor of

Atlanta, and the US Ambassador to the United Nations. The kids from Indiana made up a softball team, and with my Butler background, I became the pitcher. We played almost every afternoon against other state teams, and I had a great time. On my return to Niles, I stopped in Chicago and Uncle Royal showed me some of the museum sights.

In the fall of 1948, JoAnne was a senior in high school, and I was a senior at Youngstown with just one semester to go. But when I registered, I discovered I needed one additional 400-level course to graduate. I had taken a class in photography the first year at Youngstown, which was only a 200-level course. But that was alright with me because I would be around Niles for the spring semester and could be with JoAnne till the fall of 1949. If I were to finish in January, I had thoughts of then going on to seminary in Lexington, Kentucky.

CHAPTER 17

Ordination and Seminary

Along with the original plan of finishing my undergraduate work in December of 1948 and going to seminary the following January, we had also been planning my ordination upon completion of my college work. I was admitted for an ordination interview with the Disciples ministers of the Warren Niles Youngstown District. We had also been in touch with Harold Monroe and his calendar, to be the preacher and person to convey the ordination. And of course, I had served the Hanoverton and Augusta churches for a year and a half and had been granted standing as a licensed minister in Ohio. This was before the region established the Ohio Commission on Ministry.

On January 3, 1949, in a worship service at the Niles First Christian Church, I was ordained. Herold B. Monroe preached, Grandmother Humbert gave the ordination prayer, and Howard Jones, President of Youngstown College, brought greetings and elders from Hanoverton and Augusta. President Jones and his wife were members of First Christian Church in Youngstown. I had taken her course on Marriage and Family Life at the college.

It was a deeply touching experience of inspiration and commitment for me. Afterwards at home, Mother told me that after their marriage she had prayed that she would become pregnant with a boy and prayed that he would go into the ministry. She had kept this in her heart all these years.

My last semester of college beginning in late January 1949. I had a light load with one 400 level course that met Monday,

Wednesday, and Friday mornings. I had been a mail carrier during Christmas time for two years. The post office needed a carrier for a shorter route that would be carried twice a day. The post office was half a block from the church parsonage. The route commenced just half a block from the parsonage, went past the west side of the high school, and then over towards Gramma Angie's grocery store. It proceeded back toward its end on the other side of the high school. Gramma Angie Trimbur, was JoAnne's grandmother. She and Wade Trimbur, JoAnne's dad's brother, had established the store together. Angie Trimbur was a strong leader in the Niles First Christian Church and a trustee. It was unusual in that day to have a woman as a trustee.

I was granted the route carrying one trip on Monday, Wednesday, and Friday afternoons, and both routes on Tuesday and Thursday. Mail was delivered twice a day then. Concluding my route, I would deliver special deliveries, often to Niles's factories. I was in the habit of whistling while walking. I became known as the "whistling postman." In May, the high school opened its windows to the nicer weather. JoAnne's late afternoon class met on the side of the building that I came down to deliver toward the end of the route. I whistled songs along the way, and JoAnne's classmates would whisper, "JoAnne, there comes Johnny!" I really enjoyed the job, getting to know the people on the route, especially the children. And of course, I continued serving Hanoverton and Augusta churches.

As the spring arrived, with it came the preparations for graduation and the senior prom for Niles High. JoAnne's mother felt she should have the experience of her high school prom. Of course, I couldn't take her. The word was that John Hlay, the star running back for Niles McKinley High, would like to take her. (He would later star as a running back for Ohio State.) That possible development left me cold. As it turned out, my Youngstown College prom was the same night as Niles's prom. Beatrice relented. We attended the college prom, and then joined JoAnne's high school friends for a celebration at one of her classmates' home.

We were all together for the rest of the night. (I had become friends with all JoAnne's and Peggy's classmates.) Then we had breakfast at the Trimburs' at 815 Robbins Avenue.

JoAnne graduated from Niles McKinley High School with all the surrounding social events. I graduated from Youngstown College, with Dr. Russell Humbert, Senior Minister at Trinity Methodist Church in Youngstown, giving the commencement address.

For the summer, JoAnne did some modeling for JCPenney and worked in her dad's office. I carried the mail full time.

In the fall of 1948, I had applied to attend the College of the Bible, the seminary in Lexington, Kentucky. Fortunately, the seminary had endowment funds for scholarships and there was no tuition. As my plans changed to arrive in the fall quarter of 1949, George Moore, the regular professor for students' church placement, would be on sabbatical. Dr. Howard Short would be in charge. He had been pastor of our church in Cuyahoga Falls, Ohio, a professor of religion at Hiram College, and was a ministerial colleague and friend of Dad's. I received word in July that the seminary and the Kentucky Region would be working together in supplying a ministerial student as pastor of the Shepherdsville Christian Church in Shepherdsville, Kentucky. This church had been employing ministers from our Independent Church of Christ Bible colleges. They felt that that leadership was not sufficient and desired to be a fully Disciples congregation with students from Lexington. Dr. Short recommended me for that position and urged me to consider it. The congregation's proposal was for the student to arrive on Friday evening, do pastoral work on Saturday, lead two services on Sunday, and then return to Lexington Sunday night. And in the summertime they would live in Shepherdsville full time.

Meanwhile, as JoAnne and I looked forward to the fall of 1949, we hoped that we would both be going to Transylvania University and to seminary. JoAnne and Peggy were in the same class and had become good friends. Peggy was going to Transylvania, our fine Disciples college. However, JoAnne's parents thought that since I had been monopolizing her time for two years, she should have an opportunity to be out on her own, to meet other people, and Transylvania was out. She had visited several schools, applied to Mount Union College in Alliance, Ohio, and was accepted.

I visited Shepherdsville. Arriving there, I was put up at a hotel that was not attractive at all, much like this small town that had been through the 1937 flood. The church was a one room building that had been damaged by that flood and was literally leaning. The thought of being here without JoAnne and living in Shepherdsville all summer the next year overwhelmed me to tears. But they extended the invitation after I had an interview and offered a pay of $45 a week. I said I would give it some serious thought. I was to begin in late September as the school year commenced.

I came back to Niles discouraged and downhearted. We had a family time in August at Chautauqua planned. Fortunately, JoAnne's grandmother, Angie, was going the same week, and JoAnne could come with her. We were all staying at the Disciples House at the Institution. JoAnne and I used our family motorboat for long rides together. We had a good time with my sisters, our parents, and with Gramma Angie. Another guest that week was Homer Carpenter, the iconic minister of First Christian Church, Louisville. Shepherdsville was the seat of Bullitt County, just south of Louisville. I told him of my call. He was very enthusiastic. "John, you come down to Shepherdsville and we'll do it together. John, we'll do it!" He was very enthusiastic, but it sounded a bit overboard to me. Nevertheless, I had to make a decision. I had the "call." Both the Kentucky Region, who would be partially paying my salary and to whom I would be reporting, and Dr. Short and the seminary were strongly encouraging me to accept. It was a "bird in hand" and I needed a church for the experience and the income to survive. JoAnne gave me her blessing. When we returned to Niles, I gave Dr. Short the word that I would accept the call.

Just before I was to leave for Lexington, I was having car trouble with the engine of my 1937 Oldsmobile purchased from my parents. I had the motor overhauled just two years before. This time it was too much. The Olds garage had a 1947 Olds '88 for sale that I bought with payments to take to Kentucky.

The College of the Bible was located in the library building of Transylvania College. Housing for single students was in Ewing Hall on one end of the building nicknamed by Transy students as the "angel wing." I had my own room with my own sink. Restrooms and showers were down the hall. I moved in and then registered for my classes. My first quarter I was taking Early Church History from Dr. Short, an Old Testament class, and Christian Education with Myron Hopper who had been on the faculty at Wilmington Conference. It was great to be focusing on preparation for ministry courses after my broader liberal arts studies. The faculty and students together were a warm and stimulating community. I joined the seminary octet which sang together for chapel and visited Kentucky churches, promoting the seminary. Dick Dodson, now considered part of our family, was now in his senior year, and was also in the octet. He also had a room in the "angel wing". His friends Bernie and Dudy Davis became my friends as well. A group of us including Don Ramsdell, Reed Carter, Bernie Meece and I went over to the University of Kentucky daily to eat lunch at the university cafeteria.

I began my ministry at Shepherdsville the first Sunday in October, driving the 109 miles on Friday afternoon. The church arranged for me to room at Miss Mary's house. She was a maiden lady whose home was on Main Street, just north of the main district part of the town. She was not a member of the church. There was no office at the church since it was a one room building, so the mimeograph was brought to my room. I would cut the stencil with my portable typewriter and print the bulletins there.

I began visiting members of the church in their homes on Saturday and Sunday afternoons and preaching twice on Sunday.

I was invited to different homes for Sunday noon dinner, though not as regularly as in Hanoverton and Augusta.

I learned early on that the congregation was looking forward to selling their Main Street property and their "leaning" one room church building and erecting a new building on already purchased property just off Main Street, very near where I was rooming. In fact, they had engaged Ed Gregg, an architect from Louisville, to draw the plans for the building. That was an exciting prospect. I went to visit Mr. Gregg in his office in Louisville and enjoyed surveying the plans. The congregation was planning to move forward with construction of the new building. We contacted the Board of Church Extension for financing, with the modest funds already raised.

In October, the International Convention was held in Cincinnati. It was an opportunity to help the congregation with knowledge about the polity of the Disciples, something new to many of the members since they had definitely been leaning strongly toward the independents in their leadership. I would be attending and needed to be in Cincinnati for Sunday. My mother offered to be the substitute preacher, and the elders accepted. This would be my fourth International Convention after Des Moines in 1934 and Columbus in 1944 and 1946.

I attended the convention Friday through Sunday, but with seminary classes not meeting the early part of the next week, I just had to go see JoAnne in Alliance. We had a wonderful reunion. We attended chapel, where JoAnne was singing in the college choir.

I was able to get back to Niles for Thanksgiving, driving back to Shepherdsville on Saturday with a stop in Lima, Ohio, to sing for Bernie and Georgia's wedding, and a late arrival with preaching on Sunday. JoAnne and I were together for a few days at Christmas time in Niles. By this time, in our minds, we were engaged.

I played on the seminary basketball team and was the leading scorer. In one game I had thirty-nine points, shooting sixteen for seventeen from the field, and seven for seven from the free throw line. It was fun. I was also the shortstop on the seminary softball team in the Transy Intramural League.

By the third quarter of classes, I had decided to major in church history with Dr. Howard Short as my major professor. I would write my thesis on the history and development of the church through the early centuries. I also was stimulated by Christian Education with Dr. Myron Hopper and nearly had enough courses to major in that field. One second quarter course in Church and Society opened for me a lifetime of commitment and action to social justice.

Finishing my first year in seminary classes, the summer stretched out before me in Shepherdsville, without JoAnne. I lived at Miss Mary's, worked at getting better acquainted with churches in town, with town movers and shakers, and just folks. I was invited to play shortstop on the Woodman of the World softball team, accepted, enjoyed getting to know some of the young men, and getting to be known as the "home run preacher" in the weekly league games. I also discovered that the principal restaurant on Main Street was owned by a Butler University graduate and basketball player. In fact, when my Butler team came to play the University of Louisville my freshman year, he came to our dressing room before the game to wish us well. When I mentioned that fact to him, he remembered the moment but not me personally, although I scored ten points that night.

We had our vacation Bible school early in the summer. The women leaders used our one room sanctuary and storage garage creatively. I helped out at their direction. We also appointed a building committee, hoping to break ground in the fall of 1950 for the new building. The Board of Church Extension was most helpful with the plans and financing.

My parents celebrated their 50th anniversary that summer. The congregation gave me time off for a trip back to Niles in July. It occasioned time for JoAnne and me to be together. Every moment was treasured.

She had also been working on her parents to allow her to transfer to Transylvania College in the fall. She had fulfilled their wishes to be on her own, meeting other peers, dating, and sorority life at Alpha Z Delta. They now accepted how seriously in love we were. Our relationship had survived the year's separation. They relented and allowed JoAnne to come to Lexington in the fall.

With great joy, we drove to Kentucky to begin the year in proximity. The seminary had completed new buildings across town from Transy, adjacent to the University of Kentucky on South Limestone. Angel wing was close to us. I found new lodging at Mr. Charles's where Jim Faulkner and I shared a room, and Don Ramsdell and Reed Carter, friends from Bethany College, shared a room. My room's front windows had a view across the street to Hamilton Hall, the Transy's women's dorm. JoAnne's room window was opposite mine, distanced by about 250 yards. There was great joy in seeing each other after classes.

The dorm had restrictions on weeknights, men out by 9:30, and times to be back in on weekends. Getting permission to go with me on a weekend to Shepherdsville, with specifics about where she was to stay, etc. was taxing.

It was not easy to leave her in Lexington when I left for the weekend for Shepherdsville. She went with me on about three occasions that fall and stayed with Woodrow Masdon's parents. I have to admit I sometimes would not leave for Shepherdsville until early Saturday morning.

It was a busy fall. I was the new manager of the seminary bookstore with a small honorarium. I worked at the Jim Nix Cafeteria downtown. I had the church on the weekends, sermon prep, classes, papers to write, playing on the seminary basketball team against church teams where students held pastorates, and courting.

CHAPTER 18

Tuberculosis

From Thanksgiving to Christmas time, I had a cough, sometimes severe. Jo and I were in Niles for Christmas vacation. On the day before Christmas Eve, I awakened coughing up blood. Mother had an appointment with her doctor in Youngstown that day and I accompanied her. I was directed immediately by her doctor to a chest specialist. I went, was x-rayed, and was diagnosed with a tuberculosis cavity in my left lung. In a state of shock, I was admitted immediately to Youngstown North Hospital. There I was told that I would have surgery on the phrenic nerve in my neck, crushing the nerve which controlled my left diaphragm, enabling my left lung to be collapsed. I would then be transferred to the Trumbull County TB Sanatorium where I would probably reside for twelve months to heal.

My emotions hit bottom. Seminary, the seminary bookstore, Shepherdsville Christian Church, what would happen? I mentioned those first, but what really hit me was JoAnne and me. We had hoped to be married that next summer of 1951. I knew that JoAnne's Dad's first wife had died from TB. What would JoAnne's reaction be to my illness? Would I be sickly all my life? Mother left me in the hospital, went home to share the news with dad and my siblings. Then they went together to the Trimburs to share the news with JoAnne and her family. That evening as I lay in an isolated room, lost in the ruminations of my life's activities closing down, my family brought JoAnne to the doorway of my room. I say doorway because they were not permitted to come into my room. Even at the doorway they were dressed in white gowns and white masks. I was so moved with love to see JoAnne there to support me and love me across the room. Saying goodnight in those moments was dreadful. I spent a fitful night trying to sleep. My future was suddenly shattered. One year in a tuberculosis sanatorium!

On Christmas Eve morning, I went into surgery. Christmas Eve my parents brought JoAnne and my sisters to see me, and JoAnne showed me her present for me. I say showed. It was from the doorway, and I was not permitted to touch the beautiful blue sweater.

Christmas morning the doctors arrived with some sort of contraption with an air pump. I had not been told about the next procedure. It was to pump air into my abdomen to create enough pressure to force my diaphragm against my lung to collapse the lung. He injected Novocain into my belly, then made an incision, and through that, with the large, long needle he went into my abdomen. He pumped air till he was satisfied, and then told me they would be doing this every day for ten days.

The pressure created pain above my left shoulder along with some difficulty breathing since one lung was collapsing. I lay there with some real discomfort. But later that day I could hear a radio with the announcer calling the NFL championship game between the Los Angeles Rams and the Cleveland Browns. It was the first year for the Browns in the NFL, after four years as champions of the all-American Conference. No one thought the Browns could stand up to the NFL. In fact, they scheduled the Browns first game against the previous year's champions, the Philadelphia Eagles. The Browns won that game. Now they were in the championship game. The Browns were behind 28 to 27, with just seconds to go when Lou Groza kicked a field goal to win 32–28. The cheering in the hospital hall was loud and long. The nurses were permitted to join in the celebration. It was an absolute thrill for me. I had listened to that opening game against the Eagles in a Kentucky State Park with my Shepherdsville CYF.

The day after Christmas, Dad brought JoAnne to Northside Hospital. I was to be taken by ambulance to the Trumbull County TB Sanatorium. JoAnne rode with me in the ambulance on a cold, snowy day.

Arriving at the TB sanatorium, we were greeted by the head doctor and head nurse as I was taken by the ambulance gurney to my room. It was a private room, absent of any decorations, but with French doors opening to a large screened-in porch. JoAnne immediately wanted to make it more attractive with curtains at the doors, but was told that was not permitted. Curtains might hold the tubercular germs.

The head nurse helped me get settled with hospital pajamas. My only baggage as I arrived was the hospital gown I was wearing and my dopp kit with my toothbrush. As I was settled into my bed, JoAnne and Dad were politely informed it was time for them to depart. They were given the sanatorium visiting instructions. Visiting hours were Wednesday afternoon, Friday evenings, and Sunday afternoons only! For a guy whose life and future had just been turned upside down and needed his beloved with him as much as possible, this sounded bleak. Add to that JoAnne was to be tested for TB. For months while I was developing TB, we had been kissing regularly. I feared for her health. Immediately she was tested and fortunately she was negative.

After JoAnne and Dad left, the nurse let me know that I was to be bedfast for the foreseeable future, only getting out of bed to be taken by wheelchair into the treatment room for the procedure of pumping air into my abdomen. I would use a bedpan and a urinal for elimination while in bed. My food would be brought to my bed where I would eat all my meals.

Shortly a wheelchair arrived to take me to the treatment room for the pneumoperitoneum treatment. The doctor was a hail-fellow as he used the large, long needle, now without any anesthetic, to enter my abdomen to pump the air. This was to occur every day, for nine more days, and then twice weekly for the rest of my stay in the sanitarium. The idea was to collapse my left lung to place it in a state of rest, so that the TB cavity in my lung would heal.

Back to my room and in bed, my fellow patients who were ambulatory drifted by to meet the new guy. They were amiable in our mutual situation. What I would learn later was that the guys in the ward down the hall were taking bets on how long I would live. My first night there, the man in the room next door died. At any rate, my lunch came shortly, and it was really pretty good. After lunch I was a bit shocked to learn of another aspect of the sanatorium treatment. At 2:00 p.m., the nurse came in and threw the French doors wide open and closed the door to the hall. Every afternoon except Sunday and Wednesday when visitors would be present, we had fresh, frigid air in our room from 2:00 to 4:00 p.m. This December 28 was during the frigid winter of 1950–51, which had record snow and cold. And in the mornings from ten to noon, it was also fresh air time. I snuggled under my covers.

The next day was Tuesday with the daily air pump, but no visitors. I had a phone, but we were not supposed to use it for prolonged chitchat. Dad surprise me by stopping in for a visit after 4:00. He used his pastoral role as a way to call on me. I was glad to see him. I was trying to begin reconciling this traumatic drastic change in our lives, for JoAnne, me, and my family, who also were suffering with me. I was struggling with the big why! Why, oh God, when I've committed my life to serving you! I'm here suffering while all those people out there who are living wild, crazy, and selfish lives are going merrily on their way! But I knew why. I had been working too hard with all my jobs, schoolwork, courting, and not getting enough rest. I was physically rundown, not taking care of myself, and the TB bugs that reside in everyone could have their way with me. Plus, the town of Shepherdsville, where I was the student pastor, was written up in a national magazine as being one of the worst communities in the country for germ-filled open street side ditches. It was not God's fault! I had played a major role in the why! And I believed that the doctors and medical people had begun to set the physical circumstances where the healing power of God, which is placed in our bodies, could do its work.

JoAnne was my salvation! She transferred from Transylvania back to Mount Union College in Alliance. She was in Niles then until the second semester began at Mount. She came to see me on Wednesday, Friday, and Sunday during regular hours. We also received special permission for Saturday evening visits. In the midst of my bleak existence, her coming to my bedside sustained my life. When school started, she came home every Friday for the weekend to sit with me Friday and Saturday evenings and Sunday afternoon till she had to ride back to Alliance. She gave up her college weekend life to sit by my bedside. Some dates for a college coed!

I was completely bedfast for one month. On the 30th day of my stay, I was allowed out of bed for the first time. Running and jumping on the basketball court just prior to this hospitalization, I found it now difficult just to walk. Freed from my bed, I was allowed to walk to the dining room for my first meal seated at a table.

I found that one of the privileges of patients who were ambulatory was that Friday night after our visitors had departed, we could go to the dining room to watch the Pabst Blue Ribbon Friday night fights. Hard to fathom it now, but there in the dining room was the one and only black-and-white television set on the sanatorium premises! It was a big deal!

Being up and about, I began to get acquainted with the other patients, forming some real friendships. Pete's room was across the hall. He was an ironworker with the most profane vocabulary I had ever heard. This was the third time in his life that he had broken down with TB. This time he had been in that room for seven years. We became good friends.

One of the big social events was the Friday morning weigh-in. One of the goals for all patients was to keep their weight up in the face of the disease laying waste to their bodies. In addition to our meals we had mid-morning and mid-afternoon snacks, with milk. We all gathered around the scales each taking our turn weighing in with the results recorded. I had first weighed in at 160 pounds. The big thing among the guys was to see who won the weekly weight gain. I began to gain and was often the winner to much acclaim! In my four months in the sanatorium, I advanced from 160 pounds to 215 pounds of solid flab!

A major development was that after the first three weeks I no longer had tubercular cells in my sputum and was not contagious! The staff monitored my progress, looking through the fluoroscope at my lung, seeing some progress with the healing of the tubercular cavity.

By Easter time, I had made enough progress that I was given a week away from the sanatorium at my parents' home with instructions for at least two hours of bed rest in the mornings and afternoons. Oh joy! JoAnne was on spring break from Mount and was also home. We could see each other every day!

At the end of April, I made enough progress that I was released from the sanatorium to my parents' home with the proviso that I would report every Friday to have an injection of air into my abdomen to keep my lung collapsed for continued healing. I was to have bed rest for two hours, mornings and afternoons. I continued in this manner from April to December of 1951.

JoAnne finished her second semester, and enrolled in summer courses. She was on her way to finishing her college work in three years by the early summer of 1952. For all that time, she arranged to come home on weekends to be with me. She loved me back to health!

By November, I was well enough to resume normal activities with the prospect of working around Trumbull County from January until our planned wedding on July 26, 1952. Dad Trimbur gave me a job in the County Auditor's Office, where he was County Auditor. I began in January of 1952 auditing tax returns in the Personal Property Tax Department. Every Friday morning, I returned to the TB sanatorium for injections of air.

In the spring of 1952, Dad accepted the call to a church in Harrison, Ohio, near Cincinnati, with their move scheduled just after Easter. With my parents moving, the Trimburs graciously invited me to live with them until our marriage in July. After our wedding and honeymoon, we planned to move to Lexington, Kentucky, where we would live in the seminary apartments. I would resume my seminary education and have a student ministry. JoAnne had applied to teach in an elementary school.

In early summer, JoAnne and I with my dad and mother went to Kentucky for the dedication of the church building in Shepherdsville and for an extended weekend. We went to Fox Creek Christian Church to meet with the Church Board as a prospective minister. My friend Reed Carter was the student minister. He was graduating and going on to the Christian Church in Bowling Green, Kentucky. I had been to Fox Creek my first year in seminary, singing with the College of the Bible octet. After TB, I weighed 210 pounds. An elder, Brother Carter, who I had met before, remembered me from my first visit and noting the difference said, "Law, you sure have fleshened up right smart!" The "fleshened up" seminarian was hired to begin as the minister in the fall.

I enjoyed my time working in Dad Trimbur's office. My fellow workers were people I had met prior to this time. I enjoyed my time around the courthouse. On one occasion, a couple came to be married, but wanted a minister to perform the ceremony rather than a judge. With the Courthouse's knowledge that I was at least a licensed minister, the Court Clerk came to get me. I obliged and did the wedding.

JoAnne was at Mount Union during the early summer, finishing her coursework for graduation in early July. The wedding day was finally approaching. She had received word that she had a position teaching in the Fayette County school system beginning in September, which was a great relief. Her salary would be $2,700 a year. My salary at Fox Creek would be $45 a week.

CHAPTER 19

Wedding Bells and Lexington

JoAnne and her mother had chosen her wedding dress. There were several bridal showers with the Trimbur family and Niles friends. I was engaged to do the preaching at our Niles church after Dad left. I would do so till the Sunday before our wedding on July.

The wedding day approached. We could hardly believe it! The wedding rehearsal was interesting with the different ideas. Marilyn Thorp, JoAnne's sister was the matron of honor, and Dick Dodson was my best man. The brothers, Bill, Dick, and Bob plus Gene Eggleston were ushers. My sisters Peggy and Mary, Nancy Hodge and Esther Heindle were the bride's maids. Ida Mae Lease was the soloist. Dad was the marrying person. My parents provided the wedding rehearsal dinner at the church parish house. The reception was at the beautiful, large Trimbur home. Everything was ready!

The wedding was at 4:30 in the afternoon on July 26, 1952. It went beautifully, and we were husband and wife! We had the receiving line in the sanctuary in front of the west stained-glass window which was hot as the blazes. It was an extremely hot day, and of course, there was no air conditioning. But we were ecstatic!

The reception was very nice, with the cake cutting, and JoAnne feeding me the first piece. We changed and packed our things in the car and were off on our honeymoon. Married after five years of courting!! I had searched out a beautiful, new motel for our first night. It was just 15 miles away in Boardman, Ohio. (Now it is the first turnpike exist east of the Niles exit, and is a crummy, 69-year-old motel.) We had decided we would take our honeymoon in a place we would never live, with sights to see (and an airconditioned hotel.) We chose Washington, D.C.! We were in the Hilton Hotel on 16th Street, just north of the White House. It was beautiful! We had a dream car, our 1949 black Oldsmobile Coupe with white sidewalls, that I had bought from Nick Manella that summer.

We visited the sights of Washington, D.C. and Mount Vernon. We enjoyed our new adult life! And our married life! Mmm!

We returned to Niles in time for JoAnne to be in her Mount roommate Esther Heindle's wedding the following Saturday.

After a few days at the Trimburs', we packed up our car with all our worldly goods and drove to Lexington, Kentucky, to the College of the Bible's apartment building. Our apartment was on the 4th floor. It was a one-room apartment with a large closet and bathroom and a kitchen too small to have a table in it and with no countertops. A layman from the Shepherdsville Church was a foreman in a Louisville furniture factory. He helped us come over and pick out a bedroom set, which we bought for wholesale price. We used the dresser. We also bought a dining room dropleaf table and six chairs. They were all limed oak with a blond finish. We also bought a hide-a-bed for a sofa and our sleeping arrangements. We painted and dressed up the room with drapes at the windows, and it was quite attractive but small.

The last week in August, JoAnne began teaching fifth grade at suburban Kenwick Elementary School in the Fayette County School System. I began as the student minister at Fox Creek Christian Church in Anderson County near Lawrenceburg, 40 or so miles west of Lexington. I was to preach and lead a Sunday morning and evening service and make pastoral calls on Sunday afternoons. When Board meetings were held, I was to come from Lexington.

Board meetings were most interesting. After prayer, the chairman of the Board would say, "Preacher, what you got?" I would name the subject to come before us. The members, all men at that time, would talk about it and other things till I would finally say, "Well, what are we going to do about it?" Luther, the chairman, would say, "Well, I reckon we should vote on it. Preacher, you name it." I would state the issue, and Luther would ask for yeses and noes. Not everyone would vote. There seemed to be a reluctance to commit themselves.

One of the subjects they brought up was a need for the construction of a roof over the side stoop entrance to the Sunday school rooms. The question was for the two porch posts supporting the roof. Should they be brick halfway up or all wood for the whole post? They discussed the pros and cons, and finally I said, "What are we going to do about it?"

Luther said, "Well, I reckon this is too important for us to decide. We need to have the congregation vote on this next Sunday between Sunday school and church."

That time came, and I said to Luther, "You're gonna preside for the business meeting, right?"

"No," he said, "You need to name it, and take the vote."

So, I named it, and opened it up for discussion. No one responded, and I asked again, if anyone wanted to speak to the choices. No one responded. I then took the vote. There were probably 85 people present, and wood posts all the way up won by a vote count of three votes for the wood posts and two votes for the brick halfway. JoAnne was sitting down front and didn't see it, but she cast the deciding vote. Out of 85 people only five would commit themselves to register an opinion.

One Sunday, a gentleman farmer member told me on the way in that he had brought us a chicken to take back to Lexington that night. He had put it in our car. When we went to the car after the morning service, there on the floor in the back seat was a live chicken, in a paper sack with her head sticking out. When we arrived at Bill and Georgia Elliott's for Sunday dinner, Georgia took the chicken and turned it loose in her chicken yard. "We'll take care of it after Sunday dinner," she said.

After dinner, Bill and I went to the church croquet grounds at Luther Baxter's home, for a game of croquet with some of our church men. I held my own, thanks to Grandfather Longston's tutelage. Meanwhile, Georgia wrung the chicken's neck and taught JoAnne how to pluck the feathers and dress the chicken, which accompanied us back to Lexington that night, after the evening service.

JoAnne was teaching her fifth grade class at Kenwick School. On occasion, I was able to help by going on a field trip with the kids, getting to know them. Some of the girls said to me, "Mr. Humbert, Mrs. Humbert is so beautiful. You should give her a break and let her go to Hollywood." JoAnne also said that she could look at her class, raise an eyebrow, and they would get quiet.

I was glad to finally return to my classes in seminary. We were on a quarter plan: fall, winter, and spring. In the spring, I was surprised to be nominated and elected president of the seminary student body and president of the student council for the 1953–54 academic year.

By February, living in a one room apartment and sleeping on a hide-a-bed felt a little too confining to JoAnne. A teacher colleague at school lived in a nice, new building with four apartments in the Chevy Chase section of Lexington. Its location was closer to JoAnne's school. One apartment was open for renting. We went to inspect it. We were delighted with it. It featured a good sized living room, a nice sized kitchen, a dining area, a very nice bathroom, and a bedroom with a sizable closet. We had a fourth of the basement for a washer and dryer and storage. In addition, we had a stall in a four-car garage. The rent was only $85 a month, which was within our financial capabilities. We signed for it and moved in in early February 1953. We were absolutely delighted with what felt like our first real home.

The summer of 1953, there was no summer school at the seminary. JoAnne was out of school for the summer as well. I had my student ministry at Fox Creek on Sundays. But I was free on the weekdays. I answered an ad in the Lexington newspaper to be a Fuller Brush salesman, going door to door. I did very well, and after three weeks, I was the top salesperson in our district. "Fuller Brush Man, with a free sample for you, ma'am." And I named the number of free samples we had. "Which one would you like?" "OK, I'll just step in and get it out for you!" The sample, of course, was in the bottom of my case, thus showing all the products prior to the gift.

With part of my earnings, we purchased our first television set, with the huge antenna on the roof and a motor to turn it from WLW, a Cincinnati station, to a Louisville station as the two choices. Awesome!

The fall quarter began with additional responsibilities beyond my class work. As president of the student body, I presided in chapel whenever we had guest lecturers or preachers which was once or twice a week. We had chapel every day, Tuesday through Friday. I did the invocation, selected hymns, and introduced our guest. Other chapels were by students designing worship and preaching.

Every two weeks, I went to the Fayette County TB Sanatorium for air in my abdomen.

Practice preaching, with Dr. Dwight Stephenson, was a helpful class in developing my preaching. I preached to the class in the chapel, receiving their critique on assigned points like developing the text, illustrations, delivery, developing the thesis sentence, the conclusion. Then the student would sit with Dr. Stephenson to listen to the taped sermon together with his critique. Challenging! My first sermon after being elected General Minister and President was at University Christian Church in Fort Worth, Texas, where the retired Dr. Stephenson was a member and was in the congregation. I was so conscious that he was there. I think this was the first for us thirty-two years removed from that homiletics class. He greeted me afterwards, warmly, but didn't comment on the sermon.

I finished my class work in the winter quarter of 1953-54. That spring, free from classes, I finished the draft of my thesis "Gnosticism, and Its Impact on Christianity." I had decided to major in Church History with Dr. Short. All along the way, I researched and wrote papers on various aspects, all of which were helpful for the finished product. I rented a typewriter with large English print and typed the 130 pages in book form.

CHAPTER 20

Kettering and the New Congregation

In the fall of 1953, Herold Monroe, our Ohio State Secretary, arrived at seminary to visit with the Ohio students. In our visit, he asked me what my thinking was about my future ministry. I shared that pastoral ministry in a county seat town church setting was my sense of where I could best serve because that was my life experience growing up. He said that Ohio was launching a New Church Program, anticipating founding new congregations in suburban Cleveland, Cincinnati, and Dayton. I said I'd never experienced city life firsthand. "Well," he said, "the new suburbs are just about like county seat towns. I would like you to consider being a founding pastor in one of those settings."

The thought of support from the Ohio churches and being the founding pastor of a new congregation did sound like an exciting challenge. After talking with JoAnne about the prospect, we decided to go forward with that prospective ministry.

As spring moved toward graduation, the Dayton situation in suburban Kettering became our destination. The minister of Santa Clara Christian Church in northern Dayton was moving to Cleveland as the new church pastor in Westlake. The proposal was that we would attend the State Convention of our churches in Dayton and meet with the Santa Clara elders as a candidate. We would serve that church as interim minister, half-time, living in their parsonage, and begin work on the new congregation. After we met with the elders, they voted for us to do that, with the church and the state each contributing half of my salary. The salary was $3,600, and the parsonage allowance was $1,200. The Santa Clara parsonage was a very pleasant home. JoAnne was pregnant. We planned for our first child to arrive in October or November. She enjoyed the summer off from teaching. We found a builder and planned for our first home in Kettering.

I was preaching half-time, doing pastoral calls, and becoming acquainted with the Santa Clara folk. A committee of representatives from Central, Santa Clara, Hillcrest, and Summit Christian Churches, who I would be working with, had been formed. The ministers graciously gave me the names of their members who lived in the Kettering and Oakwood areas. Many were inactive, but some were good solid church folks. I began calling on those people with news of the new church, inviting them to consider being a part of the exciting venture. I also went calling door-to-door in an extensive new development of homes in the Kettering general area where there was land for a possible church site.

As we moved to town, we were most cordially received by the Santa Clara people. And the other Disciples ministers were most gracious, welcoming, and friendly. Maurice Fogel at Central, Eli Wilburn at Summit, and Edsel Pugh at Hillcrest became great friends. Ed and Ann Pugh along with their children were so wonderful, helping us settle into the Dayton community. John and Joan Albrecht were members of Santa Clara, about our age, and we soon developed a warm friendship that would last a lifetime.

One of the leaders at Central Christian Church, Jim Henry, an engineer at Wright Patterson Air Base handy with tools and building on the side, helped us find a builder who was constructing a neighborhood of prefab homes in Kettering. National Builders was a company from West Lafayette, Indiana.

My parents loaned us $3,000 for a down payment, and with a loan, we had a three-bedroom house built on a slab for $10,200. I served as the painting contractor to save $500, so our final cost for the house at 5535 Reardon Drive just a few blocks into Kettering from southeast Dayton was $9,700. We moved in the third week in

October. JoAnne was very pregnant and due the first of November. We were the first house finished on our block. We had no phone and our partial electricity came from an extension cord from the builder's construction shack behind our house.

I was a new church pastor organizing a projected first gathering of prospects and interested folks in December. I was still the interim at Santa Clara, with use of a phone there. For two weeks we had a retired couple, where the wife would receive calls from folk who wanted to reach me, and I would check in with her every day by pay phone or the builder shack office phone. We got full electricity in a couple of weeks and our phone installed on November 15. I worked from home as JoAnne's due date approached.

On November 6, JoAnne gave birth to John Dale Humbert on a Saturday afternoon. The labor was hard, and when they let me see Johnny, he had a pointed head, but all his fingers and toes! I was so glad to see JoAnne. Though she had been through agony and pain, she was beautiful! I called our parents from the hospital.

Because visiting hours were over, I had to leave the hospital, and I went to break the news to the Albrechts. They lived in a four-apartment building in Oakwood. As I came in hooping and hollering, they were playing cards with neighbors in the building, and lo and behold, the other couple was Earl Gardner and his wife. "Red" Gardner had been the star basketball player for DePaul University in Indiana when my Butler team played DePaul. He then went on to play for the Minneapolis Lakers in the NBA. Wow! I had played against him! He was now a teacher and coach at Oakwood High School.

On Sunday morning, I preached in Santa Clara, then went to Miami Valley Hospital to see JoAnne and our new son. They were strict about visiting hours, so I told them I was her minister. Well, I was! For the first of many times, too many, I had to leave her to make a speech in Cincinnati on behalf of the New Church Program. I was kissing her goodbye when the nurse walked in wide-eyed. She wondered, no doubt, if I finished all my pastoral calls with a kiss. (I did explain.)

My mother and dad and Mother and Dad Trimbur came calling. JoAnne and Johnny had to remain hospitalized for a week, as was the custom then. Bea and Bill were there for the homecoming and stayed for several days. Johnny was so good coming home and into his crib. I had bought a miniature baseball, basketball, and football for him. I was showing him the little football and it slipped out of my fingers and accidentally dropped on his nose. He started crying and didn't stop for three months. He was a colicky baby.

Meanwhile, I continued to work toward the first gathering of people interested in the new church. The Dayton Disciple Union committee met a number of times in our living room. Finding a location for worship in a public school was not easy. The fast-growing city of Kettering was fertile ground for the denominations to establish new congregations. The Kettering school system established the rule that new congregations must have their architectural plans for the building first in order to use one of the schools for their first meeting place. We were not that far along, of course. We finally negotiated for a meeting place at Benham's Catering Service, located in Oakwood at 2419 Far Hills Avenue, Oakwood's main street. It was just north of Kettering. The rent was $15 a week. They did not serve meals at the main location. It provided us with two rooms at street level.

Our first gathering was a snowy Sunday evening, December 19, 1954, with thirty-five people present, including five members of the Disciples Union committee. James Henry, an elder from Central Christian and resident of Oakwood, was appointed chairman. The First Christian Church of Kettering was chosen as the name for the new congregation and planning was done for the first worship service on January 2, 1955.

Our first Christmas in our new home was so special with our Johnny who was nearly two months old. We were alternating

Thanksgiving and Christmas at our parents' homes. We were at home for Christmas, then went to Niles immediately to be with the Trimbur clan. Then my family came up to Kettering from Harrison, Ohio, for a few days.

The first worship service for our new church was held on January 2, 1955, with forty-eight people present. Attendance increased each Sunday, until there were eighty-four attending within the first month. We held several fellowship dinners and meetings in Kettering neighborhood churches, with welcoming courtesy by their ministers. I became a member of the Kettering Oakwood Ministerial Fellowship.

Jim Henry had become a strong help, friend, and leader, and was chairman of the congregation. In early spring there was a shocking phone call. Jim had had a heart attack at his desk at Wright Patterson Airfield. He died in his desk chair. With his help in finding the builder of our home and working closely on all the arrangements in finding our worship place, we had become fast friends. He was only fifty-two years old. I had become close to his wife, Ruth, and two high school-aged daughters as well. It was a great loss for the people who had begun life as the new congregation. Pastoral care for Ruth and her family and the funeral were most emotionally challenging for me.

Doyle Mayberry became the new chairman of the congregation. We would work well together.

We held a chartering service on Easter Sunday, April 10, 1955, at Oakview Grade School in Kettering, with a hundred members signing the charter. Herald Monroe preached and dedicated the charter. JoAnne led the robed junior choir in singing "Open the Gates of the Temple." It was a great and inspiring day.

On May 13, at the State Convention in Cleveland, the First Christian Church of Kettering was formally recognized as part of the regional church. Six of our members were present.

Prior to this on April 24th, we reached into the community and took a religious census of the southeast area of Kettering with

Disciples from Central, Santa Clara, and Hillcrest Churches, as well as our folks cooperating.

That spring, having heard of the Disciples' drive-in service in Daytona, Florida, I proposed we have a drive-in service on Sunday mornings after our regular service. The Skyline Drive-in Theater was located in south Kettering. I persuaded the owner to let us use his facilities, including the sound system to the automobiles. I led the service from the rooftop of the concession stand with a tape machine at hand. I taped the prelude, hymns, and postlude ahead of time. We handed bulletins to the drivers as they arrived. It was blazing hot on that roof! But I did that from July 3 until Labor Day with probably eight to ten cars each Sunday. The drive-in services were not as successful as we had hoped, but we presented the name of our church before the public. We had one family of three come and join the church as a result of these services.

In September 1955, there was a development that would ultimately affect our life in ministry in profound ways. I was appointed Assistant Program Director and Platform Host for the 1956 Des Moines, Iowa, International Convention, working with Ben Moore. I would have the privilege of working with many of our international leaders in that capacity. Gaines Cook was the General Secretary of the Convention. He was a good friend of my family, and as I said earlier, the vesper speaker for four years at the Wilmington Conference. He had moved to that post as I began at Butler. The Cooks had invited me to Sunday dinner.

For the congregation, we were planning ahead and working on acquiring our building site. A beautiful piece of property at Stroop Road and Southern Boulevard in Kettering was most enticing. Herold Monroe came to town to consult with us. A whole new development of 250 homes had been built nearby. He said, "Let's see how promising the location would be." So he chartered a four-seat airplane to overfly the area. He was in the rear seat by the open door, leaning out with a camera. I was in the copilot seat. We discovered that west of this lot, not even a mile away, was a huge area of industrial development, including the site of the huge Frigidaire plant and multiple train tracks. To the east, only a block away was a sprawling 18-hole golf course (one that I would enjoy later.) These surrounding areas were not and would not contain homes and prospects for membership. However, this was my first airplane flight, very exciting to me! The pilot, in mid-flight said to me, "Would you like to fly it?"

"Yes!" I said. So he turned over the controls to me for a while. Wow! At any rate, we rejected what on the surface was a beautiful site.

We became really good friends with John and Joanne Albrecht. We got together almost every Friday night at our house since we had Johnny. They had no children at that point. The summer of '55, we vacationed together for a few days at Chautauqua, New York, with the Trimburs caring for Johnny in Niles. The four of us ventured into our first attempts at bridge on that vacation. (JoAnne and Joanne would then take bridge lessons back home. Notice since we were both Johns and JoAnnes, he became Jack, and my JoAnne became Jo. Friday nights were for bridge and making our own pizzas.) We cut our vacation short because JoAnne was so homesick for Johnny. It was the first time we had been separated from him.

In the search for the building site, we finally settled on 7.22 acres of empty land at 4701 Far Hills Avenue purchased with Ohio Disciples New Church Program funds for $40,000, with plans to break ground in the summertime of 1956. February 26, 1956, we held the dedication of the grounds service.

Meanwhile, we found Horace Mann Junior High School, just over the line from Kettering in the city of Dayton school system, was amenable to us renting the school gym for our worship and Christian education. They had no requirement for having our building plans drawn. In the school, our attendance increased.

We engaged an architectural firm to prepare drawings for the future total building and the first unit which we adopted. We had our first building fund drive in the spring, working with Disciples' Board of Church Extension. We voted to take out a loan of $55,000 from Church Extension, with the cost of the first unit estimated at $75,000.

Deborah Jo Humbert was born on Monday, July 16, 1956. Joanne Albrecht stayed with Johnny during the birth day. Johnny seemed delighted to have a baby sister. Her first days and months were so much easier than Johnny's had been. No colic!

August 12, we had our groundbreaking service for the new building. A great picture was taken of Johnny, standing on the spade with my steadying hands, and Dad kneeling beside Johnny!

We had our first "Every Member Canvas" to raise funds for our $26,223 church budget in the fall of 1956. On January 1, 1957, the church would become self-supporting, meaning my salary that had been paid out of the New Church Program funds of the state society would now be paid by the congregation. Since my time as founding pastor would expire at the time the church became self-supporting, at a congregational meeting on November 25, 1956, I was given a call to remain as pastor for an indefinite period. I was happy to accept the call.

In December, we voted to sponsor a German refugee, a good sign for our sense of mission. During 1956, we had 51 persons join the church, and after two years our membership was 156.

Construction was moving forward fast on the first unit of our building. May 12, 1957, we moved into and worshipped in our new building. What an exciting day! For the first time, I wore my new pulpit robe given to me by the congregation. In the afternoon, we had our first baptismal service with four candidates, two youth and two adults. Then on May 26, we held the dedication service with Herold Monroe preaching. Twelve people joined that day bringing our membership to 205.

As we moved into our new building, we also purchased an Allen Electric Organ. We employed Gini Robertson as our organist. Her husband Doug Robertson came too, along with their two sons.

Doug, who in his previous Methodist life thought he was a really active member because he played on their softball team and made a few annual calls on their stewardship drive, was quite surprised to discovered what "being involved" comprised. He ultimately became an elder, member of the Board, Superintendent of the Sunday school, Chairman of Evangelism, and third baseman on the softball team. The Robertsons also became fast friends, joining us on Lake Michigan and Daytona Beach vacations. Gini belonged to PEO, an educational and philanthropic sorority, and recruited JoAnne for her first membership, which would ultimately be a lifetime pursuit.

In 1958, we participated in the Bayne Driscoll Evangelism Program with the other Disciples churches in Dayton, with the goal of seventy-six new members by the first Sunday in March. We all worked hard at it, especially the minister, and we received one hundred new members.

We were very conscious of working our way into the life of the Kettering-Oakwood community. I enjoyed entering into the life and fellowship of the Kettering-Oakwood ministers group. We began having a joint annual Festival of Faith worship service at the Fairmont High School football stadium, which I chaired. I participated in the leadership of the community Thanksgiving services. I gave the sermon at Oakwood High School's baccalaureate service, which was big in those days. I spoke at the annual Fairmont High School football team's closing dinner. I was a board member of the Kettering Oakwood YMCA and was on the Board of the Dayton Council of Churches. With Ed Pugh from Hillcrest, I attended the Dayton gatherings of American Baptist ministers.

For my own continuing education, Dayton's Bonebrake Seminary was a source for the library and lectures both by faculty and guest lecturers such as Roland Bainton from Yale. I also attended the New York UN Seminar held by the Department of Social Justice of our United Christian Missionary Society. We actually sat in on sessions of the UN General Assembly and then discussed what we had seen and heard.

The 1956 International Convention in Des Moines, Iowa, was thrilling and informative, as I worked as the assistant of Ben Moore, Program Director and Platform Host. I saw behind the scenes for the first time. My first International Convention was the 1934 Des Moines, Iowa, event. I was six years old that fall. Dad had gone to Drake University in Des Moines for seminary, and he took the whole family to the convention. I remember hanging out in the exhibit hall, especially at the slide shows of the Christian Board of Publication. Then Dad took us to a Drake University football game against Grinnell University, and it rained and rained!

In September 1958, I remember putting JoAnne, Johnny, and Debbie on a flight from Dayton to Youngstown as I awaited my flight to New York for the UN Seminar. She had news for her parents. She was pregnant with Jeffrey William Humbert. He would be such a gift to us. We had planned for Johnny and Debbie, but this was a blessed surprise. JoAnne's mother Beatrice's response to the news was, "Oh Joanne, not again!" Ironically, part of the Trimbur-Humbert family lore was an occasion after Bea had given birth to her third child, Dick, just 13 months after brother Billy's birth. JoAnne's Uncle Wade, her Dad's brother, made a solo visit to Bea at the hospital. His declaration was, "Now Bea, this has got to stop! You can't be having so many children so close together. No more!"

Jeff was born January 11, 1959, our third child born at Miami Valley Hospital in Dayton.

In 1959, First Christian Church in Flint, Michigan, came to call. They contacted me, asking that I be a candidate for their position of Senior Minister. Two members of the Pulpit Committee came to Kettering to see us. It was a large church with multiple staff and the prospect of a much larger salary. It piqued my interest. JoAnne and I agreed to come meet the congregation at a dinner meeting. On the Sunday night, the day before the evening congregational dinner in Flint, our Church Study Committee on the future's report came to our Kettering congregation with a report that said, "If we are to continue to grow, it is crucial to plan immediately for the building of an additional education building, our second unit." Herold Monroe was at that dinner. Afterwards I had to talk to him. I told him of my dilemma, going to meet with the Flint folks the next night. "What am I going to do?" I asked. He replied, "You'll have to go to Flint tomorrow night, and let it wash over you, and then, make up your mind what you see as God's will for you."

So we went. The Flint congregation and staff were most gracious. A straw vote was taken after the meal. Out of some 200 people, all but two voted in favor of our coming.

We came back home "considering the alternatives." They wanted us in Flint. It would be an advancement in salary and the size of church to serve, with the stimulation of the new setting. It was tempting. But I knew that if I left Kettering, the addition to the building which was so needed would be postponed. I felt a strong loyalty to this congregation. We were happy here. We had to stay. We decided we needed warmer floors in our home and two bathrooms for the five of us. We had signed a contract to build a new, enlarged brick home, and it was currently being built. We had a cash buyer for what my dad called our "knock down house." For the first time in my life, I had symptoms of stomach ulcers.

So, we stayed! We planned and built the addition to the building, completed in the spring of 1960.

Then, we made an announcement to the community: "Sunday school will be held for the first time in nine additional classrooms, including nursery through the high school age groups. This new unit marks the inauguration and expansion of the adult education program, with the launching of three adult classes in the Sunday school hour."

We moved into our new home on Bending Willow Drive in February of 1960. At that point it was our dream house: a 12 by 24 feet living room, a dining room, 3 bedrooms and two baths, a separate family room, a large garage (instead of a cold winter's air carport), all on a larger lot in a neighborhood of beautiful new brick homes.

In the early summer of 1960, the Board of Church Extension came to call, inviting me to come join their staff in Indianapolis, Indiana. The work of that Board, and the major increase in salary was worth exploring. We visited with the staff in Indianapolis and saw the offices, exploring the city of Indianapolis. However, the position involved leaving JoAnne and the kids, with lots of out-of-town travel. The thought of leaving JoAnne and the family for all that travel was just too much. I loved being a local pastor, so I ultimately declined. And we loved the comfort and beauty of our new home and neighborhood.

CHAPTER 21

NORTH CHEVY CHASE

In the early fall of 1961, a phone call came, ironically when I was in a meeting with Herold Monroe. It was from Dr. Joe Van Boskirk, regional minister of the Capital Area, inviting me to consider being a candidate for the position of Senior Minister of North Chevy Chase Christian Church in suburban Washington, D.C. As JoAnne and I talked about Washington and the information about the church, it sounded intriguing. We told Dr. Van Boskirk we would be interested in following up on the invitation. We spoke with the pulpit committee chairman, Art Brasse. The committee then sent two members of the pulpit committee to Kettering to interview me, meet JoAnne, and hear me preach. Jack Anglin worked for the CIA, and Harry Search for the Internal Revenue Service. (Interesting name "Search," working for the IRS!) We seemed to be nicely copacetic. Then they invited JoAnne and me to come to see the situation and be interviewed by the full committee. The neighborhood was tree-lined with beautiful homes. The church building, just four years old, was a fine facility with a beautiful Gothic sanctuary. The committee was most welcoming and gracious. We were wined and dined. The Washington, D.C. ambience was very special. They took us to the Supreme Court to meet a church member, Peggy McHugh, Executive Secretary to Chief Justice Earl Warren. She took us on a tour of the court. Impressive! The Supreme Court! (The Chief Justice was not in, but we would later get to meet and visit with him on several occasions.) The church said they would either rent a home for us or build a new parsonage on a lot across the side street from the church. If we sold our $19,000 house in Kettering, we still could not have afforded a house in the Village of North Chevy Chase.

While there, the committee voted to forward our name to the congregation. My mother was in Kettering staying with our three children, but had to leave to go be with my sister Peggy's children while Peggy gave birth to her fourth child. That meant JoAnne had to go back home. I stayed on for a congregational gathering for worship. I had brought no sermon with me, so I had to reconstruct one for the occasion. Then John Shytles, an elder in the congregation, took me to Mrs. K's Toll House for dinner before the evening service. I preached in the evening worship service. The congregation voted unanimously for me to be their new minister.

Leaving Kettering was most difficult. The experience of being the founding pastor of a growing congregation with deep friendships and moving Johnny and Debbie from first grade and kindergarten and their neighborhood friends all made it hard. We put our house up for sale, but a number of Air Force people had been transferred at the time, making for a glut of houses on the market. After not receiving any offers we felt where sufficient, we decided to offer our home for rent as its source for our mortgage payments.

We had purchased the table and chairs of a dining room set for our new Bending Willow home. There was a beautiful buffet that went with the set we wanted to purchase before we left. The price was $600, which we couldn't quite swing at the time. We borrowed it from JoAnne's folks anticipating that at the going away church dinner they would give us a cash gift. At the church dinner, when it came time for the going away gift, they presented us with a beautiful complete silver tea service. We were really glad for the tea service. It was a lovely surprise!

On the day of the Kettering congregation's farewell dinner, two events of note occurred: John Glenn circled the earth in space, and a hurricane struck the Atlantic seaboard. The hurricane battered Bethany Beach, Delaware, the town founded by Disciples from Bethany College and the location of the Capital Area's Conference Center. A workday to clean up the Conference grounds was held in May. I accompanied fifteen men from our congregation on the trip. We had a strong men's group and it was an opportunity for me to mingle, work with, and get to know our men.

Ironically, the older mother of one of our Kettering families had a beautiful beach home right across the street from the Conference Center. She had been in our Kettering farewell dinner the evening the hurricane struck her home. One of her neighbors had ridden out the storm next door in her own second story bedroom. She had watched the floodwaters and a loose rowboat banging up against Mrs. Frank's garage door. Suddenly, the banging rowboat struck the garage door. The door flew up! The floodwaters rushed in, picked up the car, and swept it right out of the garage.

In late February, we moved into a rental home in the Village of North Chevy Chase, Maryland, just one block from the North Chevy Chase Church. It was a very nice, three-bedroom home on Kensington Parkway with a large backyard. We were just three blocks from North Chevy Chase Elementary School where Johnny and Debbie would be in the first grade and kindergarten. Debbie made the school transition fairly easily, but Johnny not so much. One morning during school hours, three-year-old Jeff revealed that Johnny was down in the basement. Johnny had left for school out the front door, then entered a side basement door, and hid in the basement. Getting to the bottom of it, it seemed that at recess Johnny, being tall for his age, was being taunted by some second grade boys who were saying that he must have failed first grade, that he was dumb and had been held back. After a conference with his teacher and her help at recess, he settled in. In fact, in the second grade he became "engaged" to Mary McGovern, the daughter of Senator George McGovern, who of course would later run for president. The McGoverns lived in the neighborhood, right next door to Senator Hubert Humphrey, of later vice presidential fame. Living next door to the church on the north side was Senator Gaylord Nelson, former governor and senator of Wisconsin, whose daughter became a good friend of Debbie's.

The congregation had been located in northwest Washington and was known as Columbia Heights Christian Church. After relocating to North Chevy Chase and moving into their beautiful new building in 1958, it was now known as North Chevy Chase Christian Church. The minister whom I would be succeeding was a retired army chaplain, who was well-loved, but had moved on to retirement. Prior to that, one of their ministers was Harry Bell, who years before had immigrated from Australia. He had come to the United States to study at Eugene Bible College in Oregon. At the time my grandfather G.S.O. Humbert was Vice President of the school. Harry's first night in America was spent staying in my grandparents' home. Then when Harry got married, my Aunt Madge, an accomplished organist, was the organist for the wedding. Harry previously had been pastor of First Christian Church in Marion, Ohio, near Bellefontaine when we were there. Our families visited when I was in high school. The Bells' sons, Wayne and Keith, would become prominent Disciples ministers.

The church had a wonderful and efficient secretary, Mary Arnot. Roy Harlow was the business manager. Mary's husband Ray was in the Army Signal Corps. He lived at home and was attached to the White House and President John Kennedy as one of the three men who carried the little black box with the nuclear signal button. I found that probably 70 percent of employed members were working in civil service positions in the federal government. Later, Ray was with President Kennedy in Dallas when Kennedy was shot. I had left the office to go calling when I heard the tragic news on the radio, turned around and returned to find Mary talking to her husband on the phone. He was reporting to her that there was no way the president had survived. That was not yet public knowledge. We all remember the national pain and grief over President Kennedy's assassination. Chester Miller was an elder. He was in charge of the records of persons who had threatened the President. The day of the President's assassination, he was in a seminar in Baltimore and was not with the protection group in Dallas. After, he quickly returned from Baltimore and worked on details at the White House. He stopped by our home to see his pastor. He was in deep distress over the President's death. Subsequently, they learned that the FBI had Lee Harvey Oswald's name as a threat but did not share that information with the Secret Service. There was some competition and jealousy between the two branches, where the exchange of information broke down. Chester was later transferred to San Diego as the Chief of the Secret Service in that region.

I also discovered that, while I thought we were moving East, Washington, though it was cosmopolitan with people from all over the world, was really a Southern city. A major part of our members' attitudes toward race were very southern. They were very gracious and welcoming to us, with southern hospitality, but a number had fled from the spread of expanding African American housing in D.C. The church had members all over the suburbs of Virginia and Maryland.

In the sixty-day interim between accepting the call and arriving, I had requested from Mary Arnot a notebook with the members listed by area for efficiency in making pastoral calls. I wanted to get into as many homes as possible, as soon as possible. Our first Sunday was March 15, 1962. In the beautiful sanctuary with wonderful choral music, the elders and deacons' service and communion well-done, it was an inspiring service. JoAnne and I warmly placed our membership at the invitation hymn. A coffee hour reception followed and they welcomed us graciously.

Two Disciples ministers were members of the congregation: Joe Van Boskirk, regional minister of the Capital Area, and Virgil Lowder, the head of the Church Federation of the District of Columbia. They were very receptive to my leadership, and Dr. Van Boskirk became a good friend, along with his wife, Irene.

I spent my mornings in my newly paneled pastor's office working on moving into knowledge of the structure and working culture of the church with great help from Mary and Roy. And, of course, I spent my mornings there studying and "sermonizing." I went home for lunch with JoAnne. Early afternoons, I phoned members in one of the areas to make appointments for pastoral calls. I spent the rest of the afternoon with a map finding my way to folks, facing D.C. traffic, and learning geography in the process. For hospital calling, I found my "flock" could be in any one of six hospitals in D.C., Virginia, or Maryland. One afternoon I made pastoral calls on seven members in six different hospitals, in all three.

At one of the social events early in April, Peggy McHugh told me of one of the practices of the Supreme Court. The Attorney General of the United States customarily argued just one case before the court during his term. She said that Robert Kennedy would be doing so in two weeks. Jackie and Ethel Kennedy and their children would be attending, and sitting in the special side front section of the court. (I called it the silent "choir loft.") She invited me to join them for this historic occasion. I was more than delighted to accept. I was thrilled at the prospect! However, two days before the date, a funeral home in D.C. called to say they had scheduled a funeral for me to conduct at the very hour I would be at the Supreme Court. I asked about changing the time, but the details were set, including an escort service to lead the procession of cars across Washington to the grave site. The woman who died was an older lady, longtime and well-known member of the church. At thirty-four years old, I was the first young minister for the congregation, and I knew that there were some who wondered how well I could be a pastor to the members of advanced age. I was really torn. No, I could not tell them to get some other preacher. In the end, I had to do the right thing and forgo a lifetime experience of privilege, meeting

Jackie and Ethel Kennedy and experiencing a Robert Kennedy case in the Supreme Court.

That spring of 1962, our youth group from Kettering came on a field trip to Washington. We went to the Supreme Court, and Peggy took us on a backstage tour, including the gym on the top floor. At the end of the tour, she said, "If you have time, the Chief Justice would like to meet your group and have some time with them." We had time! We were ushered into his very private office where he visited with the group for over half an hour.

On another occasion, my parents were visiting, and after listening to the court in session from the "choir loft," we came out into the back hall. The case before the court was on the water rights between Arizona and California, which had begun when Earl Warren was governor of California. Hence, he had recused himself from the case. Peggy said, "The Chief Justice is in his office and would like to meet your folks, if you have time." He received us, and he and my parents exchanged stories about their grandchildren.

When the landmark court decision on prayer in schools was announced, I believe in June of 1962, the Chief Justice had Peggy call me. He had received a strongly worded letter from a Carl McIntyre and the US Council of Churches excoriating the court for the decision to deny prayer in schools. The question was, "Is this the voice of the major Protestant denominations in the United States?" Well, Carl McIntyre was the right-wing neoconservative who led a small band of rabble rousers, a kind of precursor in the '60s to the later Moral Majority, with a name similar to our National Council of Churches. I assured the Chief Justice that this was not the voice of major Protestant denominations.

I did have an opportunity to meet President John F. Kennedy. I attended an annual Congressional Prayer Breakfast at one of the downtown hotels that spring. John Kennedy attended and made brief remarks. When he finished, I had just gotten up to leave for another appointment. By the time I worked my way to the exit of the ballroom, the presiding senator asked that all should remain seated while the President left. I went on out through the doors into the ballroom hall. To my surprise, President Kennedy also came out into the hall, all alone! There was one other gentleman in the hall near me, and the President approached us with his animated smile and greeted us. We shook hands and exchanged pleasantries. There was such an "aura" about John Kennedy that was so attracted! I did tell him I hoped he would work hard to push the Civil Rights Act through Congress.

Preaching to the congregation, with numerous federal government leaders, the regional minister, and the Director of the Washington Council of Churches was a challenge. Thinking about that, I decided that if the church had wanted Joe or Virgil to be their ministers, they could have called them. But they had called me, and I would do the best I could to preach and lead.

The years 1962 and 1963 were special for the Civil Rights Movement centered especially on Martin Luther King Jr. The historic "I Have a Dream" speech occurred on August 28, 1963. Along with thousands of others, I heard it from beside the Reflecting Pool in front of the Lincoln Memorial.

Two weeks later, during Sunday school, a Baptist Church in Birmingham, Alabama, was bombed. Three little girls were killed. I was deeply moved and was convicted, and felt called to write and preach this sermon the next Sunday.

Visions of Understanding

Acts 10:1–36   by John O. Humbert

You sigh as you take your place in the seat in your Sunday school class. What a job it is to get the family ready and off to Sunday school. This morning you were just about ready to leave, when you discovered that your daughter's Sunday shoes were a mess. "You can't go to Sunday school with shoes looking like that," you rebuked her. Off she went to shine them. Finally, everyone was ready, and here you are. You made it. Your mind comes back to attention as the teacher enunciates the theme of the lesson, "The love that Forgives."

From Matthew come these words of Jesus: "I say to you, love your enemies and pray for those who persecute you, so that you may be sons and daughters of your Father who is in heaven."

Suddenly, with split-second unrealism, there is a shattering roar, the whole building shudders under the impact. You will never forget the unspoken apprehension that became vocalized reality as it flashed through the people "bomb,"... the growing, clutching, stomach knotting, desperate fear that burgeoned with every step, the wrenching confirmation that it was her room, the frantic, soul searing, incredible disclosure of your child's emaciated death, the shoe, the unremembered flight to fresh air, just to get out! And here you are, clutching her shoe in the sunlight of a Birmingham Sunday morning - the shoe that had to be polished, now a dust covered token of your dead child, shining only where her blood and your tears intermingle on its leadened toes.

It might have happened that way. It did happen!

If the events of the past three years, or of this summer of discontent have not convinced us, then the events of a week ago should have pointed up several facts quite dramatically. It has placed a burden upon my heart, and with Simon Peter, "I cannot but speak of what I have seen and heard."

The first fact is that we are living in the midst of a revolution in America.

We may not like it. We may not want to face it. We may wish it would go away. But the facts are there – the African American people are precipitating a social revolution.

Basically, they are seeking six points of accomplishment:

1. Voting Rights
2. Public Accommodations – the right to service from discrimination in business establishments and public accommodations, including places of worship.
3. School desegregation
4. Equal employment opportunity
5. The right to secure housing where their dollar will buy it, like any other citizen
6. Acceptance as a full citizen of the United States

This is the aim of this movement to social change.

Furthermore, there are several ingredients in this revolution that we must note.

The first is, there is a new generation of strong, committed leadership among the African American people that is not content with gradual and token change toward their goals.

Second, the new leaders of the African American people have discovered that they have new power, when they unite – economic power, and the power of nonviolent demonstration.

Third, there is coming in this revolution a new focus of determinism. For nearly 100 years the white community determined when it would dole the African American a token of new freedom. For the last year or more, the focus has changed – the African American with his newfound leadership and economic and nonviolent power now initiates the action, and the white community responds.

Finally, the present Administration, here in Washington, is the most active in civil rights of any recent Administration. This is not a political judgment – just a fact of the times.

All of these facts add up to one looming, larger truth – there is no longer any question as to <u>whether</u> there will be a revolution to a desegregated America. The looming question of our day is what kind of revolution will it be – peaceful, or bloody. We <u>are</u> living in the midst of a revolution!

The second primary fact that must be pointed up is this:

We should not be too surprised at this revolution, for our Faith, Christianity produced it!

After all, the Roman world was getting along fairly well when Jesus came. There were the aristocrats and the middle class of Roman society, enjoying life. There were the subservients, who for the most part knew their place. Once in a while, one got out of line a little bit, and you simply had him tortured, cut off his hands, or had him killed and went on with it.

But Jesus Christ came quietly thundering into their world, saying that all people are God's children, that love and goodwill must reign between all people. Anyone in need is our brother, or sister whom we must love, even though he be Jew or Samaritan, aristocrat or subservient.

Then came Simon Peter, the preacher of Pentecost, one to whom a Gentile was unclean. You would not want to live next to one, and you certainly would not visit in his home. If you did, you had to go to church and be cleansed. But Peter was called to the home of one Cornelius. Before Peter went, he had a dream, however that taught him a great deal. So that as he arrived, he said to Cornelius' household,

"You yourself know how unlawful it is for a Jew to associate with or to visit any one of another nation; But God has shown me that I should not call any person common, or unclean. (10:28) In solemn truth I can see now that God shows no partiality, but that in every nation the person who reverences him and does what is right, is acceptable to him! He has sent his message to the sons of Israel by giving us the good news of peace through Jesus Christ – he is the Lord of us all! (Acts 10:34-36)

And then came the Apostle Paul, writing in the Ephesian letter concerning the cleavage between peoples –

"For now, in Christ Jesus, you who once were far off have been brought near. For he is our peace, who has made us both one, and has broken down the dividing walls of hostility. So then, you are no longer strangers and sojourners, but you are fellow citizens with the Saints, and members of the household of God." (Ephesians 2:13, 14, 19)

Listen to this further word from Paul to the Galatians: revolutionary stuff

"For in Christ Jesus, you are all sons of God, through faith. There is neither Jew nor Greek, there is neither slave nor free, there is neither male nor female, for you are all one in Christ Jesus." (Galatians 3:26, 28)

Christians have been going around preaching this Bible truth for 1900 some years now, and subservient people are beginning to believe it – we are all one. And so, you see why it is the African American Christian leadership of the church in America that is leading this revolution. They take this kind of Bible teaching seriously.

And my friends, what about us?

We are in the midst of a revolution that our Faith has created!

Where do we stand?

We may be a part of the anti-revolutionary force, and stand with the Wallaces and Barnets, squarely in the path of the African American in his March to freedom. I pray that I may seek somehow to understand those who do. There are people whom I love who feel this way. I know that they have had drummed into them by people they loved and respected that the African American is an inferior person, a kind of unclean sub-human that is not fit to live near. And they can cite individual example after example that seem to confirm that the whole African American race is inferior.

But while I pray that I may understand my brothers and sisters who feel strongly this way, I pray also for them for a vision of understanding like that which touched and converted Simon Peter, to know "God has shown me that I should not call any human being common or unclean."

Or with Paul, "You are all one in Christ Jesus." I pray that they may come to see that the substandard behavior people they cite, may be accounted for, not on the silent basis of race, but on the basis that some people have not yet taken the will of God for the value that activates them.

The revolution is here, and we can stand in the way and determine that it shall be a violent one.

Or we may simply busy ourselves with other things and hope that the nasty mess will go away while we ignore it.

I want to share with you a statement made in Congress this week by a Southern Congressman, Representative Weltner, of Georgia, that speaks to this point:

"Mr. Speaker, there was a time when the southerner was moderate for what he did not say. There was a time when silence amid the denunciations of others was a positive virtue. But, in face of the events on Sunday, who can remain silent?

Those responsible for the deed in Birmingham chose a Sabbath morning as the time, the House of God as the place and the worshippers within as the victims. I do not know what twisted and tortured minds fashioned this deed. But I know why it happened. It happened because those chosen to lead have failed to lead. Those whose task it is to speak have stood mute.

And in so doing, we have permitted the voice of the South to preach defiance and disorder. We have stood by, leaving the field to reckless and violent men. For all our hand wringing and head shaking, we will never put down violence until we can raise a higher standard.

Though honest men may differ as to means, can we not affirm as a great goal of this Republic the concept – equality of opportunity? Mr. Speaker, we need not so much new paragraphs on the books of law, as new precepts in the hearts of men. We need to raise, and to follow, this standard – as old as Christianity and as simple as truth – Let right be done."

Indeed, it is time to speak. I pray that for Christians there will come the kind of vision that Peter had to change minds and hearts to understanding, so that with him we can proclaim:

"God has shown me that I should not call any person common or unclean."

You will be given an opportunity to give concreteness to this commitment soon. Our denomination will join with other Protestant, Catholic and Jewish groups on October 20th and 27th in receiving an offering to aid those who are in need because of their stand on this issue – who have suffered economic and physical reprisal. It will be an offering of "Concern" for the rights of freedom, in which you will be given an opportunity to share.

Could it just be that since this revolution which is upon us is one that grows out of our Faith and Christian orientation of life, that rather than standing against it, or remaining silent, we were meant to lead in understanding?

The coffee hour after worship was rather quiet, though a number of people thanked me for addressing the issues head on. However, one member, Congressman Shadaburg—an ordained UCC minister from Wisconsin, and surprisingly, a member of the House Un-American Activities Committee—was disgruntled and complained to Joe Van Boskirk, "Oh, he just got that from the National Council of Churches."

In the spring of 1964, the regional assembly was to be held in Baltimore at Christian Temple. The business resolutions to be considered were forwarded to the congregations for consideration and study. The Capital Area Region was a delegate assembly. We had three voting representatives from North Chevy Chase Christian, though all members could attend. I decided our church board should study the resolutions during its April meeting. One was from the National Council of Churches, the thrust of which was to confess the church's culpability and complicity in racism with regard to African Americans. Quite an emotional discussion ensued. One prominent elder who would be one of the delegates proclaimed, "I'm not guilty of racism."

Of course, after the previous minister had preached against racism, that elder had invited the minister to accompany him to a pond in Rock Creek Park. There the elder pointed out how the white ducks were not swimming with the black ducks, and said that was the order of things. However, the minister noted that that the ducks didn't read the Bible.

The result of the discussion was a motion that passed to instruct our three voting representatives to vote against the resolution at the assembly. Normally the minister would be one of the voting representatives, but I could not vote against the resolution in this case, so I declined to be one of the voting representatives.

At the assembly, when the resolution was presented, our Chevy Chase elder got the floor and explained how he loved black people, but he wasn't going to confess that he nor was his church was guilty of racism. The North Chevy Chase Board had instructed their three representatives to vote against the resolution. I was able to get the attention of the presiding officer during the elder's speech and was recognized next. "I'm John Humbert, minister of North Chevy Chase Christian Church. I strongly urge the adoption of this resolution. Obviously, I cannot speak for my congregation, but we all know that Sunday morning at 11:00 is one of the most segregated hours of the week. If we love our African American brothers and sisters, they should be welcomed to full membership and life in our congregations. We need to confess the sinfulness of our life and practices." Others spoke in support of the resolution as well. It passed by a vote of 74 to 3. Obviously!

As part of the assembly on Sunday morning, ministers exchanged pulpits. I preached at our church in Alexandria, so I was not back in Chevy Chase for morning worship. On Sunday evening, John Shytle, chairman of the board, called. He said, "The Chairman of the Elders, Deacons and I would like to meet with you tomorrow evening at the church at 7:30." "OK," I said. The next twenty-four hours were spent with some trepidation, wondering what the "tone" of the meeting would be. John Shytle opened the meeting saying, "We heard what happened in Baltimore Friday afternoon. It was reported what you did, and what you said on the floor. We learned the resolution confessing the churches' culpabilities in racism passed by a vote of 74–3. Obviously our three representatives were the only ones voting against it. I've been thinking a lot about that. It seems I've been leading our church in the wrong direction. I want to apologize to you. It took courage for you to do and say what you did. We want you to know this." After more conversation, we left the meeting with hope for moving forward.

My commitment in ministry as pastor of North Chevy Chase was for the church to be a serving church, serving the needs of folks in our community. We found that the YWCA of Montgomery County needed space for their educational programs for women. We offered our building for those programs and served in that manner. We also became involved in the "Patterning" rehabilitation program for children with brain development delays. It involved five volunteers per child, inducing movement for the children and simulating crawling. This took place in our fellowship hall. We had volunteers from our church, including JoAnne, working with crews from the community every day of the year, including Thanksgiving and Christmas. Our program was one of only two locations in the whole Washington area for this.

Several years into the program, I received a call from a woman who lived in Chevy Chase asking if she could come to visit with me. She came to my office with a request. She had heard about the patterning program and our church's openness to serve. She was the President of the National Autistic Society. The world was just then discovering autism as a specialized condition. The headquarters of the society was in her home. Her request was to establish the office headquarters of the National Autistic Society in our church building. I took the proposal to our church board, and it was approved.

Subsequently, we worked with the Autistic Society as they founded an experimental school for two autistic children, with seven staff from NIH, Johns Hopkins, and George Washington hospitals. The school occupied several rooms in our new educational wing.

A number of our people volunteered in serving during the altercations and riots following the assassination of Martin Luther King Jr. A number of supermarkets in D.C. were burned in those days. Martial law was declared, with National Guard troops guarding the main thoroughfares of D.C. We had volunteers collecting food and transferring foodstuffs to centers in the city. We also had volunteers taking coffee, donuts, and cookies to the troops down Georgia Avenue into the heart of the city. For the 2:00 a.m. to 6:00 a.m. shift, we had no volunteer so our Associate Minister, the Regional Associate Minister, and I took that shift.

One of the additional things that people of North Chevy Chase were involved in was volunteering to serve in Martin Luther

King's Poor People's Campaign, supplying and delivering food and volunteering for transportation of leaders. When the huge rally on the National Mall was to take place, a number of Disciples came to Washington to participate. We met at the 12th Street Christian Church, an African American congregation in D.C. The congregation had arranged for transportation to the Mall. Dale and Betty Fiers, John Compton, and I wound up riding in a Cadillac limousine. As we approached the Mall, we tried to persuade the Disciples driver to let us out a couple blocks from the platform area where the rally was to take place, so we could walk the rest of the way. He would have none of it and insisted that he drive the limousine right to the spot. Needless to say, we were more than a little embarrassed to arrive at the Poor People's Campaign rally in a limousine.

My real concern was finding a way in which North Chevy Chase could actually accomplish something that would alleviate poverty. I preached a sermon calling on us to serve in that way and invited anyone in the congregation who would join me in that cause to come to the church that very night at 7:00 p.m. Forty-five people showed up. I led them to commit to finding the best local program or group already working in this area with whom to participate rather than striking out on our own for something new. On succeeding Sunday nights, I arranged for different groups to present their programs. We settled on working with Montgomery Housing. They were working with families to help them break the cycle of poverty with counseling and rent supplements. They had a hookup with the University of Maryland to train economic counselors and would receive our financial gifts for rent supplement. Two of the couples in our group committed for training at the university to be counselors, and we all made pledges to give each month toward the rent supplement. We were doing something!

Through the years, I was working hard with our evangelism committee to reach new members. We averaged about forty-five new members each year. Between 1962 and 1969, we grew from

285 members to 445 active members. Our fellowship program was really uniting. One of the features was our yearly Shrine Mont retreat the weekend after Labor Day at an Episcopal Retreat Center in the mountains of Virginia. About 120 people attended.

Barkley Brown was our first student associate from Wesley Seminary in D.C. He and his wife Joyce really became a part of our family. The youth groups flourished under his leadership, and the whole congregation was taken with his abilities. With his graduation, Ed DeLong followed Barkley's success, with excellent work with the youth groups, Christian education, and personal friendships. I received training at the seminary to become accredited with the Methodist Church as supervisor to help with their movement toward ordination. Bob Spaulding followed Ed. Barkley and Ed considered becoming Disciples ministers, but went the Methodist route. Bob Spaulding did work with the Disciples region's Commission on Ministry and did become a Disciples minister.

During our Chevy Chase days, JoAnne worked with the regional Chi Rho camp, training as a director. We both led family conferences at Bethany Beach in which our whole family participated. I then directed a CYF Conference at Bethany Beach each June.

Our church had a day care for preschool children. When Jeff started kindergarten, JoAnne began working part-time as one of the teacher/leaders. Then when Jeff started first grade, she decided she would like to return to full-time teaching. She applied to the Montgomery County System and was hired. She would be teaching in Potomac, Maryland, in a school which had been acclaimed among the top ten elementary schools in the United States by *U.S. News and World Report*. They were teaching using "learning centers." It was a real challenge to move into that type of teaching, but she adapted very well. Later, she brought that method to Cleveland Heights in her teaching at Noble Road Elementary School. To arrive at her school in Potomac, she had to drive partway on the Washington Beltway, where she had some adventures in rush hour traffic. The church and our parsonage were just inside the Beltway, off Connecticut Avenue.

Our family spent spent many August vacations at Bethany Beach, enjoying several with Bill and Nancy Trimbur and their children, Billy and Carrie.

For the final two years in Chevy Chase, I was trained and volunteered as a chaplain at the Montgomery County Detention Center. I would lead worship for the inmates once a month and have a period when anyone of the prisoners could have a personal visit with me. Only one inmate told me he was guilty of the crime for which he was incarcerated. The rest claimed innocence.

In the region, I served as Vice President for two years, and as such, attended the denomination's Home and State Missions Planning Conference in Saint Louis. I was a member of the Regional Board, later Chair of the New Church Committee and Chair of the Christian Education Committee.

I continued to serve as the Assistant Program Director of the International Convention, which met every year. But in 1966, I became the Director.

In 1966, I witnessed a landmark event. Dr. Virgil Lowder, Executive of the Washington Council of Churches, was a member of the congregation. In 1966, the NCAA college basketball Final Four was played at Cole Field House on the University of Maryland campus. Dr. Lowder had an extra ticket for the breakfast of the Fellowship of Christian Athletes at the university held the day before the tournament began. He invited me to attend with him. As it happened, we sat with several college coaches, including Dave Strack, coach at the University of Michigan. Coach Strack said he had to leave that day and had two tickets available for the semifinals and the final game. I bought them.

The final game was much noted as historic. To this day, it is still referred to as iconic. The game was between the Wildcats of the

University of Kentucky, an all-white team including the renowned Pat Riley, and Texas Western. I was sitting in the midst of college coaches who were doing a lot of grumbling about the Texas Western coach and what he had done to college basketball. For the first time in the history of the NCAA tournament, Texas Western started an all African American five! In 2006, much note was taken of the 40th anniversary of that breakthrough in the makeup of the squads of college basketball teams.

In the 1968 International Convention in St. Louis, Missouri, the Convention adopted the "Provisional Design of the Christian Church (Disciples of Christ)." The Restructure committees had been working on this design for a number of years, so this was a historic event. The Convention broke out in singing "The Doxology." On the final day of the International Convention, after we had adopted the Provisional Design, the president declared that the General Assembly of the Christian Church (Disciples of Christ) was now in session! Henceforth, the General Assembly would now meet every two years.

In 1969, the General Assembly was in Seattle, Washington. My duties at the Assembly would take about ten days. We decided we would take our monthlong vacation in conjunction with the trip to Seattle. The church gave us an extra week, so we would be gone about seven weeks. We decided we'd take our tent and camping gear and camp along the way. The kids could choose where they would like to stop. Debbie chose New Orleans, Jeff chose the Alamo, and John chose Mesa Verde. Bill and Nancy Trimbur would take care of our poodle, Pierre. We drove to Bellefontaine, Ohio, to see my folks, then on to Davy Crockett State Park in Tennessee. New Orleans was next, celebrating Debbie's thirteenth birthday at the Court of Two Sisters Restaurant. From there we went to Dallas, to visit my cousin Mary Ellen Garrett, her husband, Jack, and their five children. While there, we watched Neil Armstrong's landing on the moon! Then off we went to Mesa Verde (we didn't make it to the Alamo), Four Corners, and the Grand Canyon. We camped above San Bernardino in the mountains. Then we were on to San Diego where we spent a week with Chester and Ruth Miller. While there, we took a side trip to Tijuana, where we bought our famous lamp. It returned to Washington in the trunk of the presidential limousine, courtesy of Chester Miller, who was the Director of the Secret Service in San Diego.

Up the West Coast we went, with stops in Los Angeles, San Francisco, then the coast of Oregon. The family stayed at a resort while I went on to Seattle to prepare for the Assembly. In Oregon, JoAnne and our three children were with Chuck and Peggy and their family in condos arranged by Aunt Jessica. Then they all rode together to Seattle, and we stayed with Aunt Jessica in her beautiful large home on Lake Washington. I served the Assembly as Program Director, while the family enjoyed the amenities of the lakefront with Jessica's adopted children. After a few more days, we left for Manson, Washington, to visit my Uncle Bob, Mother's brother, on Lake Chelan. Several enjoyable days there, and then we ventured up into Canada and the East, with a notable stop at Lake Louise, which included canoeing on the beautiful lake and spending the night in the Canadian Pacific Hotel. We camped our way across Canada and into Minnesota, and then headed for Chevy Chase from the family trip of a lifetime.

CHAPTER 22

Euclid Avenue Christian Church

Beginning our fall work in 1969, I learned that Charles Malotte had left Euclid Avenue Christian Church in Cleveland to become the regional minister in the Pacific Southwest Region of the church. In early October, I received a phone call from Dr. James Farmer, Chairman of the pulpit committee of Euclid Avenue Church. He said my name had been given to them in their search for a new minister, and he was inquiring whether I would be interested in being a candidate. I noted that I was in a unique setting with a growing congregation and was happy at North Chevy Chase Church, but I would consider it. He said he would follow up soon.

The next Sunday, a couple who lived in Silver Springs, Maryland, visited the church for worship. We visited, and I learned they had grown up in Euclid Avenue Church, were married there, and had been active members before moving to the Washington area. Good prospects, I thought.

That week, Dr. Farmer called to say that he and another member of the committee would like to come to Washington the next Sunday to worship and hear me preach. I agreed to that. I learned later that the visitors, the Sunday before were actually the "advanced scouts" to see if a pulpit committee's visit would be worth their time! I was later happy that they didn't turn thumbs down!

Jim Farmer and Carl Lindberg showed up on Sunday morning for worship. I greeted them as visitors, and the service began.

During the offering, one of the women in the congregation fainted in their family pew. None of our doctors were there that day, but knowing Jim Farmer was a doctor, I asked if there "was a doctor in the house." He responded. They carried the lady to my office sofa while I began the sermon he had come all the way from Cleveland to hear. She revived and said she had been bitten by her cat and had a tetanus shot that week. It was thought that this was a reaction. So, Jim returned to hear two-thirds of the sermon.

After worship, the two came to coffee hour where Joe Van Boskirk and a few other savvy members surmised they were from a pulpit committee. They came to the parsonage, and we went out to dinner with the whole family at Mrs. K's Toll House. Before they left, they invited JoAnne and me to come meet with the full pulpit committee, which we did while staying with the Lindberghs. We had a good visit with the committee. We mutually agreed to move forward with the next step: for us to meet the congregation. On the Sunday before Thanksgiving, we flew to Cleveland for me to preach at a Sunday evening gathering of the congregation. A congregational meeting to vote on my call followed. The vote was to invite us to come. We accepted.

I needed to give a sixty-day notice to North Chevy Chase, so it would be January 20 when I could begin in Cleveland, a good time for our kids, starting a new semester.

We spent Thanksgiving in Niles with the Trimburs. Then on Friday and Saturday, Sally Farmer and a real estate broker took us house hunting. They had a parsonage but would sell it. Part of my contract in coming was that the church would lend us the full amount to buy a home at 3 percent interest. The children loved looking at the houses in Cleveland Heights, and when we entered the Demington Drive house, a beautiful 1928 Tudor home with amazing woodwork and other unique features, we were all excited about it. Moreover, there was a secret closet. The older lady who had lived there had hidden expensive jewelry somewhere in the house, but the family had never found it. The kids were tantalized. The deal was signed. Following Christmas, we spent four days working on the house in Cleveland, staying with the Clark Hungerfords in their beautiful Heights home. We spent time painting, taking apart the old kitchen sink, taking down old drapes, etc. I also measured the kitchen, including the slope of the kitchen floor, for new cabinets that would be built in Maryland, courtesy of a contractor in the Chevy Chase church. We would be moving everything, including the kitchen sink.

It was hard for the children to leave their friends in Chevy Chase. They were in nineth, eighth, and fifth grade. We were "ruining" John's life! He was in love with Maeda Metz. Debbie had several eighth graders from church who were in the same classes with her. Roxboro Junior High School was in the neighborhood, right across the street from the grade school. John struggled till spring break when he went back to see Maeda. He stayed with Obi and Fran Weir, but discovered it wasn't the same and began settling in. John and Debbie's school had a cafeteria for lunch, but Roxboro Elementary school did not. Jeff had an hour for lunch, so he came home. JoAnne had decided she would not teach the second semester to be available at home as the kids settled into Cleveland Heights. JoAnne and I were working on the house together. Sally Farmer and Bill Knapp had done some beautiful wallpapering with paper we had chosen before we moved in, especially in the octagonal breakfast room and dining room. JoAnne and I were a good team at wallpapering in the kitchen and bathrooms. We had the back entrance made into a laundry room, and I broke through the back kitchen brick wall and installed two glass French doors taken from the living room as the back exit.

The slate patio behind the sunroom (off the living room) was in need of repair. Our neighbors behind us, the Schuberts, had built a swimming pool in their side yard with sand left over. They let me use that sand to level the slate. John Schubert was an English teacher at a local Catholic high school. He was also the author of two published novels. His grandfather was one of the founding partners of 3M, the major manufacturing company.

They were a wealthy but very down-to-earth couple. One of their philanthropic interests was supporting the U.S.' participation in the Davis Cup tennis tournament. The amazing thing was that a tennis stadium seating 12,000 people was built at the Roxboro Junior High School playground and playing fields. The Davis Cup world finals between the U.S. and Germany would be played there in our neighborhood that summer of 1970. The Schuberts had two tickets, but John was not going to the opening session on Saturday afternoon. Barbara Schubert invited me to go. JoAnne gave me permission. Barbara and I walked to the Davis Cup final! What a thrill to be there. The U.S. won that year. Later, when the Australian and US women played their tournament, I watched sixteen-year-old Chris Everett practice on the junior high side tennis courts.

I came to Euclid Avenue Christian Church following a great parade of outstanding ministers: Jacob Goldner, from 1900 to 1945, President of the International Convention; Dale Fiers, who moved from Cleveland to be President of the UCMS, and was at that time the General Minister and President; Walter McGowan, who had gone on to be Senior Minister of the very prominent First Christian Church of Oklahoma City; and Charles Malotte, now regional minister of the Pacific Southwest.

The church had also had a series of outstanding associate ministers: Howard Spangler (Chuck's uncle) from 1920 to 1952, and my friends Donn Ramsdell, Ed Bartunek, and now Terry Van Heyningan. Terry had come from Christian Theological Seminary, graduating in 1968, and had been there for two years.

Terry was doing very well when Charles Malotte was senior minister. He lead in education, social action, evangelism, membership development, and youth work along with a strong Chi Rho and CYF. He was preaching occasionally. When Malotte left, there was no interim, so Terry had been handling the whole spectrum of leadership. I came with my guitar, driving my Midget MG, to be the Senior Minister. We shared leadership roles.

Terry and I met every Monday morning to agree on our responsibilities for the week, including our writing for the weekly church newsletter. We shared hospital and evangelism calling assignments. We divided major committee assignments for programs. We agreed on his preaching Sundays, about once a month. It was an adjustment for Terry since he had been in charge and leading everything, but I tried to be supportive of his share.

The Director of Music and the organist was Joy Lawrence. As I arrived, she was preparing a youth choir of about forty voices for a great presentation on a special Sunday in the spring. She invited me to do the narrator's part of the program. It was so outstanding that it became the Sunday afternoon program for the Louisville General Assembly in 1971. All three of our children, John were in the youth choir. The church music program had a large choir and paid soloists leading each "section." Two years before, a marvelous Casavant pipe organ had been installed.

Arriving at Euclid Avenue following the turbulent 1960s and with civil rights and the Vietnam War still boiling, there were some real tensions between persons committed to social action and those committed to a classical music program. The point of interaction was the budget for the music program and the very costly pipe organ. Those were both very real at budget time and symbolic of the further tensions. Also, when Charles Malotte was in his first year of ministry at Euclid Avenue, there was a civil rights confrontation with protests on Murray Hill, the Italian neighborhood down Mayfield Road, near University Circle area. A Case Western Reserve University chaplain had been killed by a bulldozer during the protests. Charles Malotte was there when it happened. He had been painted as a "radical," a label which for some he never outlived.

When we were spending time with Sally Farmer looking at real estate before we moved, I asked her what she thought the church needed in the way of ministry. She said, "We just need someone to love us." I could do that. I was able to let them know I loved them and worked hard to help them realize we could be socially active in the larger community and have beautiful worship services in the sanctuary. I worked hard calling in homes, becoming acquainted with folks, and preaching. I also emphasized *koinonia*, the loving community that would reach out to the Heights community for peace and justice. We were among the leaders of the churches in Cleveland Heights and the inner ring of suburbs surrounding the city of Cleveland. It was an area being integrated with special care to maintain integration without "white flight." Oliver Schroeder, elder and distinguished professor of law at Case Western Reserve Law School, was at that time the Mayor of Cleveland Heights.

We were also part of the Cleveland Disciples Union, working in a special partnership with Dunham Christian Church, an African American congregation in the Huff area of Cleveland, where the riots had occurred just years before. We worked together on issues of poverty and justice in the inner city.

In the Heights, we operated a children's day care and education program in the Oakridge wing of our building. Our building hosted the meetings of the Cleveland Stroke Club, Gamblers Anonymous, and Alcoholics Anonymous.

We had a strong education and fellowship program for adults led by Terry Van Heyningan, with small study groups meeting weekly in homes during the Advent and Lent and other seasons.

The strong leaders of the church were my age, midforties: Jim and Sally Farmer, Don and Jeanette Barclay, Clark and Ginny Hungerford, John and Patty Hungerford, Bryon and Helen Wheeler, Jim and Janet Graff, Duane and Eleanor Mayhew, Earl and Jean Shirey, Vi Anderson, and George and Nancy Womer. The men had all grown up in the church, and their parents, now in their seventies, were the respected seniors—active, steadfast, and supportive "saints." We all worked well together and formed lifetime friendships.

Duane Mayhew's uncle was a leader in the Ravenna church when Dad was there. In fact, it was in Frank Mayhew's Feed Mill where we kept our cow, and where the twin calves were born. Duane was a teenager, and his vacation from Mantua was a week spent in Ravenna with Mr. Mayhew and his son, Ellis. He knew my father and remembered those days fondly.

As a youth, Oliver Schroeder had gone to Hiram CYF Conference, where my father was a counselor. Ollie remembered him with admiration and appreciation.

When Dad was ill and out of the pulpit for a year in Ravenna, a retired minister, George Townsend, had been the interim. His son, Norman Townsend, an executive with General Electric in Cleveland, would come to visit his father with their son, Norman Jr. On those occasions, I was invited to come play with Norman Jr. We all remembered that. Norman was now a strong elder and leader in the church.

When I came to Euclid Avenue, all the elders and deacons were men. I hoped to lead us into the inclusive age of women being in those roles. In my second year, I proposed that we elect honorary elders, women, who if eligible would naturally have been elders. The nominating committee chose seven such women as honorary elders, some of whom had been adamant in opposing women being elders (including Mary Farmer and Vi Anderson). The seven accepted. The next year, we succeeded in electing two women elders, Eleanor Mayhew and Vi Anderson (who would become Vi Radamilovich). Women as deaconesses followed.

In 1972, our former Chevy Chase neighbor George McGovern was running for President of the United States. McGovern's Cleveland headquarters was across the street from Cleveland Heights High School. John was then a junior. Because of his friendship with McGovern's daughter Mary, plus his strong liberal tendencies, he was a volunteer worker at the headquarters after school. I read in *The Plain Dealer* that George McGovern was hoping for an invitation to make an appearance in Cleveland. I wrote to his campaign headquarters to invite him to speak as our "special layman," in October or whenever. I received a letter in response thanking me for the invitation, but noting that other plans had developed.

Meanwhile, John had secured a "MCGOVERN" bumper sticker, and stuck it on the rear bumper of my Midget MG sports car. Terry had been interviewed by the newspaper, *The Plain Dealer*, and was quoted: "Well, we don't mention candidates specifically from the pulpit, but they can gather who we support from our bumper stickers." The Plain Dealer did a full-page story on ministers and politics for the Saturday edition. In the middle of the page was a photo of my sports car with "MCGOVERN" loudly proclaimed. The following Saturday morning, Norman Townsend, Sr., came to my office. "People are saying that they are unhappy about the article in the paper and your car."

"Well," I replied, "I haven't spoken of McGovern from the pulpit, but I'm certainly free to choose a subject for my bumper stickers."

Norman would, on occasion, come to see me and say, "People are saying..." Everyone knew that he was actually speaking for himself without trying to expose his own view.

Those were the years when the ecumenical Consultation on Church Union (COCU) was having its heyday. A plan of union was proposed and published for the nine denominations involved. For our small-group studies that spring, we joined with Forest Hills Presbyterian Church to study the COCU proposal for "United Congregations." It was a congenial and interesting study with some Presbyterian polity glitches and some Disciples "emotional" glitches.

Oliver Schroeder was a member of the Executive Committee of COCU. Back in the 1966 International Convention in Dallas, he was asked to represent COCU in a speech to the Convention. I first met him then as I served as Program Director of the International Convention. COCU was developing concepts for the "middle judicatories" (Disciples regions, for example). There was consideration about the leaders of that level of the polity all being called "bishops." Disciples were mumbling about that. But Ollie Schroeder, among other things, brought down the house by proclaiming, "If you think the Episcopal Bishop of Virginia has more power than Herold Monroe in Ohio, you've got another think coming!"

The 1966 International Convention passed the first key element of restructure by creating a representative General Assembly, where every congregation would have at least three designated voting representatives. All Disciples would be invited to the Assembly, but just designated voters would vote on business items.

We continued to emphasize study and fellowship in small groups which Terry lead. In 1973, Terry left to be the minister in North Royalton Christian Church, on the southwest side of Cleveland. After a search, we called Fred Gee to be our Associate Minister. We were a good team. His wife, Sharon, and their children became part of our church family for three years. He went on to be a member of the associate regional staff in the Upper Midwest, in Des Moines, Iowa.

Our children all enjoyed church and school events. Fortunately, some of their good friends were in youth groups in the church, and they were motivated to come for church and evening youth groups to be with them. Debbie's best friend was Rose Gutfeld, from a Jewish family, who went on to Cornell to study journalism. She later served as a Washington editor for *The Wall Street Journal*. John and Bill Knapp, Jr., were good friends as were John and Tom Griffith. Jeff's good friend Jamie Graff and he rode their bicycles from Cleveland to Bethany, West Virginia, in one day. Jamie went on to Ohio University for journalism, subsequently serving as head of *Time* magazine's Paris office, then as Senior Editor for *The Wall Street Journal*. Jeff and his classmate Matt Eisenberg were inseparable. Our two families enjoyed good times together. Matt's father was a rabbi at the major Fairmont Jewish Temple. Matt later became the rabbi at a temple in the suburb of Beachwood.

John had a great baritone voice. He was soloist in the Heights Men's Chorus. He was a swimmer in events, as well, and a lifeguard at a condo development. Debbie was in the Girls Glee Club. She was on the Heights' field hockey team, volleyball team and basketball team. She was the first of our children to win a Heights athletic varsity letter. At Alleghany College, she was a starter on the varsity volleyball team.

In 1975, we had a number of younger couples in their thirties who were coming to church and were prospective members. I invited them to join me as I led a Sunday morning study group. It developed into a good group with social and party times together. They all joined the church. One time near Christmas, we had a "progressive dinner," eating different courses in different homes. Dessert was at the Humberts'. One of the young men played the guitar, as did I. He insisted that we were going to sing Christmas carols with us accompanying on the guitars. The group did some good-natured grumbling. Finally, we dragged them through the first verse of a carol, and just as we finish the verse, our French poodle, who was lying on the floor in the middle of the group, threw up and walked out of the room. The timing was perfect as far as the hilarious group could see, and they laughed so hard that that ended the singing!

In the fall of 1974, the Cleveland Heights churches called for a conference of all the congregations to send seven members of each church to "a gathering to consider together the human needs in our community and how we might act together to meet them." We were there, as was a group from a "house church" who had separated from the Church of Christ (non-instrumental) just one block from our location. They had been "churched," cast out, because they were studying the social needs of the community "instead of the Bible." I made a special effort to visit with them at the gathering. They were great people. They were meeting on Sundays, alternating in one another's homes.

Growing out of my conversation with them, I was invited to one of those Sunday worship gatherings on a Sunday evening after

Christmas. After worship we had a wonderful discussion about the Disciples' theology of the church and its life and mission. One of the persons was a professor of religion at Cleveland State University and was a leader of the group. One of their concerns was that in their house church there was a lack of peer fellowship for their children and youth. They had the feeling of missing the full fellowship of a large community of the church.

I didn't hear anything more until later in the spring. Bill Edwards called me one day and asked if a delegation from the group could come to my home and visit with me. The group came. The gist of the meeting was, "What would you and the church think and feel, if we came to Euclid Avenue Christian Church?" I replied, "I'm sure our folks would be delighted to have you come. If you came to join us as individuals in Christ, you would be most welcome. If you should come as a church body, to remain as a church within the church, turning inward as a distinct group, they might wonder about that."

They began to attend worship. One of the ladies said that the first notes of the organ were a test of her faith and emotions. They were Bill and Carol Edwards and family, Carol Wright, Jim and Janet Klein and family, David and Karen Shumway, and Ed and Ann Myers. They came. They placed their membership in Euclid Avenue Church. They became strong, faithful, and key leaders in the church for years.

I felt called to be involved in the Heights and Cleveland community. I was elected President of the Cleveland Disciples Union. I was on the Board of the Cleveland Council of Churches and, as such, was appointed Chair of the Finance Committee, working with a staff person responsible for finance, Joan Brown Campbell. I was also on the Board of the Shaker Heights/Cleveland Heights YMCA.

The nearest hospital to our church's location was Huron Hospital in East Cleveland. East Cleveland had become predominantly Black almost overnight. The people in the neighborhood were using the emergency room of Huron Hospital almost as if it were their family doctor. It was a busy place. The head of the hospital appealed to the ministers of the neighborhood to take some brief training and become voluntary ombudsmen in the ER. Several of us did so. We were to represent the patients and family to the staff of the ER and represent the ER to the rest of the hospital. Emergency rooms were the "stepchildren" of the hospitals they served. I served as an ombudsman every Wednesday afternoon for two years. It was a needed and rewarding service.

As the leader of the Cleveland Disciples Union, I felt called to pull together our Disciples ministers for fellowship and study. I invited one of the religion professors from Hiram College to lead us in a three-session study series of current theology with the ministers chipping in to provide an honorarium. It was great. Then I engaged Oliver Schroeder to lead a three-session discussion in his field, the ethics of medicine. To those, each minister was asked to bring a doctor from his congregation. We provided Ollie with an honorarium, as well.

In the Ohio Region, I was a member of the regional board and instructor and vespers preacher at the Ohio Adult Conference at Otterbein College. I also served on the Ohio commission on the ministry, and as such was a counselor to candidates under care, including Janet Long, Tom Jewell, and Glenn Stewart, who later became regional ministers. Joan Brown Campbell, when she became a licensed lay minister, was later ordained, and became General Secretary of the National Council of Churches. After retiring from that position, she was the head of the religion programs at the Chautauqua Institution in New York. Our paths crossed many times.

CHAPTER 23

Indianapolis and Deputy GMP

During my Euclid Avenue years, I also continued to serve as the Program Director for the General Assemblies in 1971, 1973, and 1975. As such, I was involved in the preplanning of the assemblies. In an Assembly Committee meeting in September 1976, the group went to dinner. Ken Teegarden, GMP, and I were the last to leave the tables. As we were leaving the restaurant, Ken asked, "How long have you been at Euclid Avenue Church?" I replied, "Six years plus."

He said, "Then you could consider becoming the Deputy General Minister and President, couldn't you?"

I stopped dead in my tracks! "You're asking me to consider...?" I was stunned! I had come to know Ken, working with him since his election as GMP in 1973. The other Deputy, Howard Dentler, and I had worked together since about 1960 and had become fast friends. Bill Howland had become Deputy in 1973 but had now left to become Senior Minister at National City Christian Church, in Washington, D.C.

We walked together for several blocks back to the meeting place. I responded that I was truly honored to be asked to consider the invitation. I had always felt my calling was to congregational ministry. But I certainly would think about it with JoAnne, with a great deal of prayer. We spoke of details such as the time to consider it in the month before Ken was at a COCU meeting in Dayton. The Administrative Committee would be in November, with an interview with the Executive

Committee, and then election by the full Administrative Committee. (I had been elected to the General Board and Administrative Committee at the 1975 San Antonio Assembly.) I let Ken know that if I did accept, I could not begin a move to Indianapolis until Jeff finished his senior year in high school, next June. He said it was acceptable.

I sat through the evening session of the Committee in a haze. When I returned to my hotel room after the session, the phone rang. It was Howard Dentler. He knew Ken was going to extend the invitation, so had stayed downtown for the night at the hotel in case I wanted to talk. I wanted to talk. But first I had to call JoAnne and tell her what had happened. Which I did, with the bombshell! Then Howard came to my room and we talked about my many questions about the position. I assured him that one of the great pluses would be coming to work with him. His part of the work was managerial, overseeing the staff of the Office of the GMP, arranging for hotels, places of meetings, budgets, etc. My calling was to the pastoral side of the office in relationships with general units, the regions, the people, the program of the General Assembly, and with the Task Force on Renewal and Structural Reform. One factor was that, when I was working in the office and not traveling, I could be home for the evenings, which was different than being in a local pastorate.

I flew home the next day to JoAnne. We had long conversations. What are the alternatives? We took long walks in our Demington/Fairmount Boulevard neighborhood in the beautiful fall. We spoke of our beautiful Euclid Avenue church culture, of her teaching career at Noble Road Elementary School. The prospect of my travel loomed. Jeff would go off to university, and we would have an "empty nest" as we moved. I would have to resign at Thanksgiving time, and I wondered if the church would let me continue ministry till June.

Finally, we decided we would accept Kenneth's invitation. I flew to Dayton to meet him, give him my answer, and discuss the work we would be doing together. I would come two days early to the Administrative Committee meeting in Indianapolis, two weeks before Thanksgiving.

The meeting arrived. I was interviewed by the Executive Committee and the next day elected as Deputy General Minister and President, to begin serving June 15, 1977.

The week before Thanksgiving Sunday, I met with Duane Mayhew, Chairman of the Board, to tell him that I would present my letter of resignation to the congregation the coming Sunday. I asked if it could be effective June 15th, 1977, with two weeks of my coming vacation being June 1–15. He was surprised, understood about Jeff and his senior year, and thought it would be acceptable to the Board. They would need to meet and take action on it. But it would mean they could begin the process of finding a new minister in that period. It would make for a shorter interim time.

At the close of worship on November 1977, I read my letter of resignation to the congregation. It was an emotional time for me. I had preached and received the call to Euclid Avenue Church on the Sunday of Thanksgiving in November 1969.

That afternoon, a member of the church called who had formerly been a real estate broker. She said, "I hope the call is not inappropriate, but a former client has long wanted just the right home in the Demington Road area. Could they come see your home the next day?" I accepted the proposal. JoAnne was aghast. There were all these things we needed to do before we put it on the market. Besides, we would not be vacating the house till the end of June. The couple came, looked at the house, and said, "We'll buy it. How much do you want for it?"

We had paid $40,000 for the house in November 1969, and I had no idea how much it was worth now. We asked for time to explore the question. Investigating with another young realtor in the church, we settled on $88,000, with no realtor's fee. We named it; they accepted it. The proviso was that it wouldn't be available till June 25, 1977, to which they agreed. They gave us $5,000 cash to hold the sale.

At Christmas, during Jeff and John's vacations (John from Kenyon College), we went house hunting in Indianapolis. Debbie was in France for her junior year study abroad at the University of Dijon. The broker had been engaged earlier in November. On the day after the Administrative Committee meeting, she had taken me for a ride in northern Indianapolis, seeing some streets near Butler University. She had an itinerary of houses set up for us this time. We saw seven houses, and when we came into the home on a cul-de-sac on Surrey Hill Circle, and toured the house, we knew it was the one: "country French" stone house, kitchen eating area leading out to a screened porch, living room fireplace, family room brick fireplace wall, two bedrooms on the first floor, one large master bedroom with master bath, large closet, dining room, two bedrooms and full bath upstairs, nice full basement, air conditioned, $72,000. They were willing to wait till June to close. How fortunate we were in this arrangement on both houses!

Jeff was doing well as a tight end and defensive end, punter, and place kicker on the Cleveland Heights football team. On Wednesday evenings, the coach would show the last week's game films for the parents. But the school did not want the expense of being open in the evening. I offered our fellowship hall, and the Coach accepted. I also was an official for home games, manning the downs' marker on the sideline of the field.

In March, Ken Teegarden invited me to attend the meeting of the General Minister's Cabinet, on the last Monday of the month. The day before, traveling through an intersection on the green light, a car driving at full speed crashed into my vehicle, shattering glass, some into my face. With the exception of a few particles of glass in my cheek, I was not hurt because I was wearing a seatbelt. But I was in a state of shock. A policeman took me to the Huron Hospital emergency room for the removal of the glass. JoAnne and Jeff were coming home from church and they passed my car sitting there on the side street with the shattered glass everywhere.

I was nowhere to be seen. They were really concerned and wondering how I was. I was able to call them from the ER to let them know that I was OK, but was having little pieces of glass taken out of my cheek. JoAnne was concerned about my attending the Cabinet meeting, but after letting the shock wear off, I decided to go.

The Cabinet meeting was my first experience viewing the interaction of the presidents of the eleven general units of the church, and it was their first time looking me over as the new Deputy GMP. I knew them all, having interacted with them at General Assemblies. The dynamics between Bob Thomas, President of the Division of Overseas Ministries, and Ken Kuntz, the President of the Division of Homeland Ministries (DHM), was especially noteworthy.

I continued to serve Euclid Avenue through to June. Jeff had a great senior baseball season and was chosen to be the shortstop on *The Plain Dealer*'s Cleveland area all-star team. He also was awarded a scholarship to Cornell University in the hotel management school. We had two graduations, John from Kenyon, with acceptance into Case Western Reserve Law School, and Jeff from Cleveland Heights. Debbie returned from her year in France at Dijon.

We closed on both houses, Cleveland and Indianapolis, one on May 25, the other with the proceeds of the first on May 27. We could stay in our Cleveland home for the month of June. I finished my work at Euclid Avenue on June 1. My income began from Indianapolis on June 1 with two weeks to work on our new home.

I went to Indianapolis beginning on the first, with tools in hand to work on our new home, painting and moving two sets of bookcases from the living room to the family room. We had chosen Williamsburg paint colors and wallpapers. I stayed at the Dentlers' home while they were on vacation, as I worked on our Surry Hill Circle home. I came back to the Heights for the weekend, then back to Indianapolis for another week of house prep.

I began my work as Deputy General Minister and President on June 15, 1977. Ken and I went to the chapel service held every morning Monday through Friday at 8:00 at the Missions Building. After chapel he said, "The Board of the Division of Homeland Ministries is meeting today. I want you to develop a relationship with that division for our office. Why don't you spend the morning with them and then we'll go to lunch?"

That was an historic morning. DHM's Department of Education was presenting a General Assembly study document on homosexuality. The Office of Communication released that information, and the TV and radio news reported it that evening. *The Indianapolis Star* carried an article about it the next morning. The study document would go to the General Board and on to the General Assembly, which, if voted to be issued, would then go on to all congregations. The premise of the study was that new developments in psychology and biblical studies called for new consideration of the question of homosexuality. DHM voted to forward the study to the General Board with the recommendation that it be forwarded to the Kansas City General Assembly to be issued in October.

On Friday June 17, I spent the day in my first meetings with the Board of the Division of Overseas Ministries (DOM).

I had spent the week settling in with my secretary Dorothy, who had worked with Bill Howland for two years. I went back to Cleveland on Friday afternoon for our final weekend in the Demington Drive house, then back to Indianapolis for my second week in the office.

On one of our visits in Indianapolis around buying our house, JoAnne had visited with the head of school staffing for the Washington Township School System. She had in hand recommendations from the Cleveland Heights system, since we had hoped for a teaching position in Indianapolis. This was especially important to us since I would be traveling out of town about a third of the time. It looked promising. As it turns out, the head of personnel for the system became the principal that fall when she began her teaching position in Greenbriar Elementary!

The General Board meeting was scheduled for the end of July in Chicago (during our 25th wedding anniversary, July 26). All resolutions go to the General Board for their action and recommendations for General Assembly business. Ken and Howard wanted me to have exposure at the Board as the new Deputy GMP, so they recruited me to play the guitar, lead the singing, and plan the opening worship on Saturday and Sunday morning. I invited Herold Monroe to preach on Sunday morning. That all turned out well.

Howard Dentler saw my role as being available in the evenings to be a listener and sounding board for Ken Teegarden after General Board sessions. JoAnne came to Chicago with me. The three of us had a wonderful dinner at a famous beef restaurant before the meetings began. We had the Presidential Suite together at the hotel, Ken with the downstairs sleeping room, and JoAnne and I upstairs. In the evenings we were together with Ken for ice cream cones and visiting. Ken had lunches and dinners with church staff and folks. They were both pastoral and strategy sessions related to the business items regarding homosexuality. JoAnne and I had time to ourselves for meals, especially our anniversary dinner at a marvelous Magnificent Mile restaurant. We also shopped for a new wedding ring for me. My original wedding ring had come off in our Demington front yard when I was throwing the football to Jeff. We were not able to find it, though we continued to search for it. In Chicago, we found a replacement that we had engraved with our initials and 7/26/52, the date of our wedding.

Publicity around the "Study Document on Homosexuality" had resulted in letters and phone calls from throughout the church—individuals, congregations, even some regional staff. Comments such as these were typical: "We don't need to be studying homosexuality. Everybody knows it's a sin. Just look in the Bible." Several resolutions were spawned. Resolution

7760, Concerning Homosexuality as a Lifestyle, from Southside Christian Church in Kokomo, Indiana, said: "Be it resolved the assembly oppose homosexuality as an alternative lifestyle open to Christians." The Board recommended it be disapproved by the General Assembly. Resolution 7742, Concerning Christian Morality, from First Christian Church of Shelbyville, Kentucky, said, "whereas present American society is described as permissive towards divorce, sexual relations before marriage, homosexual activity, childbirth out of wedlock, freedom of speech about pornography. Since the Bible prohibits divorce save for unchastity, homosexuality, fornication; therefore, be it resolved the Assembly reaffirm its commitment to New Testament morality." The Board recommended that that resolution be disapproved saying, "The question of morality is much broader than the resolution indicates."

Resolution 7744, Concerning Ordination of Homosexuals, from First Christian Church of Santa Maria, California, proposed that "The General Assembly strongly urge all of its divisions, regions and local congregations to deny ordination status to any candidate who declares that he or she practices or prefers homosexuality as a lifestyle." The Board recommended the resolution be referred to the Division of Homeland Ministries for further development and brought back to the 1979 Assembly.

Resolution 7747, Concerning Civil Liberties of Homosexual Persons, "while neither approving of nor condemning homosexuality, urges the passage of legislation on local, state and national levels which will end the denial of civil rights and the violation of civil liberties for reasons of sexual orientation, and calls upon its members to advocate and support the passage and maintenance of such legislation." This was from the Division of Homeland Ministries. The Board recommended approval.

The Board also recommended that Study Document 7750, "A Study Document On Homosexuality and the Church," be issued with the following provision: "This document is issued by the General Assembly of the Christian Church (Disciples of Christ).

It is not to be construed as an official statement of attitudes or policies of the general board."

Following the Board meeting, Ken Teegarden, Gertrude Dimke, and I worked through the changes the Board had made to the resolutions. They typed in the Board's recommendations, preparing the copy for printing by the Christian Board of Publication in St. Louis. The rules called for the docket for the General Assembly to be prepared and printed, and then for copies to be sent immediately to every congregation.

(As I said above, my relationship with Gertrude Dimke went back to my high school Wilmington Conference days, before she moved to Indianapolis to serve as Gaines Cook's secretary when he became General Secretary of the International Convention. She had served as the Secretary of the International Convention and now the General Assembly since 1945 and had worked with Howard Dentler since the early '60s. But she considered me to be one of her "Ohio boys," like Ben Moore and a select couple more.)

The business docket went out to the congregations. The letters began coming into our offices. One of the congregations that was really upset about the Study Document and our attention to homosexuality was First Christian Church in Collierville, Tennessee. The minister Terry Reister, an old friend from my Maryland days, needed help. He appealed to the GMP. Ken sent me to Collierville for my first assignment of a pastoral nature. They had a fellowship dinner and then discussion afterwards. I listened. "What is this study document and what is this on civil rights for homosexuals?" I shared that this study document is a study and analysis of the ethical, moral, and religious considerations that are important to help members of the Christian Church (Disciples of Christ) be more thoroughly informed. It is an aid to help individuals and groups form their own Christian opinions and judgments about this important issue. I told them about the process involved in the General Assembly issuing a study document. I told them that it was a study document only and should not be construed as an official statement of attitudes or policies of the Assembly. I said that we were facing the issue of homosexuality in the church more and more and that new developments in psychology and biblical studies of the original texts are being explored. If the Assembly issues it as a study document that means that congregations and individuals can study it and make their own conclusions.

Any group or organization in the church can submit a resolution about a moral, ethical, or religious matter confronting the church, the nation, or the world, to the General Board and Assembly. Resolutions are developed for the guidance of the church in its program operation or for the consideration of congregations and individual members and for Christian witness to the world. If approved, it is for your study and consideration. It is not binding on you or your congregation. But when several thousand Disciples come together from congregations in the Assembly to vote to approve a resolution on an issue, then we in congregations ought at least to consider the issue too. Civil liberties for homosexual persons is one of those issues.

I gently listened throughout the discussion. The heat that was evident as we began had tempered measurably as we discussed the process of the items, and of course, I reminded them that they had the privilege of sending two voting representatives to the Assembly that fall in Kansas City. I think the fact that someone from "Indianapolis," from the office of General Minister President had come to visit them helped.

Shortly after that, I had my first meeting of the Task Force on Renewal and Structural Reform as a staff person. We worked on the final presentation of the "Provisional Design of the Christian Church (Disciples of Christ)," which had been adopted in 1968. The Task Force observed that the "Provisional Design" had proved to be a workable document that offered flexibility. Hence the judgment was that the church at this time may not be served best by writing a constitution. They worked to make the language more inclusive and made revisions consistent with changes which had already occurred or were in process. They also recommended dropping "Provisional" from the name of the design and postponing the writing of a constitution "until some further time as might be authorized by a General Assembly."

At home, JoAnne and I wallpapered the dining room, front hall, and stairs with the Williamsburg paper. In our nice large master bedroom, we papered with roses and had rose colored carpet to match. We were copying John and Patty Hungerford's bedroom back in Lyndhurst.

We had a black cat adopt us and then leave us. We said we wanted a dog anyhow. We visited the Humane Society and chose a beautiful mixed breed Saint Bernard and Collie found wandering on a main highway, with nothing to indicate the owner. They named her Heidi. The Society did do a home study on us. We passed, but an outside fence was required. I built a fenced pen, but she dug her way underneath the fence. So, I completed a wooden panel fence on the total circumference of our beautiful big backyard, with the gate to the driveway. Heidi was satisfied with that. She was the sweetest, most beautiful housebroken dog. We loved walking with her in our beautiful neighborhood. And when I traveled, she was good company and a safety feature with JoAnne. She didn't have the drooling qualities of a full Saint Bernard. She was a big dog, but she thought she was a lapdog and acted it out to our pleasure.

One of the things that helped settle us in Indianapolis was bridge. We played with Howard and Mary Lou Dentler. Our friendship was helpful in making the move. JoAnne and Mary Lou became close. Howard and Mary Lou were members at Allisonville Christian Church. They invited us to join a bridge club with other members of that church. It met once a month. One of the members was Virginia Spradlin along with her husband. She was a staff member of the Christian Church Foundation. We enjoyed that group for a number of years.

We ultimately settled on joining Northwood Christian Church. We joined an adult class, the Home Builders, where we made friends. And we made friends in our new Surry Hill neighborhood as well. JoAnne joined the neighborhood garden club. The lady who lived next door was a leader in that club.

The weekend beginning August 21, I had a week of vacation. JoAnne and I went to Cleveland on Friday, the 19th, spent time with the kids, then went to Chautauqua, New York, for a few days. We had rented an apartment. Debbie and Jeff were with us. Then we went on to Ithaca, New York, for Jeff's entrance to Cornell University. Here was the "unloading college entrance ritual" for the third time. When we said goodbye to Jeff, I sat in our car and cried. It was such an emotional goodbye. Indianapolis was such a long way from Ithaca. I had not missed a football game he played in his whole career from junior high to the varsity in high school.

The weekend after Labor Day, the Upper Midwest Region held a regionwide educational day for laypeople in Des Moines, Iowa. I was drafted to lead morning and afternoon sessions on the polity and structure of the church, in preparation for the Kansas City Assembly. There were representatives from the church in Exira, Iowa, who remembered my father being their minister when he was a seminary student at Drake. Before I flew back with several others from the Missions Building, Bob Thomas, President of DOM, asked if we could sit together and get acquainted. We had some nice moments together. It was the beginning of a long friendship.

The General Cabinet, of which I was now a member, met in Indianapolis on September 13, with lots of discussion about where we were with General Assembly business and congregational response. The next two days, Ken and I met at an airport motel with the Executive Committee of Regional Ministers and Moderators. This would be a major relationship for me, with their annual full gathering of regional leaders in St. Louis every December. The evening of the fifteenth, Oliver Schroeder came to Indianapolis for a consultation with me. The General Board had appointed a committee to study the place and function of our Disciples seminaries, with the charge to design funding criteria for Basic Mission Finance for the support of seminaries. I was to be the staff person to work with the group. At my suggestion, Oliver Schroeder was appointed chairman. Another member was Duane Cummins. Working with Duane in this group was the beginning of another long friendship.

Jim Moak, Regional Minister of Kentucky, was the Moderator for the Kansas City General Assembly. Bob Kirkland, from Louisville, a classmate of mine at Butler University, was parliamentarian. They came to the Missions Building to meet with Ken, Howard, and me to go over arrangements, especially parliamentary procedures. We looked at the function of the different microphones on the house floor for debate. We outlined motions, signals, and procedures that needed to be in place for what in the Assembly business sessions would no doubt be somewhat contentious. Bob frequently was happy to remind me that he was a candidate for Euclid Avenue Christian Church before I was and could have come, but turned it down. I thanked him. Jim Moak left feeling somewhat better about his role as Moderator of the Assembly with Bob Kirkland's support.

October began with a preaching appointment at Arkansas City, Kansas, flying there on a Saturday evening and back to Indianapolis on a Sunday night. Thursday and Friday the Seminary Study Committee met at the Holiday Inn in the Indianapolis airport. Then JoAnne and I drove to Kettering, Ohio, and stayed with John and Joan Albrecht as I preached for First Christian Church. It was nice that JoAnne and I could get together with old friends in Kettering.

I had the Cornell freshman football team's schedule on my work calendar. Jeff was the starting tight end and punter. That weekend they played Ithaca College. In the Ivy League, freshmen were not eligible to play on the varsity.

JoAnne came back to school on Monday, and I went to the Airport Rodeway Inn for the Christian Church Foundation board meeting. I had been elected to that board in 1974, so I was well acquainted with its functions, the staff, and the board members. Jim Reed was President. As Deputy GMP, I was now an ex officio member.

The General Assembly began on Friday, October 21. I arrived in Kansas City on the Wednesday before, to get ready to direct the program with all the stage settings, etc. The Assembly opened magnificently with music and singing, worship, and sermon by Jim Moak. The Saturday morning men's breakfast was at 7:00 in the headquarters hotel. Jim Moak was the speaker. I was supposed to accompany Jim from the banquet room to the Convention Center hall to orient him regarding his place, the various microphones for debate, and their functions in the business session. On the way down from the top floor, the elevator suddenly stopped dead still. The door opened to a brick wall! I couldn't get it to move at all. Fortunately, there were only six of us as passengers, Jim Moak, Mr. and Mrs. Verlin Petrie, Mr. and Mrs. Fred Warren and me. I pulled out the phone and the operator answered. My claustrophobia was beginning to kick in.

"We are trapped in the elevator between floors 11 and 12. We need help," I said. She said, "I'll call for help," and hung up. We could hear people outside the elevator wondering why the elevator didn't come to their floor. We waited. Nothing. I called the operator.

She said, "We can't fix it. We've called the elevator company to send the repairmen."

"We have the Moderator of our Assembly on board who needs to get to the Convention Center. Can you call the Convention Center for us?" I asked.

"Well," she said," I have other calls that need attention," and hung up. I called her again. "I need to call my wife's room so she can get word to our leaders."

"What's your number," she asked.

"I don't have a phone book in here," I said. "She's at the hotel across the street. Would you please dial the hotel?" She did and I got through to JoAnne. "I am stuck in an elevator, honey!" (My other passengers are laughing in the background about our situation.) "Sure," she said mockingly. "No, I am stuck in an elevator with the moderators and four new friends! We've got to get word of our plight to Howard Dentler." Howard Dentler later said that when JoAnne came into the Assembly Office, she was a woman on a mission, with fire in her eyes. She demanded, "You've got to get John and the Moderator out of a stuck elevator at the hotel!" Howard, who worked with all the hotels, called the General Manager, demanding action. As time went on, they started the morning session with Ken Teegarden doing the honors for the Moderator. Finally, after forty-five minutes, the elevator moved and opened on the 10th floor. With relief we were set free! People were rushing to get on, but we advised differently. I finally did escort the Moderator down another elevator and across the street to the Convention Center, where he began presiding I began directing the program.

With my claustrophobia I survived the ordeal better than expected. I was busy on the phone, and I think that helped. There were only six congenial people, not a stuffed, crowded elevator.

This was the third time I had worked on the Program Director's staff for a Kansas City Convention or Assembly—1961, 1968 and 1977. In '61, I was the assistant. My father and mother were there. On Sunday, Ben Moore gave me an afternoon off and I accompanied my parents out to Richmond, Missouri, for worship and Sunday dinner at the church my father had served when I was born. I had not been there since our family moved to Ohio when I was one year old. It was a special thrill for Mom and Dad, but I really enjoyed it too. It was a strong church. George Beasley, the noted President of the Council on Christian Unity, had served there following Dad. By the 1968 Convention, Bill Robertson was there. He would later serve a church in the Chicago suburb, Arlington, where he built his own home. JoAnne and I were guests when I preached there. Then he and his wife "Bunny" moved to Indianapolis and lived in our neighborhood while he was Vice President of the Christian Church Foundation.

On Sunday of the Assembly in 1968, Robert Ramsey from Atchison Kansas, Mother's first cousin, President of the chain of Ramsey's Department Stores in Kansas and Missouri, took the three of us to the exclusive Kansas City Club for Sunday dinner. It was the first time I had met him.

One of the days of the Assembly in 1977, October 26, was my 50th birthday! I was born in Kansas City, never lived there and had only been there on a few occasions surrounding a Convention or Assembly. Ironically, here I was on my 50th birthday! During the business session, the eight thousand people sang "Happy Birthday to John." Afterwards, good old Ken Kuntz complained to Teegarden. "That was giving too much attention to one of the deputies."

The program went well, with no glitches by the Program Director. I gave the invocation at the Lexington Seminary luncheon on Tuesday.

At the beginning of the business session, a procedural motion was presented to the General Assembly. It was business item 7770, the Limitation of Debate at the Kansas City General Assembly. It was a plan used successfully at the 1975 San Antonio Assembly. It proposed the total time on any business item as recommended by the General Board to be 48 minutes, 24 minutes, or 12 minutes, according to anticipated debate time. It was approved. It also provided that each person would have 3 minutes to debate and may speak again only if all other representatives desiring to speak have had the opportunity. The provisions for debate were most helpful for the debate that followed.

The Business Sessions were well-attended, with discussion from the floor strong and often emotional.

Resolution 7744: Concerning Ordination of Homosexuals. It urged against ordination of practicing homosexuals. It was referred to the DHM for further development. It was to be reported back to the General Board, and then to the 1979 Assembly.

Resolution 7760: Homosexuality as a Lifestyle. It resolved that the Assembly oppose homosexuality as an alternate lifestyle open to Christians. After extended emotional discussion, the Assembly voted to disapprove.

Resolution 7747: Resolution Concerning Civil Rights of Homosexual Persons. It was approved.

Resolution 7750: A study document on Homosexuality in the Church was approved to be issued by the General Assembly, with a statement to appear as part of it. "It is a study document only. It is not to be construed as an official statement of attitudes or policies of the General Assembly."

Resolution 7771: Resolution Authorizing Conversations toward Possible Union of the Christian Church Disciples of Christ and the United Church of Christ. There had been informal conversations on this subject during 1976. The 1977 General Board took action to instruct the Council on Christian Unity to pursue these negotiations and bring to the 1977 General Assembly a description of the process by which these conversations would continue. The Administrative Committee of the Disciples and the Executive Committee of the United Church of Christ would facilitate resolutions to go to the Disciples General Assembly and the UCC General Synod, calling for two-year exploratory conversations at all levels of the church. The Council on Christian Unity and the Council on Ecumenism of the UCC were to facilitate the conversations and would be responsible for reporting their implications to the 1979 General Assembly and General Synod of these churches.

The Resolution was approved. At that point in the Assembly, it was my privilege to escort the newly elected President of the United Church of Christ, Avery Post, and his wife, Peg, from their seats in the audience to the Assembly platform. It was the beginning of long years of growing friendship for JoAnne and me with Avery and Peg.

We came home to Indianapolis for Halloween. (On Friday, November 4, Jeff was playing for Cornell at West Point against Army, the Plebes team.) I didn't have an out-of-town trip until JoAnne and I left to see Jeff for the last game of the season for the Cornell freshman football team. It was the only Cornell football game we would see Jeff play. They played Milford Academy at 7:30 on Friday evening, November 11. At tight end, he caught three passes and punted well. It was so great to see him. I had missed him so much.

The drive to Ithaca through Pennsylvania and New York was beautiful. Driving back to Indianapolis, it was back to school for JoAnne and my first meeting with the Disciples Commission on Budget Evaluation at the downtown Atkinson Inn. At that meeting, we began our long friendship with Dan and Mary Lee Loving.

The next weekend I drove to Lisbon, Ohio, for the 150th anniversary of their congregation's founding. There was a celebration worship on Saturday night with Herold Monroe preaching. The two of us suffered through a solo by a beautifully dressed lady, a halftone off-key through all four verses. She turned to me after the service, obviously expecting a compliment. I said, "You obviously enjoy singing." She seemed pleased.

I preached on Sunday morning and celebrated with them all afternoon. Then I drove to Cleveland for a meeting of the Consultation on Church Union Middle Judicatory Commission, Monday and Tuesday of Thanksgiving week. Jeff flew to Cleveland and he, John, and I drove to Indianapolis for Thanksgiving. Debbie had taken a train from Pittsburgh with David Ellis. This was Debbie's senior year. It was so great for JoAnne and me to have all of us together.

The week after Thanksgiving was the annual meeting of the Council of Ministers (the Cabinet and Regional Ministers) all day Monday and Tuesday, nine to twelve. Then immediately, Ken and I went into the Executive Committee of the Regional Ministers and Moderators. Then the whole Conference met till Friday noon. The meetings were all at the St. Louis downtown Rodeway Inn.

Getting to know the thirty-six regional ministers and Moderators in these annual meetings was a joy and honor. They became my friends. It was also an entrée to invitations to regional assemblies to speak and mingle with the church folk, which was central to my ministry as Deputy General Minister and President.

It was really great to work with Ken Teegarden. Our friendship was a delight. I had already known Howard for years. We were good friends and really worked well together. I had never been an Assistant Minister before and wondered how it would be. But it was great the way Ken and Howard "let me in." They had been working together for four years before I arrived. We went to lunch together every day we were in town and had great fun doing so. Ken and Howard both appreciated humor, and laughter was regular while working and in leisure moments. We all took our work seriously, but we did not take ourselves so seriously.

Sunday, December 4, JoAnne and I went to Dayton for a concert by the Allegheny College Choir in which Debbie was singing. As a freshman at Allegheny, she studied voice. In a voice competition, she won first place and an award of $200. She later sang in *The Three Penny Opera*, in which she had a leading role. JoAnne and I were able to attend and were delighted at her performance.

In order to get to know the Missions Building staff, JoAnne and I joined the fall Missions Building bowling league. For the first time in any move to a new situation, JoAnne and I didn't have a congregation ready and eager to greet and welcome us. It was especially noticeable for JoAnne. I had the Missions Building staff, but she didn't. The move was tougher on her. She did have fellow teachers at her new school, but that did not equate to a congregation.

Ollie Schroeder and the seminary study group came to Indianapolis for another meeting at the airport Rodeway Inn. I enjoyed working with them.

We had our first office Christmas party on December 9. It gave JoAnne an opportunity to be with all of the General Office staff and spouses. We went to Cleveland for Christmas with all the family, which was such a joy.

From January 22 to the 25, I attended the annual Ohio Pastors Conference in Columbus, Ohio, where I had always found inspiration as a pastor. Back home, we had a huge snowstorm in Indianapolis. I was supposed to fly to Sarasota, Florida, on Saturday to preach at the First Christian Church on Sunday. Old friend, Bernie Meece was the minister, along with Georgia, his wife, and my long-time friend, as well. Even with the help of my neighbor's 4-wheel drive Jeep, we couldn't get out of our cul-de-sac because of the deep snow! I was scheduled to give three Bible lectures Monday through Wednesday evenings. I did make it down Monday morning. Ironically, it turned out JoAnne's school was cancelled all those days and she could have been with me.

It was my first visit to Sarasota. I was really impressed!

I stayed with a family who had been members of North Chevy Chase church, and one afternoon he and I played golf! I did give the lectures Monday through Wednesday evening.

On Thursday, I flew to a meeting of the Board of the Christian Church Foundation in Pass Christian, Mississippi. JoAnne flew down and joined me for the extended weekend. We really enjoyed the members of the Board and the family that hosted us in their beach home.

The Administrative Committee met in Indianapolis the next Sunday through Tuesday. It was memorable because on Sunday the launching of the space mission ended in a terrible disaster, as the capsule exploded with the three astronauts on board.

JoAnne and I had the pleasure of driving to Niles for me to speak at our home, First Christian Church, for their annual meeting. It was a wonderful occasion because all of our family could get together.

The Black Ministers Retreat was held in Kingston, North Carolina, which was one of my pastoral relations responsibilities. Before it began, I preached at the First Christian Church in Belhaven, North Carolina, where they were having difficulty with the study document issued by the Assembly. It was an interesting discussion.

Later that week, JoAnne and I drove to Guelph, Ontario, for a weekend meeting with the all-Canada Disciples Committee. Among other things, I learned how difficult it was to have a region of the church stretching from Nova Scotia to the far western provinces. The Commission on the Ministry's extent of care for candidates for the ministry was limited to correspondence because of distance and financial limitations. But they were a committed people! I preached on Sunday at the Guelph Christian Church, and then we drove back to Indianapolis.

The Program Committee for the next General Assembly met in St. Louis, March 16–18. Ken, Howard, and I had agreed that it was now my Assembly responsibility to develop the morning opening sessions and the evening programs and worship for St. Louis in 1979. We met to develop the general theme with suggestions for evening speakers and morning preachers. I led a discussion with the committee on the elements of worship and the manner of expression of those elements. The theme was chosen, "Proclaim Christ Lord." Judge James Noe from Seattle and Second Vice Moderator, Joy L Greer, a banker from Little Rock Arkansas, had become good friends and coworkers. Samuel Hilton, minister in St. Louis, was First Vice Moderator. He had been my classmate at Butler University and a special colleague and dear friend. They were such a marvelous working group with Ken, Howard, and me for the two-year cycle and beyond.

Through all these months from June through March, in my pastoral, relational role as Deputy GMP, I spent a great deal of time with staff and board meetings of the general units: DHM, DOM, the foundation (where I had been a member of the board previously), Council and Christian Unity, Church

Finance Council, Division of Higher Education (with its Council on Theological Education), National Convocation (with its board), Black Ministers' Retreat, and NEA. These relationships continued for the eight years I served as Deputy.

A major pastoral role was with regions. I served ex officio on the Executive Committee of the Conference of Regional Ministers and Moderators, which met several times a year. I was involved in the program for the Conference almost every year. As I was present with these groups, whether they were functioning in an administrative or program setting, I felt called to focus on relational aspects and developed individual friendships with the regional ministers. During the eight years as Deputy, I traveled to and participated in meetings and events in thirty of the thirty-five regions, including regional assemblies and youth retreats as well as major congregational celebrations such as anniversaries.

Ecumenically, I was one of the Disciples' delegates to the Board of the National Council of Churches and was on its Executive Committee. On a number of occasions, when Ken was tied up, I headed the Disciples delegation to the Board. I served on the Middle Judicatory Commission of the Consultation on Church Union all eight years.

At the meeting in Cincinnati for that group on November 21–22, 1977, I was suddenly called back to Indianapolis because of the tragedy of the Jonestown Massacre.

Jim Jones had been an effective minister in Indianapolis. In fact, he had been a member of the mayor's Committee on Fair Housing. The whole congregation, led by Jim Jones moved west to a farm near San Francisco. They lived as a commune, taking care of each other with the proceeds from the farm. The Commission on the Ministry California/Nevada called Jim Jones to come for an interview concerning some of the things they were hearing about his work. He refused. The Commission made the decision that they could not remove his standing without a personal interview, so they took no action. But again, they called for him to come for an interview, which he ignored. The government was pressing him about taxes and other points of contention. He suddenly took the whole group to Guyana. Again, the Northern California Region called him to return for an interview regarding his standing as a Disciples minister, which he ignored. Then there was "Jonestown." And Jim Jones was identified as a Disciples minister in all the press.

Both Ken and Howard were out of town, and Bob Friedly and I had to handle all the frantic and angry phone calls. Bob handled the calls from the press, and I handled the calls from church people. It was a real baptism by fire for a deputy general minister and president in office just five months.

The other major administrative responsibility was with the Task Force on Renewal and Structural Reform. One key thing for the Assembly was to develop three new categories for business—to be more specific in the types of business to replace the more generic "resolution." We developed the three: (1) a Sense of the Assembly Resolution, (2) an Operation, Policy and Organizational item, (3) and an item for Reflection and Research. We also wrestled with the financial system and the work of allocations to the various parts of the church, the constant and everlasting question with which we struggle. We proposed several changes throughout those eight years in ways the Commission on Finance could work with the regions and units in arriving at their shares. In each case, I shepherded the proposals through the Administrative Committee and the General Board.

JoAnne and I were delighted with her spring vacation from April 1 to 9. We visited John in Cleveland, and then headed to Ithaca, New York, and Cornell. We were able to watch two Cornell varsity baseball games, in very cool weather. Jeff played third base. It was great to watch him play and great to be with him. As it developed, we witnessed his final Cornell athletic event. As he left Cornell that spring, the football coach told him that if he worked hard all summer, staying in shape, he would have a very good chance of being the starting varsity tight end in the fall. However, later that summer he received a letter from Cornell stating that he had not made a C average in his course work, hence he could not come back to Cornell in the fall of 1978. Having been in the Cornell highly regarded School of Hotel Administration for a year, he found jobs in Indianapolis hotels for the next year. He lived at home in Indianapolis until enrolling and attending Indiana University in Bloomington, Indiana, in 1979.

Jeff's credits transferred from Cornell at less than a C, so he wasn't eligible for varsity sports at IU. He raised his grade point in four years at IU but had to get at least a B in his last summer course in order to graduate, which he did, with a major in General Studies. After answering a corporate inquiry, he was employed by the Marriott Corporation as an assistant manager with the Roy Rogers Restaurants in Baltimore, Maryland.

In my relationship with the Division of Overseas Ministries, I was a member of the Japan North American Commission on Mission. Bill Nottingham was secretary for DOM for that part of the world. The next meeting was to be in Tokyo from April 24–27. I flew to San Francisco and stayed one night to break up the trip. On Saturday morning, I came down in the elevator and on my left were Pete Rose and the Reds announcers Marty Brenneman and Joe Nuxhall, the old pitcher. To my right were Geronimo and Dave Concepción. I told Joe Nuxhall, "I remember when you pitched your first game for the Reds." (He was a sixteen-year-old high school student at Hamilton, Ohio. It was during World War II). Pete Rose said, "Nobody's that old!" Then I met Ted Kluszewski in the hall and visited with him. Cool!

Bill Nottingham joined me for the flight to Japan, departing San Francisco at 1:00 p.m. I kept a journal of my trip, which follows:

> The time changes in flight are mind boggling. We left San Francisco at 1:00 PM on Saturday, April 21st. We flew 6 and a half hours at 500 miles an hour and reached the international dateline. We arrived in Tokyo at midnight San Francisco time, 3:00 AM Indy time and 5:00 PM Sunday evening in Tokyo. Boggles!

We were met by Rick and Pat Spears, a young couple from Chicago who finished CTS just the previous summer and were commissioned to Japan. They have a 5-month-old little girl. The three of them met us and we rode the Monorail and then took a taxi through Tokyo to the International House. It was so neat riding above the streets and canals by the Bay of Tokyo on the Monorail, and then zooming through the streets of Tokyo.

They drive on the left side of the road and barrel it! There was less traffic on Sunday so they could move.

We checked in and showered quickly, then went to eat in the dining room with the Spears and Aiji and Kiyo Kamikawa, an American couple of Japanese parents, who have been missionaries in Japan for 29 years. Someone asked me where I had been before my present job, and when Kiyo (Mrs. Kamikawa) heard me say where, she exclaimed, "That's my church!" She was a member of Euclid Avenue from 1942 to 1945 during college days and was there for Dr. Goldner's last three years, and when Dale Fiers preached his first sermon. Holy cow! What a small world it is, even in Japan, sitting there with those folks. We finally went to bed Sunday night at 10:00 PM which was 8:00 AM Sunday morning in Indy.

Monday morning, we had breakfast at the "I" house and then caught taxis to the Japan Christian center. We wandered our way through Tokyo with the city much more active than on Sunday evening: shopkeepers sweeping the sidewalk and curb area; people walking everywhere; bicycles and motorbikes and much more traffic.

We met all morning with the National Christian Council of Japan, equivalent to our National Council of Churches, they, telling us the program they carry on. The United Church of Japan, or Kyodan, while being the majority in the NCIS/J, is joined there by churches not in the Kyodan, such as Lutherans, Episcopalians, and a few others. We spent the morning and had lunch with them. For lunch they brought in these little porcelain stacked boxes with two layers and a top. In the bottom little box was rice and in the top all sorts of little delicacies, including two little, tiny fish, some meatballs, vegetable cooked balls of some kind and a little salad. And of course, there was a cup of tea. We ate with chopsticks. Delightful.

After lunch we changed rooms and went to meet with the Christian Social Work Association. The President, a very handsome man, spoke of their work in Japanese which was translated to us. Most of the denominational execs for Asia/Japan were former missionaries in Japan, so they spoke Japanese. But then the rest of us, including Bill, needed the translation.

At 3:30 we left the Japan Christian Center by taxi to go to a Chinese restaurant to meet with the Council of Schools and their guests for dinner. There were 62 Christian schools in Japan, with a 12-person council as a kind of governing and spokesperson board. They wanted to pull out of a Cooperative Council and were presenting their case to us. The political ferment of the church community there, with some strong factions pushing and pulling was really something.

After dinner we caught a taxi back to the neighborhood of the I House for a reception at a school with all the missionaries in Japan, plus Japanese leaders of the church. I rode in the taxi with three of the denominational execs, people who all speak Japanese. They were chatting with the taxi driver and sharing with me the conversation. Tokyo by night is really bright, with all sorts of signs and lights of all colors and shapes. There were cars, motor bikes, bicycles, and people everywhere!

We returned to the International House at 9:30 PM and visited with the Dean of Union Seminary in Tokyo, a Disciple by background, and a bright young Ph.D. Professor, whom we helped finance in Tübingen, Germany, for graduate study. I went to bed at 10:30 and was dead to the world. Bill said I never bothered him with my snoring.

Tuesday was another day of continuous meetings. The morning was spent with leaders of the Kyodan, The United Church, listening to their report on the status of their work, and current complicated relationships of the Association of Schools and the Christian Social

Work League in an organization where they come together called the Council of Cooperation.

The afternoon and evening were spent with our reports from participating groups, including my report from the Disciples. I sat with Nakajima Musaki, the General Secretary of the Kyodon for the afternoon and evening sessions and for dinner. Early in his career, he was a pastor in Westwood, New Jersey, for three years, as a kind of international intern.

One of the missionaries who came for the meetings, is a man named Harry Burton-Lewis, who graduated from Wesley Seminary with Ed Delong, and sang at North Chevy Chase Church with the seminary singers while we were there. He also knew Barkley Brown well.

We spent the day at the I House in meetings, which was a good stroke of fortune, because it was impossible to get anywhere that day. The streets were jammed with cars because of the strike of railroad and subway workers. Taxis were in real demand, and they said they could barely move in all the traffic. Half of our people were staying at Asia House, which is a mile and a half away, and finally just walked to the meeting.

After the meetings at night, six of us decided we needed a walk. It would be the only time we could see anything in the neighborhood. We walked four blocks down to the main street near us and turned right. About 5 stores down we ran into a very familiar sight—a Baskin-Robbins! I had a double-dipper Jamoca almond fudge. It was much the same as at home. But we decided that was too American, and we needed to find a little Japanese eating culture. We found a little restaurant down a flight of stairs from the sidewalk. The seating was in little booths which looked like pens, with four seats, around a table that had an 18 x 18-inch cooking grill in the middle. We decided we should have noodles and saki. Paul Gregory, the United Church of Christ Asian Chief speaks Japanese, so he ordered the cooked noodles. They brought these spaghetti-kind of noodles and popped them on the grill, mixing in some vegetables and greens, mixing them around as they cooked. They brought us chopsticks and a tray with three little ceramic containers filled with heated saki, with little cups with which to drink. The noodles were good, and we relaxed nicely with a second round of saki!

Wednesday, the Commission was moving to Osaka. We left the I House for the airport at 1:00 PM on a chartered bus. We were very fortunate to get out of Tokyo because there were only four JAL planes flying that day, since the airlines were now on strike. Ours was a big 747, which was chartered by a Travel Agency, and fortunately, included us. We had about 8 other people with us from Tokyo who were on the Missionary Maintenance Committee in charge of the missionaries' housing and questions of salary. Among them was Kiyo Kamikawa, our friend who was a member of the Euclid Avenue church.

Osaka is in the south from Tokyo. It was 70 degrees when we arrived on a bright, clear day. On the way down, we flew by Mount Fujiyama. What a gorgeous sight, with a volcanic top all covered with white snow! We could see it vaguely in the distance from Tokyo the previous morning, which is unusual, they say, because the Tokyo smog usually obscures it. The Korean Christian Church of Japan arranged the bus for us at the Osaka airport to bring us to our hotel.

Osaka is the third largest Japanese city—5 to 6 million people. Industry, homes, and little garden plots are all mixed together, all the way in from the airport.

We didn't see a single open field. Everything was very close together, on top of each other. It was funny to see that every so often along the freeway there were these mammoth nets about 3 stories high and 70 or 80 feet across, surrounding an area about that size. They are golf driving ranges in the middle of the teeming city. There are even very small versions of these enclosed nets, about 12 x 20 feet on rooftops along the way. The city of Osaka is a strange mixture of very old and rickety and ultra-modern, technologically advanced buildings. The "Bullet Train" traveled from there to Tokyo, and got up to 160 miles an hour! I had reservations to ride on it from a town further south back to Osaka early the next Thursday morning to catch a plane to Tokyo and head home.

We arrived at the Hotel Lutheran after slow-going through the crush of rush hour in Osaka, picked up our keys to our room and had 10 minutes till dinner! We each had our own rooms so Nottingham could sleep in peace! My room was very compact. But it was all very new and modern, and everything worked when you deposited two 100 yen coins. Handling money was easy because everything was counted in yen. The exchange rate at the time was 220 yen to 1 dollar. When some of our church reports were written just back in January the dollar was worth 275 yen! So, the decreasing value of the dollar to the yen was really a problem in all our budgetary considerations. We had to raise $90,000 more the following year for Japan just to keep our present missionaries there at the same level they began in the current year. I didn't have a chance to get acclimated that evening because we were due for dinner. After dinner, we went right into meetings on missionary housing and salaries. It developed into quite a discussion, with some of the missionaries on the Missionary Committee taking strong issue with some of the North American Asian Secretaries. The meeting lasted till 10:30.

On Thursday, the day was very moving. We spent the day with the Korean Christian Church of Japan. There are about 650,000 Korean people in Japan who are just kind of "non people" for the Japanese, with raging discrimination against them. We started the morning with worship led by the Moderator of the Korean Christian Church, a pastor from Osaka. Then we heard from a young mother of five. Because she was Korean, she was not allowed to go to public school beyond the 3rd grade. Then she had to go to work to help her family eke out a living. She told how she felt she could trust no one as she grew up, but finally agreed to attend a church. Because of the persistence of people in the church, she became a Christian. But she told of the pain of having to struggle so very hard to overcome her bitterness and hatred of her enemies, but that she had succeeded in doing so. She said that she believed, as a Christian, it was her responsibility not to accept discrimination. Then we heard from the director of the Korean Christian Center, a social service agency in the midst of the Korean community. His story of discrimination was also deeply moving. Then the General Secretary of the Kyodan responded, with a formal, but very moving expression of deep anguish for Japanese oppression. The General Secretary of the Korean Church responded that this was the first formal acknowledgement by the Kyodan at these high levels of official life, that the problem had even been recognized and commitments formally made to seek remedy in the church and Japanese society. It was a remarkable and historic occasion!

We ate at the Hotel Lutheran and then divided into groups of four to visit Korean communities and churches. The small group I was with was taken to a section of Osaka called Morro Bay, where the taxi drivers will not take passengers because it was thought to be a distasteful and dangerous section of town. We went with the General Secretary of the Korean church, who once was pastor there, and met with about five deacons and an elder. Among the laymen was the brother of Kim Chui Hyun, one of the most celebrated prisoners in South Korea in this part of the world. He was suddenly arrested as a spy for North Korea and sentenced to death. Bill Nottingham and others from this Japan North American Commission had recently gone to Washington to persuade our government to intercede on Mr. Kim's behalf, and Mr. Kim's death sentence was commuted. But he remained in prison. His brother spoke very movingly through an interpreter to the four of us from JNAC, thanking us profusely for our work and our prayers which he believed had saved his brother's life. He pleaded for our continuing concern and activity.

On our way back to the Lutheran Hotel in rush hour, we were really in a traffic jam, with cars all around us in line to get on the freeway. The lines in front of us were three and four across as far as we could see. We were just creeping along when I looked up at about 10 cars in front of us and there was a big truck with large letters in English, with the name of a company boldly across the back, one word "FORWARD!" We laughed a lot about that in Korean, Japanese and English!

After a couple of hours in traffic we went to the Korean Christian Center and met till 7:00 sharing all our experiences of the various groups. Then we ate a Korean meal with chopsticks. It was kind of strange. The ladies brought our plates. Then they had all sorts of greetings to the group, which for dinner had been expanded to include many Korean pastors and laypeople and their spouses. I thought to myself, the women at Euclid Avenue would have killed me if I did that after they put the plates on the table and the food was getting cold! After what seemed a long time, we finally took up our chopsticks. All the food was supposed to be cold! The beef was in small slices and was absolutely delicious! There were all sorts of little servings of vegetables. One was some cabbage. I took a bite, and "man alive," it was so highly seasoned! In about two seconds I felt like I was breathing fire. The Koreans and Japanese at the table had just been waiting for me to take a bite and got a big kick out of it. I was sitting next to the President of the Christian Social Work League, Abe Shiro, the fellow who spoke to us on Monday. I spent the day with him in the group of four. What a neat guy! He studied at Union Seminary in New York for a year.

Following dinner, there were more greetings and much singing of folk songs of Koreans who live away from their homeland. One was a haunting tune that I wish I could remember to play and sing on the guitar. We sang it several times through the evening. After all the greetings, there was a Korean dance group which danced for us in very colorful costumes, each of the girls with beautiful pink fans, delicately and beautifully used in graceful movements. After other greetings and farewell, we concluded the evening.

Friday morning, we held the formal meeting of JNAC, setting budgets, next meeting dates. etc. We invited the executive committee to meet the following January in Indianapolis. Our ecumenical partners, whose US offices were on Riverside Drive in New York City or, in the case of the American Baptists in Valley Forge, PA, just outside of Philly, kidded us: "Where is that?" and "Can you really fly to Indianapolis?"

After lunch we had another field trip in Osaka to the Buraku Liberation Center. The "buraku" are outcasts, Japanese people who the aristocracy decided would do the leather tanning, meat slaughtering, human executions, tending of cemeteries, etc. They were declared unclean people, a very low caste, required to live in designated areas of the cities. We spent the afternoon in that section and at the Buraku Center. The plight of these folks was impossibly dire. The Liberation Center worked in support of justice for these people, and provided assistance and support to those who sought to move beyond the buraku status.

That evening we met with the Kanzai Urban Industrial Mission organization. They work with labor unions in helping them know how to organize and work effectively. They also work in evangelism with laboring people. Johnny Walker, a young Disciples missionary came over from Kobe and we ate with him and some newly introduced Japanese leaders.

On Saturday, we met Johnny at the train Depot and took one of the commuter trains to Kyoto—the place everyone says you must see in Japan. Wouldn't you know it though, all week it had been sunny, with blue skies, and today, when we were out and doing some sightseeing for the first time, it was raining. We arrived in Kyoto and took a taxi to the International Center for the Study of Japanese Religions. We met with the director, Dr. Matoshi Doi, a small, wizened, scholarly looking man out of a picture book, that you just knew was a scholar! They have fellows from all over the world who come and live there to study Buddhism, Shinto and all the variations. We spent about an hour with them. Then we went by taxi to the outskirts of Kyoto to an area just under the shadow of one of the surrounding mountains, to the Kanzai Seminar House, a beautiful facility of the group we had met with the day before. It was a very modern facility, a conference and seminar center where people meet about all sorts of things, including technology and society, medical ethics, rights of women, other minority issues, the labor movement, etc.

Behind the very ultramodern building was the original Japanese house, with the Japanese garden and ceremonial tea house! The director, Satoshi Hirata, was a most charming and able man! We took off our shoes when we reached the front door (we did that also at the Korean Church) and put on slippers. Then when we walked into the Japanese garden, doffed slippers and put on a kind of wooden clog. Lovely, lovely garden! Johnnie Walker worked there part-time. He invited JoAnne and me to come and stay there sometime.

Mr. Harata invited us to his home to eat with him and his wife. It was our first time in a Japanese home. We wound through very narrow streets where cars looked like they would hit you head on. Then we went through a Shaji Arch over their section of the city, and to their home. Lunch was waiting. We took off our shoes, put on lovely slippers, and went to the traditional dining room with mats and all. They did have a pit in the floor so your feet could dangle into it, with your slippers off. Over the table was a lovely cloth and a wooden tabletop on top of that. You lifted up the cloth and put your feet and legs under it, put that cloth over your lap, and, lo and behold, there was an electric foot warmer under a grill under your feet. It was a cool day, and it was warm and cozy! Mrs. Harata was an excellent cook. We had shrimp tempura that was out of this world. We used ivory chopsticks. They complemented me on my ability. I wondered if they said that to all their guests. We had all sorts of delicacies with the shrimp, and huge strawberries for dessert—and I mean huge! Johnny said, "This may be a small island, but we make up for it in the size of our strawberries!"

Though Mrs. Harata was a great cook, she wasn't a "typical Japanese housewife" in other ways. She was a graduate social worker and was very active in working for change in women's rights.

After lunch we met Billy Walker, Johnny's wife, at the community center for teaching adults where Billy and Johnny worked.

At about 2:30, we took Johnny to the train to go back to take care of their children in Kobe where they lived. Billy stayed with Bill Nottingham and me to be our guide as we did some sightseeing and some shopping. She took us to see the "Silver Shrine" of Kyoto. It was breathtaking, even though it sprinkled some and was overcast. It was a holiday, the "Emperor's Birthday," so lots of people were in the gardens. Still, it was so peaceful and beautiful.

We ate dinner in a little restaurant, once again, on mats in the old traditional style. Then Billy took us to a theater in which the performance included a flower arrangement done on stage to Japanese music, a dance in traditional costume, and a big puppet performance. Then there was a performance that included a ceremonial tea. Of all things, as part of the performance on a side stage, Billy and I were chosen from the audience to be served! It was quite an experience.

It was time to go back to the train for Osaka. Billy was returning to Kobe. When we got to Osaka, Bill and I had our first experience trying to communicate to a taxi driver that we wanted to go to the Hotel Lutheran. We had little success at first, until another Japanese person who spoke English helped us. The following day, Bill preached and we moved down to Hiroshima for two nights.

On Sunday morning, Bill tried to call me. They told him that I had left the day before, checked out! He finally figured out where I was, after knocking on the door where they thought I was. They had me in the wrong room the whole four days! There was a big discussion with the desk clerk, between me in English and him in broken English about my not having my bill taken care of on Saturday night by the JNAC Treasurer. They insisted I owed them 3,800 yen. I finally paid it and got a receipt with someone else's name on it: Jack McIntosh, a Canadian missionary of the Presbyterian Church. Bob Nordyke from the US Council of Churches, who was shepherding us on this trip, arrived to get us to go to the church where Bill was preaching. He worked on the problem in Japanese. After a long discussion they straightened it out, and I got my 3,800 yen back. But we were running late for the Korean Church Service. Jack was tooling along through a wide thoroughfare with little traffic. We looked up ahead, and about a block away, 6 policemen with flags came into the middle of the street. I thought maybe a holiday parade was coming across the intersection, and they were waving us to pull around the corner. But that was definitely not it! It was a speed trap! We were clocked and pulled over! We pulled around the corner into a line of cars. Jack had to get out and go over to a regular kind of "patio court" they had set up and were processing all the speeders. There would be a fine. He was doing 25 kilometers over the limit and would have his license taken away for a month. We really felt bad! It took a while for Jack to get through the court. When we reached the Korean church, the service had just begun. As we came in, they were singing "Holy, Holy, Holy" in Korean of course. The service was much like ours in order of worship. Jack sat next to me and explained what was going on. Among other things, when the offering came, I noticed there was definitely a women's side and a men's side. In fact, women deacons took the offering on the women's side and men, on the men's side. Jack said that in Korean life, the women could not even sit in the same room with the men in meetings. The church was the first place where women ever sat with the men, and at first, they even hung a curtain down the middle of the sanctuary. Later they were able to take the curtain down. That day, there were some younger married women sitting with their husbands on the men's side. People wore their shoes in the church, but when the pastors and Bill went onto the chancel, they put on slippers. They asked me to bring greetings. The slippers were used up, so I went into the chancel in my stocking feet! There were two padded mats behind the pulpit. Preaching is going to the mat, as they say!

There was a mother and father there that day, with a baby they were bringing to church for the first time. The custom was for the mother to bring the child to the chancel for the pastor to give a special prayer of blessing.

I spoke in English when I brought greetings, and Sam Choi translated into Korean. They also had a person in another room translating into Japanese from Korean. The translation was going to a number of people in the congregation who had earplugs and a wireless transistor to hear the Japanese. When I said something that amused them, some caught on and chuckled when I spoke the English, then some with the Korean translation, and then a little later, some with the Japanese. Three chuckles on the same line is pretty good! Bill preached an excellent sermon.

We ate with the congregation after the service. We had rice and highly seasoned little strips of dried fish, along with soup with peas and noodles. The people were most gracious. Jack Macintosh then took us to the train depot where we caught the bullet train to Hiroshima. It was a wonderful ride sometimes up to 160 miles an hour. The tracks are all elevated so you cross no roads or streets, and they can really roll!

We were going from Osaka further west and a bit south, through some of the best agricultural areas in the country. I saw fields with farmers out with cultivators and small tractors working the fields. I thought of our garden at home. They make their rows mounted with little ditches between them where they run in the water. Then there were the flooded rice paddies where in their straw hats farmers were wading along transplanting the rice plants. It could have been in another century. There was such a combination of the ultramodern and the ancient in Japan.

We arrived in Hiroshima and took a taxi to our hotel. It was really good to have Bob Northrop with us, because he speaks Japanese.

Hiroshima!!! I cannot believe it! A city where every building in the city is new. I could not believe I was there! But I feared it would become a heavy burden on my heart!

The sun came up that Monday morning over Hiroshima, just as it did on Aug 6, 1945. But unlike that day of the Enola Gay, when at 8:15 AM from three blossoming parachutes there suddenly erupted a new fireball, with an epicenter of 7,000 degrees centigrade, marking the dawn of a new era. The sun that May day would caress the abundant azaleas of Hiroshima, set in the new city, the Phoenix arisen.

We went to the Peace Memorial Hall and watched as the motion picture before us told the grim and deathly devastation of the atom bomb of August 6, 1945. The place where we were sitting was under the epicenter of the bomb where the ground the temperature was 7,000 degrees centigrade! Thirteen-and-a-half square kilometers were obliterated, and fires and radiation raged beyond so that the whole city was destroyed. 200,000 people died instantly, cremated, some with no remains to be found. But they were the fortunate ones! We saw the makeshift hospitals where children, adults and old people were treated. Eighty percent of all the nurses in the 450,000 population had been killed. Doctors who were still alive, many of them terribly burned, were treating horrible burns on countless others. The tears flowed down my cheeks at the hell of human suffering.

I fought nausea as the horror of survival was documented before our eyes, with days and weeks bringing sudden unexplained death to mothers and children from the "bomb sickness." The movie ended, but not the burden of what we had seen. The final understated words kept ringing in my ears. After seeing all this hell of suffering and death, then word came: "And now, we have bombs with a force of 2,500 times as powerful as this Atom bomb." We could scarcely move or speak.

Almost unable to speak, except tor exclamations of pain, we filed through the museum viewing the evidence of the madness of nuclear war. We stood above the museum's diorama of the city of Hiroshima with the graphic portrayal of its destruction.

We walked among the monuments to the children, to the teachers, to the mothers, and to the people. The A Bomb Dome stood skeletal against the blue sky in the midst of the steel and glass of the new city, surviving in its broken form as sole witness to the catastrophe. Can it really be that we seriously argue whether we have enough nuclear weapons? It is absolutely insane!

Hiroshima, the event, became even more poignant because of our experiences here with people yesterday and today. Sunday evening when we arrived by train, we taxied to the Hiroshima Central Hotel. There was not an old building around! We were soon met at the hotel by two missionaries, Mary McMillan and Doris Hartman, and Mary's Minister, Pastor Sonehara. Mary has been in Japan for 37 years, with the Methodist Board. She came to Hiroshima in 1936 to teach in The Hiroshima Girls School, "Jogakuin," and was here until March of 1941, when the US Denominational Boards, in conference with one another, brought their Missionaries home to North America. She is from

Florida and spent the war years in the US. What grief and anguish she bore on August 6th, 1945, when the Hiroshima Jogakuin was destroyed and 320 girls and 20 faculty, her beloved friends and colleagues were killed instantly in the A-bomb fireball. She came back as soon as she could after the war, in 1946, and has taught English, Latin and has been a counselor in the college ever since. She is 65 and will teach two more years and then go home. As you might well guess, she is active in the peace movement!

Doris Hartman is the Pastor of a new Japanese congregation. She has her M.R.E. from Hartford seminary, and an M.Div. from Union. She's been here about 17 years. She has worked with congregations of the Kyodan all that time, and now is pastor of this new congregation.

After dinner Doris took Bob, Bill, and me to the World Friendship House of Hiroshima, where people can come and meet and stay overnight, who are involved in study, discussion or concern with the cause of peace. It was begun by Barbara Reynolds, who with her husband owned the "ketch," *The Phoenix*, which sailed into the areas of Russian and American nuclear testing in protest, was towed out, with the Reynolds being held for their actions. They publish a bulletin which addresses itself to nuclear disarmament and peace. The Director is currently an American from Philadelphia, Maureen Parker. We spent about 2 hours visiting with Mrs. Parker, who will be leaving later this year. There is an American Mennonite couple now in Japanese language training school in Tokyo who will be taking the position later this year.

Today after our stunned sojourn in the museums and among the monuments, Doris Hartman met us and drove us to Nihon Kurosutokyodan Hiroshima Ushita Church, where we met Mrs Sonahara and the Sonahara children. We sat in the beautiful Chapel of the Ushita Church in our slippers, read the church bulletin, and listened to the lovely little three stop German pipe organ, all self-contained, as Mary played hymns. It was much needed after the day's shocking jolt. We went into the Sonahara apartment, above the other buildings of the church complex, which also houses the Christian kindergarten for 140 children. Families in the neighborhood are on a waiting list to get into the excellent kindergarten, of which pastor Sunahara is also the Director. He is a brilliant young Pastor, with an excellent grasp of theology, with a library of classical theology that would be rare in an American pastor's study!

We went to dinner with Pastor Sonahara in a Japanese restaurant, with all the delights of raw fish and a "tempura" dinner. Shrimp and delicate little vegetables were all done with tempura "deep style" cooking. I prudently took the side against the wall and leaned, as we talked theology, with Bob Northrup and Doris interpreting. After a stroll back to the church, we came back to the hotel and had some refreshments...and wrote to President Jimmy Carter and Secretary of State Cyrus Vance, with all the fervor we could muster, hoping that the Hiroshima postmark would underscore our plea for nuclear disarmament! It is time to end nuclear madness!

Tuesday morning brought Reverend Sonahara to the Central Hotel for a morning visit to the State University of Hiroshima, where Bob talked with a distinguished faculty member involved in an Institute for University development in Asia. Bob wanted information to pass on to International Christian University. From there we went to see the Radiation Research Center on top of one of the surrounding mountains, and then on to Hiroshima Jogakuin Christian College.

There we met with the President of the College, Morsoyuki Imaishi, and a lovely lady, Dr. Hamako Herose, President Emeritus. Dr. Imaishi's secretary brought in tea, as they have done everywhere we visited in an office. We bowed and exchanged our cards. Another oft repeated ceremony. We had a delightful visit. We learned that Jogakuin College is 92 years old, with the current enrollment of 1,200 students in this new location on one of the many mountain sides that surround the city. The High School and Junior High are downtown in the old location, with 700 girls enrolled in each. The girls in the school were moving about the campus. They were lovely, friendly, and charming. And to think that in August 1945, our A-bomb killed 320 girl students just like these, and 20 faculty members. We walked the path further up the mountain to the garden, where the Ashes of those young girls and teachers mingle in memorial, midst the lovely blooming azaleas.

After lunch Pastor Sonahara delivered us to the Jugakuin High School where we met Bill Baldwin, Canadian Episcopal Missionary who is the Rector of the Parish of Hiroshima and overseer of "Serendipity," a Coffee House, 40 miles away in Iwakuni. We needed some kind of emotional release from the "heavy stuff" we had been through, and his car provided it. It was a tiny little station wagon. Our invalid, Nottingham, with his phlebitis, of course, had to sit in front with Bill Baldwin. That left the back seat, and three inches between for Bob Northrup and me. Claustrophobia!! Pain! And much joking and laughter! Riding with Bill Baldwin in his green bug was like Camino Soto, "the village of the turtle," for we were "those who creep slowly." The traffic and Bill's light foot made the 40 miles West on jammed roads an experience. But the scenery was great, for we traveled the edge of the Inland Sea, with mountain islands across the channel of water, pontoon platforms dotting the bays where oysters are cultured and grown, and fishermen plying the channel with their little old boats. I was watching one such boat as we were stopped in the line of traffic, when suddenly the fisherman came rushing out of his little cabin, the inside of which was suddenly and completely engulfed in flames. He began furiously to drop a bucket in the sea, fill it and dash it on the flames. Other boats came rallying around as the plumes of white smoke billowed from the oily cabin. As traffic moved us on, we watched helplessly as it appeared the poor fisherman might lose the vehicle enabling his livelihood. We'll never know what became of him.

It was a sunny, breezy day and with Children's Day later this week (May 5th) the Japanese custom of flying the colorful paper kite like carp from a mast outside the homes, makes the countryside even more colorful. The tradition is to fly one for each child, so they say you can tell the number of children in the household by the flying fish.

We arrived at "Serendipity." "Oh, shoot, are we already here?" says I. Ooh!! I waddled around like one of the little old bent over Japanese farm ladies!

"Serendipity" is sponsored jointly by the National Council of Churches of Christ in the USA in affiliation with the National Christian Council of Japan as a coffee house just outside the gate of Iwakuni US Marine Base, where we have a Fighter Wing based with 3,000 Marines. "Serendipity" is there for those young Marines away from home. The program Directors are Douglas McArthur, and his wife, Robyn. How about that. He has returned!

While we were there for about four hours several of the young Marines wandered in and we drank coffee and talked with them about many things. One of our Disciples Chaplains is stationed here at Iwakuni, Commander Joseph D. Cox. Doug phoned him on the base. I talked with him, suggesting we get together, and we decided it would be easier if he came to "Serendipity". He did—on his bicycle. We talked about him and his family, his work, and the church. He grew up in San Angelo, Texas, a block and a half from Joy Livingston Dodson, my sister-in-law. His older brother dated Joy during high school days! Holy smokes!

After dinner we took the train back to Hiroshima, rather than the green turtle!

Incident: Tuesday morning we ran into a guy staying at the hotel who was from Panama. We had read that Jamie Rios, former junior flyweight champion of the world, was in Hiroshima to fight the champion, a Japanese boxer on Sunday, May 7th. In Spanish, Bill asks this guy about it, and he said yes, he was here to fight on Sunday. So, I opened my little black book to Leon Spinks autograph (Leon Spinks was the heavyweight champion of the world and I had run into him in the airport parking lot at Hilton Head and got his autograph). So, I rub Leon Spinks autograph with my fingers and rubbed his shoulder. Bill says, "Why don't you get his autograph beside Leon Spinks?" So, I asked him to sign my book which he proudly does. I thanked him as we left and wished him well. When we got outside, I looked at my book and there is his autograph—Luis Urriola! Incredible! Luis Urriola indeed! Goodnight! Desecration! It wasn't Jamie Rios.

We arrived back at the Hiroshima Central Hotel after the train from Iwakuni. Who should walk in but the real Jaime Rios! You could tell. He had his name across his shirt. Bill heard our old friend Luis Urriola, say in Spanish, "There he is! That's the guy!" Whereupon the ex-champ (and champ to be, he confidently predicts, according to *The Japan Times* comes over and wants to see my date book and Leon Spinks' autograph. I obliged, and the real Jamie Rios autographed my book—right under Luis Urriola and Leon Spinks! Go Luis! I mean Jamie!

We finally had a leisurely day on May 3. We wandered around Hiroshima, shopping and enjoying the many people on the street for another holiday, Golden Day! Had fruit and coffee for lunch and then we went to a nearby park that was absolutely exquisite! It was named for a special tea that grows there, and was being ceremonially picked, "ground" by kneading, then brewed and served to all of us. There was a ceremonial tea, then, with all the Japanese costumes of yesteryear.

We left Hiroshima, but Hiroshima will never leave me! What a lovely spot in the world—such beauty out of such awesome tragedy!

We wound our way West by train to the southernmost island, Kyushue, to Kokura this afternoon. We have managed to work our way some 625 miles west of Tokyo in our travels. With my meager knowledge of geography in Japan, I never dreamed you could go 600 miles west of Tokyo, and still be on land. We met with the Korean Christian Church in Kokuro. It was a time of heartbreaking testimony of discrimination as we met with their leaders in the winding, back streets of the city. We were delivered to the hotel by a German speaking Japanese, who has married a Korean wife.

I'm tired, and it is 12:30, but I am packed and eager to go home. I have had my mind expanded beyond imagination, my emotions stirred wildly with pain, my horizons to Japan and the world lifted beyond description. I dearly love Japan. But I dearly love home, and I am ready to go.

In the morning I awaken at 5:15 AM and will travel for over 24 hours by Shin Kansan, or Bullet Train to Osaka, some 300 miles; by plane to Tokyo, some 300 plus miles; by air to San Francisco, some 5,800 miles; and by air to Indianapolis some 3,000 miles. 9,640 miles in one day! Unbelievable!

I am so glad to be home with JoAnne! But immediately, we are off to Niles, Ohio, on the weekend for our niece Jill Thorp's wedding. Great family time.

The Seminary Study Committee had its penultimate meeting, without their staff representative, while I was in Japan. That raised Howard Dentler's eyebrows a bit. They presented the report then to seminary heads for comment in Indianapolis before the General Board meeting, June 17–20.

Meanwhile, we drove to Allegheny College for Debbie's graduation weekend. We picked up Mother Trimbur on the way. It was a thrill to see Debbie complete her college undergraduate work, with all the pomp and circumstances of graduation. Debbie had been dating Greg Long for some time her senior year. She let us know that it was very serious. However, they wanted to be sure they would have a successful marriage, so they would live together to find out if they were compatible. They were moving into the Cleveland Heights apartment rented by John in his first year in law school.

During the spring when I had been in Cleveland for a speaking engagement, John and I had dinner out downtown. He was very excited as he announced that after completing his first year of law school, he would take a year off and go to the Virgin Island's Saint Croix for a year's sabbatical. He was more excited than I was, wondering how that would turn out with regard to money in the islands and his finishing law school. He was a waiter in a fine restaurant in University Circle working to support himself in law school. We had established with our children that we would pay their expenses for undergraduate school, but they would need to support themselves in graduate school. We had accomplished that with John and Deb, primarily with JoAnne's teaching salary. For three years, John and Deb were both in college. John assured us he would return and complete his law degree and would find a job when he got to the Virgin Island's Saint Croix. He had saved enough for a round trip ticket to Christiansted. Our stipulation was that he be sure to save the return ticket as security till he was coming home.

Deb and Greg shared the apartment with John for the summer, then sublet the apartment from John for the year. Debbie was applying for a French teaching job in the greater Cleveland area. Greg, who had great ambitions as a lawyer, found a job in a hamburger place, "Yours Truly."

John left for Saint Croix in the fall. As he arrived in Christiansted, it was not yet the "high season." Jobs were scarce. His money ran out. He cashed in his return ticket. Finally, in the nick of time he got a job as a bartender to keep life and limb together.

Subsequently John met a lawyer who invited him to join his firm as a clerk. So John was fortunate to have income and experience with the law. Before he left Saint Croix, the attorney invited him to come back and join his firm after graduating from law school.

I had good experiences with five constituency gatherings in June, July, and August. The first was with the Church Women's CWF Quadrennial. Every four years 7,000 Disciples women gather at Purdue University, with outstanding programs and speakers, stretching our Disciples women's world view of the mission of the church. JoAnne had attended one of the first of these.

The second was the Division of Homeland Ministry's Department of Church and Society happening downtown on the Circle. It was a gathering to protest apartheid in South Africa. The crowd of people were holding signs of protest, and I spoke about the church's support of Nelson Mandela's African National Congress.

The third constituency was the Disciples Youth Congress gathering of Disciples' CYF from across the church at the University of Nebraska in Lincoln. I was there with my guitar to lead some of the singing for the 250 teenagers. It was my introduction to our outstanding youth leaders.

Flying home from Lincoln it was another weekend family wedding, this time in Bellefontaine, Ohio. Our niece Kim Spangler wed Greg Bachman, a great addition to our family.

The fourth was Adult Conference in Ohio. Laypeople in Ohio churches had a great tradition of friendship and commitment and gathered each summer at Otterbein College for four days of study, worship, and inspiration. In my Euclid Avenue years, I had been on the faculty each year. I led a class on worship and celebration and one year was the vesper preacher. JoAnne and I were there together this year, 1978. I was back as the vesper preacher, enjoying old friendships, and making new friends.

The fifth was the Assembly of the National Convocation in Little Rock, Arkansas. The Convocation is the African American Disciples constituency. Ken and I sat with the Executive Committee, which meets for a day before the Assembly. It was my opportunity to be with some people I had come to know and really expand my relationship with many Disciples. I also could experience the culture and worship style of our African American Disciples and be with them.

At the July General Board meeting, I completed my first year as Deputy General Minister and President. I had truly developed relationships with general and regional leaders of the church. Along the way I had an expanded knowledge and friendships with Disciples layfolk.

The year had been a blessing for me with my leadership. For JoAnne, my frequent trips away were times of adjustment and loneliness. I missed her and home too, but I was always with people in activities, which was so different than her being home alone. It helped that she was teaching and making some new friends among the faculty, at church, and in the neighborhood garden club. But I was always so glad to come home to her for our reunions.

We marked the year with another trip to Chicago for the General Board, with a beautiful hotel suite.

The last week of August was our first week of Sarasota family vacation at the beach of Siesta Key. We were infected with Sarasota fever that would last a lifetime.

In the fall, I was exposed to the mission financing "system" of the Disciples with the meeting of the Commission on Budget Evaluation. All the heads of the general units, regions and representatives of higher education were gathered at the Essex Hotel in Indianapolis. Dan Loving, a dentist from Dumas, Texas, was chair of the Commission. He and his wife Mary Lee Loving were good friends of Ken Teegarden. Dan had been Moderator of the Southwest Region when Ken was regional minister there, just prior to his election as GMP in 1973. We had met the Lovings at an election celebration then. One evening of the week of these meetings, the Lovings were our guests at Surrey Hill Circle. They would become good friends for years to come, with our visiting them in Dumas. Dan would be elected Vice Moderator of the General Assembly in San Antonio.

One of the key elements in our Disciples life is the church's recruitment and education of our ministerial candidates on their way to ordination. One of my treasured experiences in my Ohio years was being a member of the Ohio Disciples Commission on Ministry and meeting, interviewing, and relating to the college and seminary students "under care" of the Commission. The general church's part in this was through our colleges, universities and seminaries. But a feature of this was the Middlers' Seminarians Conference. With the ministerial candidates halfway through seminary, we provided the opportunity for them to be exposed to the function and work of the general units.

The seminarians gathered first in St. Louis on September 26, 1978, for time with our St. Louis general units: the Division of Higher Education, National Benevolent Association, and the Christian Board of Publication. I was there to greet them and participate with them. They were in St. Louis for two days, then on to Indianapolis and the Missions Building. There I had the privilege of welcoming the seminarians with an opening session.

With the help of Neil Topliffe, I developed a parody of our work in Missions Building with a series of slides in which I fell in a creek while playing golf. Then we got serious.

Each of the Indianapolis general units presented their work—from Homeland Ministries to Overseas Ministries to our financial units and the Pension Fund. I mixed with the students for two more days, which was most enjoyable, and made memorable contacts for the next thirteen years.

A fun thing the first Saturday in October was to be the guests of Howard and Mary Lou Dentler at a Purdue-Wake Forest football game in West Lafayette. JoAnne and I were really enjoying our friendship with Howard and Mary Lou.

It was time again for the Administrative Committee meeting—on my birthday, October 26, in Indianapolis. When I was elected Deputy, two years before, I had some idea about the work and responsibility of the Deputy position but didn't really know the extent of events and meetings from one to the next. I wondered when I considered the job, how I would enjoy constant work in the office and sitting in meetings, especially as I had come to meetings in Indy, then had come back to the parish and had to adjust from traveling and the meetings. In the pastorate there was a nice variety: in the office in the mornings, out calling in the afternoons. I was usually home for lunch and made a point to be home for dinner with the family. Many evenings were for group meetings and pastoral calling. In my work as Deputy, I found that the many meetings and interactions with the people involved was stimulating. I seemed to have adjusted to the travel. And one of the really positive elements was that when I was working in the office and in Indy, my evenings were free to be at home with JoAnne. This position was the right one for me!

I accepted an invitation to preach on the outskirts of Augusta, Georgia, and to be with the congregation for four nights, Sunday through Wednesday night. I stayed in an economy motel, and the minister and I ate many meals at IHOP. For evening dinner, we were hosted by families with delicious southern meals. It was a treat to get to know the folks over four days. He and I made some pastoral calls together. I have to admit my acceptance of this preaching event, somewhat like southern churches' evangelistic meetings, had something to do with the location of the Augusta National Golf Course. I was hoping somehow to get to view the clubhouse and the Amen Corner of the Masters Tournament. I was rewarded. A gentleman in the church worked for Coca Cola. He supplied all the Coca Cola for the tournament and for the club when it was open. He took me on a tour of the course. I stood in the famous spot at the Amen Corner, where you can see the three crucial 15th, 16th and 17th holes. Wow!

On Thursday morning, having finished my preaching the night before, I flew to Fort Worth, Texas, for a meeting of the Disciples Council on Theological Education of the Division of Higher Education. It met from 1:00 on Thursday through lunch on Friday. I left before lunch on Friday and flew to Hutchinson, Kansas, for the Kansas Regional Assembly. Ronnie Reed was the Kansas regional minister and an old friend from Ohio. He had been the minister in Kent when my sister Mary had gone to Kent State, and lived with the Reeds in the parsonage. I preached on Sunday morning and after the Sunday lunch banquet flew home.

The next day I met with the Division of Homeland Ministries Board through Wednesday. Thursday, I drove with Ian McRae to Chicago for the Hoover Lectures at the Disciples Divinity House at the Center for Continuing Education of the University of Chicago, then home in the same day.

On Friday, I had an early flight with Ken and Howard to St. Louis for Saturday and Sunday meetings of the Local Arrangements Committee for the 1979 St. Louis General Assembly. Howard had developed an amazing organizational plan for the help of some 800 volunteer Disciples in the location of an Assembly. I would now develop the program and worship elements from the local arts and music resources, working with the stage union for the staging technology. We were in worship at one of the St. Louis

Disciples churches with meetings in the afternoon and then home.

It was some November, but it gives an idea about life as the Deputy GMP. December had much less travel to out-of-town meetings and events, with the exception of the first week in St. Louis for the annual Conference of Regional Ministers and Moderators.

We joined Northwood Christian Church. Paul Stauffer was a good preacher and the music program was outstanding. We enjoyed the Home Builders Class and made friends there. I taught the class occasionally, as did Lester Palmer. JoAnne served as chair of the Education Committee and the Worship Committee. She was also a deaconess. I was an elder, serving on Sunday morning and taking communion to shut-ins scheduled around my travel.

My year of 1979 began in St. Louis, working with Mary Jane Shoop, wife of Minister William Shoop. She knew the music resources of St. Louis. Among St. Louis's music personalities was Russ David, a member of Webster Groves Christian Church. Among other things, he had composed the famous tune accompanying the Budweiser Percheron horses towing the beer van, which was Budweiser's signal TV ad. We would work together extensively. The Shoops' daughter was a student at TCU and a modern dance performer we would use in worship. Bill, Mary Jane, and their daughter would become good friends. We made progress on powerful opening night music ideas, with brass, organ, and ideas for an all-St. Louis Disciples choir, which would rehearse ahead of time, singing Friday night and Wednesday night, opening and closing the Assembly.

April was a unique month as the Deputy GMP's schedule was unfolding. The first week was JoAnne's spring break vacation which we spent together. I had a meeting at Christmount Christian Center the weekend of the 31st, so JoAnne came with me to Black Mountain, North Carolina, and we spent our week at Christmount, enjoying North Carolina folk life.

We came back and I worked in the office and came home for dinner in the evenings, until the last weekend. There was much to do designing the program and worship for the October Assembly and recruiting personnel to fill the roles. It was my full responsibility.

On the 27th, I flew to Tucson for the Arizona Regional Assembly, Friday through Sunday. It was a Sunday of the change to daylight saving time. At the United Airlines departure desk, they gave me the wrong departure time. Sitting in the airport reading, when I returned to depart, the flight for Indy had departed. I had an important meeting on Monday morning at Mission's Building. What to do?

Well, United sent me on a flight to Los Angeles, where I had to wait for the midnight flight to Indy, arriving very early in the morning at 6:00. I disciplined my way through the Monday meeting on the ministry.

The large May event was the May 24–26 graduation exercises at Bethany College, in Bethany, West Virginia. Bill Tucker, my friend, who was President of Bethany, had invited me to give the baccalaureate sermon. JoAnne and I drove to Bethany for a wonderful weekend. I gave my sermon on Friday evening. On Saturday, the commencement was celebrated, in which I was given a Doctor of Divinity honorary degree. JoAnne's brother Bill and his wife, Nancy, brought Mother Trimbur to the commencement to witness the honors. The parties and receptions around the events were most enjoyable. The President's home, Gresham House, is absolutely stunning. Jean Tucker, Bill's wife, was a delightful lady and a fine leader in her own right, serving at one point as Moderator of the Division of Overseas Ministries.

My time was filled with preaching at a number of locales across the country, meeting with constituency groups, including the Japan North America Commission on Mission at Stony Point, New York. In the office I worked on details for the program and worship for the October Assembly. This time, I still was responsible as the Program Director, with all the production details, but now with responsibilities to design the program and worship and recruit participants. I really enjoyed the freedom to design and plan worship for seven thousand people.

It happened that the North American Christian Convention, the "Independent" church's gathering was also in St. Louis in the assembly hall we would be using, July 24–23. I wanted to see how they produced their program and worship, with their stage setup, projected images, and how effective their sound system was. I went to their convention for two days of observation. Then I was staying in St. Louis for the General Board, with resolutions to consider for the General Assembly. JoAnne joined me for the week.

For the General Board, we worked through the resolutions following the '77 Assembly on questions of the church, the Bible, and the theology of salvation, etc. I don't have the details to relate.

The first weekend in October was "Pope worthy." On Friday the 5th, I flew to Des Moines for the Regional Assembly of the Upper Midwest. Their theme was "Christ's Church for These Times." I gave the Saturday morning sermon and the after-dinner speech that evening. The request for the latter was "25 minutes, pointed but light."

Immediately after being "pointed but light," I caught a flight. This was the first time Pope John Paul II had come to the US. He had just held a mass for thousands on a farm in Iowa. The next day he was to be in a prayer service at a women's college in Washington, D.C. and then a mass on the Capitol Mall. I was to be a Disciples representative in the prayer service. My commitment in Des Moines was longstanding, and the Pope presence was a "drop in." (That was the story of my fourteen years in the office of the General Minister and President; appearances and speaking engagements well spread out on the calendar, but "drop ins" clogging up my out-of-town calendars.)

To get to the prayer service, I had to fly to Cleveland, sleep for a few hours in an airport motel, and then catch a 5:30 a.m. flight to Washington. Some teenagers, fellow passengers, were loudly and joyfully proclaiming in the Cleveland airport, "We're going to see the Pope!" Me too, I thought.

When I arrived at the Saint Mary's College in Washington, I discovered I was going to be with the Pope. Growing out of our official dialogue with Rome, we were invited to participate in the service. Ken Teegarden had been in events the day before, but had a conflict on Sunday, asking me to be our representative.

Other churches had representatives as well. We robed up and waited. I visited with the Secret Service Agent there to see about the Pope's safety. The Pope was delayed in another meeting. I didn't say the Pope was late. I'm reminded of a story of a local parish where an older Italian woman cooked and cared for the priest and really supervised the Father. One Sunday morning he was slow in getting to the sanctuary for the first mass. The Italian woman was fretting as time went by. When the priest appeared finally, the woman said, "Father you're late!" And the Priest replied, "Oh, has the mass begun?"

The Pope was not late! The mass had not begun. Berobed as we were, we finally gathered on the sidewalk awaiting his arrival. On both sides of the wide walkway leading to the chapel, bleachers were set up. They were filled, I think primarily with college-aged young people. They gave a mighty cheer as John Paul II exited a limousine. We joined the Pope in the procession and accompanied him to the chancel, seated there surrounding him, for the service of prayer. He gave the sermon in English, an aid handing him a manuscript. We joined him in the recessional and stood on the sidewalk. The students in the bleachers were repeatedly cheering, "John Paul II, we love you!" He came over toward me, we shook hands as I said, "God bless you." Paul Stauffer, there representing the Council on Christian Unity and our Disciples/Roman Catholic Dialogue said, "We are the Disciples of Christ, and it's good to see you again." The Pope replied, "Ah yes, last year in Rome." In a minute, I thought to myself, "My goodness, I just blessed the Pope with my GMP ring." (Which by the way, Ken had given to me by tossing it on my TWA seat tray table.)

With the St. Louis General Assembly, we began for the first time with image magnification, arranged and managed by Neil Topliffe. He became more and more involved with the program production and management through Anaheim in 1981 and by San Antonio in 1983. Because I had expanded responsibilities in the GMP office, he became the Program Director.

The prelude was organ and brass, with the Visual and Performing Arts High School Brass Ensemble. With the theme, "Proclaim Christ Lord," it was followed by dual pianos, "Jesu, Joy of Man's Desiring," with Pat and Kendra Noe, Moderator Judge Jim Noe's wife and daughter. Judge Noe called the Assembly into being. The introit followed with the St. Louis All-Assembly Choir and the Brass Ensemble performing "Thou Art God," where near the finale, the congregation joins in with the choir and brass, singing, "Oh God our help in ages past…" The ascription followed, in unison from the Preamble of the Design:

"As members of the Christian Church, We Confess that Jesus is the Christ, the Son of the living God…We Proclaim Christ Lord."

The processional was the All-Assembly Choir and Brass presenting, "Enter His Sanctuary Singing." The whole seven thousand individuals, accompanied by organ, the brass, and the choir, then joined in singing, "Come Christians, Join to Sing," a great hymn. The Assembly was off to a celebratory and powerful beginning. (Mary Jane Shoop and I had worked to put it together, and it was thrilling).

Sunday evening the worship theme was the International Year of the Child. On the program was printed the UN Declaration of the Rights of the Child. After a Woodwind Ensemble, augmented with a double string quartet of the St. Louis Youth Symphony, which was beautiful, the arena went dark for the call to worship. On the large screen it showed elderly people in a nursing home, seated in a circle, all sitting, slumped over and asleep. Into the room burst an invasion of young children carrying daffodils, who presented the flowers to all the elderly. They came alive with laughter and joy, with the children dancing around in delight.

After the excerpt was the solo, "Come as a Child." The houselights came up, and 125 children scattered around the arena and around the worshippers handing out daffodils. The mood was one of delight. Then came the congregational hymn, "Come as a Child." Following Litanies of Confession, Robert Zimmer, first violinist in the Cleveland Orchestra, accompanied by Betty Zimmer, pianist (both members of Euclid Avenue Christian Church), were instrumental liturgists. After the Litanies of Reconciliation and Assurance, Bob and Betty played again.

The address was given by Jean Childs Young of New York City, chairperson of the UN International Year of the Child and wife of Andrew Young. The postlude was by the ensembles of the St. Louis Youth Symphony. It was a powerful evening. Mary Jane Shoop had secured the musical groups. I worked with a laywoman from Union Avenue Church, who recruited 125 children to participate. We had a rehearsal late Monday afternoon. I had the children each with a parent scatter about the arena. I told them that after the solo, the house lights would come on. I told them they would have flowers and should burst around giving the daffodils to people. They should be in these same seats at 7:15 p.m. with flowers they had picked up in room 628 at 6:30. They performed beautifully.

We had the Jarvis College Choir in the Assembly on Saturday evening. We had the Eureka College Choir on Monday evening for the worship. The Shoops' daughter was a lead liturgical dancer in the dance company leading the opening of the Monday evening service. With the theme, "Christ is Lord for Peace and Justice," the address was given by Dom Helder Camara, Archbishop of the Roman Catholic Diocese of Recife and Olinda, Brazil, a world leader for peace and justice.

Thursday evening, the prelude was by Russ David's Dixieland Band, with Robert Kintner, the Assembly organist. Russ was a fine composer and musician who brought together his musician friends for this special occasion. At one point he thought Tex Beneki was going to join them. Tex had been one of the key soloists in the iconic Glenn Miller Band, and was then the leader of the continuing Miller band. I was so excited about that, but it didn't work out. At any rate, Russ David and his "Dixielanders" brought the Assembly to swinging life. They accompanied the hymn singing. After the address by Governor Robert D. Ray of Iowa, member of University Christian Church in Des Moines, Russ David's band then played the postlude, and with the encouragement of the crowd kept going. Several of us, JoAnne, and I included began jitterbugging between the stage and the front row of seats. We were joined by many more, and a great time was had by all. Thank you, Russ! He and I had had lunch several times leading up to the Assembly and became friends.

We closed the Assembly on Wednesday night, with the All-St. Louis Assembly Choir and Fred Craddock preaching.

From all the months of details of designing worship, bringing so many people together, working with many volunteers – especially Mary Jane Shoop with the local music participants, and Robert Kintner, Guy Aydelott, Brett Stratton and Ladonna Gooden – it all came together in a wonderful way. And I made lifetime friends.

I included lots of details here as examples of my work as Deputy General Minister in my role with the GMP.

In November, we commenced the two-year cycle looking toward the July 1981 General Assembly in Anaheim, California. On the evening of the eleventh, we had a Sunday evening dinner and Monday morning orientation of the new General Assembly Moderators: Moderator, Tom Youngblood, Minister of Central Christian Church, San Antonio, Texas; first Vice Moderator, Charlotte Emel, laywoman from Sullivan, Illinois; and Second

Vice Moderator, my old friend Oscar Haynes, a layman from 12th St. Christian Church, Washington, D.C.

After the annual first week in December meeting with the Conference of Regional Ministers and Moderators, December is usually quieter. Congregations celebrating Advent and Christmas usually don't invite "church bureaucrats." The last Sunday of the month, however, I was invited to Kettering, Ohio, to preach for an ordination. Keith Odit, who had been a young CYFer in the First Christian Church new congregation when I was there, had just finished seminary at Christian Theological Seminary, and would be ordained at Central in Kettering. It would be special. Keith and I had lunch during his seminary career on a number of occasions. The minister at Central was Ted Faulconer, cousin of my seminary roommate Jim Faulconer, and friend in his own right. Plus, we still have many friends and acquaintances in the church in Kettering. It was a wonderful event, with the joy of knowing him as a teenager and now participating in Keith's commitment and ordination to ministry.

Another Ohio event was coming soon. The second week in January, after sharing in leadership in the New Regional Ministers Orientation and the General Cabinet, JoAnne and I drove to Cleveland for a dinner honoring Herold B. Monroe. Herold's health had been failing and it appeared he would be completing long and noted years as Ohio regional minister. He was the minister in Hamilton, Ohio, and Director of Recreation at Wilmington CYF Conference in 1942, my first year at the CYF conference as a fifteen-year-old. He then went on the staff of the region, succeeding Albert Starne in Christian Education in 1943, still being on the Faculty Conference. Then when Gaines Cook left Ohio to be General Secretary of the International Convention in 1945, Herold became Secretary of the Ohio Christian Missionary Society, the predecessor name for "regional minister." When I was ordained in 1949, he gave the ordination sermon.

Herold Monroe had been a major player in my life and ministry. It was a privilege to be one to speak and honor him at his very special dinner. It was not to be a "retirement" dinner, because we all thought he might never retire. And he didn't. It wasn't until illness made him bedfast that he finally had to let go. As one of his "boys," now Deputy, I came to see him, bedfast, in a pastoral call before his death. I regretted that I was out of the country and was unable to come to his memorial service.

As Deputy GMP, I along with Howard Dentler, was a member of the Religious Convention Planners Association. Howard had been one of the two or three founders of this association. It was composed of people like us, responsible for the details of planning large conventions for denominations. It also included large city convention bureaus interested in landing their cities as hosts, with millions poured into their city economy. The third group was hotel representatives eager to have convention headquarters located in a particular facility of their chain. The convention bureaus took turns in providing meals for the attendees, in return for presenting their "pitch" to sell their city as a site for our conventions.

My first time to attend the Religious Convention Planners Association was to be January 21–25, 1980, in Anaheim. It just so happened that the Super Bowl was to be played at the Rose Bowl January 20, the day before our meeting. We wanted to go to the Super Bowl! We had no tickets! Howard and I took an early morning flight to Los Angeles. We rented a car, which we would need for the week, drove to the neighborhood of the Rose Bowl, parked on the street, and arrived around 1:00 p.m. The game was at 5:00.

I had made a sign, "Two Hoosiers looking for tickets! Indy 500 in return?" People walk by. "You really have Indy 500 tickets?" "No," I said, "But we can get them." It wasn't long before a gentleman walked up and said, "I used to live in Bloomington, Indiana. I have two tickets and I'll sell them to you for face value." We bought two tickets for $25 each! The game was between the Los Angeles Rams and the Pittsburgh Steelers. The Pittsburgh Steelers won, darn it! But it was a good game. I called JoAnne at halftime from a phone booth under the stand to let her know we had made it into the Super Bowl.

The program for the Association began on Monday with seminars for the church planners. It was interesting meeting staff from all the different denominations. The seminars covered topics such as what can you expect from a hotel which becomes your assembly head hotel; what do you look for in choosing a city for your meetings; what help will you receive from a convention bureau when you come to their city for your meeting; what help will a large arena offer when you meet there; and what to look for with the stagehand's union in the staging of your event. It was interesting and helpful for me. It was old hat for Howard.

Our Disciples process for selecting a city, hotels, and arena included Howard working with our General Assembly's Time and Place Committee. He would be working up to three assemblies ahead, making site visits, exploring the city's facilities and possibilities, including the strength of our congregations there, from which we would need eight hundred local volunteers for an Assembly. Then Howard would have two or three cities' convention bureau and hotel people make presentations. The committee would then make a decision on which city would be chosen. I remember the time in later years when Louisville, Kentucky, made their presentation. They brought Louisville slugger baseball bats for the male members of the committee. One young woman on the committee, a strong person for women's liberation, spoke up, "Where is my bat?" Louisville did not fare very well in the vote! Of such is the kingdom of heaven!

Incidentally, I discovered that the Secretary of the Planners Association's son was the radio voice of the Oakland Raiders NFL team. The Secretary, with inside information, directed the meetings of the Association to Super Bowl cities in 1980 and 1982, the week after the game. Luckily, Howard and I would go to the Super Bowl at the Rose Bowl in 1980, then the New Orleans Superdome in 1982. The Association met every other year. Alas, in 1984 we would be in freezing Detroit in January, with no Michigan Super Bowl.

Before the next annual February General Administrative Committee, JoAnne and I traveled to Cleveland for the weekend to see Debbie and Greg. Debbie was very pregnant, expecting the birth of Jessica within days. I remember the tender feelings for my dear Deb, realizing that probably before I would see her again, she would have gone through the miracle of giving birth to a new life. Back home every day we awaited the good news, without results. But I was at home for JoAnne's February 13 birthday and Valentine's Day Celebration. Hooray!!

The next Saturday, I had an engagement with the First Christian Church in Wilmington, Delaware. The congregation was celebrating its fifteenth anniversary. I had a hand in its founding as the Chairman of the New Church Committee of the Capital Area Region when we were in North Chevy Chase. Leaders of the church were friends, and I was invited to stay overnight with one of the families. After the anniversary dinner, in their home, I couldn't refrain from sharing about Debbie's impending delivery. I preached for the anniversary Sunday service the next morning. Following worship, we were proceeding to the fellowship hall for a potluck fellowship dinner when the teenage son of my host family called me to the church office. He said my wife was on the phone with urgent news. He escorted me to the office and heard me exclaiming over the news of Jessica Anne Humbert-Long's birth. He went on to the dinner while I learned the details. When I walked into the fellowship hall glowing, the congregation was standing and serenaded me with, "Happy birthday to you…" What a sweet moment.

I had flown into the Baltimore airport on Saturday. I had a late Monday flight back to Indianapolis because I was to have lunch at the White House on Monday with Jerry Parr, head of the White House Secret Service. Jerry was an elder at North Chevy Chase Church and a good friend. He and his wife Carolyn had joined the church while I was the minister. I called the White House to tell them I had more important things to do. I caught a flight home early Monday morning, and JoAnne and I drove from Indianapolis to Cleveland to greet our Jessica Anne and her mother. That was even sweeter!

JoAnne stayed because of Deb's request for help with the baby's homecoming. I flew back to Indianapolis, leaving the car for Jeff and JoAnne to drive back to Indianapolis later. By this time, Jeff was a student at Indiana University.

I needed time in the office to prep for four intense March leadership roles. For the first in St. Louis, I was to be the liturgist and worship leader for the Christian educators joint planning event with the Division of Homeland Ministries Education staff, the Christian Board of Publication Editors, and regional education staff—about seventy people. That was four days.

The second followed the next day, a regional youth retreat for the Alabama Northwest Florida Region in Shady Grove, Alabama. It was for two interactive times with the kids about our "Christian heritage," and the Sunday morning sermon with the youth and the members of the Shady Grove Church.

The third was the Monday through Wednesday meeting of the Program Committee for the Anaheim General Assembly. We would choose the theme, and major evening speakers, with lists of primary choices and priority of seconds, in case needed. Key meeting!

The fourth event, the weekend of the twenty-first to the twenty-third, was the Florida Youth Assembly at the Florida Retreat Center for an opening speech and then two Bible lectures. I was just into my Friday evening discourse, beginning at 11:00 p.m. when we heard a loud, loud, loud howling, and a huge dog entered the room. I told the story of our adopting Heidi, our Saint Bernard, concluded a very short summary of a point and said goodnight. But it wasn't good night! There was music and dancing and refreshments to follow. A good time was had by all.

I was back in my office on Monday till Thursday, when JoAnne and I flew to Tokyo for the gathering of the Japan North American Commission on Mission. This time we departed from Chicago, flying over the North Pole directly to Japan. Departing Chicago at 1:00 p.m., we arrived on Friday at 5:00 p.m. Fortunately, the meeting coincided with JoAnne's spring school vacation.

We were met in Tokyo by Jane, the wife of the treasurer of JNAC. He was a Japanese layman. She was an American who had come to Japan as a missionary, working with the Christian schools. She escorted us to Tokyo's International House.

When our meetings began, JoAnne was escorted around Tokyo by Jane, using subways with the "pushers"—the subway staff who pushed the last riders in to fill the subway car. She had wonderful sightseeing times. She also was given a rare opportunity to be taken to the home of the famous artist Watanabe and his art exhibit. She was able to purchase two of Mr. Watanabe's drawings, which we subsequently had framed.

One of the evenings we had a reception and dinner with the Christian Schools' leaders. Another was with the Korean members of JNAC. A third was a seven-course dinner at an exclusive Chinese restaurant located in a high-rise building in downtown Tokyo. What wonderful Chinese cuisine, and what a wonderful view of Tokyo.

The meetings then moved to Kyoto, a beautiful city with blooming flowers and trees, with gorgeous architecture where we stayed in a "businessman's hotel." The room was small, and at one point in the middle of the night I woke up feeling really closed in, with a touch of claustrophobia. JoAnne helped me open a window to put my head out and get some fresh air.

The meetings ended on Thursday. JoAnne and I remained in Kyoto, taking tours and sightseeing in this beautiful setting, till Saturday. We took the bullet train back to Tokyo. Quite a ride. Sunday was Easter. We worshipped in a Kyodan, United Church of Japan congregation on Easter. We caught a limousine for the Tokyo airport about 40 miles from downtown Tokyo.

Our flight departed at 4:30 p.m. on Easter Sunday afternoon. We flew for six hours, and at 11:30 p.m. when we crossed the international dateline, it became Easter Sunday at 12:01 a.m. We landed in Chicago, then caught a flight arriving in Indianapolis at 4:00 p.m., Easter afternoon. We had spent 47 and a half hours of Easter Sunday! Jeff met us at the airport.

I don't know how JoAnne was able to go to school and teach the next day, but she did. I went to my office in Missions Building, but I was zombielike. I didn't have to travel for another ten days until I would go to the Northern California Region's Assembly at Asilomar in Pacific Grove, California. It was an iconic retreat setting. My cousin Ted Denton lived in Pacific Grove. He had been in the Navy. In World War II, his duty was on landing craft boats. He had been on the first wave of US landings at Anzio, Italy. I had time to visit with Ted and his wife Connie, give two speeches, and mingle with the folks of Northern California and Nevada.

One of the kind of independent yet historic organizations relating and reporting through the Division of Homeland Ministry was the National Evangelistic Association (NEA). Their leaders had the very public attitude that Indianapolis, especially the office of General Minister and President, didn't give attention to evangelism and church growth. I attended their board meetings and related in a supportive way as deputy GMP. They were holding an evangelism workshop for four days in Amarillo, Texas, May 5–8. I needed to be a "presence" there as Deputy GMP. On my way, I would help lead a retreat of the Ministers and Mates in the Kansas region. I did that and went on to the NEA "big tent." Dan and Mary Lee Loving invited me to stay with them in their home in Dumas, outside of Amarillo. We attended the opening session together. John Bridwell was the Amarillo Church's minister and a longtime friend from our Ohio and Capital Area days. He later became President of the NEA. I mingled with the NEA folks and listened carefully to their speeches and ideas.

Memorial Day in Indianapolis, as you might well imagine, is alive with the Indy 500 race! The area of the racetrack is called Speedway. We have a strong Disciples congregation there. On race day they suspend worship services and park cars in their parking lot for a fee. Our Missions Building with the General Offices got into the spirit with a breakfast, cooked by the male staff of our offices, served by the men, and cleaned up by the men. It fell on the Friday morning before the race. In 1988, May 23, I was a waiter. In later years, I advanced to cook and chief bottle washer. But it was always a nice and fun affair.

JoAnne was out of school after Memorial Day and free to go with me to visit the Canadian churches in the Toronto area. We drove to Toronto and environs. After our visits, we went on to Glasgow in the Kentucky Lakes area. I was preaching for our strong church there in Glasgow in celebration of their 150th anniversary.

Bert Smith was Senior Minister, and J. Hunter Jones was Associate Minister and Minister of Music. Hunter Jones said to me, "Before I die, I want to lead the singing at the General Assembly." Little did we know what that would mean later. When Bert had called me months before with the invitation to preach for their anniversary, I spoke about a vacation on the nearby Kentucky Lakes. He said one of the families in the church had a lake cottage in the area. Turned out, he arranged for JoAnne and me to have that cottage, rent-free for the week after my preaching engagement. We had a wonderful week's vacation in a large lodge-like cottage, playing some tennis and renting a boat to enjoy the water.

The Youth Ministry Congress met for five days through a weekend at Texas Christian University. I was a liturgist and Sunday morning preacher. I led devotions to begin every morning. Sarah Webb, of Virginia, a freshman in college was the Youth Moderator and later attended seminary, committed to ministry. I always have regretted that I had a prior commitment when I was invited to preach for her ordination and had to decline. She was also an accomplished mime. This was the second Youth Ministry Congress I had participated in. I appreciate and admired Suzanne Martin's leadership, as head of the Youth Education Department of DHM.

General Board and then the National Convocation were both held at the Cincinnati Netherlands Plaza Hilton Hotel. Growing up living in Bellefontaine, north of Cincinnati, I knew of that hotel as a really classy place. I think Howard negotiated a special deal by scheduling the Commission on Budget Evaluation there as well. Howard really knew his way around the hotel business. He owned a motel in Jacksonville, Florida, before being called to the ministry.

Eureka, Illinois, had become a special Humbert family location. By 1980, Uncle Royal had been head of the Eureka College religion and philosophy department for nearly thirty years. Aunt Lois, a fine musician, was a music professor at the college and an organist at the Eureka Christian Church. Aunt Madge and Grandmother Humbert had been at the nearby Jacksonville NBA Christian home. Madge was on the staff and Grandmother, a resident. When I was at North Chevy Chase, the Eureka church was in the search process for a new minister. The Humbert clan there thought it would be outstanding if I would consider coming to Eureka to serve that church. It was a fine church in a Disciples college town and had family, but Washington, D.C. was somehow a bigger draw than Eureka. I was reminded of an observation by a Disciples historian, "Our church-related colleges were founded in small countryside villages, away from the bright big city lights, which would tempt our students." Eureka fit that bill!

At any rate, on September 14, 1980, I had a preaching date at Eureka. By this time, Aunt Madge and Grandmother Humbert had both passed away. On Friday evening, JoAnne and I drove to Eureka to enjoy the weekend. Saturday evening was a fellowship dinner. We were very graciously received by the congregation with expressions of great admiration for Royal and Lois. It was a joy to worship on Sunday morning, with Lois's marvelous organ, and Royal seated in the front row along with my niece and her husband Terry.

In September I made a trip to Anaheim for work on staging the 1981 General Assembly. Getting to know the Stagehand Union folks we would be working with was crucial. Familiarizing myself with the setting in the arena, the stage lighting we could put in place, and communication with the technicians was important. We also had supplier companies to engage for organs and pianos.

Image magnification had become crucial to the Assembly, with the need to engage the company to do that. I also needed to meet Robert Hasty, the Local Arrangement Committee's Music Chairman, and get on the same page with him. After the September General Cabinet Meeting, I flew to Los Angeles from the seventeenth to the twentieth.

I combined that trip to Texoma Lake on the Texas-Oklahoma border for a consultation on women in ministry at Texoma State Lodge, along with a trip to Dumas to preach. Dan and Mary Lee Loving were leaders in that church. Houston Bowers, who followed me at the Euclid Avenue church, had been the minister. After preaching and between the invitation hymn and the benediction, I had the distinction of being elevated to the designation a "Ding Dong Daddy from Dumas." Then I was elevated further when Dan took me for a flight in his single engine airplane, with him as the pilot! Incidentally, he had flown the family, Mary Lee and daughter Dani, to the Kansas City Assembly in 1977. But at the conclusion of the Assembly, the weather was so bad they could not fly their Piper airplane back home. They took a commercial flight home to Dumas, and later with better weather, Dan flew back for the return flight of the family airplane.

In October, my birthday month, perhaps fittingly, I returned to the place of my childhood to preach at the First Christian Church in Ravenna, Ohio. Remember, I was a one-year-old when my father came to be their minister in 1928. To the ninth grade, I grew up in this church. I stood in the chancel looking out at my father's youth group, who came to our house on Sunday nights, who knew me as a child – all of us now with gray hair. I could look from the pulpit across the chancel stage to the spot where I gave my first public speech on Children's Day, bouncing back and forth from one foot to the other, as an eight-year-old.

Afterwards my mother told me I needed to learn to give a speech without dancing. That day I preached with my feet firmly planted behind the pulpit. Mostly!

From my roots in Ravenna, I traveled to the Florida Regional Assembly for two sermons, the Illinois Regional Assembly as the Bible lecturer, and the Georgia Regional Assembly for two sermons in Macon, Georgia. While I was staying in the Macon Hotel, a man was shot and killed in the room right above mine on the next floor. I was questioned by the police as to whether I had heard anything. I sleep soundly without my hearing aids and had heard nothing.

On my three-year calendar, which we needed in the General Office, with dates far out ahead, I counted the 1980 days out of the office in the "field." I found that I had been out of town on assignments over 106 days. JoAnne was with me on thirty-three of those days. That meant, of course, that we had been apart seventy-three days in 1980.

The January Super Bowl in New Orleans between the Oakland Raiders and the Philadelphia Eagles was a nice way to begin the year. One of the Raider's stars, Willie Brown, a defensive cornerback who would later be enshrined in the NFL Hall of Fame in Canton, was the brother of Julia Brown. She would later become Julia Brown Karimu, President of the Division of Overseas Ministries and Co-Executive of Global Ministries with the United Church of Christ. The game was great, with our seats given to us by the New Orleans Convention Bureau. They were actually extra tickets from IBM given to the Bureau and passed on to Howard and me. The Raiders won.

The Religious Convention Managers Association meeting was the reason we were in New Orleans, and it was both helpful and enjoyable with work and fun. The Indianapolis and Louisville Convention Bureau staffs were special friends.

I have shared about the Middlers' Seminarians Conference in St. Louis and Indianapolis. That's easier to get to for many Midwest seminarians. But we had a number of seminarians in graduate schools in the East: Yale, Harvard, Union, and Duke. So, we had a special Eastern Seaboard Conference in Washington, D.C., at National City Christian Church. I went to Washington to help lead with a presentation, "Ministry in the '80s." I had called Jerry Parr, Head of the White House Secret Service, to let him know I would be in town. He invited me to the White House for lunch and a tour. I spent the morning with the seminarians, and then left for lunch with Jerry. I went to the North White House Gate House and told them I was to be Jerry Parr's guest. They phoned him and he came to meet me. We walked to the West Wing and to the White House lunchroom. The lunch was good and the company great, as we renewed our friendship. Jerry took me on a tour. It was rather special to be wandering the halls of "the house," going into the Oval Office, standing and gazing around. We visited the Roosevelt Room and the President's private dining room. Then Jerry took me to the lower subterranean rooms, the Situation Room, the level where the President would go in case of emergency, the Security Room, where the Secret Service can watch the perimeter of the White House grounds and see if someone even touches the outer fence.

After we had toured, we went out in the Rose Garden by the Oval Office. Jerry called a White House photographer to join us. She was very pleasant as Jerry and I posed in the Rose Garden. We went back into the Oval Office, and Jerry said, "Can you stay and meet the president? (It was then Ronald Reagan.) He's now taking a nap, but I'd like him to meet you."

"I would very much like that," I said.

Reagan grew up in a Disciples church in Illinois and graduated from our Disciples Eureka College. But it was getting on toward 2:15 p.m. and I had to make my speech at 3:45, so I could not linger in the White House. Jerry walked me out to the Gate House. The picture had been developed and I carried it with me as they called a cab. The cab didn't linger either. With a call coming from the White House, it was Johnny on the spot to whisk me back to National City Christian Church for my presentation! But I had my lunch at the White House!

My presentation regarding "Ministry in the '80s" might have been an anticlimax, but it wasn't. The bright, promising seminary students and I exchanged ideas and expectations regarding that new decade of church and society.

I came home and back to the reality of ministry in the '80s with my ministry as an elder in Northwood Christian Church, serving at the communion table in the morning, and then making shutin calls with communion on Sunday afternoon.

That March was "South Carolina Month." The Black Ministers Retreat was in Charleston for four days, where preachers roused the faithful. I brought greetings the opening night and led a workshop on the organizational structure of the Disciples. It was crucial for me to be there with "presence" to make new friends and renew the old ones. I enjoyed mingling. In some free moments, I strolled the streets of Charleston, all agog at the beautiful architecture at every turn. I vowed to bring JoAnne here in the blooming springtime.

I had an engagement at the Illinois Region Men's Retreat on "Men Living Their Faith: God's Trustees," and later that month I went to the South Carolina Regional Assembly held at a conference center south of Columbia. The introduction for my first sermon was the most unique in my ministry. The South Carolina Moderator and I had become good friends. He was the Chief of Detectives for the Columbia Police Department. He produced the framed, purported "mug shot" of me with numbers across the bottom, 10261927. (That was my birth date.) A great time was had by all. I responded that the mug shot was appropriate because I was "convicted of the gospel." I preached one other time and the assembly concluded on Saturday night.

On Sunday morning I preached at the First Christian Church in Columbia. After the service, the timing was tight for me to catch my flight home. In his unmarked police car, my friend, along with his young son, "hurried" me to the airport with an occasional "flick" of his siren. I made the flight!

JoAnne's spring vacation began on March 28. One of my friends was the minister of the Ocala Christian Church. He had been a minister in Baltimore when we were in Chevy Chase. Henry had been requesting that I come and preach in his Florida church sometime. I called and said, "How about Sunday the 29 of March 1981?" He accepted. JoAnne, Debbie, one-year old Jessica, Greg, and I set out in our car for Ocala for Sunday services. Then we were going on to what was becoming a family favorite, Sarasota and Siesta Key. One of the ladies in the First Christian Church in Sarasota had helped rent a house with a pool, and this was our ultimate destination.

During my sermon, I was speaking about the importance of teaching. An illustration I used was about Coach Bobby Knight and his skill at teaching this year's Indiana University basketball team. At the start of the season they were losing and were just about a .500 team, but with Knight's teaching and coaching, they advanced to the next night's NCAA National Championship basketball game, where they would beat North Carolina. Henry was from North Carolina, and at that moment seated behind me, he said, "You wanna bet?" The congregation more than chuckled. And right there in the middle of my sermon we made a bet on the outcome.

Monday evening, after a day in the house's pool and in the sun, we wanted to be sure we were ready with the television on for the game. When we turned it on, there was no game! All the news was about President Reagan being shot. We watched the replays, and there was our friend Jerry Parr at the President's side, in the midst of gunshots, pushing him into the presidential limousine. He climbed in with him, and the vehicle sped off. I had just been with Jerry a month before. The whole of TV land was focused on the condition of the President at George Washington Hospital. We learned that Jerry Parr had not been hit by the gunfire, but one of the President's assistants, James Brady, had. There was conjecture as to whether the basketball game would be played. Finally, it was decided that it would be played with a later start. Our Jeff was then a student at IU, and after moving to Indiana, we had become IU basketball fans. It was a great game and Indiana won! Take that Henry!

The next evening, I said I was going to call Jerry and his wife Carolyn. Greg said, "Oh you'll never get through to them." I called their home and Carolyn answered. She told us all about it from her perspective. She was a judge in the IRS System. Her court happened to be directly across the street from the Hilton Hotel's special entrance where the action took place. She was at the 2nd floor window watching as the President and Jerry exited the hotel. The shots were fired, Jerry pushed the President into the vehicle, and the limousine sped off. She didn't know whether her husband had been shot. She hurried down one flight of steps to rush over to those who were left. They recognized her, but they didn't know whether Jerry had been wounded or not. It was not until later that she found out he was safe. Jerry came on the phone, and said, "You know I told you about the recurring dream I've had since I took this job, being on a mountain top with no way to descend? I felt a little like that with the shots, but pushing the President in and climbing in with him, I saw right away he had been shot and wounded. I instructed my colleague, the driver, to 'hit it' directly to George Washington Hospital."

We had a wonderful vacation week in the sun, sand, and pool at Siesta Key, with some meals out at Sarasota's great restaurants. Coming home to Indianapolis, with multiple drivers, we decided on the way to drive straight through. With short coffee and rest stops along the way, it was a 22-hour trip. Too much!

All through these months I had been working on designing the Assembly evening worship, the morning worship and devotions, and recruiting leaders. The preliminary copy for the program book was due May 18, and the finished copy was due May 29. Meanwhile, the Commission on Budget Evaluation would meet, followed by the General Board, in the Assembly year, studying resolutions and making recommendations. After the Board, I helped Ken get the changes made in the business items. The next morning, I flew to St. Louis with the final business docket, to be printed by the Christian Board of Publication.

May 20 was a huge family day of celebration in Cleveland. The occasion was the Case Western Reserve Law School commencement! JoAnne and I joined Jessica, Deb, Greg, and Jeff for John's milestone graduation. His name was called, and he walked across the stage to receive his diploma. As he exited the stage, he opened the folder and turned ashen white. We wondered what in the world had happened. There was no diploma. Instead, there was a note that he still had two books from the library. When he returned the books, he would receive his diploma! We all went out to lunch to celebrate his graduation, with a tinge of disappointment because of the library thing.

The attorney in Saint Croix had invited John to come back and join his one-man firm when he completed law school. But in the intervening two years, he had lost one client who was 30 percent of his firm's work. He could not now afford to take on John as a second attorney. But John had loved the island life of Saint Croix. As a consequence, he had decided to move to Hawaii, take the Hawaii Bar Exam, and practice law on that island. So after graduating, he headed to Honolulu.

Meanwhile, back at my "firm," May 29 was the day the final program book copy for Anaheim was due at the Christian Board Publication. I made the deadline with all the details of program and worship in place. Details, wow!

In early June, we initiated a long-standing friendship with Johnny Ray. He was the minister of our church in Oak Ridge, Tennessee. Jeff had seriously injured his ankle and was on crutches, so with Johnny's permission, JoAnne and I brought him along on our drive. We enjoyed a Saturday night church gathering and I preached on Sunday.

I participated in my first National Hispanic Fellowship Assembly, fortunately in Indianapolis, at Downey Avenue Church and Missions Building. JoAnne and I left there to go to Hiram College and the Ohio CYF Retreat for a Friday night speech and a Sunday morning sermon. On July 27, I was off to Anaheim to prepare for the opening of the General Assembly that Friday, July 31. Meanwhile, JoAnne and I had made travel arrangements to fly to Honolulu after the Assembly to spend two weeks with John. After moving to Honolulu, he had discovered that to be eligible to take the Hawaii Bar Exam, he had to have two members of the Hawaii Bar Association recommend him. We had one such lawyer, a family friend, but not the second. So he was out of luck. Jobs were hard to come by, but he was fortunate to be working as a bartender at a restaurant in Honolulu and had found an apartment he could afford. A young lady friend of his from his Saint Croix days had not been so fortunate and was telling fortunes from a setting in a shopping center.

As we moved into the Assembly, I had more GMP responsibilities but was still in charge of directing the program. Neil Topliffe had become my lead assistant, with Rick Hendricks and Ken Evans still assisting. The afternoon of the Assembly opening, I returned to the stage area after a GMP luncheon to the word from Neil that the Stagehands Union had gone on strike against the Anaheim Arena. We could not open the Assembly worship that night unless this was settled. Howard Dentler went to work with the arena with his 6'2" Germanic firmness, and the strike was settled by dinnertime. Thank God! And Howard!

The prelude by Cesar Frank was magnificent organ and brass. The introit by the Association of Disciple Musicians' choir was, as you would guess, beautiful. After the ascription by Ken Teegarden, the processional anthem by the Disciples Musicians' choir was "Fanfare and Choral Procession." The procession was led by the marshall, an old friend and former Program Director, Ben Moore, (rather the Reverend Benjamin H. Moore, who would become Senior Minister of Hollywood Beverly Christian Church).

The processional hymn was "We, Thy People, God Confessing" by John Core. This hymn was awarded first place in the then recent hymn contest of the Association of Disciples Musicians.

I had Howard Dentler reading the scripture. A solo by Ohio minister James S. Osuga, tenor, accompanied by his college son Tom Osuga on the piano, preceded the pastoral prayer by John O. Humbert. (I had read scripture at another Assembly, but this was really my first pastoral leading part.)

The Saturday morning 8:45 worship was led by the officers of the Youth Council. Jill Carney from our Northwood Christian Church was moderator and a special family friend. We were invited to her family high school graduation party and we read the scripture.

Allen Harris from the Southwest Region gave the invocation. He became a historic person and figure. Bear with me.

He was a student at TCU preparing for the ministry. As his seminary years were approaching, the Southwest Region's Commission on the Ministry felt in a quandary about his possible ordination. Allen was gay. The General Youth Council had recognized his leadership abilities, electing him an officer. Some years later, in August 1991, I was invited as GMP to come make a presentation on ordination with regard to Allen's candidacy. I was there to witness history, the movement of the Holy Spirit, and our scientific understandings of gender on the side of openness. The other leader invited to make a presentation was a Disciples professor at the University of Chicago Divinity School. His was the more traditional approach, "We don't ordain gay persons, and anyhow, they're just kids, they don't really know yet what their gender is, and they're just trying it out." I was more than surprised! This word coming from liberal Chicago!

The Commission debated this issue after my presentation and I was dismissed. However, the practice in the Southwest was that two congregations were required to recommend a candidate for ordination. When Allen finished his seminary work at Union

Theological Seminary in New York City, only his home congregation in New Mexico would recommend him. The question of ordination in the Southwest, unfortunately, was moot. With the support of Park Avenue Christian Church in New York City, the Northeast Region ordained Allen V. Harris. At the next Northeast Regional Assembly, the Latino constituency led the Assembly to adopt a resolution declaring that the Northeast Region would never again ordain a gay person.

(At this writing, in 2022, Allen Harris, is the regional minister in Ohio.)

Back to the morning of August 1, 1981, at the Assembly. Worship led by the youth introduced the Bible lecture by Dr. Jack Forstman, Dean of the Vanderbilt University Divinity School. He was outstanding. I had met him the year before at the First Christian Church in Texarkana, Arkansas, when that congregation was celebrating an anniversary. He was there as a former youth minister, during his days as a student at Phillips University, and I was there as Deputy GMP to preach. We visited and enjoyed each other's company. While we awaited flights at the airport, he laughed and told me about an experience at that church while being youth minister. One Sunday afternoon after his responsibilities were finished and before the evening youth groups, he laid down in a sanctuary pew to rest. He fell asleep and was found by an elder. He was summarily fired. But he survived! He gave the wonderful Bible lectures on Monday through Wednesday mornings for the Assembly.

Sunday evening the theme was "One in the Family," with mimes, the Jarvis Christian College Choir, and the address by John Mack Carter, editor of Good Housekeeping magazine and member of the Board of the Christian Church Foundation. Prior to the service, John Mack had his picture taken with Ken Teegarden and me. That photograph appeared in the November 1981 Good Housekeeping Magazine Editor's page.

Monday evening's theme was "Global Mission." The call to worship was by the Philippine Concert Choir. The liturgical affirmations in dance were by the Thai Dance Ensemble. The address was by Bishop Desmond Tutu!

Wednesday morning was August 5. The morning theme was "Peace," with the worship service being in remembrance of the events in Hiroshima on August 6, 1945. I had picked out a video of the devastation of Hiroshima. We showed it as an act of remembrance. Then a call to confession was given by Ed Weisheimer, a minister from Youngstown, Ohio, who was representing the Disciples Peace Fellowship. He read the confession I had written. The call to peace was a video of the legend and story of Paper Peace Cranes. As the video ended, a thousand cranes were handed out to the audience. I had had volunteers in the Southwest Region folding paper cranes for months. With my visit to Hiroshima...

The closing Wednesday evening worship's theme was "One in Christian Unity." The song fest was by Jim Manley and the Raggedy Band, closing with James Osuga's tenor solo with his son Tom Osuga accompanying. The prelude was by the host area instrumental ensemble. Ken Teegarden had the installation of the new officers. The scripture was read by an international representative. After the evening prayer, the anthem celebrated the consummation of the union of the Reformed Association of Churches of Christ (Disciples of Christ) of Great Britain and the United Reformed Church. It was presented by the Assembly Choir Instrumental and Dance Ensemble. The address was given by Phillip Morgan, a Disciple, General Secretary of the British Council of Churches in London.

Phillip Morgan had visited the Missions Building one time in Indy at the time of the Super Bowl. As was our custom we gathered at the Dentlers' for this high ritual—the Teegardens, the Humberts, and Bob and Celia Friedly. Bob was head of communications. We invited Phillip Morgan to join us, and he did. The Dallas Cowboys, Ken Teegarden's beloved team, was playing the Pittsburgh Steelers. At one point in the game, as it was hot and heavy, Dallas fumbled the ball, which bounced toward the camera, and the General Minister and President actually dived on the floor in front of the TV to recover the ball. The General Secretary of the British Council of Churches was quite amused to see the CEO of the Disciples in the U.S. and Canada prostrate on the floor without the ball. The rest of us were roaring with laughter. Without so much as a batting an eye, Ken retook his seat with a wry smile.

Regarding the Assembly in Anaheim, the arena where we were meeting was immediately across a freeway from Disneyland. At 9:30 every night, Disneyland celebrated the closing of the day with thundering fireworks, vibrating with sound through the arena. It was best that we finished worship at 9:29, or there would be fireworks!

I completed the closing details of the Assembly that were my responsibility. JoAnne and I then flew to Honolulu for a two-week vacation with John. He met our flight and took us to his apartment. From his front door on the 2nd floor balcony, we could see Diamond Head. His apartment itself was very modest, befitting his modest income. Johnny showed us around Honolulu, and of course the bar and restaurant where he worked. We had some nice dinners out at notable restaurants. With a rental car we then explored the other side of the island, snorkeling in a beautiful bay and hiking up beyond a picturesque waterfall. When we returned to our car, someone had broken into it and stolen our swimming suits and lunch.

The second week we went to the island of Molokai. One of our church friends in Seattle had given us a week's stay in their condo there. We had a great week at the beach, exploring the island, hiking and eating out at the resort on the island, where they had a show of hula dancing, fiery torches, and drums. At one time, Molokai was most famous as an island colony of people with leprosy. It was great to spend two weeks with our John. He didn't have to work at the bar in Honolulu that one week. He was with us all week on Molokai.

I returned to the office with a major project to prepare for.

Our head of chaplaincy in the Division of Homeland Ministries had worked to set up a three-day retreat for all the Disciples and UCC military chaplains stationed in Europe at Berchtesgaden, Hitler's former retreat in the German Bavarian Alps. My assignment was to prepare three lectures and a Sunday sermon for the retreat. It seemed daunting to me, and I worked hard preparing. Our military chaplains sometimes felt quite separate from the church, especially with our denomination's emphasis on peace. Ken and Howard both felt this was an important assignment, linking the General Offices with the military chaplains.

JoAnne had arranged for a week off from school to travel with me, and I was prepared. On Sunday, September 20, we flew to Geneva, Switzerland. On Monday, we visited the World Council of Churches, meeting with several Disciples on the staff. On Tuesday we flew to Salzburg, Austria, where we would spend three days. As we boarded an airport limousine, it was so crowded I decided to put my attaché case in the trunk. When we arrived at the airport, my case was nowhere to be found! I ran around like a chicken with its head cut off to see if any of the limousine riders had picked it up by mistake! No one had. JoAnne said that when we were in a souvenir shop before we left the terminal, she noticed two men eyeing our luggage, and then saw them standing by the limousine. They must have stolen my attaché case thinking I had financial papers or bonds. Boy, would they be disappointed—three lectures, one sermon, one apple, and a book by Hans Kung.

I was beside myself. I had the one set of the lectures and sermon that I'd worked so hard preparing, only one set for such an important event, gone! This was prior to computers, so there was no other set. Well, we had a stop in Zurich. As we flew from Zurich to Salzburg, we had a real treat waiting for us, but I was no fun to be with. I had gone to the airline counter with my dilemma. I described the contents. They said they would call Geneva with the request that if anyone found my attaché case that they send it on to Salzburg.

In Salzburg we would be housed as guests at a Roman Catholic seminary of the Order of the Sacred Heart. A good friend, Father Nick Arioli, Senior Priest at Mount Carmel Parish in Niles, had arranged for our stay. The iconic significance about the seminary grounds was that after World War II, the seminary had purchased the Von Trapp family home. Yes, that Von Trapp family! The seminary was in the home with subsequent additions. JoAnne and I were lodged in cells twelve and thirteen, separately. They were very gracious, and a seminarian who knew Salzburg well was our host.

The first full day there it rained, making it a questionable sightseeing day. Anyhow, I needed the day to work on the restoration of my material and my emotional state of being. Both received all morning and early afternoon attention. Then our seminarian showed us Salzburg, including dinner in a beer garden. Thursday we took the commercial tour of all the settings for the filming of the *Sound of Music*: the glass garden house for "I am 16 going on 17," the cemetery where the family hid, and the church for the wedding. The actual home the emissary purchased was not the palatial home in the film but was a large home for the large Von Trapp family.

Thursday night, I awakened three times remembering points in my lectures I had not yet included in my "restoration." Friday morning, one of the chaplains came to take us to nearby Berchtesgaden for the retreat. It began with lunch. We were graciously received by the chaplains. My first lecture was after lunch, the second, after dinner. They seemed well received. My wise JoAnne had made me promise I would not tell them my material had been stolen! Had I let them know of that dilemma, I suppose they might have thought, "Hmm...I wonder what he left out there?"

My third lecture was Saturday morning, and the retreat then had a free afternoon. The Chaplain Director, his wife, and another chaplain couple took JoAnne and me on a tour of neighboring mountain heights. What beautiful scenery and a delightful time with the other two couples.

Sunday morning, we worshiped together and I preached. It was followed by a wonderful luncheon and a time of closing. We were taken back to Salzburg where unfortunately JoAnne had to fly back to Indianapolis to her fifth grade class.

I had agreed to stay on until Friday to visit chaplains at air force and army bases. I would be traveling and visiting with a civilian rank equal to general. At the posts we visited I had accommodations of the highest rank, the General's Quarters. We visited Augsburg, then Heidelberg. At Heidelberg, a Roman Catholic chaplain who had been an associate priest in Niles and a good friend came to visit and stay the night in the general's accommodations. Our traveling group was scheduled to have dinner with the Chief of Chaplains for the whole European sector and for all denominations. My priest friend was a bit concerned, because he knew that some of his constituents on his base had reported to the Head Chaplain's office that they thought their chaplain was drinking too much. He was careful at dinner about his alcohol consumption!

We went on to Rhein-Main Air Base. I think it was on this leg of our trip that we stopped at Oberammergau, the site of the Passion Play which is produced only at ten or twenty year intervals.

Frankfort was our last stop, a major base. We visited with the chaplains there. Because of my rank, I could shop at the post at greatly reduced prices. I purchased a set of strawberry-themed Wedgewood china. I very carefully carried it home on a TWA flight to New York, through customs, and on to another flight to Indianapolis. Because of an air traffic controllers strike, we sat for five hours lined up on the runway before we could take off. I returned home to my drill sergeant as a private. (Just kidding.)

But after a wonderful reunion and the surprise gift of the Wedgwood china, I did in fact have a "list." In October, after serving at Northwood as an elder at the second service on the eleventh, I preached close to home in Richmond and Rushville, Indiana. JoAnne and I had a great weekend. There was a sweet Tennessee lady, a member of the First Christian Church in Alamo, who had her church invite me to come preach. She was also a major contributor to the Christian Church Foundation, with a named investment fund supporting missions and her congregation. The date was the last Sunday, the weekend teachers had Thursday and Friday off. Thursday after school we headed for Louisville, Kentucky. One of my friends in Louisville was the head of sales for the Galt House, a major hotel. She had arranged for us to have the honeymoon suite for two nights. We had a relaxing time together, with easy sightseeing. We drove to Alamo and stayed with our new friend. We toured her manufacturing facility and shared stories. I preached and we shared a fellowship meal and drove back to Indianapolis.

After a meeting of the National Council of Churches' Governing Board in Cleveland at the Hollenden Hotel, Ken had me head our Disciples delegation the third weekend of November. The new Moderators, Joy Greer and Dan Loving, came to town for orientation for the biennium, looking forward to the 1983 General Assembly in San Antonio. They were true leaders of the church who were now excellent Moderators with whom we would be working.

Where would you like to spend the first weekend in January? How about the mountains of Pennsylvania at the Hartman Conference Center with zero degree weather and a heavy snowstorm, for a Pennsylvania Region youth retreat? I really enjoyed being in this kind of setting with high school youth, seeing their commitment and their response to my leadership. We finished Saturday at midnight. It was a strange time to conclude. But a major snowstorm was expected Sunday afternoon, and the kids needed to be out of this mountain setting on their way home in the morning. I was dropped off at the airport at State College, where Penn State University is located, to catch a flight to Pittsburgh and home. It was below zero, and the plane I was to take was an old DC-3. I asked the desk clerk if we were going to fly. He said, "If we can get the engine started." The engine started. There was no heat in the cabin. But we hurtled off into the snowstorm.

The next Wednesday, I had lunch with Patty Hicks and Steve Hartman to talk about doing their wedding. Patty was on the staff of the Indianapolis Convention Bureau and Steve was on the staff of the Indianapolis Convention Center. This was an example of the friendships I made through my participation in the Religious Conference Managers Association, among city bureaus hotel reps and other denominational people. The wedding was scheduled for March 6, 1982.

In fact, the RCMA met the next week in Nashville. It was helpful and a fun time, with this setting being really great. We had country music entertainers. One night, after the session, I was a guest of Rick Lowery and Sharon Watkins at a Bluegrass music concert. At the time, Rick was working on his Ph.D. at Yale. Later, I was privileged to sing from the stage of the Grand Old Opry Music Hall. Not bad. We were given a tour and brought on the stage. The tour guide asked if anyone had a birthday that day. More than one responded, so we sang "Happy Birthday."

"Now you can say you sang from the stage of the Grand Ole Opry Music Hall," said the guide.

I was really glad to have scheduled to be in town for JoAnne's birthday and to celebrate Valentine's Day the next day. And she could go with me for my "Kentucky beat," two preaching Sundays, one near Richmond and another at the Beargrass Christian Church in Louisville.

The first Saturday in March, the wedding of Patty and Steve went well with all the festivities. The third week Ken, Howard, and I flew to San Antonio to meet with the Program Committee for the 1983 General Assembly. Not only was Dan Loving there as Vice Moderator, but Mary Lee Loving was on the committee itself. Ken, Howard, the Lovings, and I enjoyed times after the actual sessions.

William Fox was on the staff of the General Minister and President as Secretary of the National Convocation. His office was next door to mine. We had become good friends and were golfing buddies as well. He was retiring. A special Missions Building-wide reception was held for him April 18, 1982. I was sorry to see him go. We had a good working relationship as I sat with him in the trustee meetings for the Convocation.

The major biennial meeting of the Commission on Budget Evaluation opened on April 22. Circumstances were such that I was now taking major responsibility for our participation through the Office of the General Minister and President. The financing of the work of the whole church was always filled with issues regarding "shares" of Basic Mission Finance resources. In my work as staff with the Task Force on Renewal and Structural Reform, we proposed a new style. The Commission would meet in open session to hear presentations of requests for shares. The Commission would then make recommendations, followed by negotiating sessions for shares. Prior to this, the Commission would simply make allocations. I shepherded this new procedure through adoption by the Administrative Committee of the General Board. Now this would be the procedure. I had recruited five laypeople from across the church to be convener/moderators for the negotiations, or "Conference for Agreements." Some of these conferences were pretty tough in "cutting up the pie." What every denomination needed was a bigger pie! I was a counselor to the conveners. It had some rough spots.

I was invited to give the baccalaureate sermon at Chapman College in Orange, California, on May 23. I flew to LA on Saturday. The service was Sunday morning at 11:30. John Dale joined me for breakfast, and we went together to the college auditorium. It was really cool to see Johnny in the audience as I spoke. We had lunch together with the College Trustees and Church Relations Director. We enjoyed a relaxed afternoon and evening. On Monday, the ministers of the region gathered for breakfast, worship, and a workshop I led from 10:00 to 11:30 a.m. John and I spent the rest of the day together, and then I flew home on Tuesday.

Then came June! After Memorial Day, I flew to New York City for a meeting with the North American section of the Japan North

American Commission. From New York, I flew to Seattle for the Northwest Regional Assembly, Friday evening through Sunday, with two speeches, and then home.

I had saved the second week in June for work on the script for my part in the women's Quadrennial at Purdue later that month. The Quadrennial theme was "Follow the Yellow Brick Road to Purdue." The program at Quadrennial was always powerful and the fellowship fulfilling. The church women's staff had come to me months before to ask if I would portray the Tin Woodman as every morning comic relief, with a script but free range reflecting on the program of the day before. The presentations would also build toward the offering at the end of the week for Basic Mission Finance. He asked if I could talk Ken Teegarden and Howard Dentler into participating, playing the Scarecrow and Cowardly Lion? I did talk them into it.

So we had costumes made by the ladies. Howard Dentler was known for his authoritative pronouncements at General Assembly. Seeing all six foot two of him in costume as the Cowardly Lion was terrific for all of us! His costume was amazingly accurate. Ken's costume looked just like the Scarecrow in the movie *The Wizard of Oz*. My costume, as the Tin Man, was a silver pullover top and silver long pants, with an aluminum funnel to wear on my head, with an elastic band to hold it on. I bought an axe handle, fashioned the axe head out of cardboard and painted it all aluminum.

I was charged with writing the script for their appearances after the first day. June 15 was the deadline for the women's department and for Jean Wolfolk, President of the Church Finance Council, to see the script. She would be playing Dorothy. Jean, from Arkansas, had a unique speaking voice and was famous for calling the hogs. So, Toto, her dog would be a little pig, imagined on the length of a leash that was curved stiff with no animal on it. Jean didn't think I had written a very funny script. But I said, "You just wait and see, there is something about a crowd of five thousand people and us dignified leaders in costume carrying on, that will bring down the house." (I hoped!)

I left a copy of the script with Jean, passed out the scripts to Howard and Ken, and we rehearsed. The Dorothy sketch was only on the last day. One sequence I had for Howard was him saying as the Cowardly Lion, "I can't sleep at night. I'm terrified." And I say, "Well, try counting sheep." And he says, "I can't count sheep. I'm afraid of sheep."

A few members of the GMP's Cabinet were complaining about our lowering ourselves to do such a thing. It wasn't dignified and we would ruin our leadership with such "carryings-on."

Meanwhile, I had a commitment to give the keynote speech at the General Youth Congress at Eureka College that weekend. The theme was, "Let there be peace...and let it begin." What is the business of the church? The role of youth in the church is helping peace begin!

Back home I came, and off to Purdue in West Lafayette, I went. I was just sorry JoAnne couldn't be at the Quadrennial. She was in summer school classes at Butler working on her master's degree. The Tin Man sketch was on Tuesday morning. I have to tell you; it was a smashing hit! The next day, I made comments about the day before, even singing a little ditty, and then brought on Ken and Howard, or should I say the Scarecrow and the Cowardly Lion. We were a huge hit! On the third day, with the lights out and me backstage, I had a stagehand hold my axe just extended from the side curtain. When the spotlight hit it, the crowd saw just the axe and they roared. Then I came on, without it and stood staring at it, sticking out from the curtain. The stagehands raised it gradually to about fifteen feet as I stared at it. The five thousand ladies were gasping, laughing, and carrying-on. On the fourth day, we brought on "Dorothy." They all knew Jean Wolfolk, and it was a hoot with the four of us. She called the pig, and I brought on Toto the piglet with the stiff leash and no animal to be seen. They all roared! The offering for missions followed and was the largest ever at Quadrennial.

Forever after that, anywhere I went in the church, including when I became GMP, I was known as the Tin Man.

We went straight from Quadrennial to the General Board meeting in Chicago. My sister, Peggy Knowlton, was a member of the General Board and was there for the opening. My brother-in-law Dick Knowlton brought JoAnne up. We had our usual suite, which was delightful amidst the pressures of the General Board meeting.

Back home on July 6, I entered Indianapolis Community East Hospital for hernia surgery. I remember Bill Riggs, our minister, coming to call on me just after I had come back to the recovery room. He prayed for me and I gagged trying not to throw up on him.

I had to cancel being on the faculty for the Ohio Adult Conference which was the next week.

I did get to go to the Ohio Regional Assembly that fall in Canton, Ohio. I had a speech and a "Sharing in Missions Conference" as part of the Assembly. Since Niles was in close proximity, Keith Bell invited me to preach there on Sunday.

Bill Robertson, who had been a minister in Richmond, Missouri—where Dad was when I was born—invited JoAnne and me to come preach at Arlington Heights Christian Church in the Chicago suburb. He and his wife, Bunny, hosted us in the home he himself had built. I was fascinated. We had a good weekend with them, beginning a friendship that would last for years. Bill later came on the staff of the Christian Church Foundation. They actually moved into our neighborhood just three blocks away and around the corner from Don and Elaine Manworren.

JoAnne and I both loved theatre. The Indiana Repertory Theatre produced fine plays and musicals. We subscribed each year.

CHAPTER 24

The Election of a General Minister and President

The 1984 General Board meeting was again in Chicago on the last week of June. There was a gathering afterwards at Purdue called "Sessions 84." We knew that the Selections Committee for the Office of General Minister and President was also meeting on that June/July weekend. The goal of this meeting was to review the credentials of the 108 candidates suggested for the position and narrow the list to a manageable number to be interviewed. While they were meeting, JoAnne and I were back home in Indy. On Sunday evening we played bridge at Frank and Pat Helme's house. I had let Ken Teegarden know where we would be. At about 9:30 in the evening, Ken called to say the committee had narrowed the list to nine persons. I was one of the nine. There would be interviews the first week of September in an airport hotel in Chicago.

Meanwhile, back to the drawing board. That week we flew to Amarillo, Texas, to spend a few days with Dan and Mary Lee Loving, then on to Brownsville for the Disciples Hispanic Assembly. There we stayed with my foster brother Dick Dodson and his wife Joy. They had built a "green" home on land equivalent to the seasons in Africa where they had served as missionaries. Their purpose was to see if they could create a self-sustaining farm, with livestock and three season crops. They were working hard at it, but Joy, a graduate trained nurse from Yale, was nursing at a Brownsville hospital part-time to help support them.

With Joy's help with my Spanish, I prepared a statement of goodwill and support for when I was introduced at the Hispanic Assembly. I had many acquaintances and friends there.

The World Convention was the very next week in Kingston, Jamaica, from July 16–23. A cruise line had set up a cruise from San Juan, Puerto Rico, to Kingston for the convention. They designated one free stateroom for the cruise, free for the Office of the General Minister and President. The World Convention was rather on the edge of the structures of the Disciples in the United States. But JoAnne and I were designated to represent the Office of the GMP. We were the recipients of the free cruise. The cruise ship, the *USS Victoria*, would dock at Kingston and be our hotel for the days of the Convention. We would then cruise back to San Juan.

We thoroughly enjoyed the trip. The ship was attractive, the food was excellent, all day and evening too. In the evening, after the sessions of the Convention, a great dance band played every night. JoAnne and I danced the evenings away. Jim and Nancy Johnson were also on the cruise. We spent much enjoyable time together. Jim had just come to the staff of the Christian Church Foundation. We attended open sessions at the convention. We took a planned and directed tour of Kingston and the surrounding mountains of Jamaica. It proved to be that the World Convention was considered to be a Disciples tourist event.

JoAnne and I had attended the World Convention in San Juan in 1974 when incidentally, riding on one of the buses provided by the Convention, we met Colonel Harland Sanders. Yes, the real Colonel Sanders of Kentucky Fried Chicken fame, a member of the Disciples Church in Somerset, Kentucky, was on our bus. We spoke together about his church. His former minister had come to a congregation in the Capital Area, when we were at North Chevy Chase. We also spent the most enjoyable time in Puerto Rico with Harry and Betty Smith.

Back home from San Juan, we continued the summer with constituency groups. The American Asian Convocation was my next participation, fortunately in Indianapolis. That was followed by a trip to Montgomery, Alabama, for the gathering of the National Convocation. What a historic town Montgomery is!

Sunday, September 2, 1984, was a huge day in several ways. On Saturday night, I drove to Chicago and stayed overnight in the airport Marriott Hotel. On Sunday morning at 8:00, I had my interview with the search committee for the next GMP. It was one of nine interviews that weekend with prospects. I shared with the committee my background and ministry for the Office of GMP the last six years. I spoke of my understanding of the nature of the church, its ecumenical nature, and my hopes for the future should I be chosen or not. They had questions for me. There was one question I'm sure all nine were asked. "A young seminary student comes to you and tells you he is gay and wants to be ordained as a Disciples minister. What do you tell him?" I said, "First, I would ask him how he feels about being gay. We would talk together about feelings about himself and about his 'coming out.' I would speak frankly with him about what he would face in 1984 with the church's general attitude on ordination of openly gay candidates." The overall interview discussion was about two hours long.

At 10:00, I checked out of my hotel and drove home to Indianapolis for a huge day for the city. The Baltimore Colts had moved to Indianapolis last summer. A no-longer-in-service grade school in our very neighborhood was renovated with new artificial turf practice fields for their new home. Indianapolis had built a new domed stadium for the Sunday games. That afternoon was the first regular season game of the newly minted Indianapolis Colts against the New York Jets. JoAnne and I would share season tickets with Pat and Frank Helme for nineteen years. I had taken my ticket with me and met JoAnne and the Helmes at the Stadium.

That evening, I received word that three candidates had been selected by the Committee to be presented to the Administrative Committee in its meeting the last of January 1985. From that meeting, one candidate, chosen by a two-thirds vote, would be presented to the General Board. The three candidates were Albert Pennybacker, Senior Minister of University Christian Church in Fort Worth; Donald Manworren, Disciples Minister and Executive Coordinator of the Iowa InterChurch Forum; and me.

The names of the candidates were supposed to remain private from September until the Administrative Board meeting. Each of the three candidates was required to have a complete and thorough physical examination in the meantime. When I went through that process, I confessed to the doctor that while there had been several hard frosts, when all was quiet at night, I continued to hear crickets. I also noted that JoAnne often became tired of repeating herself. I'd been fearful that an examination would show that my hearing was fine and I just wasn't paying enough attention. Nevertheless, I did visit an audiologist, was found to have impaired hearing, with hearing aids prescribed and fitted. The first time I used them for public speaking was for my interview with the forty-five members of the Administrative Committee.

On Sunday morning, we each had two hours before the full membership of the Administrative Committee, making an opening statement and then answering questions. On the first ballot after the interviews, Albert Pennybacker received just a few votes, decided his leadership was not accepted, and returned to Texas. The votes then were cast for Donald Manworren and me. We were sequestered separately in the Hilton Hotel in downtown Indianapolis, where the Committee was meeting. JoAnne and I had no idea what was transpiring until much later in the day. The Committee had taken five ballots without attaining the required two-thirds majority. Finally, at dinner time, we received word that we each were to appear once more before the Committee for further questioning. Don and I did that separately, with the questioning in the second interview largely having to do with my ecumenical experience for the denomination. I had been a regular delegate to the National Council of Churches, heading the Disciples delegation on a number of occasions on behalf of

Ken Teegarden. I was also a member of the Middle Judicatory Commission of COCU and had attended plenary sessions of the COCU, and was a member of the Japan North American Commission on Mission with representatives and North American denominations involved in the United Church of Japan and the Japan Schools Council. The Administrative Committee went back into session, while Don and I were again sequestered. Don was by himself, but I was fortunate that JoAnne was with me all day. Finally, about 10:00 p.m., I was summoned to a meeting room. Ken Teegarden and the Selections Committee filed into the room. Ken whispered as he went by, "no emotion." Bill Tucker announced that the Administrative Committee had voted to call me to the position of General Minister and President. He asked if I would accept the nomination. I replied in the affirmative. I was then invited to appear before the Administrative Committee. On the way, I stopped to pick up JoAnne in our room, and we met the committee. My response was brief. I thanked them for the hard work they had done all day. I said I would be brief because I knew how tired they must be. I thanked them for their confidence in selecting my leadership. I committed myself, with God's help and guidance, to serve faithfully and told them how much I looked forward to working with them and the church at large in the future. Then I returned to the meeting room to meet with Bob Friedly, Director of the Office of Communication. At about 11:00 p.m., I had my first phone interview as the nominee with a national press writer.

The next morning, I met Bob Friedly downtown for breakfast and help. From a communication standpoint I needed his advice. We had become close colleagues and best friends. I'd been writing Ken Teegarden's prayers, and Bob had been writing Teegarden's monthly columns in *The Disciple Magazine*. Needless to say, I would be getting major attention now, but needed to tread lightly. I had not yet been elected.

I returned to Missions Building Monday at 8:00 a.m. for chapel. The positive response from staff at the offices was a series of wonderful moments. *The Indianapolis Star* morning edition had a front-page story about my nomination, accompanied by my photograph. The story then appeared across the country from *The New York Times* to *The Los Angeles Times*. *The Disciple Magazine* cover had my photograph of JoAnne, Heidi, and me browsing through a family album, with a nice article written by Lillian Moir.

One of the first events after being declared the nominee was the Council of Ministers meeting with the UCC comparable folks held in Savannah Georgia. Nothing was said publicly at the meeting about my being nominated, though I suppose word got around. JoAnne flew down to be with me for the weekend.

I had been working with the Illinois Region's Search Committee for a new regional minister. I had given them names, but had highly recommended Pete Smith from Lima, Ohio. He was well-qualified, and they did choose him. His installation was set for March 9, 1985. I was invited to preach for his big day and was glad to accept. It was in Decatur, Illinois, in our very strong church there. It was a great day for the church and for our friendship with Pete and Karen, which would bloom even more in later years.

The General Board met in St. Louis the first week in May 1985. The Board voted to forward my name to the General Assembly for election. Ironically, the date was May 6. One of the members of the General Board heard a radio broadcast that morning in which the announcer noted the date was significant in the founding of the Disciples of Christ. Wondering what that date had to do with our church, he discovered it was the date of the chartering of the Campbells' first congregation, the Brush Run Church.

During the period between the General Board and the General Assembly, August 3–7, 1985, attention needed to be given to two possible positions to be filled. A Deputy General Minister and President needed to be found to fill the position I held for eight years. The position of Associate General Minister and Administrative Secretary of the National Convocation was currently being filled by an interim, Thomas J. Griffin. A nominee needed to be found to fill that role on a permanent basis. I knew the leadership of Don Manworren had been deeply appreciated by the Administrative Committee, as expressed so strongly in the selection process. I felt strongly that his leadership and abilities should be utilized in the Office of General Minister and President. He was a friend and colleague in Disciples ministry and a person I greatly admired. I called and invited him to consider allowing his name to be presented to the Administrative Committee for election in its meeting the closing evening of the General Assembly in Des Moines. After prayerful consideration, he agreed to serve if elected. In a search for a new Associate and Administrative Secretary of the Convocation, Ken Teegarden and I met with the officers of the Convocation and Tom Griffin to consult with them on that selection. That group gave us the names of four persons who would be acceptable. Among the names was Cynthia Hale, who had been a member of that board and served a term as President of the Convocation. She was from a long line of Disciples families and the niece of Samuel Hilton, well known Disciples pastor in St. Louis. She was outstanding. She was then serving as a prison chaplain in Georgia. After some persuasion, Cynthia accepted. During the summer, she and the Manworrens came to Indianapolis for consultations, as we anticipated the future serving together. Don and Elaine did some house hunting and Cynthia looked at apartments.

Having gone through eight years as deputy GMP, with all the travel away from JoAnne and home, we knew that as GMP, if elected, travel and separation would be a reality. We decided to take a major trip in June 1985. We booked a TWA tour to Italy for ten days, for the first of June. We had tours of Rome, Venice (where the Pope was in a gondola parade of great fanfare), Assisi, the Isle of Capri for lunch, and Florence where the tour ended. We rented a car and drove by beautiful Lake Como, and on into Switzerland and beautiful Lucerne, with its iconic bridge, next to which was our hotel. Then it was on to Paris where we met Debbie and Tom King. I was actually driving in Paris! Wild! Debbie showed us Paris. What a treat with her speaking French. Our next direction was to the Loire Valley, with "bed and breakfasts" in beautiful mansion palaces, and on out to the sea. We left Deb and Tom then for England and London. We had traveled the English countryside in 1976, so this time we concentrated on London and the theater.

It was a wondrous four-week vacation together before I again began traveling as GMP, if elected. Up to this point, Dale Fiers and Ken Teegarden, presented as nominees, had each been elected without question. It was assumed by everyone that this nominee would be too! JoAnne had bought me a beautiful leather briefcase in Florence as a GMP election present.

At the General Assembly, Ken gave an outstanding State of the Church address and was honored with a banquet and program, in celebration of his signal leadership in Restructure and as the two-term, beloved and outstanding General Minister and President. On Tuesday morning, the business item of the election of the General Minister and President was presented to the Assembly.

The floor was opened for discussion. Some wanted more than one candidate presented. Moderator Bill Tucker explained that The Design called for a process the same as a congregational process for calling a minister: the Search Committee interviewing and presenting one candidate to the Board, and then to the congregation. Another thought that the Deputy General Minister ought not automatically be elected General Minister and President. One said they didn't know who this John Humbert was. What had he done in the church? Bill Tucker named the congregations I had served and that I had been Deputy General Minister and President for eight years. The question was called for. The vote was taken with loud positive affirmation and a scattering of nos. Bill Tucker declared, "The ayes have it. John O. Humbert is elected General Minister and President!"

I was then escorted to the stage with JoAnne and our family. In my acceptance speech, I said I wanted to focus on two needs I felt in my experience as Deputy GMP for eight years: the tension in the church between evangelicals and social action directions and the need for a feeling of openness and access to the Office of GMP.

> My commitment to excellence in administration is firm, but it will be affected with strong pastoral overtones of being with the people, sensing felt needs, of listening and learning. To that end I'm planning in the next 120 days to work with the regions in setting up eight different locations in the United States and Canada to sit with the people of the pew and pulpits, to listen and converse about the life of the church.
>
> "As Disciples of Christ, our fundamental identity is in Jesus Christ. I believe that Jesus is the Christ, the Son of the living God, and I take him as my Lord and Savior. You have made that confession, too. But we need to go further in our understanding of the full richness of Christ, for sometimes we have settled for a partial, or fragmented confession of who he is.
>
> Some of us say he is Jesus Christ, Lord of the whole creation and Redeemer of history, who has to do with more Humane social and political systems, extending social justice and liberation, redeeming the world. And we are right! But we have pitched our tents on that campground, claiming Jesus as Lord, to be the totality of the nature of Jesus person and work.
>
> Some of us say, Jesus Christ is Savior, he is sanctifier who saves a lost individual, the person's inner will, heart and desire, creating a new person. And we are right! But in our encampment, sometimes we have said, this is the totality of the nature of Jesus person and work.
>
> Both of us have rightly perceived our saying of who Jesus is as Biblical. But both of us have wrongly perceived our fragmented Christology as being the whole. Our hope is in rediscovering the fullness and richness of Jesus Christ who is both Lord of the whole creation and its human systems, and Savior and Sanctifier of

persons' lives, in whom God is reconciling the whole human family, including the family of the Churches.

I then introduced my family. JoAnne, Debbie, Jessica, and John were on the platform with me, along with my Dad whom I introduced as being eighty-five years old and still doing interims. He came to the lectern and said, as we embraced, "My little boy!" which brought down the house with laughter. When I introduced Gramma Beatrice, JoAnne's mother, after I had related how old my dad was, she was frightened to death I would tell her age.

The installation service of the new GMP was to take place in the closing session of worship on Wednesday night. Meanwhile, the officers of the Convocation, with other members of that group, had asked for a private meeting. The officers, several male ministers and some of the strong women leaders, and I met together. There was objection to the nomination of Cynthia Hale as the Administrative Secretary of the Convocation, with some declaring she was not the right person for the position. The women present disagreed wholeheartedly, retorting that the real objection was that she was not a male. I met with T.J. Liggett, the newly elected moderator for the next two years, to share this development, feeling that it was important not to be intimidated into withdrawing Cynthia's name, especially since the Convocation officers had approved her as one of their candidates. Cynthia, Don Manmorren, and I had further conversations and consulted with Cynthia to see if, in the face of this, she was willing to remain the nominee. She was.

On Tuesday night after the worship, we held a Peace March to the state capital with a Peace Bell presented by the Japanese government to the State of Iowa. While I was walking with David Cole, he informed me that a number of Black ministers were planning to "crash" the Administrative Committee meeting at 5:30 p.m. on Wednesday, where the nomination of Cynthia would be presented. Meeting with T.J. Liggett the next morning, our considered position was that we would open the doors to anyone who wished to come. The Executive Committee of the Administrative Committee met for an hour Wednesday afternoon before the full meeting. I shared developments with that group. They strongly held to moving Cynthia's nomination forward. They also strongly concurred on the nomination of Donald Manworren as Deputy General Minister and President. The plan was to announce their elections at the closing worship at 8:00 p.m. and have them share in the leadership of the communion worship.

Cynthia's name was placed in nomination in the full meeting. I explained the process, that the Convocation officers had given us four names of persons they recommended for the office, Cynthia being one. She had served as President of the Convocation and was an outstanding minister and leader.

Several ministers present made the case for the rejection of the nomination. They charged that Cynthia was not qualified for the position because of her lack of pastoral experience, and said that they were not consulted in the process. Thomas Griffin, Interim Associate General Minister and Secretary of the Convocation, told the Committee, "Hale's nomination was a return to the plantation mentality in which the great white father is telling us who we will have as our leader. The nominee knows little about the total Black constituency. No doubt she would work well with the national staff, but she would have a difficult time out in the field." Some of the Black women present again spoke of the opposition being strongly held as sexism. The males were against her election because she was not a man. "A cry of racism is being raised," said Robert E. Brown, "because an advisory committee from the National Convocation was bypassed when Hale was nominated." Discussion ranged on until time for the evening plenary communion service, without acting on either nomination. The Administrative Committee recessed until after the evening worship.

I entered the procession for the closing worship of the General Assembly and my installation as General Minister and President just as it was moving onto the platform. Thank goodness for the Holy Spirit moving me past what I had just witnessed. It was a beautiful installation service, with my family participating. At the close of the service I did as planned, entering the congregation as a symbol of my commitment to openness and access, greeting Disciples assembly goers on the plenary floor. At 10:15 p.m., we all returned to the meeting of the Administrative Committee. Following further discussion until after 11:00, I think it was Duane Cummins who spoke, making a motion to postpone action on the nomination for the Secretary of the National Convocation, since it appeared we could not peaceably come to a conclusion. At that point, Donald Manworren's name was placed in nomination as Deputy General Minister and President, with a unanimous vote to approve. Don was greeted with enthusiasm and standing applause.

JoAnne and the family were having a celebration party with close friends in our hotel presidential suite. They were having a great time. But by the time I arrived, everyone had partied and gone home, except my family. We celebrated some more, though the disappointment of Cynthia not being elected and the rhetoric directed at me and my nomination of Cynthia was certainly felt.

CHAPTER 25

The General Minister and President

The Executive Committee of the General Board had instructed Ken Teegarden to continue to follow through on the actions of the Des Moines General Assembly and to remain in the office until September 1. They had instructed me to go on retreat for the remaining days of August after the Assembly to prepare for the demands of the office. I spent the rest of the month in Indianapolis at Christian Theological Seminary. I had the library and an adjacent classroom very much to myself for meditation, reading, contemplation, study, and prayer. As I have written before, the Assembly of the World Council of Churches had met in Vancouver and had offered biblical passages for study leading up to the gathering. If you remember, a passage from 1 Peter 2:4–10 had captured my imagination for study, contemplating the nature of the church and its mission. I had written a paper on this text for the selection committee. I had also presented the paper to the Council of Ministers, composed of the Cabinet and the regional ministers in our meeting in January 1984.

I began to write based on further study of that passage in what would become my book *A House of Living Stones* published by CBP Press. Three chapters were the basis of my presentations for Bethany College's Oreon E. Scott Lectures.

T.J. Liggett, Moderator of the General Assembly and President of Christian Theological Seminary, wrote in the preface:

> The life and witness of the church is strong and vital when the leadership and the membership share a common vision of the church's essential nature and mission. The members of the Christian Church (Disciples of Christ) can be grateful that the recently elected General Minister and President has set forth his own understanding of the church, thus making that understanding available to the entire membership. A helpful approach to the doctrine the church is to consider it under the categories of being and doing. This book may be read from these two perspectives. What is the church? It is God's creation, by divine call. Humbert rightly affirms that we are called beyond individualism into fellowship and that we are called beyond autonomy into universal community that embraces the whole inhabited earth. What does the church do? The actions of the church can best be understood as ministry in multiple forms. The church's ministry finds its center in the mediation of God's grace, justice, and love. And in classical prototypes the ministry can be conceived in both priestly and prophetic terms. While historically there have been tensions between these two – the former concern about the vertical relationship with God and the latter about horizontal relationships with human beings, Humbert rightly affirms the place of both. The Sacramental life of the church and the cultivation of spirituality, in both private devotional life and in corporate worship, are affirmed as faithful reflections of the priesthood of Jesus Christ and the priesthood of all believers. But spirituality and ethics are not to be separated! The mediation of God's mercy is also affected by the witness of the church to God's mercy in a world where violence and injustice are so prevalent. When the church lives out its message of redemption through acts of service to those who suffer in acts of advocacy, to right the wrongs of society, it is being faithful to its calling to the people of God.

Dr. Liggett caught the essence of my book. As I took office, it was the declaration of what I believed was God's call for the church.

With the publishing of my book, with this theological and ecclesiological foundation for the life and mission of the church, I would address these crucial needs:

- working to bring the evangelical leaning Disciples and the social activists together, based on our common commitment to Jesus Christ and the full richness of his person and ministry as both Lord and Savior.
- the goal of bringing the whole church together for mission, with strong emphasis on pastoral care from the Office of the GMP, modeling openness and access between pew and pulpit with the general leadership of the church, bridging the perceived gap between congregations and the general life of the church.
- emphasizing for the Disciples, a global church body, making a difference in the world as a contributing force for peace and justice in the crucial issues of the day.
- further development of the "ecumenical partnership" with the United Church of Christ, adopted at the Des Moines General Assemby in 1985.
- bringing the whole General Staff together to work as colleagues with a growing sense of unified mission and ministry.
- unifying general and regional staff for ministry and mission.
- developing a greater appreciation and utilization of Disciples' institutions of higher education.
- advancing the role of women in top leadership in the church.
- fulfilling the action of the General Assembly calling for the leaders to find and develop new facilities for the headquarters offices of the Indianapolis General Units.
- bringing the church into the computer age.

Ironically, my first sermon as GMP was at University Christian Church in Fort Worth, Texas. JoAnne and I were there for the wedding of Laura Loving and Navy chaplain Kyle Fauntleroy. Dani Loving and I were doing the service together on Saturday evening, August 24. Al Pennybacker was on vacation, and I was invited to fill the pulpit in his absence. One of the incidental things of interest was that Dr. Dwight Stephenson, my seminary homiletics professor, was a member and was in the audience. I believe that was the first time since seminary that he was in an audience where I was preaching. We greeted each other effusively after the service. There was no mention regarding the sermon. I have never learned what my grade was from my beloved professor.

We returned home for Labor Day. My first day, finally ensconced in the confines of my new office with my furniture, was September 3, 1985. My trusty secretary Marlis Morgan was now in the "outer" office!

My first two Listening Conferences were the next day at noon with the Louisville, Kentucky, area ministers and at dinner in Lexington. The Fall Convocation of Lexington Seminary was the next day. I was the preacher for the day. I shared with the students how in my student days my knees were knocking the first time I spoke from that same pulpit. Dick White, who had been a fellow student (and a wicked ping pong player!) was now the professor of homiletics. He said afterwards, he gave me a "superior" on the sermon.

The new Assembly Moderators came to town for a two-day orientation for the next two years, leading to the 1987 Assembly in Louisville, Kentucky. T.J. Liggett was Moderator, Donna Albright from Seattle was First Vice Moderator for program, and Vince Martin Jr. of Los Angeles was Second Vice Moderator. (It was Donna's condo in Hawaii where we enjoyed our vacation with John following the Anaheim Assembly.)

On Wednesday I had lunch with Wade Rubik, our General Counsel for the denomination. For eight years I had witnessed what he did and didn't do for us. He was of retirement age, and I let him know he would now be able to retire. We would be engaging an Indianapolis law firm to handle the limited amount of counsel we needed.

While I had been reading, praying, and writing in August, and otherwise preparing, there were some rumblings in the Cabinet, "Where is the leadership, etc." I had set up a Cabinet retreat for four days in Brown County from September 15–18. We had 100 percent attendance. We worshipped. I shared my ten goals for the six years. We played tennis. We ate together. It was the first time the General Cabinet had gone off together like that in a spiritual retreat. Among elements, looking forward, I called for a retreat of all the General Staff from all eleven of the general units to be held in Western Indiana to bring us all together for a unifying time and to respond to my leadership on the ten issues. This was my goal number five, bringing the whole general staff together to work as colleagues, with the growing sense of unified mission and ministry.

For years, the National Council of Churches' Department of Church and Society's Washington office held a briefing for heads of communion. When Jimmy Carter was president, Ken was involved, and they met at the White House with the President. However, when Ronald Reagan, our Disciples President, was elected, he turned to the evangelist Billy Graham. The briefing continued, but now with special guests from the House or Senate.

September 18 was my first in the Capitol with a prominent congressman from New Jersey.

From Washington, I flew to St. Louis for my first meeting as GMP with the Executive Committee of the Conference of Regional Ministers and Moderators. They were old friends because I had been meeting with them as Deputy GMP for eight years. Now I was in this new relationship.

In my acceptance speech as GMP, I committed myself to work with regions in settings for eight Listening Conferences across the church. Those Listening Conferences actually took me to twenty-seven locations in twenty regions. I asked three questions: What is it that you love about the Disciples of Christ? What is it that you find helpful in your work with regions and general units of the church? What is it we could do better together as we move into the future? I listened carefully, pencil in hand, jotting down what I heard from Disciples congregations.

My Listening Conference in the Capital Area Region was at North Chevy Chase Christian Church, in the fellowship hall (the site of the "popcorn follies" dances with my JoAnne, playing games with the CYF and Chi Rho, presiding at the Annual Town Meeting.) I pinched myself! Was I really now the GMP standing in this so familiar spot with so many of my Capital Area friends? I asked the questions and listened.

One of the key adopted resolutions in the Des Moines General Assembly was number 8539, Resolution Concerning the Preservation of the Family Farm for the Sake of the World. The resolution was brought to the Assembly through the Regional Board of the Upper Midwest, Iowa, and Minnesota. Growing out of the resolution, I was going to Ringgold County in South Central Iowa to listen to farm folk in our churches. One congregation was the Disciples church at Exira, Iowa, where my father had been the pastor in the early 1920s.

With William L. Miller, Regional Minister of the Upper Midwest, I came to be with the farmers of Ringgold County, a hard-hit area with drought compounding the well-chronicled economic plight of farmers. We shared breakfast in the farm home of a Disciples family and with neighboring farmers. We learned firsthand of the pain in their community, and the liquidation and foreclosures on family farms where there had never been a missed mortgage payment, with the secondary effect of the closing businesses in town. Then we went to the fellowship hall of First Christian Church of Mount Ayr where the co-pastors, Phillip L. and Doris M. Kinton were ministering heroically. They and their congregation were working with other ministers, priests, and their parishes in the midst of people in desperate straits. I listened to the young high school officer of the Future Farmers of America in his blue corduroy jacket, standing with three of his friends. He replied to my question about the economic state of his family's farm: "We've had three years when it rained as hard as we planted. One year we had to plant twice because it was washed out. But then we had practically no rain all summer. This year we have a good crop, but it looks like prices will be down. My dad has worked hard. We'll see what we get for this crop. But I doubt we can finance planting next spring. They'll probably call our loan."

My conversation with the young future farmer was set in the midst of a luncheon meeting with these folks, along with Disciples from neighboring communities. Judgments were that the year before hope had held together as they were able to do "creative financing." But the mood of this year's harvest was deep fear.

People were withdrawing in despair, some to the point of suicide. Among the farmers, however, there was real affirmation of the church. The crisis had brought the churches together for new ecumenical alliances for mission and nurture. They were working at bonding people together out of their isolation, demonstrating they were not invisible to the church. Keeping the small churches open to support and care for people was an important element. One Disciples woman in ministry, Edie Diehl, served three congregations—Disciples, Methodist and Presbyterian churches. There was involvement and direct assistance to the people with food pantries, for the contemporary farmer is a food buying consumer too. There were eight Vista volunteers working in ten counties. The Iowa Interchurch Forum was at work in support of mental health facilities, which had experienced the caseload increase of 40 percent. The Society of Saint Andrew set up The Potato Project, where tons of smaller potato "seconds" were being shipped in for hungry families. Our own Week of Compassion through Church World Service had given funds to regional agencies working in the farm crisis states. But we also needed to work to make our economic systems and processes more humane in their implications for the welfare of people. Farm programs and banking policies have a great deal to do with the plight of the people in rural America.

But I learned as Deputy and GMP that one has to shift gears quickly. From the farms of Ringgold County, it was off to Kansas

City the next day to the NBA facility of Foxwood Springs to be the featured speaker at a banquet of the Fellowship of John. Attending were donors to this fellowship that would support Foxwood Springs, a Disciples facility for the aging. When the meal was being served there came a huge surprise! The young woman serving me and the head table was the young woman who had shared the same lunch table with her father, JoAnne, and me the previous summer on the Isle of Capri on our TWA tour of Italy. Her mother was the head dietitian at Foxwood Springs. When asked about my work at that resort luncheon, I had mentioned the Disciples of Christ, but there seemed to be no connection for that father and daughter, even though the mother worked at Foxwood Springs.

Incidentally, that evening the Kansas City Royals and the St. Louis Cardinals were playing in the World Series. As a part of my opening remarks, I shared my own interest in that event, and noted, "I think there is someone back there (pointing to a gentleman with ear buds) who could bring us up to date on the game." He called out the score! Then everyone settled in a bit more for my after-dinner speech. The next morning, I held a Listening Conference with the ministers of the Kansas City area.

In November 1985, in Geneva, Switzerland, Mikhail Gorbachev and Ronald Reagan were holding a summit to discuss the reduction of nuclear weapons. Leaders of the churches in the United States and the Soviet Union came together in a prayer summit in Geneva, Switzerland, to be held concurrently with the meeting of the heads of the two governments. The U.S. delegation included the so-called "heads of communions" and the officers of the National Council of Churches of Christ in the USA (NCC). I was part of the delegation, as was JoAnne Kagiwada, an officer of the NCC. We agreed that we would meet only for prayer and meditation in the Geneva Cathedral of John Calvin. We would not make statements or gather near the location of the summit meetings.

When the time came, we gathered in the Cathedral each day at 8:00 a.m. We observed silent meditation and prayer for peace, and each hour on the hour one of the leaders would lead in a spoken prayer or meditation, taking turns between representatives of the Russian Orthodox leaders and the U.S. leaders. We broke for lunch at noon and returned at 2:00 p.m. to this discipline until five. In the evenings, we concluded the day singing, first the Russian leaders and then the U.S. delegation. It was powerful with the full, rich, deep voices of the Russian archbishops and priests, and the mixed voices of our delegation, which included four women. One of the most powerful was combined singing together of "Kyrie Eleison," or "Lord Have Mercy." On two occasions an ABC network cameraman from the U.S. was a witness to the singing. He told us later that as he was driving to another assignment, he was singing the beautiful "Kyrie" tune with his radio on and open to the central ABC base, when the control technician piped up, "What the hell is this 'Kyrie Eleison'?"

Before we traveled to Geneva, I received a call from Washington, D.C. One million signatures had been collected on a petition calling for Gorbachev and Reagan to agree to ban nuclear testing. There would be a press conference in Geneva with an international group, including persons from England and the Netherlands, making the presentation of the petition. The document would then be presented to Gorbachev and Reagan. They were requesting that I be part of the group from the U.S., which would also include Jessie Jackson and the film actress Jane Alexander. They were requesting that I be the second national religious leader as a part of the presentation. I asked for time to contact the NCC about our commitment to confine ourselves to prayer in the cathedral. I did so, and we agreed that I would be part of the group presenting the petition at the press conference but would not go on to present the document to Reagan and Gorbachev. That was what occurred. The group was unable to get in to see Reagan, but went on from the press conference to an audience with Gorbachev, which was duly filmed for TV World News.

Reports of that summit noted that tensions remained due to fighting in Afghanistan and Central America. After months of postponement, a mini summit was organized in Reykjavik, Iceland, to open communication further. As that occasion arrived, Avery Post and I wrote a letter to Reagan and Gorbachev urging a moratorium on nuclear testing.

As always following Thanksgiving, the Conference of Regional Ministers and Moderators met the first week in December in St. Louis. And while we had the regional ministers together, we moved into a meeting of the Council of Ministers, adding the cabinet. As leader of that group, I shared my vision of the church, its work and mission for the coming days. I also shared what I was hearing in my listening conferences as we looked toward the needs of congregations.

January 1986 was the epitome of the work of the office of GMP. The General Cabinet met the tenth. I was the keynote speaker for the Christian Church Foundation's Development Conference in St. Louis, basing my speech on my experience and approach of the Fuller Brush company for my text. That night I flew to Washington, D.C., to be there for the Saturday installation of Bishop Edmond Browning, the new presiding bishop of the Episcopal Church, at the Washington Cathedral. The next day, the twelfth, was the ritual of the service of installation at the National Cathedral. On Monday the thirteenth, I flew to Washington for a Listening Conference that evening with the Seattle area church folk. The next day was a flight to Portland, Oregon, where I met the regional minister and we drove for one hour to Albany for a Listening Conference. On the fifteenth we drove to Eugene for me to meet David Wagoner, the Dean of Northwest Christian College. And then it was off for home on a 7:00 a.m. flight from Eugene to Indianapolis.

The UCC–Disciples Partnership Committee met January 19–21. The twenty-two member Ecumenical Partnership Committee was appointed and met in a retreat near Chicago. The partnership arrangement called for new relationships in three particular areas: doing mission together, engaging in theological preparation aimed at full communion, and conducting common worship with frequent sharing of communion. The news release following the meeting noted that "the importance of the two denominations relationship is underscored by the fact that the presidents of the churches are members of the partnership committee."

The Executive Committee of the Administrative Committee met at the Indianapolis Atkinson Hotel, followed by the full Administrative Committee on the 26–28. We had worked to prepare business items for this body. I gave the opening keynote speech. Of note, we nominated John Foulkes as assistant to the General Minister and Secretary of the National Convocation. He was elected.

In February, working with David Vargas, Executive Secretary for the Department of Latin America and the Caribbean, I had the opportunity to head a delegation of ten Disciples on an official church visit with the Christian Pentecostal Church of Cuba. It was in line with my vision of Disciples, emphasizing that we are a global church and making a difference as a contributing force for peace and justice in the crucial issues of the day. Because of the economic blockade of Cuba by the U.S., we could not travel directly to Havana from the U.S. But David Vargas and his staff had arranged for us to fly to Mexico City, visit church-related folks there and then fly to Havana. We left Indianapolis on February 8. In Mexico City we visited a neighborhood where Disciples were working with families affected by an earthquake. A lady who was a lay leader in a section of small, connected homes invited us into her living room. She had small children, some grade school age. She told us of being shy and introverted. But with the encouragement of our church staff, she had become a Sunday school teacher and a worship leader. She pointed out that their neighborhood school had been shaken by the earthquake two weeks before and had collapsed. Fortunately, it was early on a school day before classes began. She escorted us down the street to the next corner to see the terrible damage of the collapsed school. We spent the night in Mexico City and flew into Havana February 9.

Here is the *Disciples News Service* release regarding our visit on February 21, 1986 in Matanzas, Cuba:

> The Christian Church (Disciples of Christ) in the United States and Canada entered a new phase in a relationship with the Christian Pentecostal Church of Cuba in February. Heading the Disciples delegation was the Reverend John O. Humbert, Indianapolis, Indiana, General Minister and President of the 1.1 million member church. The 10-member delegation attended the annual convention of the church, held February 13th–16th at the Methodist seminary in Matanzas. The two-fold purpose of the trip was to explore the meaning of the Disciples relationship with the Cuban church and help Disciples discover Cuba's present reality as a country. "What shape of continuing relationship between the two churches' takes still is being explored," said Humbert. "That relationship likely will not include economic aid but it will offer spiritual and emotional support."
>
> The two churches have had an informal relationship through the Disciples' Division of Overseas Ministries. International representatives also have attended past General Assemblies of the church.
>
> Noting that since 1973 Disciples have supported an end to the economic blockade of Cuba by the U.S., Humbert said, "The Cuban church feels isolated by the blockade which cuts off free flow of traffic and trade between the two countries. The Cuban church covets the opportunity for leaders of Disciples and the Church of the Brethren to be with them and to express their Christian concern and partnership in worship, evangelism and mission." Brethren officials also participated in the convention. "Leaders of both churches want a continuing relationship between the two," said Humbert. "We are people of faith who long for a lessening of tensions between our two governments and for World Peace. Although our two governments have drawn a curtain between our two lands, our unity in Christ transcends that barrier," he said.
>
> "The 10 Disciples met for two hours with Jose Felipe Corneado, Director of the Cuban government Office

of Religious Affairs, and three of his staff members. Corneado had been denied an entry visa by the US government for a visit to Disciples Indianapolis headquarters last fall with a Cuban church delegation.

"Among the differences discussed were those related to concepts of freedom. Theirs is to have basic economic needs met and ours include political freedom and freedom of the press and ideas," Humbert observed. The revolution in the late 1950s left a socialist country with the upper middle class and wealthy leaving the country with a great deal of bitterness.

"Those who were left fit the low-income category, including the poorest of the poor," said Humbert. "Their concerns were for housing, food, education and health care. Most of the people who had been in great need before the revolution have had their basic needs met. It is obvious that the general standard of living is simple and minimal for those still there."

The negative attitude toward the Roman Catholic Church in Cuba is changing, with the church's new identification with the poor. The Protestant church generally was considered positively because it ministered among the poorer people.

When I returned from Cuba, I was in the office for a week, and then went on an extended western trip. I flew to Cheyenne, Wyoming, to preach on Sunday the twenty-third. I led a Ministers and Mates Retreat at Estes Park Colorado on the twenty-fourth and twenty-fifth and spent the evening of the twenty-fifth with the CMF of the Central Rocky Mountain Region. From Denver, I flew to Los Angeles where I met with laypeople and ministers for a Listening Conference at the First Christian Church of Fullerton on Saturday afternoon. The Chapman College Founder's Day Banquet was that evening where I was the featured speaker. I remember I said that, in celebrating its college's life, the institution needed to answer three questions: Who am I? Where am I? And what time is it? After I sat down with "what time is it?," the college's Church Relations Director presented me with a Chapman College wristwatch. It was one of those coincidentally timely moments!

Chapman College is located in Orange, California. I preached the next morning at the First Christian Church of Orange. The Orange Listening Conference was the next evening. Then I flew to Memphis, Tennessee, for the three-day Black Ministers Retreat.

I came home for the meeting of the Building Committee for the new downtown headquarters offices. I had appointed a new Building Committee. Hal Watkins, President of the Board of Church Extension had pressed me to appoint Richard Knowlton as the Chair of the committee. Dick was certainly qualified: an architecture degree from Miami of Ohio; a principal with Knowlton Construction Company; and the builder of twenty-two buildings at Ohio State and school buildings all over Ohio, with Dick the supervising architect on many of them. But he was family, my brother-in-law. Hal kept pushing, and I finally relented and appointed Richard Knowlton as chair of the Building Committee.

Friday, March 7 was to be a big weekend. Debbie and Tom King, and Tom's mother were coming to Indianapolis for a family "get acquainted" time. It turned out that Debbie and Tom would not be able to come, but Emily, Tom's mother, came on alone. We had not previously met Emily. We greeted her at the airport. After we came home and she became acclimated with her room, she came into the family room and settled in a comfortable chair. She said, "Well, what do you two think of all of this?" "All of this" had to do with the blooming romantic relationship between her African American son Tom and our Caucasian daughter Debbie. We affirmed it was fine with us. We liked Tom. We were glad for their relationship to take its course according to their wishes.

We had a warm and comfortable Friday evening and Saturday with Emily. However, I had a preaching engagement in Toledo, Ohio, on Sunday morning. The Disciples Churches of Northwest Ohio had been studying Disciples history for several weeks. On March 9, 1986, they would all come to worship at the Toledo Public Auditorium and the Disciples GMP was to be the preacher. It was an early Sunday morning drive from Indianapolis to

Toledo. I arrived in plenty of time. I had decided to preach about our basic faith using an illustration of Halley's comet. If there is one sermon preached that I wish I could have back, that was the one. I should have done something with our Disciples Heritage, but I didn't. There I have confessed!

I went on from Toledo to lead the Michigan Ministers Retreat on March 10 and 11. Ministers retreats were special to me. I felt the need for local pastors to be alive with the faith and the privilege of being a pastor and preacher. As GMP, I was committed to working at being a channel of inspiration and enthusiasm.

Easter was coming, with JoAnne's spring vacation beginning Good Friday on March 28. Jim and Nancy Johnson had offered their Florida home for our weeklong vacation. Jim was now on the staff of the Christian Church Foundation. They would be in Indianapolis for that Foundation Board Meeting until Saturday. So we would have a vacation house for a week. It was great to be together after my extensive travel during February and March. I had finished writing my book *A House of Living Stones,* submitted the manuscript to the Christian Board of Publication, and received the edited copy. I had asked Bob Friedly, head of the Office of Communications to read it and make suggestions. I had all that and spent some time during our vacation putting on the final touches. At the end of the week on Sunday morning, I was to preach at the First Christian Church in Tampa and then at a Disciples gathering at First Christian Church in Sarasota in the afternoon. That evening from Tampa we would fly north, JoAnne to Indianapolis and John to Pittsburgh. I was to be the lecturer for the Bethany College Scott Lectures. I was using three of the chapters of my book for the lectures. It provoked interesting discussion, especially the lecture and chapter "The Sacramental Person and the Community."

I came home from Bethany College with a 9:00 AM appointment the next day with Kevin Ray and Richard Bowman, the leaders of a new group calling themselves "Renewal." One of the resolutions which came to the Des Moines General Assembly in

1985 was from the First Christian Church of Decatur, Illinois. I mention it here because a consequence of this resolution would gain major attention in the years to come around Christology. The subject of the resolution was the centrality and inspiration of the Bible, urging that it be acceptable for Disciples to hold to the "infallibility" of the Bible. The General Board submitted a substitute resolution affirming the centrality and inspiration of the Bible, but refusing to single out "infallibility" of scripture for special attention. At the close of the Assembly, Rev. Richard Bowman, pastor of the submitting congregation, approached me with great emotion and disappointment. He asked why we could not adopt the original resolution about "infallibility."

My response was that Disciples are free to believe in the infallibility of the scriptures; therefore, it was the feeling of the General Board and the Assembly that we did not need a resolution singling out that position. It was the will of the body. Growing out of his disappointment and theological position, Bowman and others formed Disciple's Renewal after the Des Moines Assembly.

My meeting with the two gentlemen was a discussion about their viewpoint and the Assembly. I reminded them that it was the General Board, made up of representatives from congregations, and the floor of the General Assembly whose mood and position they were confronting. It appeared they were wanting to try to pull the majority back to "fundamentalism," claiming that was the Disciples position which needed to be renewed. But we are not fundamentalists! It was an interesting discussion, but they remained adamant in their position. They left on cordial personal terms, but with strong theological differences.

Then there was a wedding! On April 12, 1986, Deborah Humbert was married to Tom King at Euclid Avenue Christian Church, with attendants six-year-old Jessica Humbert-Long and Jay and Cathy McKelvey. The reception was held at Debbie's condo in Shaker Heights. John Dale presided over the refreshments and beverages. It was the melding of two families of varying shades with much rejoicing!

The next itinerary was to Oklahoma City for consultations on Phillips University, to the Pacific Southwest Region to consult about regional staff problems, and then the Northern California Regional Assembly on the Monterey Peninsula, April 19-20.

The meeting of the U.S. church leaders, composed of the heads of communion, including those whose denominations were not part of the National Council of Churches, met in New York City on the twenty-first and twenty second. I spoke to the opening session of the Commission on Budget Evaluation in Chicago and was then off to the North Carolina Regional Assembly at Ridgecrest Conference Center where I had two speeches.

Chris Hobgood was being installed as the Regional Minister in Arkansas in Little Rock on Sunday, May 4. I was the preacher for the occasion. The Governor of Arkansas was also on the program. He even remained for my sermon. The governor was Bill Clinton. He presented me with a certificate declaring me an "Arkansas Traveler." Henceforth, wherever I went, I was called on to promote the state of Arkansas.

To express my commitment to evangelism I proceeded to St. Louis for the National Evangelism Workshop. Changing gears, we had a Partnership Committee meeting in Indianapolis the seventh and eighth, and a Washington Congressional briefing on the twelfth and thirteenth.

It was college season. JoAnne and I went to Lynchburg, Virginia. I gave the baccalaureate sermon and received an honorary Doctor of Laws degree from Lynchburg College on May 16, 1986. We then made our way to Macon, Georgia, where I preached for the centennial celebration of the First Christian Church. Next, I went to Orange, California, for Chapman College's graduation, giving the baccalaureate sermon with Avery Post. Both of us also received honorary Doctor of Humane Letters degrees.

Oh yes, we were having a General Assembly in Louisville in 1987! So the Program and Arrangements Committee met in

Louisville. While I was in Kentucky, the night before the meeting began, I went to the retirement party dinner for Wayne Bell, who was retiring as the president of Lexington Theological Seminary. (You remember the connections between the Bells and the Humberts.)

The Committee chose the theme "Faithful to God's Claim." They were excited about the possibility of engaging Maya Angelou as a main speaker. Another was Allan Boesak from Johannesburg, South Africa, the General Secretary of the World Alliance of Reformed Churches. It would be my task to recruit them. I shared with them that J. Hunter Jones, Associate Minister of music at our church in Glasgow, Kentucky, had told me, "Before I die, I want to lead the singing of the General Assembly." I asked him to do that.

Nineteen hundred eighty-six was the year for the great International Christian Women's Quadrennial at Purdue. I was invited to give the opening keynote address on Monday June 23. I was to move from being the "Tin Man" four years before to being the serious "senior diplomat." But when I began my address, I noted to the 4,500 women who were assembled that somebody was not very neat because something was left by the lectern. I reached down and held up my silver handled axe from four years before. The women loved it.

We had, however, come into the Quadrennial on the twenty-third, just after the Division of Overseas Ministries Board, after long discussion and angst, made a decision to grant a thousand dollars from DOM funds to the World Council of Churches to Combat Racism program for South Africa. The conservative news forces had labeled Mandela's party as communist.

The morning Quadrennial began, I had written to our leaders, the Cabinet and Regional Ministers:

> I want you to be among the first to know of the action of the Division of Overseas Ministries Board on Saturday, June 21, 1986, regarding the question of the grant

from DOM 1986 budget funds to the World Council of Churches Program to Combat Racism special fund for South Africa. As you know, I wrote to all our ministers to ask their opinion on this. The response from just over 200 was three to one in opposition to the grant, but a large number suggested the alternative of designated giving. This information was carefully shared with the Board.

However, the Board under the impact of the intensity of the situation in South Africa, simply could not say no to a response to the pain and suffering of brothers and sisters in southern Africa. They voted to make the grant from DOM's 1986 monies. I am sure there was a strong sense of the Kairos theology, "the moment of grace and opportunity, the favorable time in which God issues a challenge to decisive action to end apartheid." They heard the advice and counsel from the church, struggled mightily with it, and under the impact of their responsibility and God's leading, they made this decision.

One of our tasks now is to help our people understand the positive aspects of some of the fine things the Program to Combat Racism has accomplished.

We must also recognize the utter tyranny of the South African government. It is a government of oppression. It is in opposition against the common good of the people. It has no moral legitimacy. And, as the Kairos Theology Document declares, "A regime that is in principle the enemy of the people...can only be replaced by another government—one that has been elected by the majority of the people with the explicit mandate to govern in the interests of all the people." Our DOM Board has expressed itself as saying, "The time has come for the churches to declare their alliance with the forces of liberation against apartheid."

This will not be an easy time for us. But it may be a special time for education, witness, and further action. One thousand dollars is not enough in any sense of the word. JoAnne and I plan to make a gift to the designated special fund. What DOM receives will be passed through to the World Council in addition to the budgeted $1,000.

I pray for the church and for us, that it may be a time of growth and renewed commitment.

Sincerely,

John O. Humbert

General Minister and President

With that background, I came to preach for the Quadrennial that night. With the theme "Because We Bear The Name...," the special emphasis on that night on baptism as the entrance into "Bearing The Name...," I began:

> It is almost redundant to speak to 4,500 women of water and a new creation. You have an innate sense of that from the depths of your very beings. As a woman you have a functioning sensitivity to water giving new life. For many of you, in the cycles of conception, a growing embryo cushioned and protected, immersed in the miracle of water your body has produced, carrying new life through the cycles of growth to birth, which bursts forth out of the life-giving waters of your very being, you have vividly experienced water and new life.
>
> Jesus once said, "Truly, truly, I say to you, unless one is born anew that person cannot see the loving rule of God."
>
> Nicodemus said to him, "How can one be born when one is old? Can a person enter into a mother's womb and be born?"
>
> Jesus answered, "Truly I say to you, unless one is born of water and the spirit, that person cannot enter the Kingdom of God." (John 3:3–5)
>
> The waters of baptism are elemental in conversion, and the symbolism of the new creation, a new birth in Christ. Baptism is the sign of new life through Jesus Christ.
>
> Tonight, in this opening session of the Quadrennial, under the theme "Because We Bear the Name..." we are called to reaffirm our baptism and our new identity as daughters and sons of God. In baptism, or in the

confirmation of our baptism, a new name was given to us—Christian, a new bearing in Christ, as we began our ministry as new creations in him.

The point I would make tonight is that in the story of Jesus' baptism there is a moment of powerful symbolism which informs the nature of our new bearing in Christ: that Christ's mercy and ours has to do with universal love and compassion for all people.

I begin the story, of all places, with Jonah from the Old Testament book of the same name. You can read the book of Jonah in several ways: as literal history, as many have done; as allegory, though sometimes that has been overdrawn; or as parable, which like Jesus' parables teaches a powerful lesson and makes the characters become larger than life, like the Good Samaritan.

Father Maple in *Moby Dick* by Herman Melville preaches an exciting sermon on Jonah. "Shipmates, this book containing only four chapters—four yarns—is one of the smallest strands in the mighty cable of the scripture. Yet what depths of soul does Jonah's deep sea line sound!" (Chapter 9, "The Sermon," p. 40)

It is a book of depth to fathom, with its message of God's unbounded love for all kinds of people. And yet, so great has been the controversy over the big fish, that many of us have never really heard the powerful message of the book: the clearest note of God's universal love to be found in the Old Testament.

Jonah emerges in the book as a narrow nationalist who hates the foreign Assyrians. The book confronts the difficult task of breaking the narrow nationalism which grew up in Judaism after the return from exile, between the fifth and third centuries b.c. They were crowded in and harassed by enemies. They responded by becoming exclusive, nationalistic, and vindictive toward outsiders. Other peoples and other times have known the same vindictiveness, the same isolationism, the same exclusivism. It can be one of the fruits of international strife and upheaval.

God commands Jonah to go to Assyria to the city of Nineveh and call the people to repentance. But Jonah flees to escape doing what is hateful to him.

Later, when God has overtaken him and all but compelled him to go to Nineveh, and when all Nineveh turns to God, Jonah becomes angry and petulant. He wants nothing to do with the world where both the Assyrian and Jew stand side by side in God's mercy and favor. Jonah in fact is so narrow in his sympathies that he is more concerned about a vine that grows up to shelter him from the sun and his own solitary comfort than he is about the fate of a city full of people, including children and babies.

The book of Jonah is a message of God's love and compassion for all people. And do you know what the name Jonah literally means? Jonah in Hebrew literally means "dove."

What's the point of thinking about this? Did you hear the gospel message read this evening?

As soon as Jesus was baptized, he came up from the water, and suddenly the heavens opened, and he saw the Spirit of God descending like a dove alighting on him. And a voice from heaven spoke, "This is my son, my beloved, my favor rests on him."

In the moment of Christ's baptism, at the institution of Jesus' vocation as the Christ, in striking symbolism God was proclaiming the universality of Jesus' ministry, the wideness of God's love and compassion.

Some people in times of international strife have known vindictiveness, isolationism, exclusivism, and have been more concerned about solitary personal comfort than the fate of thousands of people, including children and babies. Not so those of us baptized in Christ's name, bearing the name of him concerned in compassion for all peoples.

The author of Galatians sounded the same theme:

"For as many of you as were baptized into Christ have put on Christ. There is neither Jew nor Greek, there is neither slave nor free, there is neither male nor female; for you are all one in Christ Jesus." (Galatians 3:27–28)

Hear this: in our baptism we have a new bearing in Christ, a liberation into a new humanity in which barriers of division whether of sex, race, nationality, or social status are transcended. We have a new bearing in God's vision of the reconciliation of the whole human family, of universal peace and justice. Because of our baptism into Christ, we cannot give in to vindictiveness, isolationism, nationalism, exclusiveness or overriding self-centered concern for our own solitary personal comfort. When the fate of children, babies and people in Libya, Afghanistan, Nicaragua, El Salvador, Lebanon, or South Africa is one of pain and injustice, we must exercise love in compassion because in our baptism we bear the name of God's universal compassion. It is a word for these days!

After the quadrennial Fran Craddock, Executive of Church Women in Homeland Ministries wrote to me:

> The officers and members of the ICWF Quadrennial Assembly Planning Committee are most appreciative of you, our General Minister and President.
>
> On their behalf I want to express our gratitude for your presence and participation during the entire assembly. This meant so much to those who worked hard to make this a meaningful event in the life of women in the Christian Church (Disciples of Christ). Personally, I want also to thank you for your message on Monday evening. I feel sure you felt the response of the women. They were grateful for your openness and honesty. Because you were willing to share in this manner, women will return home as effective and informed interpreters with a little more courage to risk speaking out on major issues facing the church in our world today.
>
> Thank you for the challenge and for your leadership.
>
> Gratefully, Fran

Marilyn Moffett, ICWF President wrote:

> I want to take this opportunity to thank you again for being an important part of the Quadrennial Assembly. Your message on Monday night was very fine, reminding us of the importance of our baptism as a sending

forth for a life of response and action in Christ, and also bringing us face to face with the issues of life to which we must respond. Thank you for both the reminder and the challenge. And the special touch with the axe was great! The women loved it. We thank you also for spending most of the week with us, both you and JoAnne.

John, it's special to know the support I've always felt coming from your direction—for me personally but much more importantly for the women of the church, especially the organization of ICWF. Thank you for that. I know it will continue.

Marilyn

With Richard Knowlton, Chair of the Building Committee for the new downtown office facility, the committee met in July to interview architects, looking for "world class." We chose Edward Larrabe Barnes of New York City. He had designed the Christian Theological Seminary's facilities with heavy participation in choice and financial support from J. Irwin Miller and family. With input from the committee and Cabinet, he set out to design a building for a particular canal side lot on North Indiana Avenue, purchased with funds from an Eli Lilly grant of one million dollars. We were "high" about the selection of Mr. Barnes and his acceptance.

As I came to the office of GMP, I was committed to the inclusion of a woman in the Executive Offices of the Office of the General Minister and President. I had interviewed Claudia Ewing Grant for Deputy GMP. She was pastor of Central Christian Church, Lebanon, Indiana. She graduated from TCU and had studied at the University of Edinburgh in Scotland and received her M.Div. from CTS. She had been on the Task Force on Ministry and the Commission on Chaplaincy Endorsement, as well as the Board of Church Extension. She had just served as Bible lecturer at the Quadrennial. She had experienced the general church. She was articulate and had great pastoral and relational skills. Claudia's name was presented to the Administrative Committee in July, who forwarded her nomination to the General Board, July 26, 1986, where she was elected Deputy GMP.

At the Board meeting I shared what I had heard in the listening conferences, and we began to move toward the priority of all of us in all the parts of the church being intentional about "developing vital congregations."

Howard Dentler was retiring at the end of 1987. Don Manworren was working with Howard on all the details of meeting planning, including the vast responsibilities of the local arrangements for the 1987 General Assembly in Louisville. Claudia Grant would begin her work in the fall of 1986 in the pastoral relationship role of Deputy. She was a marvelous choice.

I was able to save the last three weeks of August for vacation. We went back to Bethany Beach, Delaware, renting the large house on the corner across from the Conference Center. It was so nice to stay together with JoAnne in one place, especially at the beautiful Bethany Beach.

For months the general unit representatives, at my call, had been planning a staff-wide retreat at French Lick, Indiana. It was one of my primary goals, bringing the whole general staff together from Indianapolis and St. Louis to work as colleagues with a growing sense of unified mission and ministry. We came together from September 3–6, to work, pray, and play. I gave the keynote speech outlining my vision of our working together on the ten goals for the six years. I hoped we would move closer to the regions and congregations and together be a church that makes a difference in the world, a contributing force for justice and peace in the crucial issues of the day. It was well-planned by staff, with small group times and openness for any staff to make suggestions as to our direction.

It was regional assembly time. Weekends were with South Carolina, Kentucky, and Oklahoma, plus the Task Force on Health Care and the Puerto Rico Joint Commission in San Juan, Puerto Rico.

JoAnne and I were able to go to New York City together October 3–5. I preached at Park Avenue Christian Church on Sunday. We visited the Metropolitan Museum of Art in the afternoon and then had a beautiful dinner at the Tavern on the Green in Central Park. We had tickets for *Phantom of the Opera* on Broadway Saturday night. It was a great weekend!

Meanwhile, with our continuing concern about the Cold War and possible nuclear agreements between Reagan and Gorbachev, Avery Post and I were attentive to their coming meeting in Iceland as a follow up to Geneva. The news release from the Office of Communication was as follows:

> Washington D.C., Oct. 9: A US – Soviet moratorium on nuclear testing has been urged of Ronald Reagan and Mikhail S. Gorbachev in a pre-summit statement issued here today by six top American religious leaders.
>
> Their "Call to Hope and Realism in Iceland" asks the US President and Soviet leader to agree to halt testing of nuclear weapons until the comprehensive test ban treaty can be concluded. It also calls for a moratorium on testing anti-satellite weapons against objects in space and a commitment to maintain compliance with existing treaties, including Salt II and the ABM agreement.
>
> Written by the Rev. Dr. Avery D. Post, President of the United Church of Christ, and the Rev. Dr. John O. Humbert, General Minister and President of the Christian Church (Disciples of Christ), the statement was also signed by four other heads of communions.
>
> "An end to testing would go a long way toward cutting off the next generation of weapons, and ending the spiraling and escalating arms race," the religious leaders explained.
>
> "Terminating or breaking the moratorium on anti-satellite weapons and such treaties as Salt II or ABM before new treaties are negotiated would poison the atmosphere and do much to destroy the momentum toward real arms control," they warned.
>
> The statement signers urged the US and Soviet heads of state to reject the "voices of fear and illusion" that

say, "do not trust the enemy" and "do not make any deals with the enemy," but instead "just string the public along."

"Peace is possible," they asserted. "It is possible to end the arms race. It is possible to develop structures of common security, structures of justice." As church people, they said, "we expect and should expect real results in Iceland...new momentum in arms control for the next summit...a nuclear freeze to be achieved and the arms race ended." The religious leaders ended their statement with a promise to pray for President Reagan and Mr. Gorbachev and for "specific and concrete steps" that could give "momentum to a new era of cooperation and common pursuit of justice and peace."

Next was the Ohio Regional Assembly, the Seminarians Conference, the Pacific Southwest Regional Assembly in San Diego, the Oklahoma Regional Assembly in Norman, a Founders Day speech at Drury College in Springfield, Missouri, and the Mid-America Regional Assembly.

In December, after the Conference of Regional Ministers and Moderators, this time in Washington, D.C., at National City Christian Church, I had the heads of communion gathering at the Episcopal Church Center in New York City, with lunch at Bishop Edmund Browning's high-rise "parsonage condo" on Madison Avenue.

I was surprised at Thanksgiving by John and JoAnne. John had arranged an island-hopping two-week vacation in the Caribbean from December 20 through January 2. We flew to Saint Thomas Island for two days. Then by seaplane, we flew to Sint Maarten through Christmas Day. But early on Christmas Day, we sailed by chartered catamaran to the island of Saint Barts to spend the day. We swam in the bay, then had lunch at Bayside in a ramshackle looking restaurant but with good food. (We have a watercolor by John Stobart in our front fall depicting that bay and the restaurant.) We sailed back to Sint Maarten in time to shower and go to a beautiful restaurant, all dressed up for Christmas dinner!

By seaplane, again we hopped to Christiansted in Saint Croix, where John had lived for one year. We stayed in a resort overlooking the sea owned by a family with whom John was acquainted. In fact, he had dated their daughter when he lived in Saint Croix for that year. JoAnne and I had a private cabin to ourselves. The resort had wonderful food. John also took us to some of his beautiful old haunts. We spent a week there, including celebrating New Year's Eve and Day, then flew home to Indianapolis after a glorious two weeks in the sea and sun. Thank you, John!

I was able to save JoAnne's birthday and Valentine's Day in '87. Then I had the Executive Committee of the National Council of Churches in New York City the twentieth, and the Assembly of High Plains District in Amarillo, Texas, the twenty-second through the twenty-fifth.

One of the pressing issues of the day was the United States and its support of the counterrevolutionaries called "the Contras" in the civil war in Nicaragua. With the encouragement of the General Assembly "Resolution on Central America, Resolution Concerning the Pledge of Resistance to prevent the invasion of Central America," with my joint concerns with the Division of Overseas Ministries, I took a strong lead and stand on seeking to change our government's policy on funding the Contras in the civil war against the elected government in Nicaragua. It was not that we were so enamored with the Sandinistas, but rather that they had been elected in a monitored free election and that Nicaragua would not be able to solve its many problems, with the United States funding the Contra war against government forces. U.S. policy adopted by Congress held that no arms shipments could be made by the U.S. to the Contras. There was strong evidence however that this was occurring and that the very aircraft that shipped arms to Nicaragua and neighboring countries were returning to the U.S. Air Force installations with drugs which were then sold in the U.S. to provide funds to buy more arms. The Christic Institute in Washington was gathering information and evidence in this regard along with information on the ties between our government and the Contras. I was a member of the Christic Institute's Advisory Board. Another member of that group was Hillary Clinton. We had been calling, writing, and visiting members of Congress to persuade them not to provide funds to support the Contras.

I had signed on to a letter to Congress that was published as a full-page ad in *The New York Times* urging Congress not to send more money to the Contras. At home one evening I received a phone call from Alan Fiers, loudly calling me out. "The Sandinistas are communist and need to be overthrown by the Contras. How do you sleep at night being active in opposing the Contras? How dare you be so unpatriotic as to challenge the President of the United States? You have blasphemed! You are ignorant of the facts." I said, "We're receiving another story from Christians in Nicaragua. The Contras are stealing drugs from hospitals and then burning them down. They have tortured and killed innocent children and adults. We don't need to be funding them."

He replied, "Well if you don't respect me, at least you should respect my father." Of course, his father was Dale Fiers who had been General Minister and President and my lifelong hero. We would learn later that Alan was the Head of the CIA Committee for Central America. (He was later indicted for lying to Congress but was pardoned by President Reagan before he left office.)

Finally, after months of this activity, it was suggested by Jim Wright, a Democrat from Texas who was the Speaker of the House in Congress, that civil disobedience might be effective.

Working with and through the National Council of Churches, the leaders of the denominations obtained a permit to hold a "Service of Worship and Confession" on Ash Wednesday 1987, on the East steps of the Capitol building in Washington. It was, as the banner we held said, a "Lenten Witness for Justice and Peace in Central America."

Several of us then determined that, following the service, we would proceed into the Rotunda of the Capital where we would kneel and pray as an act of civil disobedience, protesting our nation's involvement in Nicaragua's Civil War. Five of us did so, including Avery Post, myself, General Secretary Arie Brouwer of the National Council of Churches, the President of Church Women United, and a Catholic priest, the head of one of the Order's social action organizations.

We were arrested at about 2:00 p.m. As we were led out of the Rotunda, the crowd that had gathered began singing, "Were you there when they crucified my Lord?" We were taken to a lower level of the Capitol where we removed and left our robes. Word was that if we were booked and taken to jail before 4:00 p.m. we would be released later that night and would not be incarcerated overnight. We were also told that the jail cell would be sparse, with only a steel bunk and no bedding. I had bought a heavy knitted sweater to wear or use as a pillow if need be. We sat until after 4:00 p.m. At about 4:45, Avery Post and I were handcuffed and led out the west side of the Capitol through the doorway used for presidential inauguration participants and down a long flight of stairs to a "Paddy Wagon." They transported us to the Central Police Station where we joined the other two men. We were ushered, without a phone call, down the corridor of cells. "Humbert, in here!" I was put in a cell by myself, the others in the next cell and just beyond. The cell doors slid shut with a clank! I sat down on the slick steel lower bunk.

After some time, they shoved my dinner tray under the cell door. The food was passable. Then suddenly, the cell door slid open, and a policeman deposited a young Black man as my cellmate. We sat on the bunk together and talked. He was a security guard at one of the TV stations in Washington. He was at home that afternoon, and one of his buddies asked if he could use his new acquaintance's hose to wash his car. The answer was yes. The friend and the nice car arrived, soon followed by two police cars. It seems the buddy had stolen the car, and both young men were arrested on the spot. Of course, my cellmate was only lending his hose and water. I knew somebody was working on the outside to spring me, but what about my young Black cellmate?

We were held there until about 10:00 p.m. when we were released. We were taken back to the Capitol Building where we retrieved our robes. The next morning, we met with lawyers who wanted very much to press for a trial regarding "precedent" on "Rotunda law." However, our cause was much more focused on the funding of the Contras by Congress. We appeared before a federal judge midmorning charged with a misdemeanor. Our sentence was pronounced as time already spent in jail and court costs. My cost was $16.85. We later learned the prosecutor was seeking a six-month jail sentence for us.

Out of jail, I fled to Canada! Well, I was meeting with the All-Canada Committee of Disciples in Guelph, Ontario, for a Listening Conference and consultation. Because our Disciples in Canada are spread from Nova Scotia to Vancouver, it was expensive to gather. When a student from the West declared a calling for the ministry, the Commission on Ministry wrote her a letter of acceptance and congratulated her and wished her well. They could not afford to bring their candidates to the Canada Regional Office in Guelph for an interview.

I then crossed the border back to Michigan to preach in East Lansing and the Michigan Assembly on the morning of March 14. The next evening, I preached at Hillyer Memorial Church in Raleigh, NC, and met with Herb Miller and his "crusade" that the General Church neither knew anything about nor cared about evangelism! I then preached twice at the Idaho Regional Assembly in Boise on the twentieth and twenty-first and spoke at a scholarship dinner at University Christian Church in San Diego at 1:00 p.m. the next day before flying off to a meeting of U.S. Church Leaders in Chicago.

I fulfilled my promise to save the 29th to the 31st for JoAnne and me! It was about time!

The Council on Christian Unity had taken the lead to establish an official dialogue with the Russian Orthodox Church. The first occasion for a Disciples delegation visit was set for April 2–13 in Moscow, Odessa, and St. Petersburg. Paul Crow had set the delegation in place when Duane Cummins insisted he must include the General Minister and President. So, at the last minute I was included. But our nephew, Bill Trimbur's wedding was set for Saturday, April 4, in Philadelphia. The delegation left for Moscow on May 2. But JoAnne and I flew to Philadelphia on Friday and enjoyed the Trimbur festivities. On Sunday, JoAnne flew back to Indianapolis, and I took a flight to Moscow.

When I arrived, a host couple from the Orthodox Church was waiting for me with a "Humbert" sign in hand. However, as officials were going through my attaché case, they found a *Time* magazine that Jeff had given me that day with an article about the Soviet Union. They were agog with conversation. They sought their superior. He then sought his superior. I guess they were concerned I was bringing propaganda into the country. At any rate, their brouhaha delayed me so that I missed my flight to Odessa, where I was to meet our group at an Orthodox seminary. The greeting couple made arrangements for me to stay in a Moscow hotel for the night, the Ukraine Hotel. In the morning, after breakfast they gave me a tour of Moscow. I was surprised to see an Orthodox cathedral inside the walls of the Kremlin. That afternoon I got the flight to Odessa. I was met by the Vice Chancellor of the seminary and a seminarian. They were very, very thorough making sure I was John Humbert. We exchanged saying my name repeatedly. Then, as we drove the 45 kilometers or so to the seminary, there was much laughter between the two. When I arrived and joined my Disciples friends, I discovered a tale about the night before. They did not get word that I would not be on the flight the previous evening. The Vice Chancellor and the same student came to meet me. They met a man and with language barriers decided he was I. They got him in the car with his luggage and transported him to the seminary. He turned out to be a Swedish sailor on holiday and never expected to be deposited on his first night at a seminary. It was straightened out, and he was taken on his way.

Our delegation was meeting with the Orthodox delegation to exchange papers with the seminarians as the audience. One of our delegation was Nancy Stalcup who read one of the papers. She was from Dallas, Texas. It was 1987, a time when the TV program *Dallas* was at its height. When Nancy was introduced and it was announced that she was from Dallas, there were noticeable oohs and aahs from the seminarians. Even in a seminary in Odessa, they knew about "Who shot J.R.?"

One of the evenings, the Russians had arranged for us to attend the ballet at an gorgeous, ornate Odessa Theater. It was superb!

From Odessa we flew north to St. Petersburg. During World War II it had been known as Leningrad, where the Russian army finally turned the tide on the German advance and began driving them back toward Berlin. The historic and amazing Hermitage Museum sat by the river in a beautiful setting. The Russians had set up a guided tour for our group that took our breath away.

We were in St. Petersburg on Palm Sunday. We went to worship at the cathedral of the archbishop of Northern Russia. We worshipped with no pews, standing the entire time, for two hours. The music with the male deep voices was spectacular. The excitement and anticipation of many mothers with small children to come forward and receive the wafer and wine was palpable.

After the mass, we were received by the archbishop in the rectory for lunch. He presented each one of us a beautiful artistically painted egg. I cherished mine for years.

I came home to JoAnne, and the next weekend we went to Niles where I was privileged to speak for the Niles Interfaith Banquet. My friend Bernard Oakes through his leadership in the Niles church community had accomplished a whole new era in the unity of Catholic and Protestants in Niles. The dinner was held at the beautiful Niles Presbyterian Church. JoAnne's mother was there with her friends from the Presbyterian and Methodist churches, and she seemed to be very pleased.

Before going to Niles, I had flown to Washington, D.C., for a National Mobilization on South Africa. All sorts of folks were there from churches and organizations, including the National Council of Churches and the World Council of Churches, committed to help overcome apartheid. I was asked to give the opening prayer. All of the groups exchanged what they were doing in South Africa to try to help. Seeking to put pressure on the white leaders of South Africa, we came up with boycotting companies doing business with South Africa. The meeting was held at National City Christian Church. We were a part of the international campaign to isolate the South African government through sanctions and economic measures to force President de Klerk to open the door to political change on the way to the end of apartheid.

After preparing the business docket for the General Assembly, meeting the deadline June 18, 1987, I attended the UCC General Synod in Cleveland. JoAnne and I could stay with Debbie and Tom for the week. I gave the closing sermon on Wednesday evening. Well, no, it was Wednesday night! The closing business session went on past my scheduled time of 9:30 p.m., and I began my scripture introduction at 11:45!

A special celebration of the Humbert family took place for two days in July in Independence, Kansas. The minister and congregation invited me to a congregational dinner in honor of my role as General Minister and President and the role my family had played in that congregation. It was in remembrance of Grandfather John Longston's ministry with that congregation from 1901 to 1911 and the birth of my mother in the parsonage in 1903. Then Uncle Ted Dunton and Aunt Madge came as ministers in 1930. Upon his death in 1932, Uncle Harold Humbert came from Hiram, Ohio, to serve as their minister. Uncle Royal Humbert was then ordained by the congregation.

When G.S.O. Humbert retired from service at Phillips University, he and Grandmother Ella moved to Independence and lived with Aunt Madge. Grandfather died there and the scrapbook that they gave me about all of this had his gravestone picture. Aunt Madge and Grandmother then moved to Enid, Oklahoma, where Madge was the Director of Christian Education for Central Christian Church, and then to Eureka, Illinois, where she served again as Director of Education.

Royal and Lois Humbert surprised me by driving all the way from Eureka for the celebration. Mary Ellen Dunton Garrett came from Dallas, Texas.

They held two different receptions, one for the congregation, which had a thousand members, and one for ministers and laypeople from the community and neighboring towns. The next day I held a Listening Conference with ministers and laypeople. Uncle Royal Humbert, professor of religion and philosophy at Eureka College, sat in!

From Independence, I flew to St. Louis for the Commission on Finance Meeting, and then the crucial General Board meeting in its role of considering business items and making recommendations leading up to my first General Assembly as General Minister and President.

One of the key business items, number 8730, was the resolution concerning the Priority for the Christian Church (Disciples of Christ). The process included the Anaheim General Assembly adopted business item 8145, "Resolution Concerning the Year 2000," declaring that

> the Christian Church (Disciples of Christ) should take a leading role in preparing for the year 2000 and that the General Minister and President should explore the appropriate role of the church in the year 2000.
>
> The Des Moines General Assembly took action mandating that the General Minister and President during the next biennium follow the regular procedure for the establishment of priorities and present to the General

Board recommendations for the church's is priority during the 1989-1991 biennium.

With guidance from our planning documents, the General Minister and President has taken these steps:
- listened to laity and ministers in 20 regional conferences
- conducted "futuring" sessions with the General Board members
- studied the Division of Homeland Ministries research
- engaged in dialogue with the Council of Ministers
- shared with and received counsel from the Administrative Committee
- presented the recommended priority to the General Board for its response.

The Priority Statement

The process has led to the decision to propose that for the next 12 years bringing us to the year 2000, the priority of the Christian Church (Disciples of Christ) will be to develop vital congregations as dynamic faith communities in prophetic, redemptive, and reconciling ministries to the whole world.

Our pursuit of this priority will be founded on such Biblical images of the dynamic church as:
- a confessing community
- a teaching community
- a community of loving fellowship, of *koinonia*
- a worshiping, praying, proclaiming community, celebrating the Lord's Supper
- a giving, sharing serving community
- an evangelistic, converting community
- a healing community
- one church, with diverse faith communities, whose visible unity is a sign of the foretaste of the unity of the human family
- a community in mission, sending and receiving apostles as ambassadors of reconciliation, bearing witness to God in Christ, strengthening the church in all lands
- a community dedicated to peace with justice

The Implementation

We call upon the official bodies of all congregations, regions, and the general program units of the Christian Church (Disciples of Christ) to affirm the priority and to commit themselves to an implementation process which will move the church through the 1990s prepared to be partners with God in a ministry of reconciliation. Shared decision-making will be key to every step of the process which in twelve years will result in the realization of the priority. The General Minister and President will launch the priority by calling upon all manifestations of the church to be in a time of prayer and consecration as each moves to claim the priority as its own. On Pentecost Sunday,1988, all persons in the Christian Church (Disciples of Christ) are encouraged to recommit themselves to God through Jesus Christ, to the renewal of congregational life, and the whole mission of the church.

Resource materials will be developed to interpret the priority. Regional teams using available materials will meet with clusters of congregations to interpret and discuss implications of the priority.

A broadly representative team appointed by the General Minister and President will design a church-wide planning conference in 1988 which will bring together congregational, regional, and general unit leadership (1) to examine current programs and resources in terms of congregational life, (2) to explore the needs of congregations and (3) to project future programs along with the leadership and resources which will be needed.

Participation in the Planning Conference will be divided into working groups focused on the biblical marks of a dynamic church.

The Church Wide Planning conference held on a conveniently located college or seminary campus will be open to all Disciples who wish to register, attend, and participate in one of the working groups.

Based on the information generated at the Church Wide Planning Conference programmatic resources and materials will be developed and produced for use by congregations as they implement the priority.

Regional events will be planned to introduce resources which can be used to support the development of vital congregations throughout the denomination. Each biennium the various manifestations of the church will evaluate their progress, reordering, rethinking, and renewing their commitment to the priority.

THERFORE BE IT RESOLVED, that priority for the Christian Church (Disciples of Christ) for the next 12 years (1988 to 1999) shall be:

To develop vital congregations as dynamic faith communities in prophetic, redemptive, and reconciling ministries to the whole world.

BE IT FURTHER RESOLVED, that the implementation process move forward through the affirmation of the priority in the three manifestations of the church, the Church Wide Planning Conference in 1988 and the subsequent implementation of program and resources through the twelve-year period.

The General Board discussed the recommended priority at length and recommended that the General Assembly adopt the resolution with the implementation. It was my strong emphasis on the church-wide planning conference bringing together congregational, regional, and general unit leadership, in fact, bringing the whole church together for mission.

Also among the resolutions was number 8729, "Concerning Contra Aid and U.S. Central American Policy":

It resolved that this General Assembly opposes U.S. government legislating covert support of the Contra war in. It urged the Congress to deny all funds to the Contras, and actively seek a peaceful resolution to all the problems in Central America in concert with other nations. It further encouraged members of congregations to write to their members of Congress opposing more Contra support.

This was also the time when Disciple's Renewal presented their resolution regarding "Jesus Only." The resolution resolved that The General Assembly reaffirm the historic faith of the Christian Church (Disciples of Christ) that Jesus Christ is the only savior of the world and that apart from him there is no salvation, and that all of our churches and institutions ensure that our programs and activities are centered in Christ, and are consistent with the fact that he alone is Savior and Lord.

The General Board recommended that the General Assembly refer the resolution to the Commission on Theology, with a report to be brought to the 1989 General Board.

The first week in August began with a wonderful family time in Valdese, North Carolina. Diana Spangler, my sister Peggy Knowlton's daughter, was the minister at the Disciples congregation there. A layman from Indianapolis, Barry Crawford had moved to Valdese with his two sons, one with severe physical and mental handicaps. Now single, Barry was a really nice guy. He courted Diana. They became engaged. And after I preached in the Sunday morning service I would marry them. It worked out really well. There were some wonderful couples in the church who were most hospitable. Barry was an attorney who had arrived in Valdese with clients in that part of North Carolina.

That week I was the vesper preacher at Christmount Week, Monday through Thursday. JoAnne could be with me for that whole time, and we had a nice room to ourselves.

We returned home for a unique event, the Pan American games. August 8–16, 1987, the Pan American games were held in Indianapolis, a major athletic event in the Americas with national teams competing in track and field, baseball, basketball, softball, swimming, and all sorts of major and minor sports. In our Disciples Offices, in consultation with the Division of Overseas Ministries, we decided to invite the Cuban national delegation to a luncheon/reception at our International Offices. We were able to be in touch with the leaders of the Cuban athletes and entourage. The luncheon was held at Missions Building and was enjoyed by our general staff and the Cubans. It was a great time of fellowship. In the tradition of the Olympic Games, there were many pins exchanged; we presented the Cuban athletes with medals of "LOVE," a miniature of the well-known Robert Indiana "LOVE" sculpture at the Indianapolis Museum of Art.

JoAnne, Debbie, Tom, and I attended the volleyball games held on the Hinkle Fieldhouse floor where I had played basketball.

Early in September, I was part of the orientation of new regional ministers in Indianapolis. Then I flew to Columbia for Pope John Paul II's visit to the University of South Carolina. The university chaplain, an acquaintance and schoolmate of JoAnne's brother Dick Trimbur at Denison University, led a morning worship service in the chapel on September 11. The college hosted us for a very nice luncheon. After lunch we proceeded to the third-floor ballroom of the university president's home for the dialogue with John Paul II. He read a paper, and our representative read a paper. Following open discussion, we had an informal reception time visiting with the Pope and other heads of communion. Paul Crow also attended the event. In the evening, we worshiped in the university football stadium with 85,000 people. We heads of communion were up on the stage and participated in the service. The Pope gave the sermon. The actor Richard Thomas, actress Helen Hayes, and the NBA star Alex English had major roles in the service.

I flew to Cincinnati for the Executive Committee of the Regional Ministers and Moderators for two days, and then to Atlanta for a meeting of heads of communion prior to the National Council of Churches Executive Committee. Emilio Castro, General Secretary of the World Council of Churches, made a presentation to the Executive Committee with a reception and dinner following in his honor. There was also a dinner honoring Don Jacobs retiring as head of the Cleveland Council of Churches. Joan Brown Campbell was there as the World Council's U.S. representative and friend of Don Jacobs. I sat with her and her family. The former Cleveland Council's finance staff and the chair of the committee on finance were together again!

Wednesday the twenty-third, I was in New York for preparation of the U.S. delegation to the World Council of Church's Conference on "Sharing the World's Resources." I was one of the delegates. The conference was to be in Spain at El Escorial.

October, of course, was the General Assembly in Louisville, Kentucky. This was Howard Dentler's last Assembly as Deputy GMP. We had become close friends with the Louisville Convention Bureau and hotel staffs. They had a celebratory dinner for our staff and spouses in honor of Howard. After finishing seminary serving as a pastor of a Jacksonville congregation, he served as our Disciples chief event manager in July 1961. Drawing on his secular experience as a hotel manager prior to seminary, he had planned seventeen General Assemblies and arranged housing. He cared for the needs of 150,000 people over the years. He had scheduled facilities for more than a thousand assembly satellite meetings and for every General Board and Administrative Committee Meeting the church had held since Restructure. He had made arrangements for hundreds of committees and commission meetings. It was a wonderful dinner. Elaine Manworren and JoAnne drove down to enjoy the occasion.

I had worked hard on my Saturday morning GMP address on the state of the church. But first, came the marvelous and celebratory opening night. Don Manworren and Claudia Grant had designed the service together, with the Louisville Area Choir singing for the procession, with the offering of symbols. Then J. Hunter Jones, who had said to me, "Before I die, I want to lead the singing at the General Assembly," led the first hymn, "Called as Partners in Christ's Service." Following the invocation and choral response, it was my responsibility to introduce our international representatives to the Assembly. I had been practicing the pronunciation of their names for days. As I was introducing them and asking them to stand, there was activity on the other side of the large stage. As I looked in that direction, I saw Hunter Jones had passed out and was lying on the floor. We always had a doctor on call near the stage for such an emergency, and Don

Manworren had summoned him. I walked toward the scene and seeing what was happening I said to the Assembly, "We have an emergency on stage. Hunter Jones is ill and our doctor is caring for him. I would invite members of his family to join them off the right side of the stage. Please join me in prayer." As I prayed, they strung a sheet around him for privacy. And then they removed him with a stretcher that was always near the stage. Then, with the situation gone from the stage, I resumed introducing the international guests. The remainder of the program went well, though the shock of Hunter's being ill hung over us in the air. But T.J. Liggett's address was superb.

Hunter Jones had been the victim of a heart attack. The irony of his declaration hit me. He led just one hymn for the Assembly and died.

In the State of the Church Address on Saturday morning, I highlighted a magnificent bequest of $8 million from the estate of Dewit and Othel Fiers Brown of Charlotte, North Carolina. Their giving from income over the years had been noteworthy. But their stewardship of accumulated resources had now reached historic proportions. Her bequest to the Christian Church (Disciples of Christ) was thought to be the largest bequest to a church body in the history of Protestantism. A permanent trust fund named for the Browns was to be established and managed by the Christian Church Foundation. Think of this, a gift in perpetuity which would bring upwards of half a million dollars annually to the mission of the church.

Dr. A. Dale Fiers, General Minister and President Emeritus was the brother of Othel Fiers Brown. Think of the heritage of commitment of this family. DeWitt and Othel Fiers Brown were such an integral part of the First Christian Church of Charlotte for over forty years, nurtured by and nurturing that community. I know for certain that A. Dale Fiers' broad vision of the mission of the church and his distinguished ministry in congregations and general leadership was a key element in the formation of such immense stewardship commitment of accumulated resources.

I had asked Dale Fiers to be present to be introduced at the lectern and to speak a few words. He came with a warm reception and spoke. I thanked him profusely. I also noted the bequest was made with the continuous help of the staff of the Christian Church Foundation. Through the years, Jim Reed, Herb Barnhard, and Jim Johnson were welcome in the Brown household.

"The most important element about this bequest," I said, "may not be just its size. The largest significance may be that, in a time when people seem to prefer designated specific gifts, here was a family committed to the broad mission of the church. So committed in fact, that they were willing to give the major portion of this estate to benefit the whole, the regions, general units, and institutions of the Christian Church (Disciples of Christ)."

The discussion on the Priority Resolution 8370 was brisk for twenty-four minutes and then was adopted with its plan for implementation. I had a feeling of accomplishment and leadership having shepherded it through the broad processes to its adoption and was now looking forward to its implementation.

The discussion on the "Jesus Only" Resolution was heated as you might expect. It was finally referred to the Commission on Theology with a proviso it would bring a report back to the 1989 General Board. It was noted that the originators of the resolution would be invited to come to the Commission on Theology to be a part of the considerations.

The discussion on the Nicaragua Resolution, number 8729, was also heated. One gentleman, referring to my being arrested in civil disobedience, loudly proclaimed, "If Alexander Campbell were alive today, he would turn over in his grave!" It was adopted.

Resolution 8727, "Resolution Concerning the Bible's Teaching on Homosexuality," had been presented by the Lake Worth, Florida, Disciples congregation. It cited proof texts that homosexuality is one of the sins listed in the Bible and is an unacceptable lifestyle for Christians! The General Board had recommended it not be adopted. The discussion included statements such as "homosexuals are persons God created, loves and redeems, and are to be included in the fellowship to love and be loved." "Proof texting this resolution does not consider the context of passages cited or take into account the variety of interpretations." "Not dealing with the issue with depth or sensitivity this resolution simply divides and polarizes." It was not adopted.

On Monday of the Assembly, I was to address the presidents of our church-related colleges at their dinner. It had been a historic day—October 19, 1987—the day the stock market crashed. The presidents' conversations were centered on what happened to their colleges and university endowments in one day. They had also been under pressure by the church to divest of funds invested in companies doing business in South Africa. There were also comments about the stock market taking care of the divestment in one day! I'm not sure they heard much of what I said in appreciation of our church-related institutions of higher education.

In my monthly article in the *Disciple Magazine*, I wrote a pastoral letter concerning the Louisville assembly:

> A "win-lose" mentality is inappropriate regarding General Assembly resolutions.
>
> At the 1987 General Assembly in Louisville, Kentucky, there were a number of resolutions where feelings ran quite high, with strong personal investment in the outcome of the vote. For some there seemed to be inordinate attention to winning and losing, and the question "how did we do." As I said at the time, I believe the question more appropriately should have been, "Was our action helpful for the body of Christ in its faithfulness to God's claim?"
>
> One of the things I learned as a very young pastor was not to identify so closely with an idea or proposition I was presenting as to feel that when the idea was debated or rejected, people were rejecting me as a person. Surely when an idea or proposition is presented to over 7,000 Disciples gathered in General Assembly, one must know the reality of the risk of widely differing opinions. There is risk in submitting a resolution,

as committed and able people often advance divergent ideas on almost any topic. In preparing resolutions, I believe it would be helpful for drafters to review business items from past Assemblies, looking at the "tone" and content of those resolutions. Most often it is possible to project the General Assembly acceptance of a proposition. Thus, when groups submit a resolution, knowing the proposition will most likely be opposed by a significant segment of the church, it is hardly fair for the submitters to excoriate the Assembly for being divisive, when, in fact they themselves have tried to move the Assembly in a different theological or ethical direction. One of the beautiful things about this church is the Accessibility of the floor of the General Assembly. Any congregation can submit a resolution. My point is that if one seeks to move the Assembly from the path of demonstrably adoptable positions, the risk of the rejection of such resolutions runs high. It is not my intention to try to stifle the submission of such business items. Rather, I would plead with submitters to understand and accept the responsibility for the risk they take in presenting propositions aimed at moving the position of the Assembly to either the ideological left or right.

Propositions about God's revelation in Jesus Christ are very personal. We strongly identify with our commitments to Jesus Christ, Lord and Savior, and predictably a resolution defining the nature of Christology will by its very substance elevate feelings.

The Louisville resolution 8728, "Concerning Salvation in Jesus Christ," certainly did just that. It sought to nail down a particular understanding of Christology. In the "Be it further resolved," it advanced to creedal element when it called upon the church "to do whatever is necessary to ensure...that the position of the resolution is 'the' position of our life.' This phrase was the basis on which the General Board believed the business item to be creedal, and the language to be that of an inquisition.

The Assembly did not defeat the resolution or "table Jesus." Nor did we reject the persons submitting the resolution. Resolution 8728 was referred to the Commission on Theology and Christian Unity, calling for a report to the General Board in 1989. The suggestion that the submitters of the Resolution be heard by the Commission on Theology is fair. We do need to hear one another with Christian grace. My hope and prayer is that the Commission on Theology will be as sensitive and faithful in their word to the church on Christology, as is the Preamble to "The Design for the Christian Church (Disciples of Christ)." It expresses my own personal faith so well. When the churches' representatives to the General Assembly in Louisville stood and declared themselves in these words, I believe they were declaring their faith as well.

We came back to our office, and I wrote letters to Congress and the President, as instructed by Assembly Resolutions. I had two days to accomplish those. I was leaving on Saturday to fly to Spain for the "World Conference on Sharing Resources" at El Escorial. The Conference was from October 26–30. JoAnne was flying to join me in Spain. Her fall "weekend off" from teaching began October 29. She was taking an additional week of personal leave so we could stay on in Spain until the following Wednesday, November 4.

The Conference concerned the work of the world's churches being channels for resources for world refugees. Representatives from the United Nations were in the Conference. We in the U.S. had Church World Service and the Heifer Project. But the magnitude of displaced persons in the world called for the world's churches to find more effective ways to meet human suffering. We Disciples, of course, had the Week of Compassion working with these agencies. (I would later share seeing firsthand the work of the Week of Compassion after I returned from Nicaragua.)

During the Conference I learned that the United States delegates would be coalescing and leading a North American "Conference on Sharing" in Portland, Oregon. I was asked to chair that event, and I agreed to do so.

JoAnne flew into Madrid on Friday morning. I had an adventure riding the train and taking a taxi to meet her. I was so glad to see her, and we had a wonderful reunion at El Escorial. She attended the last two days of the Conference with me.

After the Conference we visited Seville and then back to Madrid. Dining out in Spain was an adventure. Dinner time in restaurants was 9:00 p.m. when they opened for service. The first night we ordered from a Spanish menu. JoAnne wound up with a plate full of eels!

In Madrid we decided to go to the marvelous Music Hall for the symphony. The guest orchestra that night happened to be the St. Louis Symphony from the United States. We had a wonderful time in Spain. We flew home in time for me to speak at the Kansas City Regional Assembly. Then we went on to Miami to meet our delegation to visit Nicaragua.

The news release from our Disciples Office of Communication after the visit was this:

> November 25, 1987, MANAGUA, Nicaragua – An official delegation representing the Christian Church (Disciples of Christ) visited Nicaragua November 9 to 16, amidst its renewed hope for peace in the region. Sponsored by the Division of Overseas Ministries of the church and hosted in Nicaragua by the Evangelical Committee for Aid to Development (CEPAD), the group focused on theological and practical implications for the church in Nicaragua during this critical time in history.
>
> The Reverend John O. Humbert, Disciples General Minister and President, Indianapolis, Indiana, led the delegation of eight officials of the church. The group conveyed to the people of Nicaragua, 95% of whom are Christians, the position taken by the Disciples denomination in resolution passed at the General Assembly in October 1987, supporting the Central American Peace Plan, and previous actions which expressed opposition to the U.S. funding of the Contras.
>
> The Disciples delegation visited sites in Managua, Matagalpa, and the Jinotega province. Religious, community and government representatives asked for prayers for peace, especially now during the implementation of the accords signed by the five Central

American Presidents. Responding to one of the many statements of hope made during the visit, Humbert expressed the solidarity that Christians in the United States feel for brothers and sisters in Christ in Nicaragua. He described the visit as a faith-sharing event and stated, "We want to say as church that we stand with you and support your commitment to the lordship of Jesus Christ. As Christians we are best prepared to understand what the sources of peace will be."

Visiting in the first Base Community founded 21 years ago in Managua; in health centers which have grown from 18 to 85 in one province alone since the revolution and are now targeted for destruction by the Contra forces; in an army hospital ward filled with young amputees and a prison filled with over 2,000 Mosquito and Rama Indians being held for Contra activities; daycare centers filled with children who also have access to medical attention and good diets; the delegation found friendly responses amidst conditions which reflect the hardships of war and an economy which is barely able to support the essentials of the society.

The high point of the trip was the Sunday communion service celebrated with representatives from twenty Christian Mission congregations. Communion elements used were prepared and sent for the occasion by the Memorial Christian Church, Ann Arbor, Michigan. Two new Disciples congregations, in Houston, Texas, Good Shepherd and Iglesia Cristiana El Redentor, sent new communion ware.

For a number of years money given through Week of Compassion has gone to CEPAD which represents . Protestant denominations in Nicaragua and works in over 400 locations supporting efforts of local communities to improve their material, social and spiritual resources for living. Organized in 1972 in response to earthquake devastation which killed 10,000 people and destroyed the entire center of Managua, CEPAD now supports theological training and development for pastors and lay leaders, as well as providing training and materials for the development of drinking water projects, cooperatives, housing, latrine construction, child welfare, agricultural improvements, medical care, and education.

The delegation spent the last day in Managua with representatives of the Christian Mission Church, an Evangelical denomination with which the Disciples have developed an ecumenical relationship during the past two years.

Not in the news release was our visit to the consulate of the U.S. Ambassador to Nicaragua. I presented our resolutions to the Assistant Ambassador. He reported to our group that the Sandinistas were communists, and the U.S. government was supporting the Contras to overthrow the government. I spoke to him forcefully that we knew that the Sandinistas were elected in a world-monitored election. We knew that the Contras were attacking the health centers, stealing medicines, burning down the centers, and killing civilians. The people in the churches in Nicaragua were asking us to go back home and change our government's policy of supporting the Contras.

I continued to work on members of Congress to stop any aid to the Contras. Leaders of the National Council of Churches were working with the Speaker of the House to hold a news conference on Capitol Hill to publicly air our views. That came to fruition. We had a news conference in the Senate Office Building on February 1.

The leaders of the National Council met together just before the event. I was selected to preside and make the opening statement, and then present Speaker of the House James Wright. He spoke to the Senate and made his statement in opposition to more aid to the Contras.

As we met in a large meeting room of the Senate Office Building, all the major TV networks were there recording the event. I opened, and this is the statement I made:

> In November 1987, I was part of a delegation of eight persons from our church in a weeklong visit to Nicaragua. It was not our first contact with the people of Nicaragua, for we have a partner church there

from whom we hear regularly. We were hosted by this group, the Christian Mission Church, as well as the organization of Protestant, Evangelical and Pentecostal churches, over 40 denominations in Nicaragua, called CEPAD. CEPAD works with the people in between 200 and 300 villages and communities in Nicaragua.

We were with the people of the churches in Managua and out in the countryside, including time in the war zone around Jinotega, where, not incidentally, three days before our visit the Contras had kidnapped and murdered the mayor of the town. Almost every family in Nicaragua has been touched by death in the six-year war. When we were there in November the people were living in such high hopes that the Arias Five Nation Central America Peace Plan, or Esquipulas II, as they call it, would finally end the six years suffering of war.

The people said to us, "You are our hope. Please go back and work to stop the flow of your government money and arms to the mercenaries," by which they meant the Contras. The people of Nicaragua know this is a war between the U.S. government and their government, financed from Washington, directed, and run from Washington, in direct defiance of world opinion and the World Court which has ruled that we are breaking international law with the current administration's obsession with overthrowing another nation's duly elected government. The people know that any financial aid to the Contras, either so-called humanitarian aid or military aid, will only prolong the war.

The people know, too, that the Contras are composed primarily of former Samosa National Guard, at whose hands the people suffered torture, rape. and inhumane cruelty. The Contras' standard operating procedure is to attack widely dispersed health centers and clinics, steal people's medicine, kidnap health workers and blow up the facilities, attack the rural farm cooperatives targeted for kidnapping and assassination, blow up and machine-gun civilian buses.

To call the Contras freedom fighters is an absolute obscenity!

As a military force the contras are a failure, unable in six years to capture any territory, or gain broad support of the people. As retired U.S. General Paul Gorman has put it, "The counter revolutionaries in Nicaragua are totally incapable of achieving a military victory." In addition to the injustice and evil of our funding the Contras, in strictly pragmatic military terms, our funding the Contras in any way, is a futile financial effort, like pouring money down a rat hole."

"The Esquipulas II Peace Plan," which our government claims to support, demands an end to all outside financing of military, economic and political efforts to destabilize or overthrow the Nicaraguan government. The plan was signed in August, yet the US Congress wavered and in defiance of the Peace Plan sent $22,000,000 to the Contras in late 1987. That must not happen again! Any kind of aid to the Contras will simply prolong the war.

The people of Nicaragua are living in difficult economic times and would change some things about their government's policies. But they know conditions will not improve until the war ends, and the government no longer has to spend half its national budget fighting a war with Washington. It is a government elected in an election process monitored by a worldwide team certifying its credibility. Even the American Embassy spokesman with whom we had an audience at our Embassy in Managua said it was an election without irregularities at the polling places, and conceded that if an election were held tomorrow, the Sandinistas would hold their majority in the National Assembly.

When we were in the war zone near in Jinotega we visited a truck farming cooperative. They had built their own very simple cement block homes. One young mother invited us to see her home. She let us into the bedroom where in a makeshift hammock she proudly showed us her small baby. On the wall was written "God is love." In the corner stood a submachine gun to protect them from the Contras.

In the name of God, Congress must stop the killing! No more aid of any kind to the Contras!

I then presented James Wright, Democratic Representative from Texas and Speaker of the House, to make his statement in opposition to Congress funding the Contras. Then the Democratic Majority Whip of the House from Washington State made his statement, and we were done.

CBS News aired the conference, including segments of my opening statement. Several people told me they saw it. A week later I received the church newsletter from the First Christian Church of Mesa, Arizona. In the minister's column, the pastor wrote:

> What a surprise! I was watching television news Monday evening, trying to keep up on all that is happening in the Mecham case, and suddenly there was John Humbert filling the screen!
>
> John Humbert, as I hope you remember, is the General Minister and President of the Christian Church (Disciples of Christ) in the United States and Canada. He was on television news because of being the spokesperson for an ecumenical group of denominational leaders who presented a petition to Congress asking for the cessation of financing to the so-called Contras in Nicaragua. John was also acting on behalf of our General Assembly, which adopted a resolution in October asking Congress to cease such aid and directing our General Minister President to communicate that decision to Congress, and especially to the members of Congress who are part of the Christian Church (Disciples of Christ).
>
> To many people who saw that broadcast—and maybe some of you—John was just another church bureaucrat dealing with a political issue. We've seen a lot of that lately, with mixed feelings. It seems that every group in town has a statement to make these days, and it is easy to assume that the glamour of being on television is the primary motivation. Cynicism Reigns!
>
> But John Humbert is not just another faceless bureaucrat seeking a spot on network television! He is a warm, compassionate, and caring pastor who has a genuine conviction about what is going on in our world. He also is a faithful leader of the Disciples, personally carrying out the mandate of the General Assembly, even at the risk of a great deal of criticism. He was a caring pastor long before he became our

> General Minister and President! John is also one of us. He has over the years been a good friend to many of us in Arizona, and a fairly large number of us have rubbed shoulders with him in many Disciples meetings. I know he has been a real friend to Lisa and me as we went through some of our struggles in over the past three years. And today I learned he would have a close connection with our congregation—with George Phearson former pastor and now minister of the Apache Wells United Church of Christ here in Mesa, and a good friend of John's. It is indeed a small world!
>
> I am proud of my General Minister and President, and I am proud to belong to a denomination which would elevate such a caring person to high leadership. I support my General Minister and President in his attempt to carry out the wishes of our General Assembly and to bring a Christian perspective to one of the divisive issues of our day. I pray for my General Minister and President as he continues to lead us through a most turbulent period of our history. I encourage all of you to do likewise. Our leaders in Indianapolis as well as in Arizona need our support in our prayers. They are part of our caring fellowship! – Peace, Earle

Earle Van Slyck had been the Regional Minister for Michigan but now was Senior Minister of the First Christian Church of Mesa.

A churchwide planning conference as part of implementing our priority had been my idea. I wrote the following in my *Disciple Magazine* column for March 1988.

> The Louisville General Assembly adopted the priority for the church for the years leading to the next century, "to develop vital congregations as dynamic faith communities in prophetic, redemptive and reconciling ministries to the whole world." There were two resolutions focused on this one priority, both calling for a Churchwide Planning process for implementation. The General Minister and President was instructed to appoint a broadly representative team to design the Churchwide Planning Conference, now set for June 1–5 in Lexington, Kentucky. The group was appointed and confirmed by the

Administrative Committee in Louisville. The design team has been hard at work beginning on the final day of the Louisville General Assembly to work toward this major event. The event will consist of overall program planning for the Christian Church (Disciples of Christ) for the coming 12 years, with special focus on the Decade of Discipling in the 1990s.

Every congregation has received a letter of information regarding registration for the Churchwide Planning Conference. We look forward to strong attendance of persons who are willing to register, pay their way, and participate in one of the working groups on a biblical image of the dynamic church. The sequence of the implementing the priority will be as follows:

The launch on Pentecost Sunday, May 22, 1988, as congregations and other manifestation of the church are called to be in a time of prayer and consecration.

The Churchwide Planning Conference, June 1–5, 1988, in Lexington, Kentucky.

General Board of the Christian Church (Disciples of Christ) July 23–26, 1988, to which the plans and directions for resources from the Planning Conference will come for review, evaluation, and assignment of responsibility for development.

Fall and winter 1988–89: Regional Boards and General Unit board official action to adopt the priority; congregational clusters for information and congregational official action to adopt the priority.

Fall of 1988 and the year 1989: Development of program resources for implementing the biblical images of the dynamic faith community in congregational life.

We look forward to the days ahead and the new level of faithfulness as the body of Christ.

In the letters to congregations about the Churchwide Planning event, I wrote:

> In addition to on site participation, we are planning a most exciting possibility for your participation in the process if you remain at home June 1 through 5. We

have in place now, a Disciples electronic mail and conference forum. If you have a computer and a modem in your church, or a personal computer and modem at home, you can participate in this conference. Our computer network is called DISCIPLENET. It is a part of an ecumenical computer network called ECUNET, a computer online forum that uses telephone lines and a large computer service system to link up our desktop and portable computers.

The plan is to take the discussion and day's work of the working groups in Lexington and input the material into the computer network late each afternoon or early evening. Then Disciples who have joined the network can receive that material almost instantly. Individuals can respond to the discussion of the day. Or, as one pastor has suggested, a group of members can meet at the church that evening and discuss the material. Then groups or individuals can send back their suggestions to Lexington via DISCIPLENET where it will be picked up and shared with the working groups meeting the next day.

What an exciting possibility this is! To have the participation of large numbers of people in Lexington is great. Also, to have the input of people back home across the U.S. and Canada will be wonderful. There is still time for you to sign up for DISCIPLENET in time to participate in the Church Wide Conference. You can write the Office of Communication, attention DISCIPLENET, Box 1986, Indianapolis, IN 46206, or call and phone 317-353-1491 and learn how to get online in trying to participate in the conference.

As excited as I was about these developments as another way to bring all the segments of the church together, especially members of our congregations, two members of the Cabinet who consistently were negative, moaned about having just anybody in on planning for our church.

Nevertheless, it went off exceedingly well. Here is the report.

> We came to Lexington from many places. We came from Florida and the northwest, from California and New York, from Kentucky and Tennessee, from Canada

and Texas, from virtually every region of the church. Some of us came from other lands. Some of us speak Spanish or Korean more naturally than English. About half of us are female, and over 40% are laywomen and men. About a fifth are from small congregations, and some 95% are from congregations with fewer than 500 members. About 15% are Black, Hispanic, or Asian. As for our ages, some of us are still teenagers, some of us are beyond three score and 10. Most of us are in between. This was an authentic gathering reflecting the full life of the Disciples.

The early publicity for this event indicated that this would be a working conference, intentionally bringing together representatives of the three manifestations of the church—local, regional, and general—to explore together the implications and development of vital congregations.

Our work grew out of and was in the context of worship. We began and ended each day by expressing our Thanksgiving to God for the movement of God's loving and challenging spirit among us. We were led in worship by persons who shared their talents with us through song, movement, creative calls to works, and preaching. Flowing from our worship came the vision that congregations find vitality only as they seek to discover what God is asking of them.

The work of the Conference was accomplished in groupings which focused on one of 10 biblical images of the church. Much of the work was done in small groups of no more than 25 people.

The groups provided the setting in which we were able to reflect with each other about ways in which all of us in the church can be partners together as we live out the call to be dynamic faith communities.

The priority was discussed in each of the groups. Following that general discussion, there was specific work done in small groups which concentrated on one of the given biblical images of a vital congregation. Papers on each of the images had been thoughtfully prepared in advance of the conference and were presented by their authors who reflected the richness of the Christian Church (Disciples of Christ). After conversation with the writers, workgroups convened for Bible study, further reflection, and discussion of their assigned biblical image. Each group also made specific recommendations to the conference about ways to support the 10 images of vital congregations.

Throughout the conference, God's spirit was at work among us. A sign of the spirit's present was evident in the honest conversations between people who disagree, but who nevertheless care deeply about the life of the church. They were able, out of their love for the church, to contribute together to the life of the conference.

Each of the 10 groups prepared detailed reports on these specific marks of congregational life: confessing, teaching, caring, worshipping, sharing, converting, healing, ecumenical, mission, and peacemaking. These reports, which include specific recommendations on needs, resources, and implementation, will go in full to the General Board of the Christian Church (Disciples of Christ) in July 1988 for action. Copies are being sent to all Disciples congregations. Additional copies are available from the Office of Communication of the Christian Church (Disciples of Christ).

The conference has focused especially on how congregations find a growing vitality and how the church as a whole plays its supportive part.

There were 675 Disciples meeting in Lexington. Additionally, out in the church there were thirty-seven locations where Disciples were participating daily in the Conference by way of DISCIPLENET. What a computer "step forward" that was!

Together we produced and published a document, "Needs and Actions, Based on Ten Biblical Images," which was sent to each congregation with a cover letter from the GMP.

The General Board did its work on the material from the Conference.

JoAnne and I had another wonderful Bethany Beach vacation in August with Bill and Nancy Trimbur and our kids, who are very, very congenial. Crab fishing in a rowboat was an adventure, especially if one got loose in the bottom of the boat. Debbie was great with the wooden spoon, pushing the crabs back in the boiling pot in preparation.

Work was going forward with the architect on our new downtown office building, but not on fund raising. We called Howard Dentler back from retirement to work on local corporate fund raising, working with the president of one of the Indianapolis banks. He had promised to reach out to other banks and major businesses, but even though Howard camped in his office, we got little or no response. We had the million dollar grant from Lilly Endowment but not much else. So, we thought of Bill Barnes as an ace money raiser. Jim Reed and Jim Johnson were all for that and pushed for it. I had several visits with Bill Barnes, who was a development person for Christian Theological Seminary. He agreed to be our development person for the office building and to come on my Cabinet. He began in time for our 1988 General Cabinet retreat in Brown County on September 1 and 2.

Duane Cummins was going to be inaugurated as President of Bethany College on September 10. That meant he was going to leave his position as President of the Division of Higher Education (DHE) and as a Cabinet member. That would be our loss but Bethany's gain. I would attend that very special occasion at Bethany. The first meeting of the DHE search committee was on the twenty-seventh.

JoAnne and I had a fun weekend with the Manwarrons. Don was being honored by his home congregation in Galesburg, Illinois, for becoming such a noted church leader. The four of us drove to Galesburg on Saturday, October 8, and enjoyed his honors on Sunday. We toured important Galesburg sites, seeing the landmark store of Don's mother and the farm on which Elaine grew up. We drove home Sunday night. The Seminarians Conference was coming to Missions Building the next day. That was always very enjoyable. During the conference we had some of the seminarians come for dinner and the evening. Delightful!

JoAnne and I were preparing to attend the World Convention of our churches in Auckland, New Zealand. JoAnne had arranged for two weeks off from her classroom, partly on personal leave and partly as an experience related to her class. Through my good church friends in Auckland, JoAnne had linked up with an elementary school in Auckland as a sister school with her Indianapolis class. The fifth-grade classes had written letters back and forth. I videotaped JoAnne's class in action with their greetings to the New Zealand class. JoAnne had an appointment with the Australian fifth-grade class.

Our itinerary took us first to Los Angeles where John met us. It was just prior to my birthday. We had a delightful birthday dinner. Leaving LA we flew to Hawaii, stopping over night to break up the trip! From there, we flew to Australia for a church-to-church visit with our Australian Disciples. We were shepherded about by a couple who were leaders in our Australian church, visiting several congregations who were most hospitable. They also took us to see the National Arboretum. It was their spring. The blooming rhododendrons were magnificent!

We left from Melbourne to fly to Auckland, New Zealand, for the World Convention. One of the features was the convention planned trip to a sheep ranch to see the herding and shearing of sheep. We took advantage of that and were fascinated with the exhibition.

My assignment for the Convention was a speech at a men's breakfast. I remember that one of the points I was making had to do with issues which call us to action as Christians which are more than we are capable of addressing alone, for which we need to bind ourselves together in action. I used as illustration the plight of Christians in Nicaragua who pleaded with our delegation to go home and persuade our government to stop the funding of the civil war in Nicaragua. Afterwards, a layman from the U.S. came to me complaining, "You people in Indianapolis always come around to politics!" Ah, "You people…"

We arrived at the elementary school for JoAnne's appointment with the fifth-grade class. They received us warmly. I showed them the greetings and activities I had filmed from JoAnne's fifth-grade class. They had a lot of questions about life and school in Indianapolis. Then I filmed their class in action and their greetings to JoAnne's class. It was a heart-warming experience.

We departed Auckland Saturday at midnight November 5 for Los Angeles. Our son John met us. It was his birthday, so we had a nice birthday meal together and then had a 6:55 p.m. flight for Indianapolis. I came home to the Week of Compassion Committee meeting, the meeting of the Commission on Theology, in which the representatives of Disciple's Renewal made their case, the board of the Church Finance Council, a Consultation on Clergywomen, the Division of Overseas Ministries Board, the Task Force on Renewal, our GMP staff meeting, the beginning of the Conference of Regional Ministers and Moderators leading into December, and the Consultation on Church Union in New Orleans.

Jim Reed and Jim Johnson were pushing for a churchwide capital campaign, working with a fundraising company. We were now conducting a feasibility study as to whether it would fly. One of the recipients would be the building fund for constructing our new office building downtown. The Feasibility Task Force was meeting December 19 and 20.

January began with the annual Development Conference when all of the Disciples development people from our colleges and institutions came together for presentations from leading development professionals.

This was when I had the assignment for a presentation to the Southwest Region's Commission on Ministry, which I referred to earlier regarding Allen Harris's candidacy for ministry and ordination.

February 13 was JoAnne's birthday. We had celebrated and had just gone to bed when the phone rang. It was Michelle Spangler with word that John was in the hospital with Pneumocystis pneumonia and was HIV positive. Two hours later she called again to say that he was living with full-blown AIDS. We prayed, cried, and held each other all night. In the morning early we made reservations and flew to LA to Johnny. Michelle met us at LAX. But also, there was Ben Moore. Amazing! John had stayed with Ben and Beth overnight while he took the California Bar Exam at the Hollywood Palladium. They felt close to him. Michelle took us to the hospital. At the hospital they directed us to the floor for AIDS patients. As we went by the rooms most patients were all alone. So many were from the Midwest and their parents had disowned them. We were so glad to see John Dale! We were there with him as he was hospitalized for five days. Michelle was there with us for a great deal of the time, along with his partner, Tom Alburtis. When John could leave the hospital, I brought him home in his car. On the way we stopped for medicine—a thousand dollars for a month's supply. JoAnne was waiting with a hot lunch at John's home. We stayed another couple of days to see him settled back into some sense of normal life. He was going back to work in his law office. We flew back home to JoAnne's school and a meeting with my staff. We were open about John's AIDS and I let the Cabinet know. A number came to my office to lend support.

JoAnne and I had to go about our work. I went to Arkansas on March 5 to preach at the First Christian Church at Pine Bluff in the morning and then the District Convention. The next day was a Leader Development Conference at Columbia College for two days. It was followed by a three-day event in Kansas on evangelism and church vitality. I then flew to St. Louis for an NBA celebration and returned home on Sunday.

We were so glad that John and Joan Albrecht came to see us the next weekend. They had been with us constantly as friends and neighbors since John Dale was born. They watched him grow to be a first grader. We'd kept in close touch with them through the years.

For three days prior to that, the Conference of Ministers with Large Churches was held in Memphis, Tennessee, at Lindenwood Church. I always tried to get to that event for relationship reasons. Some of the ministers ("now that they had made it") were of the mind that "they didn't need anyone else."

After preaching the next Sunday at High Street Christian Church in Akron, Ohio, I met with the Division of Homeland Ministry's Search Committee the Sunday evening and Monday in St. Louis at the airport Hilton.

With the General Assembly coming July 28 to August 2, I had to prepare the docket of the General Board to mail to the Board members on April 6. It contained all the resolutions to be considered first by the General Board for their recommendations, and then to be forwarded do the congregations for the General Assembly. Included was the development of the plan for implementing the priority. Moving this through the Board with consensus was a challenge.

One of the hot issues was with regard to South Africa and the matter of our church institutions divesting of stock of companies doing major business in South Africa. Resolution 8329 in 1983 had called for all the administrative units, institutions, regions, and congregations to divest stock of companies continuing to do substantial business in South Africa. In Kansas City back in 1977, Resolution 7757 requested our units, institutions and congregations to evaluate their investments in this light. In 1985 in debate on this issue, Texas Christian University had been singled out by one speaker. Now one resolution came to my desk to be forwarded to the General Board, "Resolution Deploring the Refusal of Texas Christian University to Divest." (Things had gotten markedly worse in South Africa since 1983 under declared state of emergency, with Blacks arrested and detained without warrant.) A second resolution came, "Resolution on South Africa and Apartheid." It called for the General Board and Commission on Finance to be instructed by the General Assembly to withhold financial support from organizations, institutions, general units, or regions associated with the Christian Church (Disciples of Christ) which had not begun to divest, and if the divestment was not 75 percent done by December 31, 1993, the funds would be allocated to other segments of the church.

I had occasion to be at Texas Christian University and in conversation with Bill Tucker, in his Chancellor's office. He asked me what I thought should be his response to the resolutions. I said, "You made your statement in the General Assembly two years ago. We'll see what the General Board does with the resolution. But I think you shouldn't get hooked on the discussion. Just let it play out without getting defensive. Then just receive the advice the Assembly gives you."

Further related to our passionate attention to the evils of apartheid in South Africa was Resolution 8935, "Resolution Concerning the African National Congress as a Means for Peace and Justice in South Africa." It declared that the African National Congress, the party of Nelson Mandela, deserves an appropriate opportunity to contribute to the search for peace and justice in South Africa. Further it called on the governments of the U.S. and Canada to use their fullest political, diplomatic, and economic strength to end the vicious cycle of injustice in South Africa. Further it called on the General Minister and President to convey these views to the President, Secretary of State and all leaders of Congress of the US and the Prime Minister and Parliament of Canada. The Africa Department of the Division of Overseas Ministries had been working with the African National Congress for justice, and we had given money for their merciful work. We felt a kinship. General Board recommended that the General Assembly adopt this resolution.

With my emphasis on addressing the role of women in top leadership in the church, having accomplish the election of Claudia Grant as Deputy General Minister and President and Carolyn Day, now as Vice President of Communication, I was supportive of Resolution 8931, "Resolution Concerning Economic Justice for Women." It called for the General Assembly to affirm and urge full and adequate support and funding for the governmental agencies and programs engaged in advocacy and the safeguarding of economic justice for women, e.g., Equal Employment Opportunity Commission. It also called for further support of Church Women United's Five Year Imperative on Poverty of Women and Children using materials available from the Division of Homeland Ministries. The General Board recommended that the General Assembly adopt this resolution.

In the General Board Meeting we developed a substitute resolution, number 8945, for the two resolutions about divestment.

> Background:
>
> Apartheid is an immoral system of minority domination that has produced overwhelming hardships for Blacks in South Africa, resulted in numerous acts of violent persecution and mass murder, and is oppressive of both the white and Black populations.
>
> The final hour for accompanying any victory over apartheid by nonviolent means, appears to be at hand because Blacks are being armed. The population of South Africa is 68% black, 12% colored, 18% white and 2% other races. Therefore, it is clear apartheid cannot continue and will be resolved either violently or nonviolently.
>
> Black church leaders of South Africa are working feverishly to keep the movement nonviolent but are increasingly losing the support of the people to trade union leaders and other groups which are not committed to a nonviolent solution. South African Black churches' leaders are asking for support of the world's Christians through divestment and other economic sanctions.
>
> Economic sanctions are having an effect on the economy. The Rand in December of 1987 was worth $0.51 against the American dollar and in March of 1989 had dropped to $0.39 against the American dollar. The economic index went from 100 in 1989 to 228 in 1986 and 265 in 1987. Exports are decreasing.
>
> The Christian Church (Disciples of Christ) has supported selected divestment and in resolution 8329

urged its related General Units, Institutions and Regions to divest. The General Assembly is gratified that in response to this resolution, the overwhelming majority of entities related to the Christian Church (Disciples of Christ) have divested, or are in process of divesting, including all General Units, 5 theological education institutions, 11 colleges and universities, 35 regions and a number of other organizations that relate to the church. However, some of our related institutions and a region have made a decision not to divest.

It is recognized that the church and the institutions of higher education are in covenant, so declared and officially signed by both parties. On the one hand, the church covenants to:

"Recognize the right, desirability and necessity of the institutions to be under the independent control of its governing board and not...the church."

On the other hand, the institutions of higher education covenant to:

"Seek to understand the churches' concerns, aware that the church and the institution hold in common the development of persons to their highest potential and the shaping of a society beneficial to all." (From "A Covenant Between the Christian Church (Disciples of Christ) and our Colleges and University.")

Therefore, be resolved, that the General Assembly affirm its stand that apartheid is a moral issue and is an evil and oppressive system;

Be it further resolved, that the General Assembly of the Christian Church (Disciples of Christ) acknowledges it stands in solidarity with church leaders of the South African Council of Churches who are working in the name of Christ to end the oppression of apartheid by nonviolent means;

Be it further resolved, that the General Assembly commends the organizations, institutions, general units and regions which have divested according to the General Assembly Resolution 8329, and as reported to the General Assembly by the Corporate Responsibility Advisory Committee, and expresses appreciation to the Council of Colleges and Universities for its commitment to begin participating in the meetings of the Corporate Responsibility Advisory Committee;

Be it further resolved, that the General Assembly, recognizing the covenant relationship with its institutions of higher education, and the "right desirability and necessity of the institutions to be under the independent control of its governing board and not... the church, nevertheless recalls that the institution has committed itself to understand the church's concern, aware that the church and the institution hold in common the shaping of a society beneficial to all," and therefore, in the spirit of covenant strongly urges the institutions and region which have not yet taken positive action, to reconsider prudent sale of stock held in Chevron, Control Data, IBM, Mobile, Royal Dutch Shell, Texaco, and Unisys, the seven U.S. companies still doing major business in South Africa.

The General Board recommended that the General Assembly Adopt business item 8945 as amended.

One of the key reports that came to the Board was the Report of the Commission on Theology in response to resolution number 8728, "Concerning Salvation in Jesus Christ." 8728 was the resolution that resolved that "Jesus Christ is the only Savior of the world, and that apart from him there is no salvation; and we should do whatever is necessary to ensure our programs and activities are centered on Christ, and consistent with the fact that He alone is Savior and Lord."

The report was a marvelous statement of the theology of God and Jesus Christ. Two key points were as follows: (1) Not the church, but God decides who will be saved; (2) Because God is who God is in Jesus Christ, Christians have reason to trust that by God's mercy, no human being is ultimately rejected and nullified by God.

The General Board recommended that the Assembly "receive with deep appreciation the report of the Commission on Theology and affirm that it expresses biblical faith in Jesus Christ as Savior which this church proclaims and teaches, and recommends this report for widespread study among congregations, regions, and institutions of the Christian Church (Disciples of Christ)."

The Task Force On Renewal and Structural Reform had been busy as we sought to clarify classification of Business Items for the General Assembly in the special rules of procedure for the General Assembly. Those rules called for four kinds of items: reports, resolutions, definitions of policy, and study documents. We proposed five, since resolution was too broad a classification;

1. reports
2. operation, policy, and organizational items
3. study documents
4. items for reflection and research
5. sense of the assembly resolutions

One of the elements proposed in classification five was key: "A Sense of the Assembly Resolution is out of order and shall not be considered by the General Assembly when it contains doctrinal statements as a 'test of fellowship' in its 'Therefore be it resolved' text. Determination of eligibility shall be by the Executive Committee of the Administrative Committee of the General Board upon recommendation of the General Minister and President."

The responsibilities of the GMP were expanded to include inviting each resolution-submitting entity to designate a spokesperson to attend the meeting of the General Board in which their business item would be processed (at the entity's expense). The GMP had already been inviting a representative of the submitting body to make the first speech in favor of the resolution at the General Assembly.

Things were really hopping after our successful General Board meeting with a crucial New Facilities Committee meeting May 11 and 12, National Council of Churches Board meeting in Lexington, Kentucky May 16 to 18, the Oregon Assembly in Portland, where I preached twice, and then on Sunday morning at the First Christian Church in Salem, Oregon.

May 21 to 25 was the World Council of Churches Conference on Mission and Evangelism in San Antonio, Texas. It was a gathering of church leaders of all stripes from all over the world. I had been chosen to serve as Chair of the U.S. Host Committee. The Committee had been meeting periodically in San Antonio and New York to be ready to host this major event. I had been working with Joan Brown Campbell, who at that point was the Chair of the World Council's U.S. Office in New York City. Her staff was really helpful in my committee work.

While in Texas, I met with Disciples ministers in the Austin area.

The General Synod of the United Church of Christ was meeting in Fort Worth, Texas, June 29 to July 4, 1989. Among other issues, the Partnership Committee was to be presented, "Declaring that the UCC would now be in full communion with the Disciples." It was crucial that I be there to respond. The resolution received good attention and discussion and was adopted. Now we were to take our Disciples positive action in the Indianapolis Assembly July 28 to August 2.

"Full communion" means

1. Both churches make common confession that Jesus is the Christ the Son/Child of the living God;
2. Members of each partner church are members of the one universal Church of Jesus Christ and thus are linked to one another as members of one body;
3. Member share in celebrating the Lord's supper/holy communion in local churches, associations/areas regions/conferences and in national and international meetings;
4. Ordained ministers of each partner church are truly ministers of word and sacrament;
5. And both churches search for mutual ways of manifesting the common mission of witness and service.

The 1989 Indianapolis General Assembly opened July 28, two days after we celebrated our 37th wedding anniversary. I'll let the General Assembly News, written by Bob Friedly, describe it:

Diverse but not divided. The words were those of a self-described conservative late in the 1989 General Assembly and they referred to a church that came into its assembly certainly diverse, with some question about the not divided.

But this was an assembly characterized by sweetness and light-sweetness despite a few pickets, hecklers, and other routine hazards of public witness in the present day and the theology Commission would say that God will be the judge as to how much light there was.

Despite emotional issues embraced by people who are poles apart, a record number of resolutions sent back for reworking and twice the normal number of General Board recommendations overturned, the 1989 General Assembly in Indianapolis will be remembered for contending spirits that were content to love and let love.

Conservatives who for years have felt unheard and unwanted beamed broadly as they shared with Administrative Committee members in shaping a response Jesus Christ issue—one which honored the Commission on Theology's report, but acknowledged other views, welcomed opposing statements, and reaffirmed that historic commitment. Jesus is the Christ...Lord and Savior of the world.

General Minister and President John O. Humbert was at his warm reconciling best. In the State of the Church, he spoke boldly in areas that he knew would draw criticism, (also 17 applause interruptions). He entreated Disciples to speak the truth with patience, kindness, gentleness, and self-control. "Let us behave in debate at least as if we have these fruits of the spirit (applause) ...though our differences are real let us love one another."

The historic passion for Unity of Disciples received a refueling. The General Assembly approved "full communion" with the Disciples ecumenical partner denomination, the United Church of Christ, portending a future of exciting and challenging new relationships.

Three thousand Disciples paraded down the middle of the street past the Indiana State Capitol and gathered on a triangle of cleared land where in about three years a seven story Disciples International Center will become a dramatic new symbol of identity, witness, and worldwide mission.

JoAnne and I drove home from the Indianapolis Convention Center with feelings of a combination of accomplishment and anticipation of our vacation together in Marco Island, Florida, with Debbie and Jessica.

In Florida we had been given the use of a condo, with only the cleaning of the facility to pay before we left. The beach was beautiful. The restaurants were plentiful. We even played some tennis. Jessica wrote a movie script that we all had parts in, and it was duly filmed on our camera with interruptions of great laughter. It was a wonderful three weeks.

Back to work, I was meeting with two search committees, DHM's presidential search, and the Southwest regional minister's position search in Fort Worth, Texas. The latter was especially enjoyable because Ken Teegarden was the interim regional minister.

The General Cabinet met for its annual fall meeting, with a special sense of good spirit after the Assembly, with the two who were sometimes hard to bring along even complimenting me on my State of the Church address and leadership in the Assembly.

In September, we began the two-year cycle toward the Tulsa General Assembly in 1991 with the orientation of the new moderators, David Cole, Moderator, Fran Craddock, First Vice Moderator, and C. William Bailey, Second Vice Moderator.

The people of the Mooresville, Indiana, Christian Church were upset about the report of the Theology Commission on Salvation in Jesus Christ and other resolutions. They called, requesting a meeting of delegations from their church with the General Minister and President at Missions Building. I responded positively, and the meeting was set for 4:30 on October 10.

When they arrived, the delegation was 15 members of the congregation and their minister. I was cordial and introduced myself to individuals as they came into our Fellowship Hall. We sat in a circle, and I asked them to tell me what was on their mind and hearts. They did.

I reminded them about Assembly resolutions: they are advice and counsel to our congregations, but are not binding. They are also a declaration to the world around us of the will of Disciples attending that particular assembly. The five thousand word report of the Commission proclaimed Jesus Christ as Savior, but also cautioned Christians about making self-righteous judgments that belong to God. The report maintains there are two themes in the New Testament, one stressing Jesus as the only path to salvation, the other that salvation is God's grace to all and cannot be earned by people's response. No human is ultimately rejected and nullified by God, the Commission found.

I reminded them that the report declared that confessing that Jesus Christ is Savior is not a test which one must pass before God will show merciful love, but a means which God has provided so that the experience of that love can be shown and enjoyed by all. Reaction of the General Assembly was to receive the report of the Commission, stating that it

> reaffirms our belief that Jesus is the Christ, the Son of the living God, and proclaims him Lord and Savior of the world. We acknowledge that no statement of faith can fully express the whole faith of the whole church. We offer this report as one source to congregations, regions, general units, organizations, and institutions within the church for study and response. We urge ongoing dialogue in searching that we may grow in our understanding of the Lordship of Jesus Christ and in our freedom to embrace all who name Jesus Christ as Savior.

We had an extended discussion. Though I'm sure there was some level of disappointment as the group left, at least the level of tension with which the group arrived was much lower. I hoped they now knew that at least the GMP was a caring person.

The following Sunday, October 15, I was invited by the presiding Bishop of the Episcopal Church to join other heads of communions for a service of prayer for persons with AIDS at the Washington National Cathedral. Bishop Browning and I had become friends and he was very thoughtful and empathetic with prayers for our son John. It was a meaningful and heartrending service. After Bishop Browning's sermon, we went to stations to receive individuals who wished to come for anointing with oil and prayer. Here is the news release from our Office of Communication regarding the service:

> WASHINGTON D.C. October 15, 1989 – One by one they came. Each with their private sorrow, each with their own pain. As they moved to the appointed station, church leaders reached out and touched them as if to ease some of their suffering and infuse the healing love of Christ in their life. They were there for the Ecumenical Service of Compassion and Healing for persons who have AIDS and their families held in Washington National Cathedral on October 15th.
>
> The Reverend John O. Humbert, General Minister and President of the Christian Church (Disciples of Christ) who was a participant in the service, described it as an emotionally charged experience. Persons suffering from Acquired Immune Deficiency Syndrome, their families and friends not only heard words of comfort at the service but experienced the laying on of hands. Humbert and eleven other leaders of communions stood at four stations in the cathedral to offer prayer and lay hands on those who came.
>
> "It was a very moving experience to meet people, call them by name and pray for them," said Humbert, who added that "many of these individuals and families have experienced rejection because of the stigma of AIDS. For the church to reach out to them in compassion and healing was affirming," he said.
>
> "AIDS: to Heal and Make Whole" was the theme of the service which was a dream of Bishop Edward Browning, Presiding Bishop of the Episcopal Church.

Browning had ministered to a person suffering with AIDS while serving a parish in Hawaii and continued to carry that concern when he became Presiding Bishop in 1986, according to Humbert. A year ago, he invited the heads of communions of National Council of Churches member churches, as well as Roman Catholic Bishops, to participate in the leadership of an ecumenical service for persons with AIDS.

After the service, the denominational leaders met for dinner to share their personal stories of ministry and care of persons with AIDS. Humbert said individually some congregations and ministers are working with those who have AIDS and their families, but after experiencing the impact of this service, he hopes it is replicated in other communities.

"Our hope is that people ecumenically in local communities will gather for worship services of compassion and healing and will seek to encourage pastors and regional leaders to become involved in AIDS care," said Humbert.

Disciples have available through its Division of Homeland Ministries a packet on AIDS and at its 1989 General Assembly passed a resolution encouraging compassionate care and love for those with AIDS and their families.

From a weekend with attention to AIDS, the next weekend, October 19 and 22, was a big family weekend! It was Jeff's wedding in Baltimore. JoAnne, Beatrice, and I drove to Cleveland and then rode with Debbie and Jessica to Baltimore and our hotel. It was our first occasion to meet Linda's parents. We enjoyed the rehearsal dinner Friday night, after the rehearsal at the Baltimore Children's Museum. This was Linda and Jeff's choice for the setting of their wedding. Linda's dad was a National Airlines pilot with the third highest seniority in the whole system. We enjoyed getting acquainted. The wedding went well, with John and his partner Tom there. I did the honors. John was an usher, Bill and Nancy Trimbur were there from Philadelphia. Barkley and Joyce Brown were there as well.

At the reception I gave a toast, as did Barkley Brown. It was a great opportunity for JoAnne and me to dance. She was beautiful! Then I invited and took Jessica to the dance floor. We danced together with her at first being a little embarrassed to do that. But it was a delightful evening and weekend.

The following Saturday was a dinner at the Adams Mark Hotel in Indianapolis to honor John Compton, retiring as President of the Division of Homeland Ministries. He had a noted and illustrious career in ministry with the Disciples:

- First Black Associate State Secretary (Ohio)
- First Black assistant to the General Minister and President (Dale Fiers)
- First Director of Reconciliation (helped to conceive it)
- First Black Regional Minister (Indiana)
- First Black General Unit President (DHM)

We had been young ministers in Ohio, he in Cincinnati and I in the Dayton suburb of Kettering. So we were longstanding friends and colleagues.

The National Council of Churches Governing Board met in Pittsburgh in mid-November. I had to be there early as part of the Executive Committee. Thinking about this reminds me of the long discussions we had over the membership of the Metropolitan Community Church denomination in the National Council. The members of those congregations were primarily gay persons. There had been discussions as to whether we would admit the denomination whose life was based on congregations being committed as people who are gay. By this time, that communion had been admitted for membership.

We had a big Thanksgiving celebration with Dick and Peggy, Debbie and Jessica, and JoAnne and me. But we also hosted the Helme family for Saturday lunch, with Mary Jane Helme and Mark Alland. They were both in school at Texas Christian. The table for our Saturday "Thanksgiving continuing food" was the ping pong table on the lower study level of the lake house, where the food was served. It was large enough to accommodate the large dinner.

The Conference of Regional Ministers and Moderators was held at Bethany College at the invitation of the President, Duane Cummins, December 2–3. Ken Teegarden was still the interim regional minister in the Southwest Region and as good friends of Duane and Suzi Cummins, he and I were invited to stay with them in the President's home in the third-floor apartment. That was most enjoyable.

The Council of Ministers followed, with this GMP presenting a keynote paper as proposed in the procedures of implementing the priority in resolution 8949 at the 1989 Assembly.

This was in the resolution.

> As part of the implementation of the first phase of the priority, the General Minister and President shall prepare a document which attempts to identify:
>
> (a) those things that would keep Disciples from being vital faith communities.
>
> (b) the vision of our mission and ecclesiology which compels us to be vital faith communities.
>
> This text should draw on the various resources, including the regional listening conferences, the CTS Conference, "Christians Only, But Not the Only Christians," and the Lexington Churchwide Planning Conference and appropriate ecumenical consultation. The text would be shared with the 1989 Council of Ministers at Bethany College, West Virginia, and after revision directed to the Executive Committee of the Administrative Committee to inform the implementation of the priority.

Not much of an assignment! I worked thoughtfully on the presentation of the (a) and (b) assignments. I shared my thinking and written sections in consultation with my friend Michael Kinnamon. It turned out to be a 33-page document. I will not include it here, but I will share the outline.

I. The vision of our mission and ecclesiology which compels us to be vital faith communities
   A. The vision and experience of our encounter with the Holy, God in Jesus Christ
   B. The vision of the church as the Body of Christ
   C. The vision of the church as the covenant community
   D. The vision of the gift of God's evangel in Christ
   E. The vision of the church involved in social concern and social transformation
   F. The vision of the church in ministry
II. Those things which keep Disciples from being vital faith Communities
   A. Our knowledge and understanding of scripture
   B. Our knowledge and understanding of Disciples tradition
   C. Our knowledge of the tradition of the church
   D. Our understanding that the faith community is God's church
   E. Our understanding of the church as the body of Christ
   F. Our understanding of the church as the people of the covenant in God's *koinonia*
   G. Our understanding and practice of witness in word and deed
   H. Our understanding of social concern and social transformation
   I. Our understanding and practice of ministry

The members of the Council of Ministers then discussed the document I presented. It was not as extensive as I had hoped. But I had fulfilled my commission!

John and his partner Tom Alburtis came for Christmas. AIDS was taking a heartbreaking toll on our Johnny. His energy was flagging; he needed to rest extensively. He was feverish all the time and he had lost weight. It was so difficult to see him failing. Up until November of 1989, he had been going into the law firm's office in Santa Monica to work. Now he was working from home. Deb, Tom, and Jessica were there for a family Christmas which had overtones of this being our last Christmas with our Johnny.

As 1990 dawned, I threw myself into the General Minister and President meetings of the Cabinet, Renewal and Structural Reform, ministers of the "steeple congregations," the feasibility study for the capital campaign, Disciples Development Conference, and the New Facilities Committee. We were not doing well in raising money for the new office building. The Administrative Committee met the last of January. It had taken action asking that I appoint a New Hymnal Committee. We had attempted to move on doing a new more inclusive language hymnal jointly with the UCC. But in conferences on the matter, personalities had "gotten in the way of the kingdom," and that possibility had been scrapped. I had presented a list of broadly representative folks for a committee, but the Administrative Committee thought I had not done enough with the representative factor. So, I continued to work through the General Board and the Administrative Committee for a satisfactory committee three times. Now finally, in the 1990 Administrative Committee, it was approved.

This meeting of the Administrative Committee became historic. During the meeting there was the recognition of the release of Nelson Mandela on February 11, 1990. A fortunate occurrence was that the chaplain of the African National Congress was present in our meeting. After making a statement regarding Mandela's release, I presented the Chaplain Reverend Fumanekile Gqiba to speak to us.

The News Release from the Disciples Office of Communication was as follows:

> Indianapolis – "The release of Nelson Mandela is the first step. It is not the end at all. The pillars of the racist system still are there," the Reverend Fumanekile Gqiba Chaplain of the African National Congress said in Indianapolis, February 12, at the Administrative Committee meeting of the Christian Church (Disciples

of Christ). "For South Africa to make progress in ending apartheid, the next step is to reform the economic policies that allow the nation's minority of whites (Blacks outnumber whites five to one) to control 87% of the land." Other steps include controlling the nation's police that Gqiba termed "ready to shoot and act beyond the law."

Calling the Indianapolis based Christian Church Disciples of Christ "partners in a mission," Gqiba said that the 1.1 million member denomination and others opposing South Africa's racist policies partly are responsible for Mandela's release.

"International solidarity is one of the pillars for combating apartheid," Gqiba said. "Our South African economy is linked to the international economy. Boycotts have placed strong pressure upon the government to reform."

"We rejoice that Mr. Mandela never has wavered in his vision of a free, Democratic, nonracial and indivisible South Africa," Rev. John O. Humbert, General Minister and President of the domination said in an address to the body. "The courage and commitment of Mandela has been a wellspring of inspiration to South Africans of all races who yearn for justice and peace."

Mandela was released from prison Sunday after being imprisoned for 27 years for helping to organize the South African National Congress, an anti-apartheid organization that until recently was banned by the South African government.

The Administrative Committee unanimously approved sending letters to South Africa president F.W. de Klerk praising his "bold steps" in moving toward a New South Africa. The letter also urged the removal of troops from black townships, an end to the nation's state of emergency, and the release of political prisoners.

A separate letter to ANC president Oliver Tambo pledged the churches "redoubled" support in ending South Africa system of forced racial separation.

I did write the letters to President F.W. de Klerk and Oliver Tambo. I received a letter from the office of the President of the African National Congress,

> Dear Rev. Humbert,
>
> This is to acknowledge, with deep appreciation and sincere thanks, receipt of your letter to our President, Oliver Tambo, informing him of how you celebrated the Release of Nelson Mandela.
>
> The release was indeed a great victory for all peace-loving people of the world.
>
> We thank you very much for your support and remain convinced that your Church will continue your support for the struggle against the evil system of apartheid.
>
> Yours sincerely, Anthony Mongalo, Secretary For Presidential Affairs.

On February 23, 1990, I met with the chairman of the new hymnal committee, Dan Merrick of Peoria, Illinois, and they then began their work.

Meanwhile, the search committee for a new President of the Division of Homeland Ministries had done its work. Anne Updegraff Spleth was installed as President at a service of worship on JoAnne's birthday, February 13, at Geist Christian Church where Anne's husband Randy Spleth was the minister. I gave the installation sermon.

I flew to Corvallis, Oregon, on Saturday, February 24. After a stop off in St. Louis for the Executive Committee of the Regional Ministers and Moderators. I had the privilege of preaching at the First Christian Church of Corvallis, where my grandparents, G.S.O. and Ella Humbert, had served as co-ministers from 1900 to 1903. Their service as ministers was recognized in worship. It was a thrill for me to be there and to preach where my grandparents had.

From Corvallis, I flew to New York City for a series of meetings for the planning of the Ecumenical Conference on Sharing of

Resources which would take place in Portland later in the year. It would be the United States follow up of El Escorial.

I was home on Wednesday, February 28, and I was off to Tulsa for the Thursday through Sunday meeting of the Tulsa Assembly Program and Arrangements Committee. By this time Don Manworren was fully in command of Howard Dentler's wonderful plan of organization of the committee structures and was doing a great job. I was just moral support and a pastoral presence. The Committee chose the theme "In Remembrance of Me." The daily themes were as follows: Friday, "Celebrate With Thanksgiving" (with communion); Saturday, "Proclaim Christ's Presence"; Sunday, "Embrace One Another"; Monday, "Share My Bread"; Tuesday, "Anticipate God's Future"; Wednesday, "Go Forth With God's Hope."

The Committee urged that in planning the worship for Tulsa, we recognize we would be in Native American country.

Interestingly, I was invited to preach for the First Christian Church in Logansport, Indiana, on March 11, 1990. This is the congregation that some months before had uninvited me from preaching for them on an appointed Sunday. This was the congregation that reacted against my being arrested in the U.S. Capitol Rotunda in my civil disobedience regarding Nicaragua. Evidently, lay leadership had changed or at least their minds and feelings had changed as well as their attitude. So, I preached for them on March 11.

The following Saturday was an ecumenical prayer service and rally in Washington with regard to our government's positions towards Central America. The service was held in a Roman Catholic Church on Capitol Hill. I was one of the speakers along with Jim Wallace, editor of *Sojourners* magazine, an evangelical publication. After the service, we marched in our robes out in the rain to the Capitol.

The next day, March 25, I was in Cleveland for the installation of Paul Sherry as President of the United Church of Christ. I flew in on Saturday night, stayed with Debbie and Tom and then participated in the service. Unbeknownst to me at the time, Bob and Carolyn and Bruce were worshippers in that service.

JoAnne's spring vacation was the first week in April. We headed for Niles to spend some time with Jo's mother, Beatrice. I had breakfast on Saturday morning with Disciples ministers from the Warren, Niles, Girard, and Youngstown area. It was a really good visit. But as we were visiting in Niles, having kept in touch with John by phone, it was clear that he was in his serious wasting away period. JoAnne said, "John, don't you think it's time that your mother should come be with you?" He wholeheartedly agreed. So, we arranged for her to fly to Los Angeles. Michelle Spangler met her and took her to Topanga Canyon, John's home, on Good Friday, April 13. By this time John was basically bedfast. The AIDS had so affected the nerves in his feet that it was agony for him to stand. JoAnne stayed with him in his home the week of Easter and for two weeks after.

It was a Godsend that I was coming to Los Angeles to lead a Pacific Southwest Regional Ministers Retreat, April 22–25. The retreat center was only a half hour from John's home in Topanga. I could spend the night with JoAnne, John, and his partner Tom, and then from breakfast through dinner time be at the retreat.

On Tuesday the 24, Tom and JoAnne were able to get John to see his doctor. It was agonizing. The doctor's word was that John could not live much longer. When I returned that evening from the retreat I sat down by his bedside. From his bed he said, "Dad, how do you get ready to die?" My thirty-five-year-old beloved son, my John.

"I can only tell you what I believe. Your life will not end. Your body won't be able to sustain your life as we experience it. But the mystery we believe from God is you will pass over into a continuing life. Some have had near death experiences where there was a passageway with persons waiting for them on the other side in a beautiful light. Jesus said he was preparing a way for us.

I believe it. We will all go through this, my beloved son." He said, "Well, I have a lot of friends over there ahead of me."

Meanwhile, I was leading the spiritual retreat, and JoAnne was sharing her love with her firstborn. She was also working with the doctor to find a nurse who would come stay with John while Tom was at work in a law office where he managed the support staff and operation. She had to return to Indianapolis on Saturday the twenty-eighth to her teaching position. Fortunately, she found a nurse whom she employed. I was leaving on the twenty-sixth to go to the Louisiana Regional Assembly in New Orleans to speak and preach.

I came back to Indianapolis for the meeting of the Commission on Finance, the big one related to the funding distribution decisions for regions and general units. It ran all week. On Friday the 4, we had our staff meeting from nine to twelve. (I haven't mentioned these meetings prior to this.) It was good for us to be together for the sake of our souls and spirits—Claudia, Don, John, Neil, Frank, and myself. We did this periodically, sharing where we were with our work and our beings as we were pulled in different directions. But my door was always open to all our staff, and they were welcomed warmly for time with me as needed. And of course, Don, Claudia, and I went to lunch every day we were in town.

National City Christian Church Board was meeting that Friday and Saturday. The National City Corporation Board was composed of several members of the congregation, plus elected members from across the church. The General Minister and President was an ex officio member of the Board. The church's stand was that it needed churchwide support because otherwise Disciples would not have a witness in the nation's capital. It was our "National Cathedral." Of course, when I was serving at the "witness place" in North Chevy Chase and there were five or six other Disciples churches in suburban D.C., we felt that position was a little extreme and not quite accurate. Now, I was related to the Corporate Board as an ex officio member. I tried not to let my feelings of yore affect my participation. This particular Board meeting was honoring Gertrude Dimke. She had moved to Washington, D.C., to be employed by National City and was now retiring again. She had been the Executive Secretary in the Office of the GMP when I came to work there as Deputy. She had worked especially with Howard Dentler, and when he retired, so did she. I was one of her "Ohio boys" from CYF Conference days, so it was good to be there for her warm accolades.

However, I needed to fly that evening to Raleigh-Durham, rent a car, and drive to Wilson, North Carolina, for a commencement address the next day in the afternoon for Atlantic Christian College. The Board was meeting that weekend with the express purpose of settling on a new name for the college. They felt that "Atlantic Christian" sounded too much like a fundamentalist moniker. But they adjourned on Saturday, unable to make a unanimous decision. In my opening remarks, I noted that this institution, by whatever name, was cherished by the Disciples of Christ in the United States and Canada. Subsequently, the name was changed to Barton College, after Barton W. Stone of North Carolina and Kentucky, the founder of the Christian Church wing of our movement. Later, one letter writer to *Disciple Magazine* noted that in naming a college after a person, it was a good thing his first name was not "Bubba." Ah, Bubba College! That has a ring to it!

I was staying with Ben and Betsy Hobgood overnight in Wilson. When we returned to their home after the graduation festivities, JoAnne had left a message on their phone. She had heard from Tom in Topanga saying that John had become delirious. At his doctor's instruction, Tom had taken him to the hospital with word that he was in his final days. I called JoAnne as we shared in this news. She made reservations for us to fly to Los Angeles the next morning. I had reservations for a Delta flight departing at 6:25 in the evening, arriving in Indianapolis that evening at 8:15. Monday morning we flew to Los Angeles. Michelle Spangler met us and took us to the hospital. We went to Johnny's room.

He recognized us as we hugged him and held his hand and spoke of our love. He knew he was dying, and we assured him we would be there for him, surrounding him with our love. JoAnne had called Debbie and Jeff, and they were also on their way.

In conversation with the doctor, he said that all John's systems were shutting down. It was just a matter of a day or two, or even just hours before his death.

We had so hoped there would be medical discoveries to save him! But it was not to be.

Debbie arrived on Monday evening and Jeff on Tuesday. We stayed with Johnny every minute, sleeping in his room in chairs and one cot each day and night. On Tuesday evening, several of his and Tom's friends came to visit. Between moments of drifting off to sleep, John spoke and even chuckled with them. The Conference Minister of California of the UCC also visited that night. He and I had become friends. The next evening, our Regional Minister Peggy visited.

One of the amazing things about his hospitalization and care regarded the nurse who was his primary nurse. She was a "traveling nurse" who had spent six months in Alaska prior to coming to this LA hospital. Of all things, she was originally from Cleveland Heights, Ohio, and was a graduate of Cleveland Heights High School, from which John, Deb and Jeff had graduated, and the system where Deb was now teaching. She gave John special care.

As Wednesday came, John was sleeping more and was almost comatose. Thursday morning, May 10, his breathing was more labored. He was not responding and able to speak. His life signs were ebbing. JoAnne and I were sitting close to him. I said, "Johnny you seem laboring to stay with us. We love you dearly, but it's alright for you to go."

Tom, Deb, and Jeff went down to the cafeteria at about noon. They needed to keep up their strength. At 1:10 p.m., John took his last breath and passed away. Tom, Deb, and Jeff arrived in the room just after he died.

After we had our last goodbyes, we left the room so that the staff could give care to his body before the funeral home took him. We stood together near the nurses' station, believing, but unbelieving that his earthly life was over. The nurse said to us, "I have never seen such love as there was in John's room as you surrounded him with your love."

John had decided that he wished to be cremated with our concurrence. We had made arrangements with the funeral home. We decided to have an informal memorial service at John's home that next Sunday afternoon. Tom let their friends and John's law office know about it. I called Marlis Morgan, my secretary, to let everyone at Missions Building know about John's death and our plans.

We were staying with Tom at John's home. We took care of arranging for food for Sunday evening following the memorial service at his home. As the time approached 2:00, lo and behold, I looked down from John's mountainside and there came Claudia Grant, Don Manworren, and John Foulkes, my faithful coworkers and dear friends. That was so very special.

The informal memorial service that Sunday, May 13, was on Mother's Day. My dear JoAnne!

We were in his yard and on his porch. I read scripture and asked Claudia to pray for us. Then I invited people to speak about John. Many of the two dozen or so friends did so, including our niece, and John's dear cousin and friend Michelle Spangler and her significant other Darrell Hodge. John's secretary was there and spoke about him. It was a time of laughter, and so moving and helpful in our grieving.

We all flew home on Monday, Deb to Cleveland, Jeff to Baltimore, and us to Indianapolis. I asked Claudia to head our delegation to the National Council of Churches Governing Board meeting in Pittsburgh, May 15–18. I cancelled my speech the next Sunday with Terry Reister's congregation at Hyattstown Christian Church in Clarksburg, Maryland. It was so good to be in town, home with JoAnne as we shared our grief. I did not have an out-of-town trip until May 30.

Of all things, John, an attorney, did not have a will. We called his law office to ascertain whether he had one in his office files to no avail. John had not done anything to give his partner Tom Albertus any legal authority for his financial details. Tom said he was going to move to an apartment in LA because of his grief being in John's home and because he now had no reason to live so far removed from his law office which was by the courthouse in downtown LA. We gave all of John's furniture, dishes, etc. to Tom.

We also asked John's firm to recommend an attorney who specialized in Topanga Canyon properties to be our agent in selling John's property. In addition to his home, he also had an A-frame house on the property. They did, and with the new firm, we signed the legal papers so they could take care of the details of the estate and the sale.

My first out-of-town engagement was at University Christian Church in Seattle, Washington. I stayed with the Bill Bailey family. Bill was one of the Moderators. They stayed in our home after the Indianapolis Assembly when Bill was ill and when we vacationed in Florida. I was speaking at a dinner for the congregation. Bob and Marjorie Thomas were members there. Bob had retired as President of the Division of Overseas Ministries. It was so good to see them.

On June 3, I preached at the Mount Lebanon Christian Church in suburban Pittsburgh. Vernon Bowers was the minister. We were old friends from our Dayton days when he was at Santa Clara Christian Church. Jeff and Linda were there, as well as her parents. Vernon had brought a group of Mount Lebanon laypeople to visit Missions Building and then invited JoAnne and me to dinner with them. I now had about five couples who were my friends in that church. We had lunch together and then went to a church about 30 miles away for a listening conference.

At the listening conference, W.H. Shanks and his wife Marcie came up with some "falderal" about finding the right classroom at Butler. "Dub," as we called him, was one of my roommates at Mr. Forkner's at Butler. And it was Marcie in whose home Betty Harper had lived as her roommate. Small world!

I had dinner with the Bowers and one of my new friends from the church, and then they took me to the airport. That morning I had told Linda's dad the flight I was on for U.S. Airways that evening. He was piloting a flight out that night, he said. He surprised me by showing up to see me off at my gate in his captain's uniform. That was cool!

On Friday, June 8, JoAnne, and I flew to Los Angeles to spread John's ashes at sea. Tom had picked up the ashes in a copper container from the funeral home. I had chartered a 38-foot sailboat at the Santa Monica Marina. On Sunday, June 10, 1990 JoAnne and I met Tom and Michelle at the marina. The captain motored out of the harbor and into the Pacific Ocean. Off the Santa Monica shore, we then shared in a ritual of commitment of John's ashes to the sea. Michelle read these words which she had prepared:

> Let our tears turn sweet with the memories of life.
>
> And let them drown the raw and heart wrenching pain at the end.
>
> Let us be joyful that he was a part of our lives, and happy that he lived.
>
> Let us not Bury our love for him, or barricade our hearts because of our loss,
>
> But let our love flow to others and flourish,
>
> So that his living and his passing are forever filled with meaning and purpose.

We spent some vacation time in California as we grieved, also taking care of details with the lawyer for John's estate and arranging to take over John's mortgage.

Quadrennial was meeting in its wonderful sessions at Purdue, June 24 to 29. JoAnne and I went up for one day. And then the United Church of Christ "Faith Works" was meeting at Indiana University, June 27–30. I was asked to give the pastoral prayer at the opening worship service. JoAnne and I went down for that service. Then on Friday, I was starting out from Missions Building to drive to Bloomington for another part of Faith Works. About two blocks from Missions Building, I was trying to fasten my seat belt and as I looked up the car in front of me had stopped. But I didn't have room to stop. I rear-ended that automobile. I didn't make it to Faith Works! Ah well!

The Hispanic National Fellowship met in Houston, Texas, July 10 to 13, at Redeemer Christian Church. It was important that I support our Hispanic constituency and be present for that event.

The Administrative Committee and the General Board met in St. Louis at the Clarion Hotel. At the opening worship, an offering was taken, and the Committee voted to designate it to a fund in remembrance of our John Dale. I asked and permission was granted for it to be a fund for research for curing AIDS. The General Board offering was also designated for that fund.

This was the Board meeting in the year between General Assemblies, hence a meeting without Assembly resolutions. It was a time to continue on the path of implementing the Priority by the general units and regions, with emphasis on their priority work.

National Convocation met in Arlington, Texas, and I needed to be there with the African American constituency. I had missed the last sessions to be with our whole family at Bethany Beach. That was just following the advancement of John Foulkes to Deputy General Minister as well as Executive Secretary of the Convocation. Ray Brown and John Compton, significant leaders in the Convocation constituency, had advanced that idea for John's position, a promotion, in essence. But a number in attendance only saw it as taking John away from his work and putting more work on the position. They were concerned about the Convocation's needs. They were not happy with this GMP. Neither John nor Raymond said anything at the Convocation. And Don and Claudia were at a definite disadvantage. So, it was very important for me to be there for the 1990 meetings.

The Assembly of the World Council of Churches was ahead, February 7–10, in Canberra, Australia. A pre-assembly meeting for delegates and Heads of Communion and National Council staff was held at the Sofitel Hotel at the O'Hare airport in Chicago, August 22–24. We were given study documents in preparation. And we were also introduced to unique songs and hymns we would be singing in Canberra. ("We are marching, we are marching, oh, we are marching in the light of God.") I still sing some of them. Joan Brown Campbell was prominent in the prep time, as U.S. Secretary for the World Council. We had seven delegates.

Meanwhile, we had a General Assembly coming in Tulsa, Oklahoma, October 25 to 30. The General Assembly worship committee met in Indianapolis at the Alverna Retreat Center, just a block from our home on Surrey Hill Circle. Claudia Grant was the lead planner for morning and evening worship at the Assembly. I had lunch with the group on Thursday.

On Friday we had a units-wide meeting at Missions Building on "computers and software." One of my goals in my six years in office was for us to bring the church into the computer age. During the Churchwide Planning Conference, DISCIPLESNET had 17 places where people could remotely participate in the conference planning sessions. It was a beginning. When I arrived in Indianapolis in 1977, the Board of Church Extension had a huge room full of one computer, with cables running everywhere under a subflooring. It was a subcorporation, doing our computing by contract. But now we needed to move into wide use of computers at every desk.

The Search Committee for the candidate to be the new General Minister and President had been appointed and was working. They were meeting in St. Louis. I was invited for an interview with the committee on September 13. They had questions about the extent of the work and relationships of the position. They would present three candidates to the Administrative Committee meeting, February first through the fourth, 1991, from which one candidate would be forwarded to the General Board meeting, July 27–30.

On September 15, I flew to San Juan, Puerto Rico for the Joint Commission of the Puerto Rico/U.S. Disciples meeting. The Board of Church Extension had been working with the congregations in Puerto Rico with counsel and loans for church construction. We were meeting to express the U.S. churches support for our churches there. We were working through the matter of recognition of ministerial standing between the United States and Puerto Rico. It was also good fellowship.

We always had Cabinet meetings the first week in September, and the meeting of the Executive Committee of the Regional Ministers and Moderators the third week.

The New Facilities Committee continued to meet with attention to raising funds for the new office building downtown, with Bill Barnes reporting on his fundraising work.

The Disciples/UCC Ecumenical Partnership Committee met the last three days in September, working on the implications of our churches having declared that we are now in "full communion." One element needed developing: ministerial standing, so ministers with standing in one were eligible for standing in the other.

October 1990 dawned with the Division of Higher Education "Conference on Advancing the Quality of Leadership" at the Alverna Retreat Center. I could walk to that conference because again because the Retreat Center was not far from our house.

On Thursday, October 11, I took our staff—Claudia, John, Don, and myself—on a lark. I invited them to Geist Lake for lunch and a sail in my 18-foot older daysailor sailboat. I bought it the year before from a neighbor. I painted it, renewed it, restored it, and berthed it at Geist Lake about 10 miles north of our home. We had lunch, and after bailing out the rainwater from the boat, we set sail from the marina. Trouble was, there was no wind, except from the smart comments of my dear friends. So becalmed, I set free my mighty two Hp electric motor, battened the hatches, and we went about for a short cruise. Fun afternoon!

I had commitments in Omaha, Nebraska, on Sunday the 14. In the morning, I would preach, with an emphasis on stewardship, at the First Christian Church where Nancy Brink was the minister. It was their Commitment Sunday for pledges. In the evening, I would preach at an Omaha Community AIDS Prayer and Healing Worship Service in a Roman Catholic Church. It was a moving experience, with very personal memories. After I preached about Jesus' healing ministry and our accepting and caring for all in his name, we invited any or all who would feel called to come to stations around the sanctuary for personal prayer and anointing with oil. As I came down from the pulpit to one of the stations, one young man came to me and told me he had AIDS. He said his father was a Disciples chaplain in the U.S. Army and had disowned him. I prayed for him and his father and family and anointed his forehead with oil. I asked if he would like me to know his name. He said yes and gave it to me. I asked if he would give me permission to talk to his father, telling of this encounter. He gave me permission. I asked him to wait for me to speak with others in line. He did, and we talked further while I received his and his father's written names.

I did talk to his father, sharing our family's story. I learned later that there had been a reconciliation between the father and son.

From Omaha, I went to St. Louis for the opening sessions of the Seminarians Conference with St. Louis general units NBA, Division of Higher Education, and the Christian Board of Publication. I rode from St. Louis back to Indianapolis in the Lexington Seminary van packed with their students. We had a rollicking good time!

I joined the whole group of the conference for two more days giving a meditation in recognition of this being the annual Disciples Celebration of the Week of the Ministry. It was appropriate in celebrating these young women and men preparing for the ministry.

I flew to Arlington, Texas, in suburban Dallas, to preach on Sunday morning, October 21, at the First Christian Church.

The senior minister was Art Digby. Art was Dick Dodson's college roommate at Transylvania. I had first met Art when I was a senior in high school and visited Transy.

The Southwest Regional Assembly began that evening. I preached on Monday morning.

I flew from Dallas to Chicago to an airport hotel meeting of the National Council's Search Committee for a new Executive Secretary. We had had a conference call the Wednesday before, while I was in the middle of the Seminarians Conference.

We continued to work on planning and funding for our new facilities downtown, with Jim Reed now chairing the committee and Bill Barnes serving as development officer. Obviously, one of the goals for my term of office would not be achieved; building downtown offices for the Indianapolis general units would not be accomplished during my six years. After working with the architect, Mr. Edward Larrabe Barnes on developing a building for an Indiana Avenue site on the canal and having the Indianapolis African American community reclaiming that block, we had to start over. We chose a local architectural firm of renown, resulting in a model at the 1989 Indianapolis Assembly, with dedication of new grounds with Assembly goers. But the Indianapolis business community was not responding as we and the Lilly Endowment had hoped to help finance the building. A layperson in southern Indiana with a limestone quarry had offered to donate Indiana limestone for the exterior. However, we found that the cost of preparation and installing the limestone was prohibitive.

Fortunately, I'd been able to save JoAnne's October Friday off from school. We enjoyed a beautiful Indiana fall weekend. It also happened to be my 64th birthday.

The next Sunday, November 4, 1990, I was preaching in Niles for the celebration of the 150th anniversary of the founding of the congregation. It was also a celebration of the three Timothy's of the congregation, Tom Madden, Rick Sanden, and me, all ordained at Niles. After worship, Bernard Oakes, good friend and Senior Minister of the church, had set up a congregational luncheon in our honor. It was good for JoAnne and me to be in Niles with Debbie and our three nieces, Lynn, Joyce, Jill, and their families.

On Friday I was scheduled to receive a six-member delegation from Lindenwood Christian Church in Nashville, Tennessee at 2:00 p.m. Lindenwood was one of our largest congregations. But large or small, I wanted to meet and visit with folks from any of our visiting churches. I was glad for those occasions. (Maybe with one exception, when Ken Teegarden and I were having the watermelon seed spitting contest, and one such group came into our offices' hall.)

After the celebration of the 150th anniversary in Niles, the next Sunday I went to a much younger congregation to preach. On November 11, the Radford, Virginia, church was celebrating their Centennial. One of the elders in that congregation was Moderator of the Virginia Region, and we had become friends. He was a professor at Radford University. He was most hospitable after I flew into Roanoke, Virginia.

I flew to New York on November 13 for the meeting of the Governing Board of the National Council of Churches. This was the meeting in which Joan Brown Campbell, a Disciple, was elected General Secretary, the CEO of the Council. This was a cause for celebration. As a member of the search committee, I had urged her selection.

Following the Governing Board meeting, I had a two-day meeting in New York, regarding the planning for the Consultation on

Sharing Resources to be held in Portland, Oregon, which I was chairing.

The annual Conference of Regional Ministers and Moderators that year was in Los Angeles at the University Hilton near the University of Southern California. I remember enjoying the friends in the seventy-two people attending and feeling the reality of this being the last such meeting of my nearly fourteen years serving in the offices of the GMP. I was beginning to feel the "lame duck days." The Council of Ministers followed with that same feeling.

I left these meetings and flew to Washington, D.C., for the meeting of the U.S. Conference of the World Council of Churches, looking forward to the World Assembly in Canberra, February 7–13, 1991. And back to Indy, I came for the Executive Committee of the Convocation Trustees the first weekend in December.

The next weekend was the meeting of the UCC/Disciples Planning Meeting for the General Synod/General Assembly meeting together in 1993. Talk about a "lame duck!"

We set aside December 19 and 20 for our GMP staff meetings which included Communications and the Office of Research with Frank Helme. The practice was also to have coffee hour with all the GMP staff folks every morning at 10:30. The whole staff really enjoyed one another. Then Don, Claudia, John, and I, whoever was in town, would go to lunch every day. It was a wonderful working fellowship.

And of course, we had our office Christmas party. One of the years, the Indianapolis Convention Bureau and the Convention Center sponsored our party, with a free dinner for us at the Convention Center. It happened that there was another public event that evening. Some Disciples from a suburban church attending the other event wandered by, saw the staff of the GMP's dinner party, and the word spread that the GMP's staff was living it up with a cocktail party out on the town. Ah well. Howard Dentler did get the word to the congregation from which the "cocktail party" story emanated about the nature and support for our staff dinner.

One unusual event occurred January 25. I preached in Indianapolis for the Church Federation Week of Prayer luncheon on "Hallelujah" from Psalm 117. I say it's unusual because I had preached all over the country outside of Indianapolis but not much "at home."

The International CWF Cabinet was meeting at Missions Building over the weekend of January 25. They invited JoAnne and me to dinner that Monday evening. They were expressing their appreciation of the support they felt from the office of GMP during my time of service.

That weekend was the beginning of the Administrative Committee's major task of selecting one nominee for GMP for the next six years. On Thursday evening January 31, we had dinner for the Moderators and our executive staff—Don, John, Claudia and me. We had lunch with the Executive Committee on Friday, February 1, then discussed the process. The Administrative Committee began on Sunday, and then went into Executive Session through Monday to select their nominee. Roy Griggs and Michael Kinnamon were two who were presented by the Search Committee. The candidates were interviewed during the morning hours. Late in the afternoon while the Committee was making the decision for the one candidate to be presented to the General Board, JoAnne and I had invited Roy and Michael to have dinner with us while the discussion and decision was being made. We remembered what it had been like during the long day of the decision of the Administrative Committee in my case and thought it might be helpful for both Roy and Michael to have some company. We had dinner at one of the airport hotels near another hotel where the discussion was taking place. Word came to us during dinner that Michael was chosen on the first ballot! JoAnne and I were both pleased for Michael and for the church. Roy would have been excellent as well.

After dinner we spent some time with Michael answering questions and discussing the ministry of the GMP. This was not our first discussion. Once before at a dinner with him and his wife, the three of us had talked about the probability of his being a GMP candidate for the next six-year term.

Administrative Committee ended after lunch on Tuesday, February 5, and my journey to Canberra, Australia, for the WCC Assembly, February 7–20, began that evening with a flight to Los Angeles. I rested well on the flight from LAX to Canberra, but it was such a long trip!

One of the functions of the WCC, according to its constitution, is to express the common concern of the churches in the service of human need, the breaking down of barriers between people, and the promotion of the human family in justice and peace.

The Christian Church (Disciples of Christ) in the United States and Canada had four official delegates: Bonnie Fraser, International CWF President, from Oklahoma; Patrina Tallie, a medical student at Cornell University; Dr. Paul Crow, President of the Council on Christian Unity, and me. In addition, another twenty North American Disciples attended in various roles and categories from advisers and accredited visitors to stewards and staff. About one thousand official delegates of the more than three hundred WCC member churches came from all over the world, with another thousand in other categories. Under the theme "Come Holy Spirit – Renew the Whole Creation," Bible study and worship were central. Daily worship took place three times a day under a tent on the campus of the Australian National University in the Federal Capital City.

As you would surmise when representatives from the churches around the world gather, they bring many perspectives. Since the last WCC Assembly in Vancouver seven years earlier, several streams of concern for God's world and the mission of the church had been moving through world conferences toward Canberra. I was involved in two of those, the 1989 Conference on World Mission and Evangelism in San Antonio, Texas, and the 1987 Conference on the Ecumenical Sharing of Resources in El Escorial, Spain. The third prominent stream in movement toward Canberra was the 1990 Conference on Justice, Peace and the Integrity of Creation in South Korea. In Canberra we considered the following subthemes under the overall Assembly theme "Giver of Life – Sustain Your Creation;" "Spirit of Truth – Set us Free!;" "Spirit of Unity – Reconcile Your People;" and Holy Spirit –Transform and Sanctify Us!"

For the first time in the history of the World Council, the churches from what had been the communist bloc were out from under such authoritarian government.

On Sunday February 10, Bill Nottingham and I attended a Canberra Disciples congregation. We were cordially received and went to Sunday lunch with one of the families.

Back home in the United States, I wrote in my column for the *Disciple Magazine*:

> We were meeting during the height of the bombing and missile sorties of "Desert Storm," with the ground war imminent. The war in the Middle East was the dominant issue. United States delegates met three times, with discussion of the work of the leaders of the churches attempting to avert war, and with our position regarding "Desert Storm" front and center. The Assembly itself voted to make public statements on eight issues, with statement number one on the Gulf War, the Middle East and threat to World Peace. The Public Issues Committee spent one entire evening in an open hearing attended by the majority of the delegates, on the subject of the Middle East and the war. Debate and amendments occupied a full morning and a portion of the last afternoon as we worked to perfect and adopt the statement. With Christian representatives from all over the world, the view of the situation had many different "focal lengths."
>
> Metropolitan Mar Gewargis Sliwa, Archbishop of Baghdad, spoke to the United States delegates. He told

of the Christians of Baghdad living in hope for peace. On the Sunday before Christmas, he began serving communion at 6:30 AM outside the Cathedral because so many were coming. They served the Eucharist constantly until 11:30 at night. The people's prayer was one, "Please God, avoid us this war."

My friend, Jean Zaru, a Quaker Christian from the West Bank, a Palestinian with whom I have been in several WCC meetings, told the United States delegates of her worry for the safety of her children and grandchildren on the West Bank. The scud missiles were falling on her people as well as Israel, with little thought of the suffering of Palestinians. The curfew imposed by the Israelis where people have been prevented from going out to buy food and medicine, has created not only hardship but death. She recognized the illegality of the occupation of Kuwait, but forcefully called our attention to the 42 years of Israel's occupation of Palestinian lands on the West Bank. UN resolutions for negotiating settlement of disputes bear as much weight as those regarding Kuwait and Iraq, she reminded us, with no corresponding action by the community of nations.

Even as I write, the U.S. military victory over Iraqi forces in the cease fire had been declared. What now will we do with the power in our hands in the Middle East? There can never be peace with justice in the Middle East until all parties Iraq, Kuwait, Jordan, the Palestinians, Israel, Lebanon, Syria, Saudi Arabia, Egypt, and even Iran, can come to a diplomatic, negotiated state of international agreements. As we have taken the lead in war, I pray that we will undergird and support the work of these nations and the UN in working for peace!

I had returned to the U.S. to the Arizona Regional Assembly in Mesa and then home again, for a Monday Missions Building Community Life Committee meeting. During all of our travel, we always gave attention to the *koinonia*, the community life of the staff of our general units, by sharing refreshments and giving attention to elements of our life together. We were colleagues, from secretaries to unit presidents.

We invited Michael Kinnamon to town to meet with the GMP staff for conversations about his impending role. He was firm about wanting Don Manworren, Claudia Grant, and John Foulkes to stay on. He had lots of questions about details of the work and ministry of the office of GMP. It was helpful for all of us to be together.

On Saturday, March 16, I flew to LA for the Pacific Southwest Region's Youth Retreat at Chapman College. When I spoke to the young people about serving as pastor in Chevy Chase, they said they didn't know there was a place named Chevy Chase. I told them about pumping gas at a gas station at the corner of Sunset Boulevard and the Pacific Coast Highway and looking to the next pump and seeing the comic actor Chevy Chase pumping his gas.

Easter week, April 1–7, JoAnne and I had a wonderful week together in Indiana's Brown County before I went into a flurry of events and GMP trips.

The New Regional Ministers Orientation was Monday, April 8–9. I flew to Kansas City for lunch with UCC and Disciples area ministers with UCC President Paul Sherry. We spoke about "Discovering Our Partnership." That evening we also met with laity from the congregations around Kansas City, on the same theme. I flew home at 6:30 a.m. for our GMP staff meeting the twelfth, from 9 to 4.

On Saturday, JoAnne and I drove to Carbondale, Illinois, stayed with the pastor and her daughter, preached on Sunday morning and again in the afternoon for the gathering of the Southern Illinois cluster of churches. Concluding at 7:00 p.m., we then drove home. Monday was a Church Finance Council Board dinner with JoAnne invited. Friday the 18 and 19, the Council on Christian Unity Board, met with me participating in a World Council of Churches panel. Sunday the 21 at Euclid Avenue Congregational Church in Cleveland at 5:30 p.m., there was a sermonic dialogue with Paul Sherry on our "full communion." On Monday, I traveled to Tulsa, Oklahoma, for dinner and preparation for the Assembly. I flew home early Tuesday, the

23, for a meeting of the Christian Church Foundation Board on Tuesday and Wednesday, with JoAnne invited to come for dinner. Wednesday afternoon I flew to Chicago's Woodfield Hyatt for the Nominating Committee of the National Council of Churches Governing Board and flew home on Friday. Saturday, JoAnne and I drove to Shepherdsville, Kentucky, to preach and visit with Shepherdsville Christian Church, my old stomping grounds during my first year in Seminary. That was my April 1991!

The first week in May, I was fortunate to fly to Williamsport, Pennsylvania, the home of the Little League World Baseball Championship. From my room in the motel, I looked out on the street and down into the iconic baseball diamond of the championship stadium. I was there to preach for Sarah Webb in her congregation and then go with her in her role as Associate Regional Minister to a District Assembly at Johnstown's First Christian Church for an afternoon "state of the church" speech and an evening sermon. Having seen Sarah in her role as Moderator of the Youth Ministry Council as a college student, it was great to see her in these ministries "all grown up."

Back in the office I worked to prepare the docket for General Board to be sent to the printer. I accomplished that by May 13. Then I flew to New York for the installation of our own Joan Brown Campbell as Executive Secretary of the National Council of Churches. As Disciples GMP and member of the Search Committee, I had a part in the service at New York City's Riverside Church.

That Sunday I preached for my old friend Terry Reister, at Hyattstown, Maryland, and stayed for a potluck dinner. If you remember, I had canceled preaching for Terry and his congregation right after our John died. Terry had been on the faculty for the first CYF conference I directed in 1963 at Bethany Beach. Later, he was minister at Collierville, Tennessee, when I came down to visit the church when they were upset before the 1977 Kansas City Assembly, my very first church visit as Deputy GMP. Now he was back serving in the Capital Area Region.

The next day Joe Jones, President of Phillips University in Enid, Oklahoma, came to see me over the financial straits of the university. Both the university and its seminary had been at the historic heart of our Disciples church. At one point, so many of the leaders in Missions Building had graduated from the Phillips University and seminary that people kidded about "the Phillips mafia." To think that our historic university was now struggling for financial support, their budget in the red, was a real crisis. We decided to gather our financial general units to meet with Joe Jones and representatives of the Phillips Board of Trustees for a consultation in Oklahoma City.

Michael Kinnamon came to town again to meet with the staff. Don, Claudia, John, and I had a good time meeting with him. That night JoAnne, Michael, and I went to a baseball game in the really great new ballpark of the Indianapolis Indians AAA team. We just happened to buy the seats reserved for major league scouts right behind home plate. Michael is a big baseball fan, and he and I love to trade tales of baseball history! And, of course, JoAnne kept score! When she and I were dating, going to Cleveland Indian ball games, I taught her how to keep score. She had been doing that ever since, including at Jeff's high school games. We have a notebook full of her scoring of Jeff's Cleveland Heights Tigers' baseball games.

The program committee for the joint gathering of the UCC General Synod and Disciples General Assembly in 1993 met the next day, June 1. It was good to see everyone, but I was really just a bystander as they did their work. And of course, we awaited the election of the officers of the next biennium.

The General Synod was in Norfolk, Virginia, July 1–4. JoAnne came with me. It was great to be together with me having little responsibilities on what I thought would be my last General Synod. It was always special to be with my UCC friends I had made through the years on our way to "full communion."

General Board and associated meetings began in Schaumburg, Illinois, at the Woodfield Hyatt Hotel on July 24. This would be the Board Meeting to which Michael Kinnamon's nomination would be forwarded, with a two-thirds majority vote required to send it on to the General Assembly. Between the time of his being named the nominee and the General Board meeting, opposition had been raised by some over his membership in the Gay Lesbian and Affirming Disciples (GLAD) organization and his limited experience in congregational life. Floyd Legler, an Indiana trucking company owner, had published and sent his objections widely to congregations. A group called "Disciple's Renewal" (an oxymoron) was also active in its opposition to Michael's selection.

Michael had visited with Floyd Legler to no avail. Michael had traveled widely at the invitation of regional gatherings to answer questions and engage in dialogue. A financial grant for travel expenses was given to him to cover the cost of traveling extensively for folks to meet and hear him. He went to fifteen different regions.

On Saturday morning, before the Board meeting began, Michael asked for a private time with Robert Welch and me. He was concerned that his nomination would be too divisive for the church and seriously wondered if he should withdraw his name from consideration. My stance was that our church needed his leadership. The opposition was a minority that should not rule. The Administrative Committee had overwhelmingly chosen him on the first ballot. We should let the duly elected members of the General Board consider his nomination, with that body making this decision. Robert Welch concurred. Michael finally agreed to move forward with his nomination.

Michael made a fine presentation to the Board. A period of discussion with the Board members raising questions followed. The Board then went into an Executive Session, with time for their comments and discussion. A vote was taken with the "Ayes" far exceeding the two-thirds majority needed.

The Resolutions submitted for the General Assembly to be reviewed by the General Board were wide ranging. Several related to human sexuality. The Disciple's Renewal congregations submitted one for the Operational, Policy and Organizational Items category and another for Concerning Homosexuals and Ministry. It resolved "that the General Assembly ask Regional Commissions on Ministry to make policies rejecting the ordination of professed and practicing homosexuals and lesbians, and that this be done with appropriate compassion and concern..." The Executive Committee recommended it become an item for "Reflection and Research."

First Christian Church of Decatur, Illinois, presented a business item, "Disciple's Renewal Report on Salvation in Jesus Christ." Recognizing that the report would not fit the category of an item for "Reflection Research" as presented, we worked with the congregation and the Executive Committee. If the submitters had presented one or two paragraphs setting forth the issue, it would more readily fit the category. So together we wrote the item for "Reflection and Research" as follows:

> The church of Jesus Christ confesses as its foundational truth that Jesus Christ is Savior and Lord. The Christian Church (Disciples of Christ) joins with the Christian community of all times and places in confessing this truth. We wish to encourage our church to reflect more deeply in its historic confession of faith in Jesus Christ and what it means for the life of the church today.

It was recommended to the Assembly that this be adopted. So, this was a win-win.

The report of the Corporate Responsibility Advisory Committee of the Christian Church (Disciples of Christ) was submitted. Six resolutions concerning South Africa were approved by the Committee for submission to thirty-four companies regarding doing business in South Africa, asking that they withdraw or sever all economic ties to the apartheid government. Twenty-three resolutions were sent to ask companies to report progress they had made in being ecologically responsible. Twenty companies were asked to share information on their fair employment practices and on their operations just outside of the U.S. known as "maquiladoras," or factories.

The conclusion of the General Board demanded a quick turnaround to follow up on changes made in resolutions by the Board. I designated contacts to be made, taking the first and most tenuous myself, and directing the efforts to get the docket ready for printing to go to every congregation. We finished our work in two days, August 1 and 2.

Michael Kinnamon came back to town for more meetings on the fifteenth, with a conference call with the Moderators and then further discussions with Claudia, Don, and John.

I went to St. Louis for my final meeting with the Board of the Christian Board of Publication on August 28. The General Cabinet met September 4–6. It was my last presiding with the Cabinet. It consisted of the heads of all eleven general units, plus the head of the Office of Communication, the three Deputy GMPs, the Development Officer for the new building, and of course the General Minister and President.

The Ecumenical Partnership Committee met in Cleveland the second week in September. Again, special attention was given to the "mutual recognition and reconciliation of ordained ministers." The ecumenical partnership model for ecumenical reconciliation of denominations provides for each denomination to retain its own identity and structure while recognizing among other things it's ordained ministries. This would be worked on pointing to 1995 for some seemingly overly ambitious, for others much too slow.

The General Cabinet held an appreciation dinner for the retiring GMP and his bride. Bill Nottingham, President of the Division of Overseas Ministries, was asked to speak for the Cabinet. He said:

> Last night I was watching Laurence Olivier's magnificent movie Hamlet on the Bravo station. It led me to think of a number of things that I could say in tribute

to John. I thought about "Goodnight, sweet prince, and flights of angels sing thee to thy rest." But Patty said that was no good because it was too strong for retirement. Then I stumbled on "to be or not to be." Then I thought it might be well just to talk about what John has been, for me.

In the first place John has been outstanding as a pastor. The finest compliment I ever heard Bob Thomas give anybody was after his stay in the hospital in March 1983, and John Humbert, who was then Deputy General Minister and President, came to see him. He gave a prayer that Bob said was just exactly right for Bob's situation, his temperament, and his faith.

But I've also seen John in pastoral situations that were important to me, such as a surprising decision of the DOM Board of Directors to authorize the support of the Program to Combat Racism in the World Council of Churches around 1987. Charlie Bayer, Chris Hobgood, and I had all counseled against it, following the advice of most of you. But the Board decided otherwise, and we realized that they had been right. But it was John, going straight from there to the ICWF Quadrennial Assembly at Purdue who had to interpret that action to four thousand women, and not just to justify it, but to celebrate it as a responsible witness in the name of Jesus Christ. He was pastor to us all.

In the second place, what John has been was a person committed to world mission. His commitment to the world mission of the church showed when he went to see what missionaries were involved in and to express the solidarity of our church with leaders. I was with him in Japan and in Nicaragua. I remember in Japan I had phlebitis and had to sit with my foot out, so I sat behind him in a little car going from Hiroshima to Iwakuni with my foot in his back, so he was cramped up against the dashboard. When we got out, he limped more than I did. In Hiroshima in the same hotel, there was a boxer named Jaime Rios who attracted a lot of attention. Two years later, I found a newspaper clipping saying that he accused someone of having drugged him, so he lost the fight. John and I thought it might have been just the dining in our hotel that got to him.

In the third place, I think of John as someone solidly in support of human rights and truly repulsed in the center of his being by torture and inhumane treatment.

In Nicaragua, we stayed in Jinotega, where the mayor had been kidnapped just the week before, where there was still bombing once in a while, and we stayed in a wreck of a hotel. Marcelina Davila, the old man who had founded the Christian Mission Church among the poor, wrote a poem, because he was so moved that the head of our church would come and make such a visit. Then John was arrested in the Rotunda of the Capitol in Washington, praying for peace in Central America, and showed thereby the kind of commitment that has been appreciated through our work. Therefore, I want to say to him, "thanks."

In returning to Hamlet, I want to paraphrase a line; "Gold good old Yorick, I knew him well.

JoAnne and I went to Philadelphia for of a celebration of our niece, Carrie Timbur's wedding to Michael Kelly on September 28. It was a great family weekend with both Debbie and Jeff there.

October opened in Dallas, Texas, for the Christian Church Foundation Board meeting. I had been elected to that board in 1975 when I was still minister in Cleveland and continued participating in their Board meetings ex officio for sixteen years. It was great to see the success of raising resources by the staff, and the support of the board. It was a celebration party and work time. It was creating resources, the interest of which would support the whole church.

I was in the office for most of October prior to the October 25–30 General Assembly in Tulsa. There were a number of meetings. I had time to perfect my final State of the Church address. It was a time of reflection and nostalgia, as I was concluding fourteen years in the work of the Office of the General Minister and President. It had been a great eight years as Deputy serving with Ken Teegarden. We had had a great relationship of loyalty, trust, and enjoyment. I fully believed I had been able to make a real contribution to the work of the general office. And the work together with Howard Dentler had been fulfilling in accomplishment and friendship. Working with the three of us together had been a joy and delight. We became fast friends. My experience as Deputy had been a great training ground for when I was elected General Minister and President. I was familiar with the work of the general office, and Ken had in fact had enough faith in me to allow me to share a great deal of the responsibilities with him. So, I had been able to "hit the ground running" as GMP.

I had written *A House of Living Stones*, my book published by the Christian Board of Publication, setting forth the theological and ecclesiological foundation for what I felt would be the calling for the life and mission of the church. I had set forth ten goals for my six-year term:

- Working to bring the evangelical leaning Disciples and the social activists together, based on our common commitment to Jesus Christ and the full richness of his person and ministry as both Lord and Savior.
- The goal of bringing the whole church together for mission, with strong emphasis on pastoral care from the office of the GMP, modeling openness and access between pew and pulpit with the General leadership of the church, bridging the perceived gap between congregations and the General life of the church.
- Emphasis for the Disciples, a global church body, making a difference in the world as a contributing force for peace and justice in the crucial issues of the day.
- Further development of the ecumenical partnership with the United Church of Christ, adopted at the Des Moines General Assembly in 1985.
- Bringing the whole General staff together to work as colleagues with a growing sense of unified mission and ministry.
- Unifying General and Regional staff for ministry and mission.

- Developing a greater appreciation and utilization of Disciples institutions of higher education.
- Advancing the role of women in top leadership in the church.
- Fulfilling the action of the General Assembly calling for the leaders to find and develop new facilities for the headquarters offices of the Indianapolis general units.
- Bringing the church into the computer age.

In my work as GMP, I attempted to model both the evangelical and justice nature of the life and mission of the church, working with Disciples based on our common commitment to Jesus Christ. This was the central emphasis of my pastoral call and care for the term of my office. I'm not sure I brought the two leaning groups together, but at least perhaps I accomplished a bit more openness for evangelical-leaning Disciples and social activists to allow the other as faithful Disciples.

I worked continually at reaching out pastorally to bridge the gap between congregations and the general life of the church. I sought and received word from congregations in the twenty-some Listening Conferences. From what I heard, we developed the priority of all parts of the church focusing with congregations "developing vital congregations as dynamic faith communities..." In the Lexington Churchwide Planning Conference, we invited all lay and clergy Disciples who wished to come to accept the invitation. Almost seven hundred people were involved on site in the daily work of that conference, with Disciples participating by internet in seventeen locations across North America on DISCIPLENET During the Louisville General Assembly, I asked the people with whom I had been present in any setting during my first two years as GMP to stand. An overwhelming number of the seven thousand folks stood. I said, "It's so nice to see you, again!" I made it a personal mission to be with the people in regional assemblies and congregations to make new church friends, bridging the gap.

The Christian Church (Disciples of Christ) is a denomination working as a global church, with missionary staff in countries around the world, in education, social service, health care, resource development, faith development, and reconciliation. Disciples, through General Assembly resolutions, speak to the world and to the President of the United States and Congress on issues of peace and justice. On behalf of the General Assembly, I worked to carry out resolutions on Central America and, in particular, Nicaragua. In addition, we were active in promoting reconciliation in South Africa with a relationship with the African National Congress. As a member denomination in the World Council of Churches, we were part of the Council's outreach for peace and justice in the Middle East.

In the further development of our "ecumenical partnership with the United Church of Christ," we brought our relationship to the point of declaring that we were now in "full communion" with the reconciliation of members and were continuing to work on the reconciliation of ministry. For the first time, we brought together all the staffs of the general units in a working (and playing!) retreat. It was both symbolic and we actually worked together with a great sense of being colleagues in the mission of the church.

In planning and carrying out the Lexington Churchwide Planning Conference, there was a great mix of general and regional staff working together toward ministry and mission.

Christian Theological Seminary's Conference on "Christians Only, But Not the Only Christians" was a great example of utilizing our higher education institutions. The Churchwide Planning Conference was hosted by Transylvania University and Lexington Theological Seminary.

With the goal of advancing the role of women in top leadership in the church, we were blessed with electing Claudia Grant as Deputy General Minister and Carolyn Day as Director of the Office of Communication.

We worked diligently on developing new facilities for the headquarter offices for our general units. When I retired, we had the lot and the architectural plans for the building. Lilly Endowment had been notably generous with the one-million-dollar grant for the property. We were seeking the support from the church at that point, with Bill Barnes as Development Officer. The General Board was presenting a resolution for approval of a Church-wide Capital Campaign, "Embrace the Future," with the goal of $30 million with $1.5 million supporting the construction of the office building. (The resolution was adopted in Tulsa.) And we were just on the edge of having a computer at each desk in Missions Building!

So there was much to celebrate as we went to Tulsa for the General Assembly to elect Michael Kinnamon as General Minister and President.

The Assembly, meeting under the theme "In Remembrance of Me," opened with dramatic Native American drums accompanied by Michael Morton on the flute. Then, the processional hymn, "In Christ there is no East or West," was sung first by the Assembly Choir, and then by the congregation of nearly eight thousand Disciples. Communion was designed by Claudia Grant. And K. David Cole, Moderator, gave a great uniting sermon!

There is nothing quite like the thrill of an opening hymn in a General Assembly with eight thousand Disciples' voices!

Saturday morning, I gave my State of the Church Address calling us to realize there is more going on in the world while we seem to be giving so much attention to sex. But more important, we must find unity in remembering our historic slogans, "no creed but Christ" and "in essentials unity, in non-essentials liberty, and in all things charity." I urged the election of Michael Kinnamon as General Minister and President, "as a person of God, immersed in scripture, with an enormous love for the church, and with marvelous gifts and vision." The Assembly newspaper summarized my State of the Church Address this way:

> Human sexuality must not become a church dividing issue, John O. Humbert warned the General Assembly

> in his last State of the Church address as General Minister and President. The retiring executive implored, "Righteous indignation is growing on all sides. But our righteous indignation must not become idolatrous, where our will is projected as God's will."
>
> Humbert noted the irony of the "current propensity for concentration on things sexual." "While the church has been riveted on sex," Humbert said, "significant things have been happening in the world. Besides the death of communism, the opposition of Russian Orthodox leaders to the attempted coup in the Soviet Union and President Bush's arms reduction proposal," to the applause of Assembly participants. He described a chaotic situation in Zaire and the need to pull church missionaries out of the country. He said the war in Iraq is not really over, that children in Iraq continued to die as a direct result, and he declared that he strongly supports the U.S. government's work on the Middle East peace conference. He declared there is a new enthusiasm for Bible study in the church and, to applause, asserted, "Many of our people are hungry for serious Bible study, and our priority of renewing congregational life rests on taking biblical truth seriously." Humbert took issue with those in the church who insist on defining correct views of scripture and how persons must believe in Jesus Christ. He called it "a throwback to a test of fellowship that Disciples rejected in 1811."

In reference to the "test of fellowship" rejected in 1811, I had shared a story with the General Board the previous summer that I now used to finish my final State of the Church Address:

> Recently Bill Moyers interviewed Oren Lyon, tribal chief of the Onondaga Indians, discussing Native American spirituality. Chief Lyon remarked that in their tribal council every decision was made on the basis of its effect on the seventh generation. Remarkable principle, that! It set me thinking of our situation in this moment in history.
>
> On May 4, 1811, the Christian Association of Washington, Pennsylvania, constituted itself a church,

the Brush Run Church. As members of the Association came forward, one by one, on that significant May 4, to qualify as members of the church, they were examined theologically as Thomas Campbell propounded to each the test question: "What is the meritorious cause of the sinner's acceptance with God?" Only two failed to give a satisfactory answer. Their admission was postponed.

The next Sunday, one of the well-known members of the Christian Association who was absent on May 4, James Foster, by name, presented himself for membership. The Brush Run charter members made the decision that with the stance of the Declaration and Address, and the principle that they were to have "no creed but Christ," they would never again ask the theological test question, "What is a meritorious cause of the sinner's acceptance with God?" and expect a creedal answer. All that would be required would be, "Do you believe that Jesus is the Christ, the Son of God." Garrison and DeGroot confidently declare in "The Disciples of Christ, A History," "The test question was never used again."[18]

The person around whom this decision was made, not to require a creedal theological statement as a test of fellowship and faithfulness, save profession of faith in Christ, that person was James Foster, my great, great, great Grandfather! That's six generations ago! How will the decision of the Brush Run Disciples move to the seventh generation of Disciples as the mantle passes from this Disciple's sixth generation?

There are some in our midst whose aim is to turn the theological clock back 50 years to what they believe Disciples were then. Truth be known they propose to turn the clock of Disciples tradition back past May 11, 1811, to May 4, 1811, and reinstate the abandoned creedal question, "What is the meritorious cause of the sinner's acceptance with God?"

May 11, last year, was one day after our son John Dale died. We were in his home. I was looking through the bookshelves in his den. One of the volumes was

---

[18] Alfred T. Garrison, Winfred Ernest, and DeGroot, *Disciples of Christ: A History*, (St. Louis: Christian Board of Publication, 1948), 153.

by Thomas Merton, entitled the "Asian Journal of Thomas Merton." Thomas Merton, you will remember, was a Trappist monk, who did so much to deepen the church's understanding of prayer and spirituality, and helped us understand that depths of spirituality lead to action for justice, reconciliation, and peace. John had placed a bookmark at page 318. The passage contains a special closing prayer offered by Thomas Merton at the first spiritual summit conference in Calcutta, India, just before Thomas Merton, himself, died.

This prayer was a gift to us from our son. It was used as a prayer in John's Memorial Service. I leave it as a gift to you now in the spirit of Ephesians, in our deep need of the moment, as Disciples gathered in the General Assembly:

Oh God, we are one with You. You have made us one with You. You have taught us that if we are open to one another You dwell in us. Help us to preserve this openness and to struggle for it with all our hearts. Help us to realize that there can be no understanding where there is mutual rejection. Oh God, in accepting one another whole heartedly, fully, completely, we accept You, and we thank You, and we adore You, and we love You with our whole being, because our being is in Your being, our spirit is rooted in Your spirit. Fill us then with love, and let us be bound together with love as we go our diverse ways, united in this one spirit which makes You present in the world, and which makes you witness to the ultimate reality that is love. Love has overcome. Love is victorious. Amen.

Those were my final words to the General Assembly as General Minister and President.

On Monday morning the order of the day, after the morning prayers, was business item 9418, Election of the General Minister and President.

That morning on one of the Assembly transportations buses, an empty ammunition box was found. With emotions running high over the GMP election, we decided to move Michael and Catherine Kinnamon backstage as a precaution.

The discussion was very emotional on both sides. People were lined up at both the pro and con microphones for the forty-eight-minute discussion. I was backstage with Michael and Katherine. Dale Fiers and Ken Teegarden joined us. We were able to watch the discussion on a video monitor from backstage.

The vote was taken by written ballot. There were 5,623 votes cast, with Michael's election requiring a sixty-six and two-thirds percent majority. We were shocked when David Cole announced Michael fell short of the required number. (He fell 70 votes short of the sixty-six and two-thirds percent required.) Before Moderator David Cole asked Michael to come to the stage, he asked Disciples to join in singing "Blessed Be the Tie That Binds" and then observe a moment of silence.

Backstage Michael, Katherine, Ken, Dale, and I locked arms in a tight circle of prayer. When Michael came on stage for a post-election statement. He was greeted with a standing ovation. He was most gracious in defeat and said,

> I am no less excited about the future of this church and no less committed to being a part of the future than I was an hour ago or a month ago, and you must not be either. We Disciples have done something significant in the way we have carried out a churchwide theological conversation around this nomination. And now we must show the world a more excellent way as we attempt together to follow the leading of God's spirit.

Further, he called for a "season of prayer" to turn the church from occupation with itself, to God's action in the world.

The Administrative Committee was charged with naming an Interim General Minister and President and was called into session that evening. The General Cabinet were ex-officio with that body. The name of C. William Nichols quickly came forward. Ironically, he was a major evening speaker earlier in the Assembly, and his crowd-stirring appeal was front and center. He had been active in all sections of the church, was an outstanding preacher, and was minister of the sixteen hundred member Central Christian Church of Decatur, Illinois, where he had been the Senior Minister for nineteen years.

Nichols was presented to the Assembly as a nominee for Interim General Minister and President. It was a popular choice, and he was elected.

On Monday evening there was a banquet honoring the retiring GMP. The Assembly News described it this way:

> A banquet honoring retiring General Minister and President John O. Humbert drew an estimated 1,400 people to hear stories on topics ranging from his childhood interest in the ministry to an encounter with the Pope. Humbert, 64, in office since 1985, was described as a guitar playing family man, a good-natured pastor, and a voice for justice and peace. Many family members were present for the evening, and about 15 of them gathered around Humbert at the podium at one point, handing him a guitar and joined him in singing the folk hymn "Michael Rowed the Boat Ashore." A book of letters of remembrances from well-wishers, presented by Harry Smith, a retired Disciples pastor from Akron, Ohio, included touching testimonies to Humbert's skills as a local pastor from 1962 to 1977. David Vargas, Division of Overseas Ministries Executive Secretary for Latin America and the Caribbean, said Humbert will be remembered for promoting connections between North American Disciples and their counterparts in Latin America and the Caribbean, and for speaking out for justice. Tributes also came for Humbert's identity as a peacemaker. Kit Fuller, a student at Christian Theological Seminary, Indianapolis, announced the creation of the John O. Humbert Fund for Peace Education, to be received by the Christian Church Foundation.

It did not escape us, the irony of singing "Michael Rowed the Boat to Shore," as I looked down at Michael and Kathy Kinnamon after the morning that Michael was unable to row ashore as GMP.

I was pleased with the adoption of a number of resolutions: 9123, Guidelines for the Ecumenical Sharing of Resources, (from El Escorial, Spain where I was our official representative); Opposition to Capital Punishment; 9132 Women's Health; 9137 Regarding our Response to Modern War and Military Action; 9144 Resolution Regarding the Church of Jesus Christ-Christian (this group is also known as the Aryan Nation, a hate group), declaring the antisemitic and racist teaching of this group to be diametrically opposed to the teachings of Jesus Christ; 9138 Resolution Concerning El Salvador and Central America, urging the U.S. government to vigorously pursue peaceful settlements and make cuts in military systems to the government of El Salvador.

On Sunday morning I participated in the AIDS worship service held by GLAD, an emotional time remembering our John.

With the closing benediction for the General Assembly on Wednesday night, October 20, I was free!

Saturday, October 26 was my 64th birthday. Now, I had finished my work as GMP! JoAnne had come home on Thursday morning accompanied by Deb, Tom, and Jeff, who went on to Baltimore. I came home on Friday to enjoy the weekend with JoAnne in our wonderful home on Surrey Hill Circle. It was such a good feeling of pressures being off, freedom, with no heavy responsibilities for the whole denomination's leadership. No events to plan, nothing where the "buck stops with me." JoAnne worried that I would miss the spotlight and special treatment. But I felt like the little boy in the family in North Chevy Chase on Sunday night, leaping up in the chair, standing with outstretched arms proclaiming, "Freedom...Freedom on the Sabbath!" I had felt it a great privilege and joy to serve as the GMP, but it was high pressure work.

Bill Nichols had told me to take my time getting my things out of the office, so I was relaxed over the weekend. But when I went in on Monday morning, a little late, Don Manworren greeted me with the word that Hal Watkins was overseeing Bill's transition into the office. Bill was to be there the next day to begin his term in office. Don had arranged for a mover to be there that afternoon to move my things, including my paneled bookcase wall. I spent the day packing up my books and stuff.

My library was not as extensive as it once had been. As I prepared to move out of the office, I had given much of my library to the Christian Theological Seminary. They would use what they could in the library and the rest would be put in their book sale to students. JoAnne said I could only bring home two boxes. I had little more than that, but not much. My correspondence would go to the Disciples of Christ Historical Society for their archives. The movers came that afternoon, November 4, 1991, and the remnants of my term of office were gone. I followed them home.

I had laid some important papers on the desk, however, to show Bill Nichols what was impending that he needed to know. He and I had agreed we would meet for a few moments the next day, early Tuesday morning in the office. That morning I thought I would get there early to get ready with those papers before he came. I arrived at 7:00, an hour before chapel, and found him seated in "my" desk chair. We chatted for a while about his living plans with the sudden change in his life direction and then went to chapel together. Afterwards we came back to the office, and I began to speak of the papers I had prepared. He said, "Well, I need to do some dictation with Mary now." It was obvious that I was dismissed so he could begin his term. I wished him well and went to see Larry Grooms at his Christian Church Services office to turn in my keys to Missions Building after fourteen years. I went to Don Manworren's office to turn in my American Express and AT&T office credit cards and went home mid-morning.

JoAnne was at home. She had been called to jury duty that morning but was not impaneled. We had lunch together! What a treat! Then she went back to school to teach for the afternoon.

It was a beautiful fall day with the wonderful fall colors of an Indiana afternoon. I went out in the front yard to rake some leaves. I had such a sense of newfound joy and the freedom from my life of responsibility and travel. I was at home with JoAnne!

The next morning, I got up before JoAnne and prepared breakfast for us. It was so relaxing for me! I saw her off to school. I took the morning newspaper and a cup of coffee into the sun-filled living room for a leisurely reading of every section of the newspaper, no longer searching for issues about which I might be consulting with someone or making a statement, or writing about in a monthly column in *The Disciple*. No more monthly columns in *The Disciple*!

I think that by noon I had adjusted to being retired!

CHAPTER 26

Retired!

As I approached the end of my term as GMP, people began asking me what I was going to do in retirement at 64 years of age. I had arranged with Christian Theological Seminary to teach a course beginning in the January semester, so I simply said, "I'm going to teach at CTS." That seemed to justify my retirement. And I admit that helped give me something to look forward to, something to work toward. It would be a new course, "The Theology and Practice of Evangelism." I had time to prepare from November to January. But I would need to do some study and reading in the field, outline my commitment and pastoral experience in evangelism, and prepare a syllabus. But not today!

I had finished my work as General Minister and President of the Christian Church (Disciples of Christ) in the United States and Canada!

I had retired, but JoAnne would continue to teach for eighteen months. I filled my days from November to January with "JoAnne's List." I also enjoyed some leisurely time at Geist Reservoir tinkering with our sailboat and our pontoon boat. I fixed dinner each evening, reveling in being at home. And, of course, I was preparing for my teaching of "Theology and Practice of Evangelism," enjoying visiting at the seminary library and working in my newly minted home office in one of the upstairs bedrooms.

The class membership numbered seven students, all over forty years of age. They were all second-career students now studying for the ministry. We met every Wednesday afternoon for three hours. It was very stimulating as we reflected on and discussed the assigned readings and their own life experiences. I shared elements of my twenty-eight years of pastoral ministry in congregations as well.

The summer of 1992, JoAnne and I joined brother Bill and Nancy Trimbur on an Alaskan cruise. We flew to Anchorage and embarked south toward Vancouver, with stops in Juneau and Sitka. It was a wonderful trip. To be with Nancy and Bill was great fun. Then from Vancouver we helicoptered to Victoria, a beautiful city, and Buchart Gardens, with gorgeous floral displays. We all enjoyed the incredible gardens but of course JoAnne with her great love of flowers was in "high heaven."

In the winter of 1992, JoAnne's partner teacher told her about her husband, John Babcock, who was the designing the show house to be built for the 1993 Indianapolis Home Show inside the Indiana Fairground's huge Exhibit Hall. He had noted that it was available to be taken apart and built on someone's building lot after the show. If someone would be willing to agree to buy this house ahead of the show, it could be bought at the builder's cost, with upgrades for all the appliances. We pursued it with the architect and the builder and secured a lot on Lake Kesslerwood, remarkably in our northern Indianapolis neighborhood near our home of nearly fifteen years. We loved our Surrey Hill Circle French Style stone home, but this looked like a retirement adventure worth taking. And we took it.

We put our house up for sale (after I worked on "the List") to make it sale attractive and worthy.

We bought the Lake Kesslerwood lot with money from the sale of Johnny's California home and our lot at Lake of the Woods near Charlotte, Virginia. And we proceeded with the details with the builder and our bank.

The house was constructed indoors from December 22 to January 28, 1993, with John Orth at the Fairgrounds almost every day, and JoAnne supervising John. We were fortunate in the sale of our Surrey Hill home. A neighborhood woman who was a real estate agent knew a young couple who wanted to buy a home in our neighborhood. She wrote letters to us and neighbors, asking if we would sign a contract for a one prospective visit to our home.

We signed that contract, and the family bought our home.

One small detail—the family needed to move in the second week in January and our Lake House would not be taken apart, rebuilt and ready for us until July!

We looked for rental property where we could lease without a long-term contract, from January 15, 1993, through the finish of our new Lake House. We were fortunate to find a home very near our Northwood Christian Church in an attractive neighborhood. The home was a two-story Cape Cod style with a dry and clean basement where we could store boxes of stuff for six months or so. It also had a two-car attached garage. The owner coincidentally had a hobby of keeping an historic record of the houses built for the Indianapolis Home Show and where they were located in the rebuild! Wow!

The day after Christmas 1992, I began packing moving boxes. I packed and packed! I filled countless black bags for trash collection. And I packed and packed! On January 14, the movers came, and on this cold, snowy day we moved. They finished moving us in to the rental at 3 a.m. the next morning in freezing weather. We had left the home where we lived the longest of our married life—sixteen years.

The rental home was cozy, though it had no fireplace. But it was several miles closer to JoAnne's school. When she came home from school, I had the newspaper ready for her so she could put up her feet and relax while I prepared dinner in what was an older kitchen. While she worked on her school plans in the evenings, I worked on drawing the plans for the great room/living room fireplace wall I would build. I drew "intimate" designs for cabinets and bookcases for either side of the fireplace. I had moved my power tools to another room in the basement where I would measure and cut the parts to transport to the lake house to install at the appropriate time.

Meanwhile, construction of the show house continued. I visited constantly and took JoAnne to see the progress after school. The building began inside the exhibit December 21 and was completed, landscaped, and decorated by January 28. It opened for showing on February 1. I was there much of the time watching 160,000 people touring the home. As some of my acquaintances came through, they were shocked that this would be our new home. The Home Show ended on February 10. The Gettum Builders Construction Company had ten days to dismantle the house, pack it in a semi-trailer truck and transport it to our lakefront building lot on Lake Kesslerwood in northeast Indianapolis.

While the building was going on at the Fairgrounds, construction was beginning on our lot. By the time the show was over on February 10, our foundation and basement walls had been poured and completed. Construction of the upper floors of the house could begin immediately. However, there was no longer the urgency of the Home Show deadline pressure for a timeline. And of course, in the Home Show "build" there was no heating and air conditioning, or actual plumbing construction, which would now take longer. Now there was also the winter weather with which to contend.

In this adventure for our new lake home, JoAnne had insisted, correctly, that we designate substantial funds for landscaping. The Ski Landscape Company had done a beautiful job in landscaping the exterior of the Show House. We contracted them for our new lakeside plantings. Its staff, John Wolski and his brother were very creative and helpful, with JoAnne taking the lead in planning.

We also were working with the decorating firm on buying drapes, wallpaper, colors, and some dishware that would match. In April,

I began work on crafting the wood parts for the cabinetry for the living room fireplace wall.

In May, with Frank Helme's help, we built the lakeside deck, stairs, and ramp to the dock. I built the floating dock on empty large juice barrels. It was such that we could dock both our sailboat and pontoon boat, one on either side. The boats were currently lodged out in the country toward Geist Lake in a boat storage area I had rented.

We watched the house come together with great anticipation, occasional frustration, but primarily, great satisfaction. The builder was excellent to work with as we arranged for some changes in the interior layout.

In the middle of May we had a large garage sale, with lots of nick-knacks, an Indiana "pie cabinet," which had been in our Demington, Cleveland Heights, home when we bought it, and an olive-green refrigerator we had bought when we moved there.

In mid-June, the living room construction was far enough along that I could rent a van and transport the parts for the installation of the cabinetry on the fireplace wall in time for the painters.

I also packed boxes with the stuff we had out for living in our rental house for five and half months, ready to move it again.

The spring semester was JoAnne's final teaching semester. There were delightful parties recognizing her retirement, including a systemwide dinner, recognizing her sixteen years teaching in the county system.

JoAnne's retirement was official on May 25, 1993. To celebrate, we made a trip to Hilton Head, South Carolina, to visit with sister Peggy and Dick Knowlton for a week. Everything was in order for the finishing of the house! The landscaping was in. The decorators would finish as the painting was completed.

So, with a combination of relaxation as JoAnne had finished her career as a public school teacher, but with incredible anticipation, we enjoyed the week.

At Hilton Head there were many art galleries. Dick guided us to a particular gallery. We selected two original paintings for our new home, one a watercolor of flowers that JoAnne really liked, and an oil of a river scene which was my choice. (They hang in places of honor today, the watercolor in the living room in memory of JoAnne).

We signed the closing papers on the house July 1, 1993. The movers took two days to transport all our stuff from the rental to the lake house. We were in by July 3. Debbie, Tom, Jessica, and Emily arrived on the Fourth to celebrate with us. They had visited for spring break, seeing the house in process, but now here it was all finished on the lake!

We had moved our boats from storage to our new dock in June, so they were there for water delight. I had also created a sandy beach by the deck, and swimming was good and fun.

JoAnne gloried in the landscape of trees and shrubs that were installed. She had joined the neighborhood garden club when we moved to Surrey Hill Circle in Indianapolis. She had won honors for her specimens of daffodils and her flower arranging. We had not yet taken the master gardener course, but she already had major floral knowledge and was ready for planning and planting flowers to supplement the shrubs and trees Ski Landscaping had installed.

That spring, JoAnne had had a "Grandparents Day" in her classroom. One of the grandfathers was very outgoing, visiting with JoAnne. He told of being retired and playing in a golf league at our nearby golf course. She spoke of my retirement and love of golf, and he invited me to join and gave her information about it. So, even before our lake house was finished, I joined that league and played on Monday mornings. I also joined the better players to play on Friday mornings.

As summer continued, JoAnne was now even more involved in the garden club. Our new home on the lake not being that far from our Surrey Hill home, it was the same garden club!

When school opened in late summer, she felt even more invigorated about being retired.

We had planned ahead for the fall, when we would both be in retirement. We were taking a two-week driving tour through Connecticut and New Hampshire, exploring the beautiful foliage of late October. As part of that trip, we visited Avery and Peg Post in Hanover, New Hampshire. When he was President of the United Church of Christ, Avery and I had worked together on many occasions and had become good friends. They had a wonderful home and retirement setting with Dartmouth College nearby. Members of their extended family lived within driving distance as well.

In December, we were invited to join the Irvington Dancing Club. It had been formed years ago by friends in the Irvington community on the east side of Indianapolis where the Missions Building, the Disciples headquarters was.

But in a large home with a third-floor ballroom, friends had formed a formal dancing club, holding dances once a month in formal wear. Subsequently, it moved to the famous Riviera Swimming Club in northern Indianapolis, not far from the Butler University campus. They hired a dance band to play "our kind of music" once a month with a dinner served to open the evening in our tuxedos and formal dresses. Quite a few men in the golf league were members, including Harry, the grandfather from JoAnne's class. We loved to dance. We accepted the invitation and joined.

As we moved toward retirement, we had been thinking about where we might want to spend our winters. We thought of Arizona and Florida. We decided to spend two weeks in January 1994 in Tucson and Phoenix to see if Arizona was what we wanted. Then we would spend two weeks in Sarasota, Florida, where we had vacationed twice prior to this. For one thing, the Superbowl was to be in Phoenix, where we had targeted to be for that weekend. We hoped against hope that the Indianapolis Colts would make it there. Alas, they lost to the blasted Steelers, who scored the winning touchdown on an illegal play! In addition, we were spending a few days with Bill and Ann Barnes in Scottsdale, a Phoenix suburb. All of it was delightful, though mornings in Tucson were a little cool for us.

We flew home to do some laundry and were off driving to Sarasota. We had rented a condo for two weeks where we had stayed before. It was located right across form the Siesta Key public beach with its broad expanse of quartz sand. The condo also had a wonderful large pool we had enjoyed on our prior stays at the location. It was within walking distance of Siesta Village with all its shops and restaurants. We enjoyed early morning walking on the beach. It was no contest with Arizona, with all the beautiful flowers and blooming shrubs, the culture of the arts we discovered, restaurants, and later the golf courses. We fell in love with Sarasota.

We came back to Indy to our Lake Kesslerwood home, reveling in the prospects and reality of spring, summer, and beautiful fall in this incredible lake and garden setting, now deciding to spend winter months in Sarasota. As spring unfolded, we enjoyed the blooming trees and spring flowers, the Irvington Club monthly dinner and dances with blossoming friendships, the golf league as the warmer weather came, the Indiana Repertory Theatre with Frank and Pat Helme, and the gorgeous home in which we lived on the . We had always wanted to live on a lake. Here it was, with lake swimming and our docked boats right at our back door. And then in the fall, season tickets with the Helmes at the home games of the Indianapolis Colts, beautiful Indiana fall foliage colors. We now could be more active in Northwood Christian Church and the trips of the "Keenagers" (which was like "Bifocals" in Beneva Christian Church in Sarasota.)

As Memorial Day approached, we heard about the big boat race on our lake. It was the Indy 4 Lapper. Like the Indy 500 on the same day, we had a boat race with our pontoon boats, with five horsepower limits on the motors. Like the big race, the day before we had qualifying runs with two laps around the marked course to determine our starting place. Ours was the slowest boat, so we got to be in first place at the start. We were off! The other boats began passing us right and left with lots of comments about our turtle-like pace. They must have souped up their motors! We finished last but it was great fun! And then we partied on land with a potluck dinner and lots of chatter.

At one of the Indianapolis Home Shows in the next year, one of the exhibitors was an Amish family from southern Indiana who built gazebos. We had talked about a screened-in gazebo. We had almost everything we wanted with our new home, but not a screened in porch. I had thought of building a gazebo myself, but the angles in constructing a gazebo were challenging. We visited with them in their booth and talked about the process of their building one for us. They would build it in their shop in southern Indiana, and then bring it to our yard and erect it in one day. We took a trip to their home shop, taking a sample of the paint specifications to match our house trim. We inspected their workmanship and models there and signed the contract. In the summer of 1994, the screened gazebo was brought and built behind the house, just off the main gravel path to the deck and dock. We spent many a summer dinner, evenings, breakfast, and lunch in our screened-in gazebo. JoAnne planned and executed wonderful flower gardens surrounding it. We had a round table and chairs along with four wicker veranda comfortable rockers and solid chairs. JoAnne had her birdhouse collection around the top of the walls. Her mother would sit lounging there saying, "JoAnne, you couldn't get another thing in here!"

When we lived in our Surrey Hill Circle home, we had adopted a Saint Bernard/collie named Heidi. She was a wonderful companion, especially for JoAnne when I traveled so much. But her life ran out, and the vet had to put her down. As we moved into our lake house, we were ready for another companion. We had a company put in an "invisible fence," an electric pet fence. We were ready for another dog. One morning, as often was the case, the newspaper told of a golden retriever that was available for adoption at the Humane Society. I said, "Let's go out to the Humane Society." We sped out there, and as we arrived and parked, we saw a man in a fenced area with a golden retriever. At the fence I asked if that was the golden advertised as available. He said yes, he had her out here to see if she would be a good dog for helping in searching for drugs. He was with the Sheriff's Department, but she was not, in his opinion, right for what they needed. I asked if he would keep her out there till I could go through the office and building and get out to claim her. He said he would. So, we went in and said we wanted to claim the golden retriever outside being rejected by the Sheriff's Department. They said yes. So, we hurried through to the waiting gentlemen. Turned out her name was "Bailey." She was a beautiful golden, friendly and receptive to us. We claimed her for adoption and filled out the papers. We called our vet to make a stop on our way home to have her examine Bailey to make sure, as much as possible, that she was healthy. She got a good report. However, when I opened my front door, Bailey was almost out the door before I could control her. She was quick and strong. She had been with a family for a year, but they had four children all under the age of six, and the mother said she could not handle another in Bailey. She was well housebroken and now I had to train her to an invisible fence. I knew the ropes, and worked at it for two weeks, training her for all the boundaries, including across the front driveway. We let Bailey out in the yard without a leash. She did alright around the yard, but she bolted to the fence in the front driveway and took off running down the very busy Fall Creek Parkway on which we lived. I charged after her. Cars and trucks stopped. But Bailey, seeing one pickup coming toward her turned back toward home. She came running and I grabbed her collar as she fell into a mud hole next door where a new house was being built. I picked her up, holding her in my muddy arms and chest and carried her to the garage house entrance and knocked. JoAnne couldn't believe her eyes at the sight of her muddy pair. I took Bailey into a first-floor bathroom bathtub to de-mud both of us! Fortunately, that was the only time she escaped like that.

One time, several years later, she had one of those big plastic collars over her head to keep her from getting at a sore on her hip and was out in the front yard. The doorbell rang. A lady had stopped and said, "Your dog has had a bad accident. She has her head stuck in a lamp shade!"

She was well trained. Her bed was in the laundry room. We could say, "it's bedtime!" and she would go right in, and we would close the door. One problem: she would lick the wall and chew holes in the plaster board. She did that for about six months. I became adept at fixing the holes. But other than that, she was wonderful. If we were sitting down relaxing in a chair, she would come over to us and sit down awaiting some "lovin'." She loved to ride on the pontoon boat. Going in the lake swimming with us was a lark.

At a Christmas party at friends across the lake, we met a new couple, Hugh and Jo Plant, who had just finished building their home on the lake about four houses from ours. We had a nice visit with them and agreed we would get together for an evening sometime. We got together to play cards. Jo Plant also joined the garden club that JoAnne was in, so they became friends there. We continued to be together playing cards, alternating homes or going on a night out for a concert or play. We became good friends. They were not attending any church, so we invited them to come with us to Northwood. They came, became more and more involved, and joined Northwood.

The next year, I began teaching a course at CTS on the "Ethos and Polity of the Disciples." I had a class of fifteen students for three hours once a week for the spring semester of 1993. It was about the spirit, history, and structure of our church and how The Design provides for how we work together as a denomination. It was right down the road of my experience, knowledge, and theological understanding of the church. I taught the course every other year until 2003. The last two times, I was joined by a minister from the UCC and it was expanded to the polity of both churches, now in "full communion."

JoAnne expanded her gardens and was very much involved in her garden club. She was enjoying her new friendship with Jo Plant and their mutual activity in the garden club. JoAnne and I enrolled in the master gardener class provided by the County Extension Department. It was very interesting and informative, with hours of community service required. JoAnne fulfilled her hours through volunteer service on flower beds at the home for hearing impaired and worked in partnership with Jo Plant. We became master gardeners!

In the summer of 1996, we took a cruise to the Panama Canal. The first evening on the beautiful *Princess Line* ship, we rode the elevator to a dinner with a British couple, Ton and Helen Beecher, who were on their honeymoon. We chatted with them over cocktails prior to the welcoming meal and were with them for dinner. We became friends, as we sometimes had a drink or breakfast or lunch and sat together for the evening showtime. The evening of the final formal dinner, they invited us to their honeymoon suite for happy hour drinks and nibbles. That was a great treat.

We enjoyed seeing the Canal, as we sailed halfway through and then back out. The cruise then visited Caribbean Island ports on the way back to Fort Lauderdale.

After the cruise, we corresponded with Tony and Helen for several years, discussing other possible trips together. That didn't work out, but the correspondence continued through 2003.

In 1998 we took another cruise, this time from Montréal down the Saint Lawrence Seaway to Québec, Halifax, Saint John, Bangor, Boston, Newport, and finally New York City. It was quite something to wake up in the morning, gaze out your porthole to see the Statue of Liberty right there. After a Broadway show, we traveled by train to Philadelphia to spend several days with Nancy and Bill Trimbur. From there we flew home to Indy. It was a great trip!

We enjoyed a fourth brief cruise to the Bahamas. It was free, but also involved a pitch for timeshares back in South Florida. We bit on a timeshare in Williamsburg, Virginia. We took a week around the Fourth of July. We enjoyed several vacations there with family.

In May of 1997, we were struck with an unimaginable tragedy. Our dear granddaughter Jessica had a terrible automobile accident and was severely injured. The call came in the evening. Debbie began to tell us about it from the hospital but couldn't finish. Tom King got on the phone and said Jessica was driving home from working in the evening at the supermarket in a severe rainstorm and crashed into a tree about four blocks from home. She didn't make it. She had died. It was almost too much to bear.

JoAnne's mother was with us. She had been with us for a six month stay, as she alternated between staying with us and JoAnne's brothers. Taking Beatrice and Bailey with us, we left as soon as we could pack a few things together. We called Don and Elaine Manworren to let them know. Before we left, they came to give us their empathy. I drove all night for us to get to our dear Debbie. It was early the next morning when we arrived. Debbie and JoAnne fell into each other's arms in terrible grief. Then I held my dear Debbie. Jessica was our pride and joy, our beloved first-born granddaughter. After Johnny's death, here was another of our beloved family passing away. It was way out of sync from the way it is supposed to be.

JoAnne's brother Dick came up to meet us and took Beatrice to their home in Girard.

The conjecture was that after the prom weekend, late nights, and lack of sleep, she had worked the evening shift as a checkout clerk. She fell asleep momentarily, lost control of the car, and crashed into a tree.

We accompanied Debbie to the funeral home to take care of arrangements. There would be an open house at the funeral home for friends to come see the family. Deb thought it best to have an open casket so that Emily, then five years old, could say goodbye.

That was also true for many of Jessica's friends. Jessica was then cremated before the memorial service.

Houston Bowers led the service beautifully. The church was full, with an amazing turnout of her high school classmates. Jessica had just completed her junior year, was in the Honor Society, and had just been elected president of "Unity," an association to promote interracial relationships for Cleveland Heights High School.

We stayed on with Debbie, Tom, and Emily for several days after the memorial service. I don't remember whether Gramma Bea came back to Indy with us that time. When she had needed help in her advancing age, we took turns in our homes. She was a delight and participated in our social life, playing cards, the dice game, going to plays, church, movies, and such. She was not a burden. We put a single bed in the den, which had a full bath next to it. JoAnne helped her with her baths. Ultimately, as she needed more assisted living, she went into a nursing home near Niles.

Though we were still living with our grief over our loss of Jessica, life in our lake house and our church and social life was idyllic. We had our winters in Sarasota as well. After adopting Bailey, we had one of my students from seminary, Suzanne Cole, house sit when we spent one month in Sarasota. However, when we went to two and three months stays, we could not think of leaving Bailey for that long. We found places to rent, for example the Banana Bay Club, where we could have Bailey with us. During the years between 1994 and 2001, we enjoyed looking at new homes during the Builder's Home Shows. We also had invested in a stock Dick Knowlton was involved in that was going to "bring our ship in." And we could buy a second home in Florida. Well, our ship did not come in! Finally in early February 2001, we visited a home within our reach. On JoAnne's 70th birthday, we signed a contract to purchase the home on 1939 Wyndham Drive in Sarasota, FL. It had three bedrooms, two full baths, living room/dining room, large eat-in kitchen, family room, outdoor room and lanai, and a 36-foot pool.

For a month, we shopped for furniture, dishes, cookware, silver, bedding, etc. We were like a couple of kids let loose in a candy shop! We simply had a glorious time. We arranged the down payment and the mortgage and closed one month to the day from our purchase on March 13. We arranged for our new furniture to arrive by the thirteenth, with the approval of the owners, even a couple of days before. Jeff and Cindy were visiting and helped put together the furniture for the lanai. Emily was given permission to swim in the pool a couple of days before we closed. So, we had our dream of our own home in Florida come true in Sarasota. We were spoiled with our beautiful lake home in Indy and now, thanks to JoAnne's touch and me on a ladder, our beautifully decorated home in Sarasota.

Moving in on March 13, we enjoyed feeling the luxury of our own Florida home till Easter Sunday. That morning we received word that Gramma Bea, JoAnne's mother had passed away that morning. The funeral would be on Thursday at the Niles Funeral Home. It happened that we had invited our Beneva Church ministers, Ed and Mary Pat Spencer to Easter Sunday dinner after church. They wanted to share some of their family problems and ask us for some counsel. So between that and the news of Beatrice's death, the occasion was dampened.

We packed the car and headed for Ohio. We stayed with Dick and Mary in Girard. I led in the funeral service at the insistence of the family, with the minister of Niles First Christian Church assisting. After a few days with family, we drove back to Indianapolis.

That fall, we decided we were free enough to go to our Florida home beyond just wintertime. So, utilizing and enjoying our new home and Sarasota, we enjoyed some October days on Wyndham Drive with the luxury of home and pool. And doing some more decorating!

Looking toward our 50th wedding anniversary on July 26, 2002, we were pondering where we might have that family celebration. We didn't want a big brouhaha, just family. We thought of

Bethany Beach, the place of so many family memories. But we decided on Sarasota, starting a new tradition in our home. We loved the thought of having the celebration dinner at Ophelia's Restaurant. We invited our family to save that week to come join us in Sarasota.

We were enjoying the early summer on Lake Kesslerwood with friends. However, JoAnne had some swelling in her left cheek. In an appointment with our dentist, he thought a tooth might be infected. He sent her to a specialist for a root canal procedure.

We drove to Sarasota. The kids all came, including the grandchildren, and we celebrated. We had a great time around the pool and lanai. We had a beautiful cake JoAnne ceremonially cut for us. We went to dinner at Ophelia's. Fifty years! Lovers and tight friends!

JoAnne was still having trouble with swelling in her left cheek. We asked our minister Mary Pat for a recommendation for an ear nose and throat physician. She gave us a name. The otolaryngologist was very thorough in her examination. She found some polyps in JoAnne's nose which needed removing. With an appointment for surgery at Doctors Hospital in Sarasota, the polyps were removed. While JoAnne was under the anesthesia the doctor went into JoAnne's left cheek and took a biopsy. It was sent to the lab. In a few days, she had another appointment. The doctor gave us the news. It was cancer. JoAnne had a CAT scan. It showed there was a mass in her left sinus and left jaw up into her cheek bone, very near her left eye. It was eroding her jaw and cheek bone. Radical surgery was required.

The doctor spoke of the outstanding reputation of treatment at the Moffat Cancer Center in Tampa. But we preferred to be back in our home in Indiana for surgery and treatment. As we left Sarasota to drive back to Indianapolis, JoAnne felt she would never be back in Sarasota.

JoAnne and I both had gone to an otolaryngologist with whom we felt very comfortable. In fact, she had operated on my nose.

We called her. She recommended a doctor at the Indiana University Medical Center in Indianapolis whose specialty was cancer surgery of this type.

We made an appointment with the surgeon, bringing the CAT scan with us. The doctor described what was needed. The tumor mass would be removed, but with it, part of the cheekbone, part of the palate, and teeth and gum of her upper left jaw, with reconstruction to follow. JoAnne was incredible with her approach to this major development, uncomplaining.

The surgery took place September 9, 2002, at the Indiana University Medical Center scheduled at 11:30 in the morning. The surgery was from then until about 5:00 p.m. By this time Chris Wratten was our minister and was with us for prayer before JoAnne went in for surgery. Our friends Hugh and Jo Plant were with JoAnne and me right up until they took her in for surgery. Don and Elaine, Frank and Pat, and Neil and Sandy stayed to wait with Debbie and me. The surgeon's associate, a young woman, came out to give us a report that JoAnne was doing well with the anesthetic, and the surgery was going well. The surgeon came out at about 5:45 to say that he had to take out half of the roof of her mouth, her left upper cheekbone, left upper teeth and jaw, and bone under her left eye. Going in, we didn't know whether he could save her eye.

I finally got to see her at about 10:30 that night. My beloved! She stayed in the hospital for four days. Peggy, Diana, and Kim came to see her. Elaine, Pat, and Sandy visited too. She healed from the surgery for one month. Then for six weeks, five days a week, she was given radiation treatment on the site at the Indiana Medical Center. During that six weeks, my Jo went from 180 pounds to 120 pounds.

She had to see the dental section of the IU Medical Center for the creation of an obturator for her mouth, to cover the openings in the palate and jaw. The doctors also operated to place soft tissue under her left eyeball and worked on the tear ducts to drain the tears from the eye. She had double vision for some time, so she could no longer drive. Reading was trying, so every night before turning out the light, I read novels to us before going to sleep. I continued to do all the cooking while she recuperated. For her it needed to be soup and soft foods.

We were able to go to our Sarasota home for the winter of 2002–2003 as she further recuperated. It was at that point, however, that we decided that it would be best if we moved our northern home from Indianapolis to Cleveland to be near Debbie and our old "stomping grounds." Among our group of friends in Indianapolis, a number had been doing that as well. The Helmes moved near Mary Jane in Fort Worth. The Manworrans moved near their son in Dallas. The Weisheimers moved to Shaker Heights and Youngstown. And the Topliffes moved to Michigan near their daughter.

Living in our wonderful lake setting with our lovely home, Jo-Anne's outstanding flower gardens, the gazebo, the sailboat and pontoon boat, and lake friends, especially Hugh and Jo Plant, was idyllic! But we put the house up for sale. We also explored where we might live in Cleveland. Tom and Debbie told us about Aberdeen in Highland Heights. John Hungerford told me about my childhood friend Doug Brown who lived in Aberdeen. On Easter Sunday afternoon when we were in town with Debbie and Tom, we visited Doug, appreciated his house, and called the builder Ron Miller. He showed us his model homes in Aberdeen Village, and we made a decision to move ahead with a particular model.

Our Fall Creek Road Lake house sold in the spring of 2003. Our new house would be completed November 15. We had to give over possession of the lake house in August. I packed 123 boxes! The movers agreed to pack our stuff in a semi and store it there until November 15. We left our lake home with wonderful memories of ten years of joy in that setting. We came to our Florida home until the October General Assembly in Charlotte, North Carolina. We attended the Assembly and then went to Cleveland, staying with Debbie and Tom from the last of October till November 15.

The builder, Ron Miller, was right on time, finishing on November 14. We paid cash for the house! Our stuff from the movers arrived November 15, right on time as well. We began settling in at 333 Burwick Road, Highland Heights, Ohio, just in front of the 15th fairway of the Stonewater Country Club in the Village of Aberdeen.

Brother Bill and Nancy arrived the next day from Philly. We all attacked the boxes. With all the boxes we could barely navigate the great room. They were a big help!

We settled in with the hanging of drapes and other things. The major settling in, however, was with JoAnne and the Cleveland Clinic. She brought all of her records with her to the Otolaryngology Department with communication from the Indiana Medical Center as well. She began with Dr. Cowper. She also was put in touch with the Clinic Eye Institute, with her left eye continuing to give her trouble which necessitated surgery on tissue around the eye. Dr. Cowper referred JoAnne to Dr. Alland. He did major surgery, taking serious tissue from her left arm, making it a flap to fill in the openings created by the first radical surgery. Dr. Alland was the major surgeon for the woman who received a whole new face transplant at the Clinic. He also took some tissue from another patient's arm and created a new larynx for that patient.

Over the next sixteen years JoAnne would have a total of thirty-eight surgeries or procedures, with a disintegrating lower left jaw replaced by a new metal jaw, more flaps moving tissues in her body, a hernia, breast cancer with one breast removed, a heart attack, cancer on the tongue, a feeding tube for four and a half years, with complications of the opening to her abdomen, and surgeries around her mouth in an attempt to help her to be able to close her mouth.

Between hospitalizations, we enjoyed our home and our Cleveland church. We enjoyed time with Houston and Mary Bowers. Houston was the minister who succeeded me at Euclid Avenue Christian Church. He insisted we should come join the church. Normally, it is not good practice for a minister to join a congregation he had served. But Houston noted we had been gone to Indianapolis for twenty-six years. Many new members would not know me as their minister. It was a real treat listening to Houston's sermons, and the music program was outstanding. Debbie was active in the church. And we joined.

Houston and Mary introduced us to Bob and Carolyn Bruce, who were regular attendees at Euclid Avenue Christian Church. The Bruces loved to play golf and they invited me to play with them at Manakiki and Stonewater. JoAnne rode in the cart with me the first time we played, but my scooting around hunting for my ball rather unsettled her tummy, so that didn't last.

In our winters in Florida, we renewed friendship with Pete and Karen Smith. We played cards and went out to eat after church. Pete and I played golf while Karen and JoAnne browsed, shopped, ate out, and played card games until we finished. It was really great to have their friendship. We also joined the Bifocal group in the Beneva Christian Church in Florida, with gatherings for the Super Bowl, Easter dinner, and a monthly get-together. It was hard for JoAnne though because after her first radical surgery she could only open her mouth a smidgen. Mary Caress saw to it that JoAnne would have soup when the Bifocals met. JoAnne's specialty for the parties was great, delicious slow-cooked meatballs.

Our friendship with Bob and Carolyn Bruce developed with cards and golf. We had something in common in that Bob had been a United Church of Christ minister and JoAnne and Carolyn had experienced the role of "preacher's wife." We invited them to come to Sarasota for Carolyn's teaching spring break. They came and stayed at the Hampton Inn. I prepared an "itinerary" designed to show them the highlights of Sarasota: the weather, beaches, restaurants, theaters, golf courses, churches, card playing, Mexican Train, and our friends Pete and Karen Smith. We kidded for years about the "itinerary."

Beneva Christian Church had some needs after our ministers Ed and Mary Pat left. At one point, Pete, Jack Collins, and I filled the pulpit in the interim. Jack and Pat Collins now were wintering in Sarasota and increased our circle of friends, Jack on the golf course and Pat with the roving ladies. The three couples of us also played cards and dominoes in the evenings.

Bob and Carolyn enjoyed Sarasota so much that when they retired in 2007 they came to Sarasota for two months. They rented a home in the first year and then rented a condo for two months in the Meadows in succeeding years. They joined the Smiths and us for cards, dominoes, and golf. And at home in Cleveland, we went to church together and played cards and golf.

In Indianapolis, I had been Chair of the Board of our Northwood Christian Church and served on the pulpit committee when Chris Wratten came to be our minister. She saw us through JoAnne's first radical surgery and radiation. It was a big help.

When we came back to Cleveland it was great to hear Houston Bower's sermons. He continued on for several years. When he retired and we were searching for a minister, Chris was dating David Eggert who was driving all the way from Chautauqua, New York, where he lived to Indianapolis every weekend. They were serious. I told Chris about our opening, and she put her name in with Bill Edwards, our regional minister, and activated her ministerial papers. The long and short of it, she became our minister here at Euclid Avenue Christian Church! She was beginning the first of January 2006. David was still working in New York, and she and David were married, but had not yet found a place in Cleveland to live. Since we would be in Florida from January to April, JoAnne offered our home to Chris and David, he for weekends since he hadn't yet retired. So that was arranged.

As we approached January 2019, JoAnne was having pain in the back of her head and neck. We delayed our trip to Sarasota for appointments January 8 at the Clinic. With a new MRI, a new mass was confirmed. We held our consultation with her otolaryngologists, Dr. La Marre, and an oncologist Dr. Koyfman. It was a major discovery.

For JoAnne and the two doctors another major surgery seemed out of the question. Furthermore, she said she was "ready to go," to pass away!

JoAnne's doctors suggested we wait and see how things developed. We made an appointment for April 23, three months hence.

JoAnne did not want to spend the winter away from family, the Clinic doctors, and our Cleveland home. So we stayed on at Burwick Road through January and February. JoAnne was enjoying playing bridge with friends from church, and they reported she was outstanding at bridge. I knew that.

JoAnne agreed to fly to Sarasota for two weeks in March. We had definitely decided to put our Florida home up for sale. We needed to gather photos and treasured memorabilia to take back to Cleveland. On March 11, 2019, we flew from Akron/Canton to Sarasota. Debbie and Bob and Carolyn Bruce were already there. Debbie met us.

It was good to be in our Sarasota home. We began collecting things we wanted to keep, and bagging things to take to Goodwill to donate with many trips. We talked to Ron Morano, our neighbor and friend who was in real estate sales, about representing us. We always felt that when one of us, JoAnne or John, was gone, we would need to sell our Sarasota home for economic reasons.

We gathered collections of cherished things in boxes. Debbie and Al, in their large-capacity auto, packed them for their drive back to Cleveland.

As we talked to Ron about the salability of our home, he recommended a new stainless-steel stove and dishwasher, attractions worth buying. Also, we knew the carpet in the living, dining, and bedrooms needed replacing. More changes would be coming! On

Friday, March 22, 2019, we signed a contract with Ron Morano to sell the house. We also signed to have the house painted inside and out. Ron was great in recruiting the painting contractor. Also, against JoAnne's better judgment, I arranged to have my 1994 Oldsmobile Cutlass Supreme convertible transported to Cleveland. On Monday, March 25, 2019, Bob and Carolyn took us to the Sarasota Airport for a direct flight to Cleveland. I left my golf clubs with Bob and Carolyn to bring back when they drove, leaving on the thirtieth. As we departed our Sarasota home for the final time, we simply left all our cherished furniture and furnishings for Ron to have an estate sale and a garage sale. It was just like abandoning everything. We did ask Ron to save and send three paintings, which he did. I especially hated to leave a beautiful corner cabinet, and the painted unique table in the entryway.

When Bob and Carolyn returned to Highland Heights they called before coming over to unload my golf clubs. They backed up to the garage as I came out. When they opened the back end of their car, there were my golf clubs and the table from the entryway in Sarasota! What a joy! And how thoughtful of them!

We were having supper at Emily's and Adams on April 1, when I received a call that the convertible had arrived. JoAnne hosted bridge on April 4 and played at Carol David's with Judy Griffith and Patti Wiley on April 18 and won. Jo and I were still playing Hand and Foot every evening after dinner.

On Friday, April 19, JoAnne had a CAT scan at the Beachwood Clinic. On April 23, JoAnne, Debbie, and I met with Dr. Koyfman and Dr. La Marre at the Clinic Cancer Center. Dr. Koyfman was gentle in saying to JoAnne, "Up to this point the doctors have pretty much made the decision for you regarding your treatments. Now, you must make your own decision. Mrs. Humbert, the mass in your neck and head has grown. On the one hand you could choose a few radiation treatments to live a little longer. But you would need nutrition and that would mean another feeding tube. On the other hand, you could choose the peaceful way of hospice. We could provide you with hospice care with the hospice nurse coming to your home tomorrow. You can be at home for your hospice care."

JoAnne said she was ready to go, and chose the hospice way, beginning Wednesday, April 24, 2019.

That Wednesday morning, I was scheduled for an interview with Rick Lowery at the United Church of Christ headquarters offices in downtown Cleveland. I was to make a taped presentation for the upcoming General Assembly. As I always did, I prepared the oatmeal breakfast for JoAnne. Then, I fulfilled my responsibility doing the taping at the UCC studio for Des Moines.

I came home, and JoAnne was still sleeping. The nurse, Margie, arrived and we sat in the living room. JoAnne came in on her walker and we sat together on the sofa while Margie explained the hospice process. Margie was sensitive and thorough.

On Friday, the social worker came to visit JoAnne and me. One of the questions before JoAnne arrived in the living room was, "Have you made arrangements with the funeral home?" I hadn't yet done so. He encouraged me to do that promptly. That made things suddenly even more imminent.

On Saturday, April 27, the young hospice chaplain, Tyler Delaney arrived. Before JoAnne came into the room, I said, "Tell me about your background." He said, "I'm a Disciples of Christ minister." I said, "I'm a Disciples of Christ minister!" And we went on from there. He was wonderful with JoAnne in their conversation.

On Sunday, Megan, the social worker, came, and we connected really well. On Friday, a substitute had come, and now Megan would be our contact.

On Saturday, JoAnne had stopped wanting to eat, and I was supposed to abide by her feelings. She was sleeping most of the time.

On Monday, Margie the nurse came again. She had a conversation with JoAnne about Jo's not wanting to take pain-relieving medicines, which was her pattern. Jo said it was because she didn't want to get hooked on pain medicines. Margie talked about this moment in JoAnne's life and noted that this would not be a problem. It was time for relief from her present pain. It was time for morphine. I was given instructions and gave JoAnne her first morphine drip in the side of her cheek. She did come to the kitchen table for some soup that April 29 evening. And though she would kind of drift off between plays of Hand and Foot, still she won again.

On Tuesday, JoAnne slept most of the day, with morphine dripped regularly in her cheek. In the evening, though she was not eating, she insisted on getting up and coming to the kitchen table for cards. JoAnne won again. It became our last card game.

On Wednesday, May 1, Jeff, and Cindy arrived from Baltimore. Debbie had been spending most of her days with us. Megan and Tyler both came that day. We were all gathered in the bedroom as JoAnne slept and occasionally awoke and tapped her cheek, a signal that I was to give her another morphine drip.

On Thursday, she was sleeping all day. She would get up and use the walker and my help as she needed the bathroom.

On Friday afternoon, Nurse Margie came. She checked JoAnne's blood pressure and heart rate. She told us that JoAnne had just hours to live. That evening as Jeff, Cindy and I were with her, she sat up on the edge of the bed, she reached out as if to reach for something she was seeing beyond us. Jeff and Cindy sought to calm her with their presence. I encouraged her to come to the bathroom with me, and she said "Why?" and "No, John," her last spoken words to me.

That night we slept quietly together. In the morning, she was breathing thinly, and she breathed her last and died at 11:30 a.m., May 4, 2019. We called hospice and another nurse came to confirm her death. I called the funeral home, and they came and took her dear body.

The memorial service was set for May 18, 2019, at our church, now named Disciples Christian Church, with Roger McKinney presiding. We chose the columbarium in our church for the resting place for JoAnne's ashes. There is room just next to her ashes for mine.

Don Manworren came to town for the service. Joyce Brown and her daughters Lara and Heather drove in from Maryland and North Carolina. Peggy, Diana, Barry, Kim and Greg, and Michelle were here. Rick Reisinger, President of Church Extension, Dick and Mindy Hamm (Dick is a former GMP), and Timothy James, Associate GMP, all came from Indianapolis.

Roger McKinney led a beautiful service, with Amanda Powell's piano and marvelous voice a comforting presence.

Speaking in tribute of JoAnne were Terri Hord Owens, our Disciples General Minister and President, Houston Bowers, Karen Smith, and Debbie. I wrote my tribute for Roger McKinney to read for me.

Debbie spoke of JoAnne being the consummate teacher, at home and at school. At home as at school, she was calm, collected, thoughtful and understanding. She was famous in our home for saying, "What are the alternatives?" In short, she led by example with dignity. She was a teacher of life. She closed talking about how our family used to sing together, and one song she remembered closed with these words:

> I think the good Lord above, put you here for me to love.
> Picked you out from all the rest,
> Because God knows that I'd love you the best.
> Thank you, MOM!

I wrote of how we met, fell in love, and cared for each other during long stints of illness. I wrote:

> You've seen how wondrous JoAnne has faced adversity and made the best of it with amazing grace and presence. Through it all she has loved us with her amazing resilience and courage, carrying us all along through

the turbulence of surgery after surgery, ravaging her face and body, but never her spirit. This time, after seventeen years, and another cancer deep in her face, she was ready to go, and was not afraid to die. With confidence she chose the hospice way of comfort, passing away peacefully. May the elegant words of George Gordon Byron, Lord Byron, be my words of love and expression of ultimate admiration for my JoAnne:

> She walks in beauty, like the night
> Of Cloudless climes and starry skies
> And all that's best of dark and bright
> Meet in her aspect and her eyes
> Thus mellowed to the tender night
> Which heaven to gaudy day denies
>
> One shade the more, one ray the less
> Had half impaired the nameless grace
> Which waves in every raven tress
> Or softly lightens o'er her face;
> Where thoughts serenely express
> How pure, how dear their dwelling place.
>
> And on that cheek, and o'er that brow,
> So soft, so calm, yet eloquent,
> The smiles that win, the tints that glow,
> But tells of days in goodness spent,
> A mind at peace with all below,
> A heart whose love has been well spent.

My dearest, beloved JoAnne, Shalom, until we shall clasp hearts and minds again.

We loved our JoAnne through these last days the hospice way.

I was dealing with all the elements of 1939 Wyndham with Ron Marano, and new flooring, new countertops, a roof leak, new landscaping, garage sale etc. The house was officially on sale on May 9, 2019.

I began work with our trust lawyer in Indianapolis, Brett Carlisle. Having set up our trust back in the '90s made financial details so much easier.

Debbie and Allen, Bob and Carolyn, and Chaplain Tyler Delaney were there with and for me in the trauma of JoAnne's passing. I renewed friendship with Joyce Brown, Lara, and Heather and Dale whom I had married some forty years ago. On June 19, I drove to Baltimore to be with Jeff and Cindy, Nikki and Allen, Isabel, and Brianna. On Friday and Saturday, I was invited to be on Dale and Heather's 40-foot beautiful boat on Chesapeake Bay. As it turned out, the boat trip was postponed, but it was nice to be with Joyce and to go to church on Sunday at Columbia, Maryland, at the church of which Barkley had been the founding pastor. I was back with Jeff and crew for Sunday afternoon and dinner and night, then left for home Monday morning.

Bernard Oakes and I resumed our lunches at the Welshfield Inn. We both, having lost our beloved wives, found solace in our long-standing friendship since 1953 during seminary days.

July 12, 2019, we closed on the sale of 1939 Wyndham Drive in Sarasota. It was a place of joy and love for eighteen years. We enjoyed it as a hospitality house, as we shared it with friends from far and wide, with laughter and fun. One of our friends called our home "the party house."

I had work done on the engine of the convertible, then had it detailed so it really "shone." Then I took Amanda Powell, Luisa, and Sofia for ice cream in Willoughby Hills on the seventeenth.

The General Assembly was held in Des Moines, Iowa, July 20 to 24. Debbie and I flew to Des Moines on Friday the nineteenth. We had a wonderful time together in the sessions, at meals, and visiting with so many old friends and colleagues. Des Moines brought back so many memories, even back to my first International Convention in 1934, days before my seventh birthday. But, of course it was 1985, where I was elected as General Minister and President that stood out. We ran into Cynthia Hale, remembering our time when the Black ministers practically vetoed my nomination of her as head of the Convocation and Associate GMP. She danced around the room in front of us in 2019, singing, "free

I was set free." In 1985, she was called to start a new congregation in Atlanta, Georgia, called Ray of Hope Christian Church. It's now in Decatur. As I write this in 2021, it has 2,531 members and 1,100 in worship! And Cynthia is still there as Senior Minister after thirty-five years. Cynthia was one of the evenings' featured preachers at the Assembly. Powerful!

I came home on the twenty-fourth, and then on Friday, July 26, remembered our wedding anniversary which would have been our sixty-seventh.

JoAnne loved to play Hand and Foot. We played every evening after supper. We played about once a week with the Bruces, the ladies against the men. After JoAnne died, Bob and Carolyn and I continued playing Hand and Foot with three, every person for themselves. When I returned from the Assembly, Bob and Carolyn were on a two-week trip to Scotland with "Road Warriors."

My "rain delayed" renewed invitation for a day on Heather and Dale's boat was for August 4. I drove to Jeff and Cindy's in Baltimore on July 30 for another visit. On Friday, Jeff prepared a sumptuous dinner, Crab Imperial, plus a steak and cheese broccoli. Wow! It was sumptuous. On Saturday, Joyce, her sister, and I spent the day at a resort on the Chesapeake Bay on the beautiful boat, crossing a section of the bay and back. I was allowed to take over as the captain steering the powering boat in open bay water! Great day! Great boat!

I was due to pick up Bob and Carolyn from their return flight to Cleveland from Scotland on the seventh at 5:19 p.m., but flights were delayed, and they missed their connection. They didn't arrive in Cleveland until about 3:00 a.m. They took a taxi home. I heard lots of stories of Scotland as we played golf on Friday, the ninth. That evening I went to dinner at Debbie's with Greg and Kim Bachman who were visiting from Springfield. Saturday morning Greg, Allen, Adam, and I played at Stonewater, our golf course. The other three guys really hit long balls! I did okay. Allen is really into golf, with continuing golf lessons from our pro, and lots of sessions on the practice range.

On August 21, I traded our 2016 Cadillac for a new 2019 XTZ sedan. This would probably be the last car I would buy!

On the twenty-eighth, the Bruces and I met Pete Smith at Belleville, Ohio, just north of Columbus, for a round of golf and dinner. We had a great time! The course was really tough, up and down the steep hills.

I made another trip to see Jeff and Joyce Brown from September 18 to 23 in my new car. It drives so effortlessly and comfortably. Had a good time with Jeff again at a golf driving range. Joyce doesn't cook, so we ate out! On my way home I stopped for lunch at Deep Creek Lake with Duane Cummins. He was President of our Division of Higher Education and in my GMP Cabinet, before he became President of Bethany College. We went to see his home after lunch. It is absolutely spectacular in the Maryland mountains. His library study has a remarkable collection of history, both secular and religious, including an amazing collection of Disciples volumes. He had my book, *A House of Living Stones,* and asked me to autograph it for him. The library is so aesthetically beautiful, with the bay window behind his desk overlooking the mountains. Wow!

In the first days of August, Greg and Kim had brought my sister Peggy as they came to Cleveland for Kim to attend a meeting. They stayed overnight, with Greg going with Kim for the meeting. Peggy and I had a wonderful time visiting.

I had several doctor's appointments in October regarding some difficulty with my swallowing. Included was a barium swallowing and then endoscopy. I had no cancer in my swallowing system, just old age. Speaking of which, on my 92nd birthday, I had dinner with the Bruces, Debbie and Allen, Emily, Adam, and Harper. (Elizabeth was with her dad.)

Receiving brochures about river cruises in Europe, I decided I wanted take one in the summer of 2020. I invited Debbie to consider going with me. She accepted. So, in October we went to see the travel agent at AAA. We booked a cruise on the Rhine River beginning at Basil in Switzerland for ten days, to Amsterdam, the Netherlands. We made a down payment. We would complete the cruise payment December 12, reserving the best two room cabins on the riverboat! How exciting!

Meanwhile, a church group in Cleveland had donated free tickets for a Cleveland Cavalier basketball game. Debbie wanted to go, but Allen didn't. Carolyn wanted to go, but Bob didn't. So, I signed up to receive three tickets. The three of us went. Just before we went through the gate into Rocket Square Arena, Debbie found she had left her new phone in the car and returned to retrieve it. While Carolyn and I were standing there, a gentleman and lady walked up to us. He said, "Would you like two tickets down by the floor? Guests who were coming cancelled out. I work for the Cavs and have these extra tickets." "Well," I said, "there are three of us, but we'll work something out." We accepted the tickets. We decided Debbie would use our tickets for the first half, Carolyn and I would use the gift tickets the first half, and then Carolyn and Deb would switch. When we arrived at the gift seats we were sitting next to the couple. I began visiting with him and found out a little about his job with the Cavs. Moreover, I found that he grew up in Chevy Chase, Maryland, just blocks from our church and our home. He knew all about what we called "Chevy Chase Lake," with the drug store, supermarket, ESSO gas station, and the hardware store. His name was Jon Horton, and his grandfather was Secretary of the Treasury under Harry Truman! He traded seats with his lady friend, so we could talk more politely, and we chatted up a storm. At halftime, the people on the other side, next to us had left. As Carolyn prepared to leave to meet Debbie, Jon said, "Here take this stub, and John's daughter can get in to sit with us, and you can stay, Carolyn." So, Debbie joined us. Jon and I hit it off. We took pictures and exchanged phone numbers and email addresses. We later connected by phone and made arrangements for lunch at Brio.

On December 11, Carolyn, Bob, Debbie, and Allen came to my home for a dinner I prepared to celebrate Carolyn's birthday. Her birthday was on the fifteenth, but we were all too busy that day. We also celebrated Bob's birthday which was on the thirtieth.

I took another driving trip to Ellicott City to see Joyce and to Baltimore with Christmas gifts for the family, including Isabel and Brianna.

I had another lunch with Jon Horton on December 30. We had become friends. Carolyn had Googled "Jon Horton," to discover that his mother's best friend was Margaret Truman, who was her maid of honor for her wedding. It was held at the Washington National Cathedral, with a packed house, including President Harry Truman. His mother and Margaret Truman had traveled together in Europe. There were letters on record from President Truman to Margaret and Jon's mother while in Europe.

New Year's Eve I had dinner with Sheila Ratcliff at the hotel dining room where she rents an apartment at 9th and Euclid Avenue downtown. It was pleasant, but we didn't ring in the New Year together. I was home by 9:00 p.m. And just so, the year 2020 began. Little did we know!

Emily and Adam had given me an outing with them for a Cleveland Cavalier's basketball game. With the whole family, Elizabeth and Harper included, we did that. The girls were great as we sat in the balcony seats with a good game down below. We won!

Every month at church during the sermon time, Roger McKinney had an interview with a member of the church about their spiritual journey. People had suggested that I might be a candidate to be interviewed. Roger spoke to me about it, and we decided we might need two Sundays for my interview. We chose the twelfth and the twenty-sixth of January. The first Sunday, I covered from birth to 1977, through my ministry at Euclid Avenue Church. The second Sunday was from Deputy General Minister and President through being GMP. It was stimulating to me to go back and remember my whole life and to try to speak about it in two sermonic times.

In the beautiful Rockefeller building, where our bank was located in the '70s, a couple of entrepreneurs had developed indoor golf. You could play famous golf courses, by hitting into a screen with simulated scenes of the hole you were playing. The impact on the screen would determine how far and where your ball was in the scene. Bob and Carolyn and I had several good times with this modern phenomenon!

Jon Horton and I had lunch together on several occasions, in conversation moving from Chevy Chase to the Trump era. He and the Cavs had "separated" and he was looking for a new position in the sporting world. Meanwhile, Debbie and Allen, Bob and Carolyn, and I were preparing for our trip and stay in Sarasota in February and March. We drove down in three vehicles. Debbie and I took turns driving my car. Bob and Carolyn were in their car. Allen Powell was driving his car. We rendezvoused in Rock Hill, South Carolina, at the Hampton Inn for dinner and the night. We then stayed at the familiar Sarasota Hampton Inn on January 31, waiting till February 1, when we could move into our rental properties. Allen and Debbie were on Siesta Key. Bob and Carolyn and I were in the Meadows.

We played a lot of golf, Al, Debbie and I, and Bob, and Carolyn. I renewed friendships with Beneva Christian Church folks, alternating with the Congregational UCC church and the Church of the Palm's with the Bruces.

On JoAnne's birthday, Deb and Allen and Bob and Carolyn were my guests at our favorite Bijou Cafe for dinner to celebrate JoAnne. In spirit, she was there with us for delicious food and a delightful dinner. As we were leaving, there was the waitress JoAnne and I always requested in long years gone by. I was delighted to catch up. She was still employed here in the fall, winter, and spring, and on Cape Cod in the summer months.

Unfortunately, Bob Bruce came down with pneumonia and was hospitalized at the Lakewood Ranch hospital. We had just begun to hear about COVID-19 in the news. Fortunately, Bob was not struck down with severe breathing problems. He was hospitalized for four days. We did not play golf that week, though I did get out with Debbie. The last Sunday, Bob did get out with us to one of the concerts at the Church of the Palms with the Sarasota County Band that we always enjoyed. It is made up of retirement age professional musicians who are quite good. One year, one of the musicians had previously taught music at Butler University School of Music. I had an interesting conversation with him.

CHAPTER 27

The Pandemic

In late January there had been one person in California with COVID-19. Then, there were sixteen cases. President Trump said, "Oh they will recover, and it will go away." Obviously, he didn't take it seriously. But it was serious! This was just a further experience of the last three years with Trump lying to us, lies after lies. In interviews published much later, he admitted this new pandemic was serious, as it was sweeping the country. Europe was also feeling the brunt, especially Italy and Britain, including the Prime Minister himself. Thousands in the U.S. were already sick, with hundreds dying.

Jo Plant came up to see me for a day. She winters in the Naples, Florida, suburbs. We agreed we would keep in touch.

One of the fun places where our Cleveland contingent met was the pizza place with a source of beer in a wall. In a wall you say? The waitress gives you a wrist band. You take the band to the beer wall. There were multiple choices of beer. You make your choice and hold your band to the wall, push that button, and with your glass held there, out comes the beer. They have really good salad with the great pizza. I also took Kitty Miller, my former neighbor, there for dinner. She lived across the street from us on Wyndham Drive and was also a member of the UCC church. We renewed friendship and had several dinners and lunches out. She had been a widow for a number of years.

Two years before, I had met Diane and Chuck Wacha, who are now living across Wyndham Drive from our former home. Chuck had graduated from Sarasota High School as an outstanding baseball pitcher. He was drafted by the Boston Red Sox. He had made it as far as their AA Farm Team. But when the Red Sox drafted another Sarasota High School pitcher and asked Chuck to return to Class A as a kind of tutor for the new kid, he saw his future making the big club as diminished. He resigned and now had a business of pool care for private family pools. He and Diane were both very outgoing. Diane, incidentally, worked in the law office through which Ron Marano completed the sale of my Wyndham home. She was very helpful to me with details of the actual closing.

Chuck had said we ought to get together and play some golf at the Meadows Highland course. I invited him to join me on February 22. We played and enjoyed nine holes. Incidentally, he had a forty-nine and I had a forty-eight. But he really hits a long ball as you might expect.

One sunny day I came down from my condo to see a gentleman eyeing my car license plate. He commented regarding it being from Cuyahoga County. "Cleveland, huh?"

"Yes," I said. "You know Cleveland?"

"I'm from Warren," he said.

"Well," I said. "I know Warren. I'm from Niles and my father-in-law was Auditor of Trumbull County for twenty-eight years, William C. Trimbur."

"Really?" he said. "My father owned a funeral home in Warren for forty-five years until I became the funeral director."

I said, "The McFarland Funeral Home?" He said, "Yes"

"I know your father," I said. "He and your mother are best friends with the realtor who sold us our home on Windham Drive. And of course, there are all the Mount Union College connections with my JoAnne, who was also a PEO. She went to PEO gatherings with your mother here in Sarasota." So, this was "Sonny" McFarland! We were in condos in the same building.

Gordon Oliver is one of Pete Smith's college roommates. It happened he winters at the town just south of Sarasota. He had divorced his wife he met at Bethany and is now married to a former nun. She was a college education professor. They met in a bridge group in a condo neighborhood outside of Detroit. Pete, Gordon, and their other roommate have kept up with reunions every year. Pete introduced me to Gordon, and we became a golfing threesome during our winter's days. We were joined by Jack Collins, another Bethanian who also began wintering in Sarasota. Pete and Karen have not been able to get away to Florida for several years, since Karen's mother was living with them. She was 102 years old and could not travel. But Gordon and I had gotten together for golf with Bob and Carolyn. We had lunch one time a season. We continued that practice in 2020.

As March arrived, with further alarm about the spread of COVID-19, Allen and Debbie had gone back to Cleveland. Bob, Carolyn, and I began to cut back on our social life, including limiting games of Hand and Foot. We did continue our golf outings, being out in the open and feeling safe. The first of March we were playing the Highlands Course at the Meadows. Since we were a threesome, they put a gentleman with us. He commented about my Ohio State sweater and his Penn State cap, and we chuckled. He and his wife, Anne, had just moved to State College Pennsylvania, home of Penn State. They had both graduated from Penn State. His daughter and family lived there. But he was originally from Kansas. He mentioned something about going to church. I told him I was a minister. "What church," he asked. "The Disciples of Christ," I replied.

He had grown up in the Disciples of Christ Church in Kansas. He asked where I had served.

"Dayton, Chevy Chase and Cleveland, Ohio," I said.

"Cleveland!" he exclaimed. "My parents were members of Shaker Heights Christian Church in Cleveland and I lived on Cleveland's West side for twenty-seven years, where I was very active in the community, serving on the school board. When I was in college at Penn State one summer, Phil Smith, Associate Minister at Heights, was taking a CYF group to Germany for two months. I went along as sort of a chaperon."

"Phil Smith," I said, "We were contemporaries in Cleveland and sometime golfers."

He said, "I still keep up with Phil and we try to play golf together once a year. And his daughter also lives in State College."

His name was D'lane Wisner. We exchanged phone numbers and email addresses. He also gave me Phil Smith's number. We invited D'lane to come join us in our next golf game at the Rosedale Golf Club. We enjoyed his company. He joined us for the second game.

My niece Kim and Greg Bachman had invited me to join them for a Baltimore Orioles spring training game with the Washington Nationals on Tuesday March 17. But by that time COVID-19 had shut down such gatherings. Kim and Greg did not make the trip from Ohio, and the game was not played.

I had another lunch plan with Kitty Miller on the nineteenth, but to be safe we cancelled that, as well.

With so many things shutting down, Bob, Carolyn, and I decided to leave Sarasota a week early on March 23. We decided we would get in one last game of golf on March 22, eighteen holes on the Meadows Highlands Course. I shot my age. I had a miraculous 42 on the front, and 50 on the back for a 92! Wow! What a send-off. Carolyn had a 94 and Bob 104. Amazing.

Well, contrary to Debbie's wishes, I drove alone, in front of Bob and Carolyn's car, all 1,134 miles back home to Highland Heights.

And to what did we come back? Quarantining! Churches were not gathering for worship. Restaurants were not serving indoors. The governor of Ohio was calling us to stay home. Jon Horton and I sat outside under the awning. He was without a job, though interviewing with several universities. I had an appointment with my urologist, and it was done by phone. Tyler Delaney our hospice chaplain was coming by, but he had a hospice call, which took precedence over our social visit.

And yes, it was too wet and muddy for golf!

Debbie and I were looking forward to the European Rhine River cruise. Considering the wide spread of COVID-19, we decided to cancel our trip, with the hope of a refund. Ironically, we learned from Dottie Humbert that she and Diana Spangler Crawford had taken that very same cruise last fall. Dottie spoke of the magic of their experience. We had to experience that trip only through Dottie's stories! We did cancel the cruise, and with the help of our travel agent received seven-eighths of our money. Part of our money down was for insurance for just such an occurrence. When our July trip date rolled around, it was a fortunate thing we cancelled. The European Union was not allowing U.S. citizens to enter because of COVID-19.

April was not a total loss. I worked long on my memoirs, making good progress! I received a note from Sarasota. A Beneva Christian Church committee was getting in touch with members to see how they were doing in the midst of the pandemic. My note was from Kim Wheeler. It included her phone number with an invitation to call her. I did, and we had a pleasant conversation. We had met only briefly at a Sunday noon potluck dinner when I was in Sarasota last winter. She asked if it would be alright if she called again in a week or so to check on me. That was fine. She did call again and we had another pleasant conversation. We spoke of our early years, hers in Fullerton, California, to the age of twelve, then two years in England when her father, an engineer, was involved in one of the world's leading companies as an executive. She told of attending a private school and a school field trip skiing in Norway! We then began phone conversations a couple of times a week.

Kim's health was rather fragile. She had breast cancer in 2000. It had metastasized now in her back. She had surgeries two years ago, long rehab, but now was able to get around and drive, but was still with tentative health. She had been a dental hygienist, graduating from Randolph-Macon College, with an advanced degree from the Medical College of Virginia. She had been in an abusive marriage which ended in divorce nine years before.

After many years in dental offices, she started her own dental ministry, "Tooth Fairy Kim." She provided care to elderly homebound patients as a mobile hygienist. With the back problems two years ago, she was no longer able to lift her dental equipment for the traveling service.

We enjoyed our conversations and began visiting on FaceTime every night through the summer months. She was attractive, with long blonde hair and blue eyes. Meanwhile, here in Cleveland, we had Sunday worship on Zoom for Disciples Christian Church. Roger McKinney was moving towards retirement. The pulpit committee had worked with our regional minister on finding a new minister, and the last Sunday in March our Disciples Christian Church met in person. On March 29, Jason Bricker Thompson was presented, preached, and was extended the call to be our new minister. Roger and Jason spent ten days visiting every church member's home for a two-minute call presenting Jason, at social distancing level of course.

When we returned from Florida, I told Bob and Carolyn I had a ping pong table in my basement without space to use it. They frequently had their grandchildren over. Would they like to have it? They had room for it in their basement. The gift was accepted.

A weekly ping pong hour was established since we would be more than six feet apart across the table. I would play Bob, and Carolyn would play Bob. Then I would play Carolyn, and then Bob. The first night, I beat Carolyn. From then on, Carolyn won every game!

During the summer we watched the number of sick from COVID-19 grow into the millions, with deaths in the hundreds of thousands. President Trump was still claiming it would all go away, with "Trumpers" claiming this was all a Democratic hoax! We had lived through his impeachment by the House, with the Senate Republicans failing to convict him. Now he was claiming the role of nominee to serve another four years. He was the worst president in the history of the Republic—not accepting the word of the intelligence agencies; disdaining climate change and proposing withdrawal from the Paris Accords; withdrawing from the seven-nation Iran agreement to control nuclear weapons; and telling lies at least four or five times a day.

A statement by Admiral William H. McRaven, Commander of the U.S. Joint Special Operations Command from 2011 to 2014, who oversaw the 2011 Navy SEAL raid in Pakistan that killed al-Qaida leader Osama bin Laden, says it all! Written for *The Washington Post*, the headline was "REVOKE MY CLEARANCE, TOO, MR. PRESIDENT."

> Dear Mr. President:
>
> Former CIA director John Brennan, whose security clearance you revoked this week, is one of the finest public servants I have ever known. Few Americans have done more to protect this country than John. He is a man of unparalleled integrity, whose honesty and character have never been in question, except by those who don't know him. Therefore, I would consider it an honor if you would revoke my security clearance as well, so I can add my name to the list of men and women who have spoken up against your presidency.
>
> Like most Americans, I had hoped that when you became president, you would rise to the occasion and become the leader this great nation needs.
>
> A good leader tries to embody the best qualities of his or her organization. A good leader sets the example for others to follow. A good leader always puts the welfare of others before himself or herself. Your leadership, however, has shown little of these qualities. Through your actions you have embarrassed us in the eyes of our children, humiliated us on the world stage, and, worst of all, divided us as a nation.

If you think for a moment that your McCarthy era tactics will suppress the voices of criticism, you are sadly mistaken. The criticism will continue until you become the leader we prayed you would be!

CHAPTER 28

The Presidential Election

Joe Biden, Democratic nominee was our hope! His selection of Senator Kamala Harris confirmed our hope. With the science, he demonstrated mask-wearing for safety. Somehow, wearing a mask became political with Trumpsters demonstrably declining. The President was renewing COVID-19-spreading, no-mask gatherings, after having been sick with COVID-19 himself. He had "triumphantly" returned to the White House from Walter Reed Hospital.

For us mortals, the way we could get out was golf. I played rounds with Debbie and Allen, then with Bob and Carolyn at Stonewater and Manakiki. To be safe, we each had our own golf cart. Allen kept taking lessons and following instruction driving at the driving range, shot after shot. He really did improve.

Allen and Debbie had begun ordering their groceries from Heinen's, having them delivered to their home. They invited me to place my order in with theirs. I did and I continued with that practice. Debbie would bring my part of the order to my front door.

Emily provided bright spots, by bringing Elizabeth and Harper out to Deb and Allen's beautiful pool for a couple of hours around their lunch time. I would join the girls at the pool. Elizabeth was learning to swim and was a real water baby. I would go and sit on the opposite side of the pool. We celebrated Harper's second birthday at the pool on August 25.

After sharing conversations every night for several months, Kim and I began talking on Monday and Friday evenings in September. She was losing strength and was taking medicine for sleep, so we moved our conversations from 9:00 p.m. to 7:00 p.m., so she could then begin earlier rest and sleep. Cancer in her back was progressing. We had become good friends. She shared a lot about her three children, Bridget, Lindsay married to Charles, and son Adam, 6 feet 7 inches tall! They were 34, 31, and 23, respectively.

I invited Jason Bricker-Thompson over for a visit to sit outside under our awning. We enjoyed getting to know each other. His experience in Hiram House and in social service with the Heifer project and Hiram Farm were not only contributions to many lives, but also invaluable experience. We had a good visit.

We played golf through September and October. Our last game for the season was Monday, November the ninth. The winter-like weather sunk in. Our clubs found their resting place for the season.

I'd been talking with Ron Marano about coming to Sarasota for the winter period. He found a home around the corner from our former 1939 Wyndham for me to rent for January through the end of March. Bob and Carolyn were talking about not going to Florida this year, but I placed a deposit with the family that owned the property. As talk of immunization with the developing science came to reality, Deb spoke to me about getting my two Pfizer shots before going to Florida. I was able to move my rental months in Sarasota to February through April.

Meanwhile, my friendship with Kim Wheeler continued through October. The last of October, she began to have hospice care. She told me then I was "an answer to her prayers." She had an abusive marriage. After her divorce, she had tried dating. That was unfulfilling, with men who were divorced and difficult. She had prayed that she could somehow finally have a relationship with a man who was kind, thoughtful, and gentle. She said she was thankful to have found that man in our friendship.

On Friday, the twenty-eighth of November, two days after Thanksgiving, we had our last real conversation, expressing our care for each other. On Monday the thirtieth, she was not strong enough for a conversation of any length. That day, her daughter, Lindsey had sent messages to Kim's friends that she could no longer receive phone calls. Lindsey also texted me that if I would call her Tuesday evening, she would put the phone call on speakerphone, and Kim and I could greet each other. I called and Lindsey did that, so that Kim and I could speak a word of warm greeting. Lindsey was in tears, saying her mother was dying.

Meanwhile, Kim's best friend Janice, who had been with her every day, along with Kim's hospice nurse, called to tell me Kim was close to death. On Wednesday, December 2, surrounded by her family, Kim quietly passed away. Janice had stayed away that day so that Kim would be surrounded by her family.

Kim had a strong faith that heaven is a perfect place, "perfection" as she put it. I knew that death held no fear for her.

Another friend from Beneva Christian Church, Marilyn Gerkin, wrote me in an email, "I'm sure you have word of Kim Wheler's death. I'm so glad you met her at that church potluck dinner last winter. I'm sure it was a God thing. You were an inspiration to her during the last months of her life."

As Janice was closest to Kim, we have kept in touch by phone. Janice is quite an artist with stained glass and watercolors. Two years before, her husband left her, and they divorced. She's also very active at Beneva Christian Church. Or was before COVID!

Christmas 2020 was dictated by COVID. We had presents to exchange. I mailed my gifts to Baltimore. They arrived safely on the twenty-third. Deb, Allen and I arrived on Christmas Eve afternoon for a brief Christmas gift exchange at Emily and Adam's new home in Highland Heights. We adults gave, received, and opened gifts. I received a precious gift from Emily. Months ago, I had given Emily one of JoAnne's closet hanging bags with yarn and the beginnings of a scarf. My Jo had just started knitting this project. The gift was the scarf, begun by JoAnne, and now finished by Emily! How precious! Emily had also prepared our traditional after-Christmas Eve family meal that we ate at Debbie's home, vegetable soup and ham and cheese sandwiches. She had prepared these for each of us to take home. In addition, she had baked our family's recipe for cinnamon rolls.

After the Zoomed Christmas Eve service, I ate my lovingly prepared meal. Then I sat on the sofa near the Christmas tree in front of the lighted fireplace as JoAnne and I always did late on Christmas Eve. I sat and remembered when there was the two of us, touching and holding hands.

On Christmas Day, I was alone, but surrounded in both love and friendship by those I had lost: John, Jessica, Tom, Neil, my JoAnne, and Kim.

All these months since returning in March to the pandemic COVID-19, I had really lived for the anticipation of finishing my memoirs. I have found purpose in my daily conversations with Debbie and then hours in my second-floor study with my computer. I had handwritten my memoirs up to January 2020. I had worked on getting it into print on my laptop computer. That was quite a challenge, but in print I had arrived at the first day of my General Minister and President retirement. I had printed out my memoir to the point when I became Deputy General Minister and President, page 241. I was editing capitals and words at the point where JoAnne was being allowed to transfer from Mount Union to Transylvania. I tapped the letter N into the computer to edit a word. A blank page appeared with only the N printed. I couldn't get back to the page on which I was working! I could not get to any page of the manuscript. Suddenly, my whole manuscript in print on the computer disappeared!

I was stunned, aghast, and sick at heart!! I mean sick at heart and soul! And angry! No! It couldn't be! Debbie, then Allen with his computer skills, and then Carolyn searched and searched to find the lost manuscript…to no avail. However, in their search they did somehow find the first 130 pages in another folder. In addition, I had printed out along the way, from page 130 to 241.

Allen set up my computer on Auto Save. With a heavy heart, I began redictating pages 242 to 394, all six years I served as GMP. Of course, I had my pencil written manuscript from which to dictate, thank goodness. But it was a tedious and long process to redictate those six years of my life and work. Finally, I did redictate my life until January 2021!

Meanwhile there's been a lot going on in the world, to put it mildly! The presidential race had been Trump focusing on himself, telling lies, and riling up unmasked crowds, spreading COVID-19. Joe Biden, wearing masks, had spoken from safe places seeking the unity of the country. As compared to Trump, he was fresh air.

When I was in Sarasota I resigned from my Florida "legal residence." Marilyn Gerkin of Beneva Church had been the head of the Sarasota County Election Bureau. I gave her my forms to take JoAnne and me off the election roles.

I received my absentee ballot from the State of Ohio. With the mail overloaded with absentee ballots, I went the route of Debbie taking me down to the Board of Elections to the drive-through drop-off of my ballot.

With hope for a new day, after four years of Trump purposely dividing our country, spewing lies of white supremacy, we anxiously watched the election returns. Eight days following the election day of November 3, Biden and Kamala Harris were declared the winners.

It is on the public record, how Trump behaved: claiming fraud, claiming the election was stolen, trying to get states to change the votes, going to courts, including the Supreme Court, to no avail. He had given the invitation to white supremacists and the Proud Boys to come to Washington on January 6 to prevent Congress from counting the electoral votes confirming Joe Biden's presidency. And when they came en masse, he told them to go to the Capitol and "fight like Hell" for his presidency. And we all saw the mob he created as they breached the Capitol and violated the sacred halls of Congress, cheered on by Senator Hawley and Ted Cruz. The worst president in history had acted to attack his own government! The halls of Congress fought back, impeaching him for the second time.

Those of us wishing for a President with integrity, seeking the truth and justice, seeking to unite the country and a return to a presence in the global community, were so filled with hope and joy on January 20, with the inauguration of President Joe Biden and Vice President Kamala Harris. What a glorious day it was!

Free! We felt free!

I will leave you with the hope for a return to America where "Black Lives Matter," where justice flows down like a river, and peace, truth and justice prevail.

Ninety-three years ago, in a letter to me dated seventeen days after I was born, Grandfather Rev. John Longston wished for me "a long, wholesome and healthy life, knowing that with my parents' loving and Christian upbringing, I would make outstanding contributions to the world."

That has been my hope, too.

Butler University 1945-1946 Varsity Basketball Team.
John Humbert, number 32

Our family, 1968, in North Chevy Chase.
JoAnne, John, Jeff, Debbie, and John

John Humbert visiting with Pope John Paul II

Humbert worshipping with other church heads in the Service of Christian Witness with the pope

Christmas in Indianapolis, 1980. JoAnne, Heidi, Debbie, Jessica and Greg Humbert-Long, John O., John D., and Jeff

The Two Deputies: Howard Dentler and John O.

My mother, Frances Elizabeth (Longston) Humbert

Morning of the election to Deputy General Minister and President by the Administrative Committee, November, 1976

Minister at Euclid Avenue Christian Church, 1971. Age 44

John O. Humbert, Minister of the First Christian Church of Kettering at age 29

The Ordination, January 2, 1949. Grandmother Ella Humbert gave the Ordination Prayer. Also pictured, Father M. Dale Humbert, the presiding minister, and John O. Humbert

John, the Seminarian

We move to North Chevy Chase, John and JoAnne

www.ingramcontent.com/pod-product-compliance
Lightning Source LLC
Chambersburg PA
CBHW060830190426
43197CB00039B/2534